Home Front to Battlefront

WAR AND SOCIETY IN NORTH AMERICA

HOME FRONT TO BATTLEFRONT

An Ohio Teenager in World War II

Frank Lavin

Foreword by Dr. Henry A. Kissinger

OHIO UNIVERSITY PRESS
ATHENS

Ohio University Press, Athens, Ohio 45701

ohioswallow.com
© 2016 by Ohio University Press
All rights reserved

Printed in the United States of America
Ohio University Press books are printed on acid-free paper ⊗™

First paperback edition printed in 2018
Paperback ISBN 978-0-8214-2343-1

26 25 24 23 22 21 20 19 18 17 16   5 4 3 2 1

Library of Congress Cataloging-in-Publication Data
Names: Lavin, Franklin L., author.
Title: Home front to battlefront : an Ohio teenager in World War II / Frank
  Lavin ; foreword by Dr. Henry A. Kissinger.
Other titles: Ohio teenager in World War II
Description: Athens, OH : Ohio University Press, [2016] | Series: War and
  society in North America | Includes bibliographical references and index.
Identifiers: LCCN 2016040527| ISBN 9780821422557 (hc : alk. paper) | ISBN
  9780821445921 (pdf)
Subjects: LCSH: Lavin, Carl, 1924–2014. | United States. Army. Infantry
  Division, 84th—Biography. | Soldiers—United States—Correspondence. |
  Jewish soldiers—United States—Correspondence. | World War,
  1939–1945—Campaigns—Germany. | World War, 1939–1945—Personal
  narratives, American. | United States. Army—Military life—Anecdotes. |
  Germany—Social conditions—20th century—Anecdotes. |
  Teenagers—Ohio—Biography. | Canton (Ohio)—Biography.
Classification: LCC D769.3 84th L47 2016 | DDC 940.541273092 [B] —dc23
LC record available at https://lccn.loc.gov/2016040527

To the men of Company L:

We are here today because they were there yesterday.

Contents

Illustrations

Foreword

My troop ship to Europe was different than Carl Lavin's. Our ship embarked from New York in a convoy of Liberty Ships and, after only some two days at sea, there was a minor collision between two of the ships in the convoy. Not much more serious than a scrape, perhaps, but the damages were such that our ship had to return to New York Harbor. Unbeknownst to us, the good citizens of New York assumed we had returned from the Front, and laid on a heroes' welcome. We did not have the heart to tell them we had only been at sea a few days and had never seen combat. Eventually we were dispatched after repairs to the ship and I joined the 84th Division in Europe. Carl did not join our division until Christmas Day 1944 when he was detached from the 69th Division and hurried to the Front as a response to the German offensive in the Ardennes.

Carl Lavin and I served together, though we did not know each other at the time. He and I were both foot soldiers, not just in the same division, but also in the same regiment and battalion, though in a different company. And shortly after he joined the division, I was transferred to Division Headquarters.

Yet reading this book, and his letters, I have the sense that I knew him intimately. We sometimes forget that the US Army was, and is, essentially a force of teenagers and young men who are required to grapple with the exigencies of combat even as they are attempting to grapple with adulthood.

I have a special place in my heart for the men of the 335th Regiment of the 84th Division. They saw some of the Second World War's more coruscating moments. They served capably and with enormous losses. And their story deserves to be told. Thankfully, this book has done so.

For me, the war was the opportunity to repay my adopted country for the safety it offered my family after we had been driven from the land of our birth. It was also a journey back to that country of birth to witness firsthand the devastation wrought by that conflict.

It was in the 84th Division that I first met Fritz Kraemer, the staid Prussian aristocrat who helped start me on the road of serious academic work.

I believe Carl also made some key decisions because of the war. He cherished the comfort and settled environment of his upbringing. He contributed to the vast postwar economic boom that propelled America to superpower status.

After the war, we went our separate ways. My calling was academia, and eventually public service. Carl returned to a family business in the Midwest and raised his family.

Though I never knew Carl directly, I got to know his son Frank through public service, as he served as US Ambassador to Singapore and later as the Under Secretary at the US Department of Commerce, and we had the chance to collaborate several times.

I am grateful to Frank for his public service, but more importantly for his work in putting together this book. He put in the work to edit and research the work therein. As I see the strength of the man in his letters, so do I see a reflection of those strengths in his son.

—Henry A. Kissinger

Preface

"There are really two wars," John Steinbeck wrote, "and they haven't much to do with each other. There is a war of maps and logistics, of campaigns, of ballistics, armies, divisions, and regiments,—and that is General Marshall's war.

"Then there is the war of the homesick, weary, funny, violent, common men who wash their socks in their helmets, complain about the food…and lug themselves and their spirit through as dirty a business as the world has ever seen and do it with humor and dignity and courage."[1]

This book concerns that second war. This is the war as seen by one foot soldier, Carl Lavin, an American teenager who becomes a combat infantryman.

This is Carl's story but it is also a broader American story, for what comes through in this narrative is how ordinary, and yet how extraordinary the tale is. Sixteen million Americans served in the military during the Second World War. They were overwhelmingly young adult males, with all the strengths and shortcomings of that group. This is a story that many of these sixteen million—or their family members—will find familiar.

This book involves only a few years of Carl's eighty-nine-year life, from Pearl Harbor through training, combat, and finally to V-E Day and the Allied occupation of Germany.

Carl enters the war step by step. Too young to enlist on Pearl Harbor Day, he signs up for the reserves when he enters college the following fall. Spring of that freshman year he is called up. The reader journeys with him through his adventures and impressions of America at war as he completes army training, is sent to Britain, then gets thrust into combat and fights his way across Europe.

From my perspective as his son, my father always struck me more than anything else as serene. A bright man, he grew up in a world of limitations, shaped as it was by the Great Depression and the Second World War. Yet he led an active and optimistic life, perhaps in part due to the trials of combat and the luck of surviving.

This book started during the summer of 2004. That year saw the dedication of the National World War II Memorial. Then came the telecast of Steven Spielberg's masterful *Band of Brothers*. Finally, there was a Library of Congress exhibit on the American soldiers of World War II. I knew, of course, that my father had served. We had talked about it intermittently over the years, and he occasionally shared a story when the lesson was pertinent. But he never seemed to particularly relish the discussions, and I never consciously sought them out.

Like many veterans, my dad seemed somewhat reticent to talk about his experience. Natural humility was part of it. His awareness of the shared sacrifice made his personal efforts not particularly noteworthy in his mind. Others suffered worse or contributed more. The goal of the war, after all, was not to revel in triumph, but to return to civilian life as rapidly as possible. In many ways, this was a typical American view of war. As the poet Karl Shapiro stated, "We all came out of the same war and joined the same generation of silence."[2]

But the events of 2004 reminded me that he had a story to tell, if only to our family, and that none of us were mortal. So I purchased a tape recorder, and sat down with my father for many hours of discussion.

Then I received a lucky break. In the furnace room, in an old cardboard box, I uncovered a trove of over two hundred letters from that period, almost all written by Carl to his mother, Dorothy. Thus his recollections were aided by a contemporaneous account—a flowing narrative containing Carl's thoughts and dates, as well as spellings and punctuation from that era.

As military mail was censored and prohibited any discussion of combat, I used official military records, government documents, private papers, and conventional histories of the period to place the material in historical context.

While Carl Lavin isn't a household name, his letters and recollections capture an extraordinary time in American history.

Let me begin the story by introducing our four main characters, the members of the family:

Carl Lavin, born 1924. A seventeen-year-old high school senior on Pearl Harbor Day, and by all accounts not a particularly motivated student.

Dorothy Lavin, born 1895, Carl's mother. Dorothy is the correspondent for almost all of Carl's letters, so her concerns, emotions, and principles run through his letters as well. Dorothy does not believe in a hands-off approach to raising her children.

Leo Lavin, born 1895, Carl's father and the family patriarch. Leo runs the family meat-packing business, Sugardale Provision Company, along with his two younger brothers. The company was started by Leo's father, Harry, an immigrant from Kiev, then part of Czarist Russia.

Fred Lavin, born 1922, Carl's only sibling. Fred is two years older than Carl and as a result of his age is able to qualify for officer's training. He is commissioned a US Navy Ensign and sent to the Pacific.

At times, the impression generated by this book is one of mistake after mistake after mistake. Readers should not let the anecdotes in this tale, even the horrific ones, obscure the fact that Americans and our allies fought honorably and with valor. Only in isolated cases did they not fully live up to their cause. The American fighting man was, and remains, the finest in the world. If there is one central theme to this history, it is that regardless of the nobility of the struggle, war is carried out by human beings, with all of their shortcomings and imperfections manifest in the moment. By the same pale light of war, however, we also see some of mankind's finest characteristics: courage, self-sacrifice, and quiet devotion to duty.

Perhaps this book will serve somewhat as a corrective for the overly dramatic view of war. There is a Hollywood version of World War II, usually based on the heroic moment, and spurred by a love interest. None of this drama is present in this tale. This tale is of an unpretentious young man, dedicated and dutiful yet critical, thrust by events into a world he did not seek. Daily attempting to acquit himself. Attempting to survive.

Historian Samuel Hynes captured this theme when he wrote, "Personal narratives…subvert the expectations of romance. They work at a level below the big words and the brave sentiments, down on the surface of the earth where men fight. They don't glorify war, or aestheticize it, or make it literary or heroic; they speak in their own voices, in their own plain language. They are not antiwar—that is, they are not polemics against war; they simply tell us what it is like."[3]

There was nothing uplifting or ennobling about war, despite the noble cause for which the United States stood. This is the World War II world of Carl Lavin, a son, a brother, a soldier, a friend—and my father.

—Franklin L. Lavin

Acknowledgments

Many people contributed to this project over the years. I am grateful to Mary Carey of the Stark County District library who helped with background information on Canton in the 1940s and Lehman High School; Mark Holland, Archivist, and Tom Haas of the McKinley Presidential Library and Museum; Dr. Robert Schmidt, the archivist at Miami University; Chad Daniels of the Mississippi Armed Forces Museum at Camp Shelby; Thomas J. Cleary from the Department of Special Collec tions and Archives, Queens College Libraries, CUNY, Benjamin Rosenthal Library; Dr. Robin Sellers, Director, Reichelt Oral History Program, Florida State University; and Dr. David J. Ulbrich, Assistant Professor of History at Rogers University, who patiently read the draft manuscript and provided helpful suggestions and critiques. Laura Dozier provided superb assistance with line and graphics editing. Edward Tufte provided the inspiration for the graphics. Megan Harris and the Library of Congress were very helpful in identifying papers and recollections from other members of the 84th Division.

I thank my mother Audrey for her support and advice during this project. Also my sister and brothers, Maud, Carl Jr., and Douglas, who added their ideas, comments, and memories.

This book would not have been written without the persistent help of Dan Kadison, journalist, writer, researcher, editor, and friend, who was my partner and collaborator throughout this project, and Gillian Berchowitz, the director of Ohio University Press, who saw in a partial manuscript the potential for a great book. She nudged, cajoled, implored, insisted, and directed me to do a better job. And she did so with a smile. So I had no choice.

A Note on the Text

This book is organized around Carl's letters, which occasionally results in some loss of detail. I took pains to keep the letters intact, dropping only extraneous phrases for which no context is provided (e.g., "Say 'hi' to Joe"). We corrected spelling errors, but left stylized spelling intact (e.g., "Willya" for "Will you"). The dates for some of the incidents related by Carl can only be approximated. There appear to be one or two letters in which the date in the letter does not line up evenly with the events described or with Carl's later memories, but we ascribe that possible mismatch to the fact that people occasionally date letters and then add to them, or simply put in the wrong date. We have worked with historical records to match the letters against historical developments. We also are aware that wartime censorship and Carl's desire not to alarm his family colored the letters, resulting in comments to the effect that there was not much going on or that everything was fine, when in fact there was a great deal going on and nothing was fine.

PART I

Before Combat

Introduction

If I were giving a young man advice as to how he might succeed in life, I would say to him, pick out a good father and mother, and begin life in Ohio.

—Wilbur Wright, 1910[1]

Growing up in the 1930s, Carl Lavin used to play tackle football in weekend pick-up games in his Canton, Ohio, neighborhood. Carl loved the feel of the football, the stiff-arm stops, the slip throughs, and the straight-away runs.

Being tall for his age, Carl also didn't mind the aggression of the game or the fact there were no pads or helmets. He enjoyed the rousing sport as well as the camaraderie and the playground heroics that came along with it.

But Carl's love for the game was to remain on the field. His mother, Dorothy, was a serious pianist. She was an immigrant's daughter who stood at average height, but wielded a big personality. She lived in a world of manners and modesty, not childish scrapes and stubborn grass stains. She was skeptical of the value of sport, and she was keen to make sure her boy did not injure his hands.

Dorothy had studied piano at a conservatory and played with local classical groups. It was no surprise that Carl was obligated to take piano lessons. Like any carefree boy, Carl never particularly enjoyed the lessons or felt he had any special aptitude for music, but such was his fate.

In 1938, as Carl was entering Lehman High, the school decided to upgrade its football team to compete as an official school sport—Canton was the birthplace of professional football, after all—and Carl asked his mother if he could go out for the team. His mother refused permission,

Figure I-1. Carl and Fred with Dorothy, c. 1930. Carl would be around six years old, Fred eight, and Dorothy thirty-five. Author collection.

pointing out that the school did not provide helmets or pads, so the game was not safe.

Carl had a choice. He could tell his mother that he had been playing tackle football without protective gear for some time now, hoping the argument would win approval for school football. Or, if he confessed this activity, he might find that she would also prohibit him playing in the weekend pick-up games.

Carl decided to keep quiet, forgoing the chance to play at school but at least preserving his private freedom to play on weekends.

That was Carl as a teenage boy. He was smart and pragmatic. He was also very funny—and a bit mischievous, too. That tells you a lot about Dorothy as well. Always seeking the best for her boys, even if it did not seem so to them at the time.

Dorothy would practice the piano for hours a day, filling the small house with classical works. But she had smallish hands; her span was limited. There was one particular part of a Chopin étude that required a reach. She would frequently miss the note and stop her practice with a sigh, only to begin again.

Every time Dorothy came to the troublesome point in the étude, she held her breath. Carl would listen as that moment grew near and hold his breath as well. Dorothy tensed and Carl tensed. When she hit the note, they both relaxed. If she missed it, he joined her in a sigh.

Besides football and piano lessons, Carl was poetry editor of the school paper and a voracious reader. While Carl was often casual about schoolwork, he possessed curiosity and imagination.

On Carl's bookshelves were the complete short stories of O. Henry and the works of L. Frank Baum. The former dealt with ironies and fatalism in the lives of everyday people, written by that well-known alumnus of the Ohio State Penitentiary. The latter dealt with the most amazing adventures possible. Get this—the hero was not a knight or a detective, but just a kid from the Midwest. This Dorothy appeared to be every bit as plucky as Carl's mother, and from the same era as well. That kid from the Midwest faced a series of improbable dangers and it was not completely clear if she would ever make it back home.

Also on the shelf was his collection of postage stamps from around the world, a typical Depression-era hobby, allowing a boy to dream about far-off lands when he wasn't able to go anywhere. Even at a young age, Carl started to develop a sense of the world just by looking at stamps from China, Argentina, Great Britain, and even that interesting stamp commemorating the 1936 Olympics, the one with the odd symbol on it; a swastika, they called it.

In December 1941, Carl Lavin was seventeen years old, standing six foot two and attending Lehman High School in Canton, a Midwest industrial town of about 110,000. Carl was a senior, and, even though it was the time of the Great Depression, he was fortunate to have a fairly worry-free

6   life. He had a loving family, a dog named Spitzy, and the entire world in front of him.

Carl's brother Fred was two years older and attending college at Miami of Ohio. Carl's father, Leo, and Leo's two brothers, Bill and Arthur, ran the Sugardale Provision Company, the family-owned business started by Carl's grandfather, Harry.[2] Sugardale processed and sold meat products and other foods, everything from ham and bacon to cheese and Birdseye Frozen Foods.

Harry had a fourth child, Elizabeth. She had married Lou Kaven and, while the couple was not involved in the family business, they lived in the same half-mile radius as the rest of the family. With Harry and his wife, Mary, their four children and their spouses, there were five households in a small area on the north side of Canton.[3]

Carl had it pretty good, considering. Lehman was a fine high school; Canton, a nice town. Life was pleasant. True, business was slow all around, and the Great Depression had gone on so long people began spelling it with capital letters, but the Lavins and the Canton community were persevering. The misery of the 1930s was receding, slowly.[4]

In fact, a few of the local family businesses had gone on to bigger things. The Diebolds' safe company sold their products around the world. The Hoovers also built their cleaner company into a famous brand. The same with Mr. Timken and his ball bearings.

Sugardale wasn't a national name, but it did its best to endure during those difficult days. The Lavins cut business hours and reduced expenses. By reducing the workweek from five days to three, Sugardale was able to survive without layoffs. Because the company endured, Carl's family was in a better situation than most. Besides, Leo made good use of the days that were closed for business by taking the train to Cleveland to watch the Indians play.

Dorothy and Leo owned a house on 25th Street. It was small, but it was paid for. It had indoor plumbing and a telephone.[5]

The house was a little more than a mile away from the home at 7th and Market where Governor William McKinley had run his front-porch campaign for president, twenty-eight years before Carl's birth. It was also about a mile away from the Hupmobile dealer at 2nd and Cleveland, where the National Football League had been established four years before Carl was born. And it was about two miles north of Nimisilla Park, where Socialist Party leader Eugene Debs gave the 1918 anti-war speech that got him arrested.[6]

The United States was a different world in 1940. Journalist Cabell Phillips offered an overview:

> The population was 131.6 million in 1940, up a scant seven percent over 1930....The GNP was 97.1 billion, with federal government expenses running at just under 10% of that amount at 9.1 billion. About 7.5 million people paid federal taxes, with the tax rate at 4.09%. Only 48,000 taxpayers were in the upper bracket of incomes between $25–$100,000. And there were 52 people who declared an income over $1 million. The average factory wage was 66 cents an hour and take home pay was 25.20 a week. Urban families had an annual income of $1,463 and only 2.3% of these families had an income over $5,000 a year.[7]

Along with a house, Leo also owned a LaSalle automobile, which he allowed Carl to drive—a pretty good deal for any seventeen-year-old boy.

One Sunday Carl took the LaSalle downtown. It was around 3 p.m., and he was headed home after having a bite at a lunch counter. As he braked for a traffic light, his uncle Bill happened to pull up alongside him, then started waving, trying to get his attention.

Uncle Bill rolled down his window, motioning for Carl to do the same.

Uncle Bill was almost shouting: "Is your radio on? Turn to the news. Pearl Harbor's been bombed."

Carl did not fully understand.

"The Japanese have bombed Pearl Harbor," Uncle Bill said. "That's ours."

On 25th Street, Dorothy and Leo also heard the news.

Dorothy, classical pianist that she was, always had Leo tune into the weekly 3 p.m. broadcast of the New York Philharmonic Orchestra on the CBS network. There was one large RCA radio set downstairs, and it wasn't a bad way to pass a Sunday afternoon while reading the paper and catching up on small talk. That day Arthur Rubinstein was to perform Brahms's Second Piano Concerto. But as Rubinstein was about to begin, CBS announcer John Charles Daly broke the news of the attack on Pearl Harbor.

8   Said Daly: "The Japanese have attacked Pearl Harbor, Hawaii, by air, President Roosevelt has just announced. The attack also was made on all military and naval activities on the principal island of Oahu."

After Daly reported for thirty-three minutes, Rubinstein conducted a spontaneous rendition of the "Star-Spangled Banner."[8]

Leo and Dorothy knew America was at war. Carl knew that somehow he would be part of it. He just did not know how downright dark and deadly it would be.

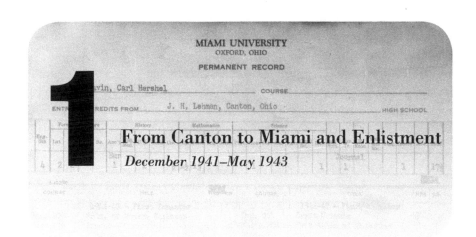

From Canton to Miami and Enlistment
December 1941–May 1943

At Lehman High School on Monday morning, the mood was electric. Students were assembled in the auditorium to hear President Roosevelt's address to Congress. America was going to war, and all the boys wanted to be part of the action.[1]

Carl was a little bit chagrined because he wouldn't be turning eighteen until April, over four months away, and everyone believed the war would be over by then. Carl was disappointed he would not get a chance to fight.

Time seemed to slow down after the initial rush of excitement. Carl still had high school to finish. For the moment, Carl's contribution to the war effort was limited to a small poem in the school paper.

> "Answer to Goebbels"
> Then have
> You seen our men
> As they walk home from work
> Each clean and dirty, weak and strong?
> You will.

The immediate optimism after Pearl Harbor faded with a string of Allied defeats and setbacks. With the fall of Hong Kong in December 1941, the fall of Singapore in February 1942, and the Japanese sweep across the Philippines, historian Paul Fussell noted that early 1942 was "close to the nadir for the Allies." *Time* magazine declared the week of February 23 the "worst week of the year." US radio stations were forbidden from using the transition phrase "and now for some good news." That week President

Roosevelt used the perseverance of Washington at Valley Forge as a theme for his Fireside Chat radio address.[2]

Carl joined the discussion when he entered the essay contest sponsored by the *Canton Repository*. On the same day as *Time*'s pronouncement, Carl won second prize in the City Division for his essay, "Right or Wrong," urging Americans to buck up:

> We have been told again and again that this will not be an easy war and that we must expect many defeats before final victory, just as we have been asked to have faith in the capacity of our leaders, our factories and soldiers, and our allies.[3]

Hometown Canton adjusted to wartime. The Hoover plant was producing hand grenades instead of vacuum cleaners.[4] Diebold was making armored cars and airplane and anti-aircraft parts. Republic Steel manufactured armor plating, ordnance, and bombs. Hercules Motors churned out engines. And Timken—whose gun barrels and bearings were vital for the war effort—went from eight thousand employees at the beginning of the war to eighteen thousand by the end.[5]

These industries made Canton part of the war effort, but Timken Bearings was the talk of the town. The fact that most of America's ball bearings were made in Canton meant the Nazis knew it as well. Everyone knew this meant Canton was number 11 on the list of German targets in the United States. Or maybe it was number 17. Anyways, it was up there.[6]

In April, Carl turned eighteen and registered for the draft. Lehman also adjusted to the war. Civics and history classes had radios for the latest war news. Defense stamps were sold every Thursday. Knitting clubs were organized.

But the seriousness of the war did not stop small-town eccentricities. The most quirky Lehman tradition for senior year was in the math department. The math teacher made a pact with the seniors at the beginning of every school year. If they could cover the entire year's requirements in the first semester, the teacher would then use the time allotted for math class during the second semester to read Victor Hugo's entire novel *Les Misérables* to his students. Carl's class, like the preceding classes, accepted the challenge. It wasn't so bad listening to and discussing the great novel as winter turned to spring.

The senior class gift was an ambulance, a converted 1940 Packard donated to the City of Canton, with funds raised through a scrap metal drive.

The ambulance was presented at the June 5 graduation. The commencement speaker's theme was the need for people of all races and backgrounds to work together.[7]

That fall it was off to join elder brother Fred at the University of Miami, just north of Cincinnati. Leo had not gone to college and was not too keen on Carl attending, but he agreed to send Carl under two conditions: that the college be in Ohio and that Carl major in business. So Miami it was, notably the Ohio college farthest from Canton.

As a freshman in the fall of 1942, it was difficult for Carl to take school too seriously. He was expecting to be called up at any moment, and he joined the army reserve program on campus, the Enlisted Reserve Corps (ERC).[8]

When Carl discussed the ERC with his mom and dad, they didn't quite get it. They asked, "Can't you just wait until you are called up?" Dorothy and Leo wanted Carl to stay out as long as he could. The draft was there and everyone was going to be grabbed sooner or later. There's no point in going in any sooner. Take your time, they said. Those words of caution might have been just what prompted Carl to join. For as soon as he arrived at Miami, he hitchhiked to Columbus to sign up for the ERC at Fort Hayes.[9]

Albeit a reservist and still a student, Carl had officially signed up with the army. Throughout his life, Carl could recite his army serial number with a bit of pride: 15140578. It started with a one, which meant he was a volunteer. The draftees' serial numbers all started with a three.

When the school year began, everything was near perfect. Carl was cheerful and proud of his accomplishments. It was good to be in college and nice to be on his own, though Carl did get homesick. Signing up for the reserves meant Carl was doing his part, at least until it came time to *really* do his part. Fred, two years older, was able to get into the V-12 program, the officer training school for the navy.

But for Carl, not much happened in the ERC. There were no monthly drills. At first, there was not even a uniform. In many respects these months had a peacetime aura to them.

Still, America was at war; talk of gas and meat rationing had begun;[10] and while Carl sent chatty letters home, some tweaking his family, Dorothy must have been worried about her younger boy going off to war. In the fall of 1942, Dorothy began saving Carl's letters.

November 30, 1942

Dear Mom,

It's probably a good thing I didn't write you last week. I spent all my time studying for the nine week exams (sounds good anyway) with these results: Business—incomplete (missed the test and took it later but I don't know my grade yet—I believe it is an A); Math, A; Geology, A; English, A; and history, A!—Honest, it was three times as much a surprise to me as it is now to you! The very worse I can have is a 3.8 average and it's *probably* 4.0. Whoppee!—but don't go expecting it every time now. I was just darn lucky.

Yes, a yellow scarf and gloves would come in very handy. And how about sending down some more ties. I need them very badly, about 10 or 12 of them. Just pick out the clean ones I've got and send 'em along. AND SEND ME THE *DAILY REPOSITORY* [the Canton newspaper]—right now!! Please!!!

I've been waiting for it for at least two or three weeks now.

I told the guys down here about your having those tickets on the Canton-Massillon game 50 yard line and not going—they didn't say anything—just ran around in circles on the ceiling![11] But I suppose the excitement down here was nothing like it was in Canton—and I also suppose that you've talked about it so much that you're tired sick of hearing about it.[12]

By the way, my roommate is now about three food shipments up on me. Why don't you send some more down before Xmas vacation? It's cold enough for orange juice to keep—and we could use some more cheese, and some meats, and some dates, and some *fudge* most of all—also anything else you can think of would be greatly appreciated.

Love Carl

P.S. Any big dances going on this Xmas?

Tell me what's going on between the U.S. govt. and the Sugardale Prov. Co., willya?

Got drunk a couple of weeks ago to see what it was like—fine, but I don't think I'll try it any more.

I went to Cinci last week and had a lot of fun—behaved myself too. Don't bathe Spitzy [the family dog] any more this winter—she can't take it. How's the gas up there?[13]

Sunday 12/13/42 only four, 4, more days (to Christmas break)!!

Dear Mom,

I hope by this time you have sent down the 25 or 30 dollars we will need in order to buy the tickets and get ready to come home. We are leaving at 8:15 from Oxford on a special to Dayton. From there we take the Cleveland train up to Crestline where we change to the Canton train. We will get in some time between six and ten o'clock, and perhaps later if we are held up so much that we miss a connection at Dayton or Crestline.

I'm not sending any of my soiled clothes home because I only have enough room for some suits and pants, and I think I'll bring home a Hudson Bay, too, because I don't need it here and I have an idea you'll be needing it there with us coming home.[14] However, I'll hang all the soiled stuff up and give it an airing out while I'm home.

I'm getting a lot of sleep these last two weeks so don't tell me I look like a fugitive from Molly Stark [mental institution] when I get home. I'm going to have a good time when I get home because this will be the last time us kids (we kids) will be together.

I'm awfully anxious to get home. Just thinking about it gets me all excited (pant, pant). The only thing I don't like about it is going around saying "hello" to everyone. Why don't all you mamas get together and work out some kind of a system whereby all that will be done away with?

By the way, ask Daddy if he knows any way of finding out about all the different kinds of services in the army and how they differ. I'd like to decide pretty soon what branch I want, because I probably won't be here after this semester. Love –Carl

Carl was back at school after the holidays. As the school year went by, the boys were disappearing; classes were constantly dwindling in size due to enlistments and call-ups. Indeed, in the course of the war, some five thousand Miami men and women served in uniform.[15]

Carl's enthusiasm of the first semester gave way to a sober pragmatism. War or no war, he needed money and food.

NAME Lavin, Carl Hershel   COURSE

ENTRANCE CREDITS FROM J. H. Lehman, Canton, Ohio   HIGH SCHOOL

English	Foreign Language				History				Mathematics				Science									Con'l Subj.	Man. Tr.	H. Econ.	Econ. and Soc.	Geog.	Speech	Misc.	Total
	Lat.	Fr.	Ger.	Sp.	Anc't	Med./Mod.	U. S.	World	Civ.	Alg.	Geom	Trig	Arith	Phys	Chem	Bot.	Zoo.	Agr.	Gen'l Sci.	Biol.								
4	2	2				Sur 1	1			½	1½	1½			1					1	1	Journal 1			1			17½

5-42-2000

COURSE	TITLE	SEM. HRS.	GR.	COURSE	TITLE	HRS.	GR.
	1942-43 - First Semester				**1946-47 - First Semester**		
Bus. 100	Prin. of Modern Business	2	A	Eng. 201	Great Writers	3	B
Eng. 100	Freshman Composition	3	A	Econ. 202	Principles of Economics	3	B
Geol. 101	General Geology	4	A	Fin. 311	Intro. to Business Finance	3	C
Hist. 100	European Civilization	3	B	Acct. 212	Principles of Accounting	3	C
Math. 131	College Algebra	3	A	Econ. 315	Intermed. Economic Theory	2	C
Phy.Ed.110	Gymnasium	1	P	Econ. 431	Taxation, Financing Gov't	3	B
		16				17	
	1942-43 - Second Semester						
Math. 113	Plane Trigonometry	3	D				
Math. 132	Math. of Investments	3	A				
Bus. 100	Prin. of Modern Business	(2)	F				
Geol. 102	General Geology	4	D				
Phy.Ed.110	Gymnasium	(1)	F				
	Registered the second semester of 1942-43, but officially withdrew on May 8, 1943. Reason: Army Enlisted Reserve Unassigned. (to receive full credit for the semester)						
	from Queens College:						
Eng. 102	Freshman Composition	3					
Math. 110	Unified Mathematics	5					
Phys. 100	College Physics	14					
Hist. 200	American History	5					
Geog. 100	Economic Geography	4					
Chem. 100	General Chemistry	12					
Phy.Educ.	Gymnasium	2					
		45					
	1945-46 - Second Semester						
Ind.Mgt.321	Indust. Organ. & Management	3	B				
Econ. 201	Principles of Economics	3	A				
Psych. 201	General Psychology	3	A				
Acct. 211	Principles of Accounting	3	B				
Speech 132	Essentials of Public Spkg.	2	B				
Bus. 371	Statistics	3	B				
		17					

Veteran - Excused from Phys. Ed. (Senate, 10/23/45)   67

67

Figure 1-1. Carl's Miami transcript, with a strong first semester and a devil-may-care second semester. *Author collection.*

——

Jan. 1943
Wed.

Dear Mom,

Here I am, back again in the old grind. Everything's just the same here—except that some of the guys aren't around any more.

I didn't get my laundry yet. I hope you sent some pajamas along. I only have one pair. My pecuniary supply is also alarmingly low. When are you going to start sending the remittances? And don't forget the $2.00 raise—due to the increase in the cost of living down here.

We arrived in Oxford at 3:00 instead of 6:00 and didn't have to wait at all in Lima. Just after we got there a train came in going to Hamilton—so we took it and we came into Oxford on a bus.

Nothing exciting happened on that trip except that I lost my hat.

I narrowly missed serious injury yesterday from a violent explosion. I opened my mailbox and the door almost blew off under the concentrated pressure of two weeks of *Repositories*. When is that supply shipment coming? This is the first time in three months that we haven't carried at least something in the larder. The whole third floor is complaining. I started off the new year here with a complete new leaf. I shifted the beds and chairs around until now we have an entirely different floor plan. Charming effect—charming.

Well, s'all now. I'll be waiting to hear from you—in several different ways.

Love –Carl

——

In January, Carl all but stopped serious academic work. As he explained later, all the guys were waiting to be called up, so they mainly played poker all day. The view was "it's going to happen any day" so students just didn't go to class. This wasn't something that Carl's mom liked to hear, but Carl, being Carl, wrote about it anyway.

——

February 1943

Dear Mother,

I can see that everything is going along very nicely back home. You seem quite serene, in fact. I think that what you need is a good war job. You need something to take care of all that spare time. I can just see you every day trying to look busy. It's bad for you to just sit around. You start thinking up ideas—such as buying stock. I'm surprised that daddy let you buy all that much and especially at that price. The market is about normal now but after the war it will go way down. If it gets around nine you'd better sell it. And don't buy any stock from my savings. That means "do not."—in other words, no. I am trying to convey a negative impression in regards to your buying more (RCA) stock for me. I trust it registered. But don't sell it either—unless it gets over eleven. By the way, I bought it at 5 ½, not 4 ½. Why don't you just buy bonds with all that surplus money? If you'll remember, every time in the past twenty years that you've had money you've invested it. Every time you've invested in, you've lost it. All of which leads to one conclusion.

I am now a pledge at *Zeta Beta Tau* [Jewish fraternity]. We have only six pledges this year. It's a lot of fun and I think I'll go active if I have the chance.

I still don't know when I'm going into the army. But I'm doing very little work and cutting a lot of classes, so it had better be before grades come out again. I don't have much to do with myself and I'm really enjoying it down here. Maybe I'll come home the week-end of the 20th. But don't expect me. I probably won't.

I just got the worst haircut of my life. I look like an egg-head now. It's a combination of a bowl and a butch. Gives a rather startling effect.

I'm not dating the gentile girl any more. It was her idea, but I guess it was all for the best.

Could you please send quite a lot of extra money? There's a prom coming up—lot of things are doing that week-end. Since you've got so much you don't know what to do with it, I'll help you spend it. Really, though, I need it—Soon as possible.

Our supplies are running pretty low, too. Please don't send any Swiss cheese this time. Don't we have American anymore? And tell me, what all has Sugardale cut out, and what's going on there, and what's been changed? Please tell me.

Has Spitzy gotten any older? Give me some more home town news.

All my love —Carl

—

Sun, Feb. 21, 1943

Dear Mom,

Well, here it is Sunday—and everything's all over. I went through more complications just getting Alice down here (for the prom). Stop worrying so much.

I needed the extra ten dollars to join *Phi Eta Sigma*, the freshman's honorary.

What prompted that heavy barrage of character-building? I don't know what I said but it must have been something—I was probably joking about something. Anyways it was unnecessary. If you'll remember while I was at home going to Lehman, and had the benefit of innumerable lectures, I stood at about the middle of my class. While here, where I am on my own, I am doing considerably better.

And now for your question: Meteorology doesn't interest me—I don't intend to get stuck in some boring hole for two years. When are you sending some more food? I also need towels and handkerchiefs.—Love Carl

P.S. The prom was pretty good. Had a swell time this weekend.— Still nothing definite about the E.R.C. I'll let you know as soon as something happens.

—

The army called Carl up in May.

—

Ft. Hayes, Columbus
Sat. May 22, 1943

Dear Mom,

Got my uniform Thursday and will probably get transferred to a permanent base around Tuesday. The chances are that I will get in

18 the administrative branch of the service or Supply or Air Corps, but of course that is very indefinite. So far Army life has been quite nice. I live with mostly E.R.C. men, so it's pretty much like college to me. Bye. Love Carl

—

Pine Bluff Ark
May 28, 1943
Thu.

Hi Maw,

Left Columbus Wednesday morning at 10:30 and made St. Louis in 8 ½ hours (420 miles). Then we went the next 110 miles in 11 hours. It is now 10:30 P.M. and we are waiting here in Pine Bluff, Arkansas (pop. 52,000) until 1:15. So far the army has been a lot of fun. And this trip has been no exception. Just finished riding for a couple of hours with Don Curtis. His dad is a lodge bro. of pop's. I'll write when I get to the base.

—

His youthful confidence notwithstanding, Carl did not know when, or if, he would ever be home again.

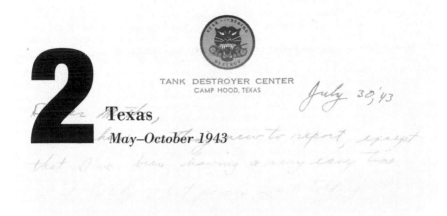

2 Texas,
May–October 1943

TANK DESTROYER CENTER
CAMP HOOD, TEXAS

So Carl was inducted into active duty, joining millions of Americans who were being called up for war.

The good news: the new soldiers were going to serve their country and join a noble cause. The bad news: the army was coming out of the Great Depression and wasn't ready for a war.

In 1940, the War Department had announced that the use of the sabers by officers on duty with troops "will be discontinued." In 1941, the department announced that the army had just supplied itself with 20,000 horses, the most since the Civil War. The army had to sprint to grow from some 225,000 regular troops in 1939 to 1.5 million troops just two years later.[1] The incoming recruits had to sprint, as well—enduring basic training in the Texas sun as they prepared for combat.

Carl was shipped to Camp Hood (now Fort Hood) for basic training. The base, located some 160 miles southeast of Dallas, had been established just one year earlier. Set upon 108,000 acres of converted farmland, Camp Hood was used to train soldiers, instruct anti-tank units and hold prisoners of war (POWs). When it first opened, 38,000 soldiers occupied the base; by the next year, 95,000 were there, Carl being one of them.[2]

Basic training is not meant to be fun. It can range from physically demanding to tedious. The rules can be arbitrary. And the weather was downright unrelenting. Those were just a few reasons why Carl wanted to get out of the infantry. Camaraderie offered a bulwark against what one writer called "this drab khaki world" with its "boredom, cold, exhaustion, squalor, lack of privacy, monotony, ugliness and a constant teasing anxiety about the future."[3] So while making the best of Texas during wartime, Carl contemplated transfers to Officer Candidate School, West Point, or

20 a college-based program called the Army Specialized Training Program (ASTP).

Yes, Carl was keen to find a way to bypass the infantry. All he needed was time—and a little creativity.

———

May 31, 1943

Dear Mom,

This makes two weeks that I have been an active member of the armed forces, and tomorrow the activity starts. So far I haven't done a thing—altogether about 14 hours' work in 14 days. It's just been like going to a boy's camp with a bunch of college men, for that is all I've associated with so far. I'm still learning some more bridge. Oops— they just turned the lights out and I'm writing this in the dark. There are a few things I would very much like to have. First of all at least six to eight coat hangers as soon as possible. Very important—I also need some of that Upjohn's foot powder.

I have to take eight weeks of basic training before I can get into officer's school or specialized training. I believe I got into something pretty good. It is connected with none of the 13 branches of the army and entirely new. In fact this camp officially opened the program.

I may not have much of a chance to write from now on as I'm going to be very occupied.

Love Carl

———

June 6, 1943

Dear Mom,

So far I've been writing you that the army is a vacation. Since last Tuesday, however, I have definitely changed my mind. Every minute of every day is taken up in either instruction or exercises. We are taking a 13 week basic training course and a Basic Unit Training Course at the same time in eight weeks, so you see we are pretty busy. Wednesday we took 50 minutes to march 3 miles in 90 degree heat with full pack. But I'm living through it good enough so don't write any letters to my company commander telling him what a sensitive boy I am.

In our barracks we have 11 E.R.C. men and 23 hillbillies from N. Carolina—all in their teens. And we really have some time together! We fight the Civil War over every day. Yesterday was a holiday and Ohio played N.C. in a ball game. We beat them 35 to 9! By the way, three days ago the banks were all closed in Texas—Jeff Davis's birthday! But that didn't affect us much because all new men are put in quarantine for two weeks. That means we can't associate with anyone but ourselves—no PX, no movies, no passes.

When I wrote last that I asked for eight hangers, and I presume you already sent them. However I've found out that I'll really need twelve so please send the rest right away. I also need some cord and a few nails and a box to keep my stationery in. Just get me a dozen or so nails from the cellar and about 30 feet of good cord. And it would be a very good idea to send some fudge in that box. I don't want a subscription to the *Rep*. but please cut out all articles that might interest me and send them along. I won't need that foot powder because they have some here—G.I. and good. But I do need an electric plug—you know, one of those things you screw into a socket. You can't get any around here and I can't use my electric razor. Better send 2 or 3 of them. There aren't any good candy bars here so if you can find some way to pack them so they will keep cool send me some Forever Yours and Milky Ways.[4] By the way I suppose you know that I can get a 10 day furlough if the Canton Red Cross is convinced that there is a sufficient emergency at home. However, *don't* get me one! I know you would have tried, but this training is very important and if I missed 10 days of it, that would very likely be the thing that would keep me out of O.C.S. So don't try anything because I know what is best, and I will let you know if anything turns up. This is us—the Tank Busters.[5] We are the toughest outfit in the army next to the paratroopers. I think I'm pretty lucky to get in this, because it's new and growing. I can't get into OCS until I've been in the army for three months and they've cut down the quota pretty much, but I'm going to try. If not that I'll try A.S.T.P. which would send me to a college—Bye now and write.

Love, Carl

June 13, 1943
         Tuesday

    Dear Mater,
    This will have to be short, and sweet, I hope. I stayed in tonight
although we could get passes because I wanted to write some letters
and do some washing. So since I didn't get a pass they chose me as
one of the guys for a special detail. We worked for two and a half
hours—until lights went out. But I'm fooling them—I'm writing
anyways. Four men could have done the same work in the same time
that we eight did it—four guys were always standing waiting. But we
all had to stay there. Now isn't that stupid and unfair? Here I and
several others had planned this evening, the only time we have to
ourselves, in a certain way, and they take this time away when it isn't
even necessary. It's really terribly unjust. And if you will remember,
it is injustice in any form or manner that affects me the strongest and
irks me the most. I can stand anything but injustice. That I cannot
stand.
    BUT—It didn't bother me at all! That has been one of the most
surprising things about army life that that I have seen. It's so terribly
unfair, and yet you don't mind it because the army is unfair to
everyone. You see unfairness so often that you become used to it. It
is only humorous, nothing more—and that because it is out of place.
That's what real humor is, you know, misplacement. That's why the
New Yorker cartoons are so good. They realize that and capitalize on
it.[6]
    Received your cookies and candy today. Very good, very good.
We'll have to finish them all tomorrow because we're moving out into
the woods Thursday. No electricity, no plumbing—but swimming.
Lots of love from Carl

———

    Once, Carl's unit was taken to a military prison to learn how not
to behave. They were shown prisoners who broke the rules. This soldier
didn't come back from leave on time. That guy got in a fight with his sergeant. That sort of stuff. The moral: You disobeyed the rules and you got
tossed in the hoosegow.
    Even the men who found themselves in the stockade didn't need
a lecture about why they were in the army. After Pearl Harbor it was

universally accepted that we were attacked, and we are at war, and war is all-out war. The national sentiment was that there was only one thing to do and that is to defeat the enemy. Everyone hung flags and draped bunting. Parents placed a star in their window for each boy in the service. Dorothy and Leo had two stars in the window.

Everyone you talked to was for military action; Carl and everyone else were very patriotic, even the soldiers in prison—no matter if the prisoners' purpose was only to serve as a bad example.

—

June 18, 1943

Dear Mom,

I'll have to make this brief because it's late and there's an ugly rumor going around that we're having a nine mile hike tomorrow.

Thanks for the stuff but you overdid it a little in places. I wanted about six nails, not six pounds; and just a little cord, not enuf to start a rug factory with. But you show the right spirit. I can hardly wait to get that fudge. I'll expect it at least in carload lots.

Hey! Where's my shoes? And be sure to send trees with them. Also as soon as possible send all my sweat socks. Most imp.

Didn't you get that picture I sent you from Columbus? It cost me 10 cents. As soon as I can get to town I'll have some good ones taken.

Just last night I saw *The Ox-Bow Incident*.[7] I suppose it's been to Canton a long time ago. If it hasn't or if you missed it once, be sure to see it. I firmly believe that it is one of the few outstanding pictures of the last few years. If you did see it tell me what you think of it.

Went out in the firing range yesterday and I didn't even get killed. By the way, don't worry about my visiting the German prisoners. I should just try to get closer than 30 yards to the camp. We also have some Italians and a few Japs. They caught two more of the escaped prisoners, also by the way.

Don't forget the shoes and socks.

Love Carl

—

To deal with prisoners of war, camps were set up across the United States. Texas held many such camps due to "available space" and because

24   the state possessed the same climate as North Africa, significant because
the Geneva Convention stipulated that any POW must be harbored in a
climate that was approximate to the place of capture.

From over 150,000 of Rommel's surrendering Afrika Korps to the
tens of thousands of soldiers who gave up toward the end of the war,
the United States housed up to 425,000 enemy combatants during World
War II.[8]

———

June 18
Sat.

Dear Folks,
Here is what we did yesterday. Got up at 0500 (5:00 a.m. to you)
which was not too unusual since we've been doing it every single
day; Reveille at 5:15 to 5:25; Chow at 5:30 to about 5:50; then try
to get washed, make your bed, clean out your barracks, prepare for
inspection, put on your leggings, fill your canteen (the water is no
good here and has to be medicated), and police the area in about 45
minutes. Then we march off to the training area with pack and guns,
either a 1917 model Enfield or Thompson sub-machine gun. From
0700 to 1100 we have classes of 50 minutes each, separated by a two
minute "wind sprint" and an eight minute rest period. The classes
are on first aid and gas, mostly, so far, but we'll be having many more
different ones. We just started motor maintenance and driving, and
we've also had military courtesy, the Articles of War (I can be put up
for life for not shining my shoes—A.W. 94—Conduct Unbecoming a
Soldier) and map reading. Then there is an hour of drill and formation
exercising. From 1200 to 1330 we eat and have a rest period, most
of which is taken up in waiting in line to get some food, waiting in
line to get seconds, and waiting in line to wash your mess gear. To
1730 we have some more classes sometimes. Usually the last hour
is spent in doing something a little more exerting, like yesterday we
had a hike. I believe I wrote before saying how hard it was marching
3 miles in 50 minutes with a pack in 85 degree heat. Well yesterday
we marched *five* miles in 45 minutes with a pack and a rifle in 90
degree heat! If you don't know how fast that is, there was a guy ahead
of me that was about 5'5" and his legs weren't long enough to go that

fast. He had to run about a third of the time. But the most fun of all
was when we double-timed the last hundred yards. Those marches
are really the only thing that I don't like about the army. And I have
a violent hatred of them. They are nothing but torture from the first
step to the last and there is no deeper discouragement than to have
your leg muscles paining and your shoulders rubbed sore, and come
to some rough or sandy ground and realize you still have four more
miles to go, but can do absolutely nothing but continue to march,
and march at top speed. Then towards the end your eyes start to
smart from the sweat washing through them, and you hope you won't
stumble because you're sure you won't be able to start up again. But
the funny thing is once you're back and you put down your pack
and gun, the relief takes all the tiredness away and you don't throw
yourself down on your bunk as you so ardently desired out on the
hike. You lay down for two or three minutes, drink a quart and a half
of water, usually, and start joking about the hike. Yesterday we got a
big laugh out of the company commander riding past in a jeep saying
"all right, men; close it up." That is we got a laugh out of that back in
the barracks; it wasn't very funny while it happened.

However, we are very fortunate in our company officers. All we
have is eight second lieutenants. One of them will be a captain soon
and several will be first lieuts. They are all excellent men, and the
older soldiers who were transferred from some other branch all say so
too.

I did start to tell you the daily schedule, so I'd better continue it;
when we get back to the barracks we have chow, retreat, mail call and
then we are off til nine-fifteen, or I should say 2115, when the lights
go off, theoretically, that is. So far in two weeks, I've just had that
period off on three different days. Somebody always gets an idea to do
something, like the night before last the sergeant had us up til about
eleven (2300) drilling because he didn't like the way we looked. That,
of course, didn't help our condition out any on the hike yesterday.
And then we were in quarantine until yesterday (2 wks) and had
to go to medics and be inspected every night. And then there were
many other things such as waiting in line for three hours to get a G.I.
haircut (Didn't I tell you I decided that as long as I could only have
an inch and a half of hair I might as well do it up good? I now have a
slight buzz on top of my cranium and look like a fugitive from Sing-
Sing.) and taking a lot of tests. By the way, they picked about 1/10 of

our company to register for A.S.T.P. and I was one of those chosen. I won't know for some time though if I'm accepted or not, so don't go telling anyone. I have another cheerful note—about a week ago one of the lieutenants called three of us from the company and told us we would "probably see a better side of the army" and to be sure and get nothing on our records.

I hope I haven't surprised you by what I said about the marches. They aren't going to hurt me. Besides I have been in perfect health ever since I got in and if it wasn't for the lack of freedom I would like this just as much as school. I'm happy, healthy, and wealthy enough.

No, I don't need anything else. In fact I don't even need what I asked for. They gave us some coat hangers, we have foot powder. I managed to get an electric plug at Camp Hood when I went to the hospital there (broke my glasses and that's the only place I can have them fixed—no they won't fix them—I take that back—they'll give me two more pairs) and my new shoes probably won't fit me. At least my old ones don't. The army knew what it was doing when it gave me a "D" width.

I can get magazines here so don't send me any. I won't have a chance to read them anyways. No, I didn't get anything from Aunt Dodo, and I'll write everybody very soon. Don't forget to keep tearing interesting articles from the *Rep*. They told us to watch out for those German prisoners, but I haven't seen any yet. Send me some gossip. A very happy birthday, Fred. Love –Carl

———

Carl was discovering what every GI discovered. As described by military historian Peter Kindsvatter:

> During the tearing-down phase, the recruit, for the life of him, could not see what any of this unpleasantness had to do with preparing him for combat. Learning to shine shoes, march, salute, pull kitchen duty, and make a bunk in a military fashion did not strike him as useful skills. After several weeks of such training the recruits hit a nadir. They were demeaned, frustrated, and angry. They had worked hard but received little in the way of positive reinforcement, and they certainly did not feel like soldiers. . . . Yet just when the trainees' frustrations hit a high point and their morale a low point, things began

to change, albeit almost imperceptibly at first. The tear-down phase ended and the buildup began.[9]

———

Wednesday June 23

Dear Mom,

I was on guard duty for the first time—two hours on, four off, and so on for twenty-four hours. It wasn't bad, but I wouldn't like to do it too often. I'm getting to be a seasoned soldier now. I've had K.P. too. It was for officers' mess and I really left a mark for myself; first by knocking over a stack of dishes, and, secondly, by running the entire length of the mess hall with a dish of mustard for one of the officers before I found out that while I was in the kitchen getting it, the major had gotten up and was giving a talk. Oh well, it's little adventures like that that make life worth living!

Fred, your daily schedule is exactly like mine—two days a month. The other two Sundays I either go into town or they think of something for us to do to keep us from getting homesick. Five of the six weekdays this week I got up at 4:30 instead of 5:00. We've been firing on the range and it takes a lot of time. A score of 134 is what we have to have to qualify. I got a 131 but if I ever get my glasses fixed, I'll get about 150. The only trouble is the noise. It's hard to hear anything for about 12 hours after we shoot. Can you imagine the noise 200 guns all shooting at once would make?

I'll probably be transferred to another unit here at camp in a week or two for A.S.T.P., Lt. E says. It'd better be soon because every week the hikes are getting tougher. We had an eight miler Thursday and it's been very warm the last few days. This time eight guys fell out. Before the hike we had some tactical maneuvering and our squad got lost and had to ford one river three times. We arrived fifteen minutes late and didn't get a rest at all before the hike and then at the beginning of the hike we had to run across a 300 yard bridge, so with the wet shoes, no rest, and all that double-timing we weren't in too good a shape to march eight miles. But we did.

If you take any snapshots send them to me. I don't have any pictures at all of anyone. We get paid in a week and I'll get some pictures taken of me then.

By the way, I wasn't one of the seven soldiers killed by the truck here, in case you're worrying. Five of them were Ohio boys, but none that I knew.

Fred, as soon as you start in your life as a sailor, write and tell me all about it. I want to know what it's like.

I'm sending this airmail so you should get it before you leave. I hope you all enjoy yourselves.

Love Carl

———

They say the one name you remember in the military is the name of your drill sergeant. But the name never stuck with Carl. What Carl did remember was that basic training was basic training. He spent a lot of time on ten-mile marches and fifteen-mile marches. Those were terrible.

Basic training included physical conditioning, close order drill, parades. The first reaction was, what's the point of this? Why do we have to march in parade—we're going to be in combat? And yet it sank in. There was a parade every Saturday. At first it was ridiculous. But then the more Carl did it, the more it sank in, the more he got the feeling of being part of the group.

A postwar study by Walter Reed Army Medical Center described basic training as a process of "learning carried out simultaneously on two levels. In the narrower sense, basic training was a straight-forward process of teaching the trainee specific combat skills. In the broader sense, basic training was an 'acculturative process' in which the trainee learned 'the basic mores, canons, and customs of the military subculture, and the arts of living and cooperating with a large group of his fellow men.'"[10]

That didn't mean that Carl, like any teenager, stopped cutting corners. Back in Canton, Carl enjoyed doing some carpentry work, almost as a hobby. He had done a bit of it before. And he could see that some carpentry work needed to be done around the place and he talked the first sergeant into appointing him battalion carpenter. Carl got razzed a bit by the other guys for it, but it spared him from some of these long marches with a full field pack.

———

Dear Mom,

My Independence Day was a little bit drier than yours. I went
to Dallas with G and we had what could be classified as a glorious
fourth. Sat. night we saw *Sweethearts* in the "Operetta under the
stars" and wandered around the amusement park that is around it.
Sunday we saw Southern Methodist and the rest of Dallas. These two
events were interspersed with steak dinners (but good), running into
guys we knew from Miami, milk shakes, and sleeping in a good hotel
bed. It took ten hours and 300 miles of traveling to get there and back
but it was worth it.

I'm glad that you're having such a grand time up there. In spite
of the fact that it's a little obvious, I'm going to say that I wish I were
with you. Did the old man keep to his plans and go back to Canton
yet? According to the good time you're having, I don't suppose he did.
If you are still there, pop, I want you to tell me what is going on with
Sugardale? How does it differ from what it was six months, one year,
and two years ago in respects to the quantity and quality and price of
the products, as well as the employees?—also what's happening with
subsidies and what's the outlook for the future? What do you have to
do exactly with the ration stamps and how are you handling them?
How does the profit and loss sheet and balance sheet compare to what
it was three months ago, in percent? Etc. I'd really like to know, pop.

Don't worry about my glasses. I'm getting two pair of G.I.s free,
but not in a hurry. There was a mix-up and now I'm supposed to get
them tomorrow. As soon as I do get them I'll send my pair back to
be repaired (one lens is out) because no matter what is wrong with
one's glasses the govt. won't fix them—they'll give you two new pairs
instead.

As for my weight, it's 159 with clothes on, which would be about
155 or 156 without. They weighed me in at the induction center
at 152. Hard work can only make you lose weight by sweating and
burning up fat. You can drink all the sweat loss back, and you can
regain the energy loss by eating the right food. Regular eating and
sleeping hours is what is keeping me in shape.

Where's the pictures of you around the Lodge?[11] Do they still
have those dances over the lake to an orchestra? I suppose it's too late

to tell you now, but remember that sun. I went out in it for an hour and a half the first time and was burned sore for *five* days.

Lots'a love Carl

———

Saturday, July 17, 1943

Hi pop,

So you finally broke down and wrote a letter! Well, I appreciated the gesture even if I couldn't read the words. I gathered that you were worried about the recoil of the big guns and about my ambition and progress in progressing. Well, my ambition is to get into A.S.T.P. or O.C.S. Since O.C.S. has been about 80% eliminated and more experience is required, I'm trying now for A.S.T.P. which stands for the Army Specialized Training Program. It is a nine months course at a college and it also gives college credit. You have to pass three interviews to get in and complete your basic. I have passed the first one so far, about two or three weeks ago. All I can do now is wait. You know the old army byword—"hurry up and wait." Anyways you have to complete your basic before you can get into A.S.T.P., which means another month or so for me.

We moved out into the woods a few days ago, by the way. It's pretty good, if you don't mind the dirt and the lack of water. There are five guys with us in this tent, all from Ohio. Three are from Akron, one from Alliance, and one from Warren. All are college boys and we get along pretty well together, and have a pretty good time.

There are two things that I'm pretty much in need of. One is a pair of shorts or a bathing suit. The other is an old worn out bag to keep my toilet articles, writing stuff, etc. in. I think there is an old gym bag around that's about one foot by two feet by a foot and a half. If so, send it on please; or any other bag of that general size. A bag is the only thing we can keep things in—a box won't do.

Pop, if after the war you can get hold of some G.I. trucks, for God's sake do it. We went on a cross-country convoy and I was in a loaded 2 ½ ton White truck. That 2 ½ ton job went up places that no car and few motorcycles would climb. Very hard to slide or overturn and impossible to wreck.

Yesterday we dug slit trenches and machine gun emplacements all day. The temperature was 110 in the shade—and we weren't in the shade!

Don't worry about gun recoils pop. We don't get big guns for a while yet anyways and if that was all I had to worry about in the way of danger it would be nice. I've learned to keep my eyes open.

On night maneuvers three days ago I was in a tactical situation where I had to lie in one spot for two and a half hours. The next day I learned that that spot was a poison ivy patch. It sounds pretty funny, but it's not to me. I haven't been able to hardly sleep since. We're having some more maneuvers tonight. This time I think I'll burn out any area first that I have to lie in.

Tell me how Sugardale is doing, old man. Take it easy.

Love Carl

———

After hot Texas runs, Carl's sweat and body salt would leave a u-shaped stain on his shirt. He was thirsty and could use a cold Coca-Cola from the drinks cooler provided at the end of the run. But since he was not usually in front of the pack, no Cokes remained. The only soda left was Dr. Pepper, a Waco drink that was a novelty for a midwestern soldier. Even decades after the war, Carl wouldn't drink the stuff. All those years later, he still associated its taste with his runs in the desert.

———

Sunday, July 25, 1943

Hi, Family! –

This letter is doing a big job. It's answering about three of yours. But our free time here in bivouac is even more limited than in the barracks. It's next to impossible to answer letters at any time other than weekends.

Hey, pop, there's just a couple of things I'd still like to know— what percent of the mortgage do you still have to pay? And what percent of normal meat sales are you selling? By the way, there isn't very much of a shortage of meat down in Texas. It's not hard at all to buy a large steak at a restaurant, although I still haven't found one yet that had the quality of Birdseye.

What do you think of my going to West Point? There's an opening for sixty-two men from the eighth service command (about two million soldiers). You have to have an aptitude test of 135 (mine is 141), be 19 to 22 (I'm 19), be in the army one year by July 1, 1944 (thirteen and a half months by then) and sign up for *eight years*. You go to a college from Sept 1943 to July 1944 and then take the test to enter West Point. It's something I'd like to get into, because the peacetime army is much freer than this, and the army interests me more than any business I know of. Of course the chances of my getting in are just about aren't, but I can try. I'm going to speak to the first sergeant about it as soon as possible. Don't say anything about this to anyone by the way.

You know it made me feel good to receive both of your last letters; you both seemed so happy. Are you still going around with the Canadian smart set, mom? And are you still under-trimming the pork loins, pop? Do you still have as many fights as you used to? I'd really like to see how just the two of you get along together.

I've been telling the fellas about your love-making efforts.[12] They've been getting quite a kick out of it. Does it take you back to your younger days? But no kidding, I'm glad you did. She seems to be a pretty swell kid. I'm still waiting for her picture, and I'm still waiting for a lot of yours. I still haven't any of me; and I'm not too sure you'd like to have me take one for awhile with my hair a quarter of an inch long, my face swollen and covered with medicine from poison ivy, and not having chewed in four days for the same reason - also a young mustache which I am experimenting with.

Excuse the status of this paper, s'il vous plait. They're Coke stains and Coke is too valuable around here to throw away. I'll just have to send it on.

Our basic training should be over in about two weeks. It's supposed to end with a sixty-five mile march (I can hardly wait) and then we'll be moved out of here. A.U.T.C. (advanced) will probably be in main Camp Hood and that's where I'll most likely be unless I start hearing something from A.S.T.P. By now you've probably gotten the idea that all you do in the army is wait. Well that's the right idea. That reminds me—I've finally gotten my G.I. glasses—seven weeks after they were promised me. They're pretty good, but they don't look so hot. Oh well, they'll blend in with the general gruesome effect of the G.I. Carl Lavin.

I guess I've been doing a lot of griping, but I'm actually quite
happy here.

Remember what you said about the army being a glorious adventure? Well it *is* a glorious adventure—in living. I've been with every type of person there is—and I'm fascinated in having some of the highest types for tent-mates, the kind you were just writing about, mother. Well, s'all for now.

Love Carl

———

There was something unusual near Carl's barrack—a group of barracks of men going through Officer Candidate School, and they were all African Americans. At that time, America was still largely segregated, and the military was no different.[13]

There were a few all-black units. There was a black tank battalion. There was a black fighter wing—the Tuskegee Airmen. But Carl's most common sighting of black people was in transportation units. They were truck drivers. Large numbers of African Americans also served in engineer and quartermaster units, among others, but there was hardly any mixing of races. Occasionally, Carl would see some black and white MPs. The camp made it a point to have one black and one white MP go out together.

It was at Camp Hood that Carl first encountered African Americans in a professional capacity, and what he saw impressed him greatly. In barracks next to his was this group of black men training to be officers. They were polished, smart, and smart-looking. Carl's conclusion: In the face of segregation and societal pressure, those soldiers had to be twice as good as the white soldiers in order to get ahead. They were accomplished, professional, elite. They were a crackerjack group.[14]

———

July 30, '43

Dear Mother,

There's nothing new to report, except that I've been having a very easy time of it lately. That poison ivy I told you about hasn't left me yet, so they put me on light duty. I'm not supposed to do anything that makes me sweat, because that's what spreads and irritates it. Yezzer, I'm leading the life.

Believe it or not, we've had a rainy spell for two days now! The temperature has gone down to 90, which actually feels quite cool, and every night we have rain, which feels exhilarating in the tents.

I guess I forgot to tell you about the long-horn I sent you. I happened to see it when I was in town and I thought it would go good with the dog and the bear on the radio. Does it?

I'm still waiting to hear something from A.S.T.P. Rumor has it that our basic will be over pretty soon. Only encouraging sign so far is that I've been made assistant squad (10 men) leader which isn't a damn thing.

Yes, I got a letter from Betty K. Can't tell much from it—seems to be pretty decent, intelligent, etc.

I received the shorts. Thanks a lot. I didn't expect you to buy some, though, with all the bathing suits around. They'll come in very handy. I'll still need a bathing suit though. How about sending me that blue pair? I didn't get the bag yet, though. If you have time and points will you make me some fudge, please? How about the *Repository*? Write soon.

Love, Carl

Aug 2, 1943
Sunday

Dear Mom,

Right now I'm having a good time doing nothing but existing. It feels damn good to do nothing and have nothing to worry about. We got paid yesterday so practically the whole company is out on pass. As a result there's a lot of extra food, which is always good on week ends, and I think I must have gained five pounds this week end. I'm using it also to get rid of my poison ivy. They told me that the sun would be the best thing for it, so I took a sunbath yesterday in the nude. After an hour of battling gnats, half-inch flies, quarter-inch ants and various and sundry other members of the animal kingdom I began to get quite warm in certain generally unexposed sections. And then when two buzzards started circling overhead I decided it was time to end the sunbath. It worked pretty good though, because I slept good

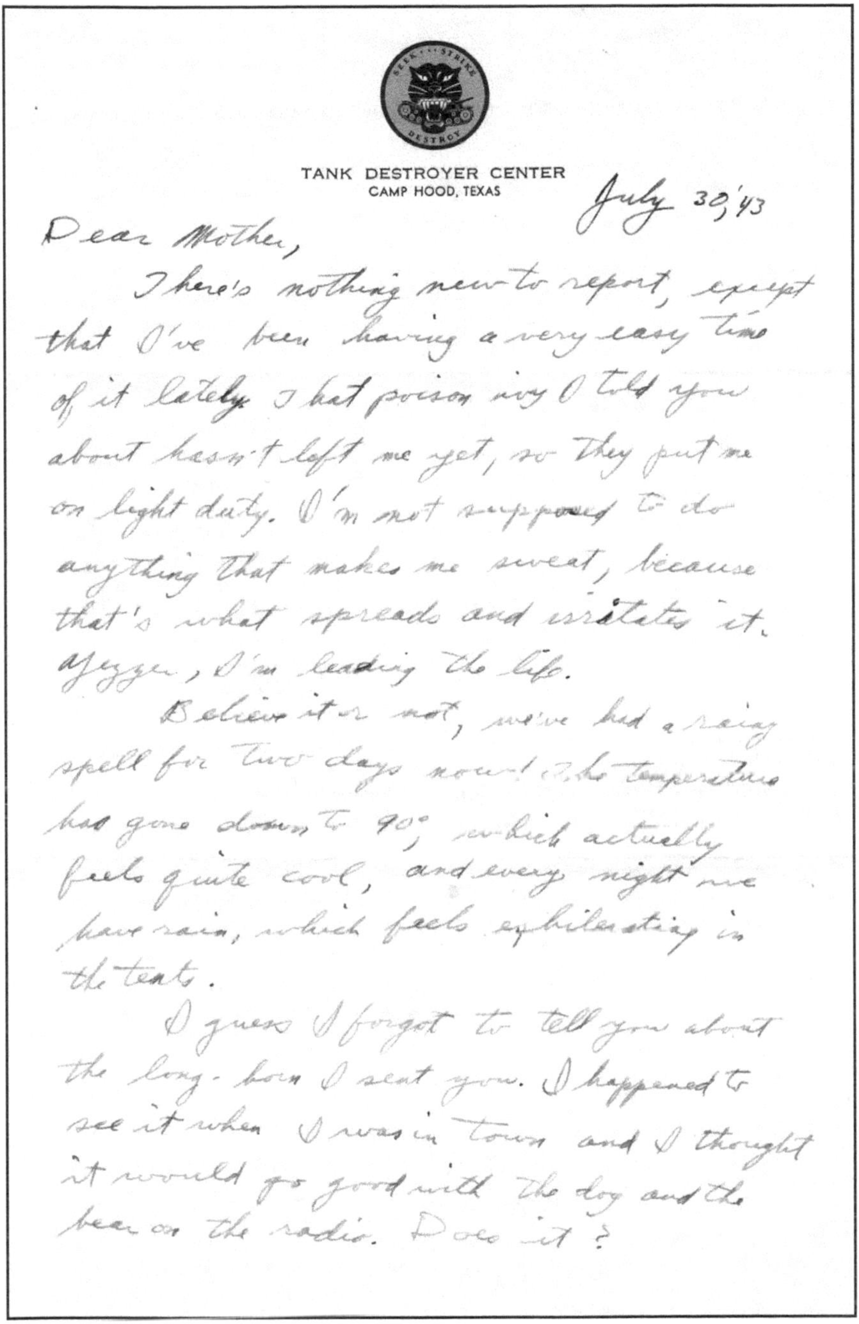

TANK DESTROYER CENTER
CAMP HOOD, TEXAS

July 30, '43

Dear Mother,

There's nothing new to report, except that I've been having a very easy time of it lately. That poison ivy I told you about hasn't left me yet, so they put me on light duty. I'm not supposed to do anything that makes me sweat, because that's what spreads and irritates it. Ayeyye, I'm leading the life.

Believe it or not, we've had a rainy spell for two days now! The temperature has gone down to 90°, which actually feels quite cool, and every night we have rain, which feels exhilarating in the tents.

I guess I forgot to tell you about the long-horn I sent you. I happened to see it when I was in town and I thought it would go good with the dog and the bear on the radio. Does it?

Figure 2-1. Tank Destroyer Center letterhead, Camp Hood, Texas, July 30, 1943. *Author collection.*

last night for the first time since I've gotten it, and that's probably why I feel so good today. All a matter of relativity.

How is everything getting on now back in Canton? Any riots, floods, fires, or explosions? Any of the kids home on furlough? By the way, send me my chess set please. I think it's around there somewhere. Never mind the board.

Take it easy. Love Carl

Wednesday August 4, 1943

Dear Mother,

Don't worry, I still have not signed my life away or at least that eight year stretch of it. I don't believe you read my letter very carefully in which I told you about getting into A.S.T.P. This is the procedure—1st – two or three interviews—2nd – assignment to a "STAR" unit, which determines which part of ASTP you are "best qualified" for—and assigns you to it regardless of your choices—3rd – preliminary ASTP which consists of 3 twelve week courses separated by a week of furlough—4th advanced ASTP which consists of from 1 to 4 twelve week courses or more. Now this kid whose letter you sent me was assigned to a medical ASTP at his STAR center because they thot he was best fitted for that, whether he wanted it or not. And that's what will happen to me—I'll be tested and assigned to what they want me. If it's something that has advanced training and if they want me to, or decide I'm good enough to, I'll get advanced training later.

Now, as for West Point. As I said, the odds are 100,000 to one against my getting in. If I'm lucky enough to get into the preliminary training course I'll have until next June to decide if I want to really take West Point and eight years. You said that if I got into that I'd have eight years away from civilian life and consequently would not know how and be afraid to conduct myself in it again. I would have wasted eight years, not be able to marry, and not be able to make a living for myself. You said my best bet would be medicine.

Well, I think you're wrong. Who are the important men of twenty years from now going to be? Not scientists—they were taken over by industry in the last war, not industry, or capital, or business—they are

all being taken over by government in this war. When peace comes
the military heroes will hold the offices, we will retain a big army
which will have a large say. The army leaders will also be leaders of
public opinion. Government will be the big thing and the army will
be the big thing in government. Let's look at it in a less general way
now. My eight years will be three years of excellent training (four,
in peace) followed by five or four years of the best practical training
in the world in handling men. Now if that wouldn't be enough to get
any really good civilian job, I'd like to know what is. But I probably
wouldn't want to get a civilian job. I've talked to men who were
in the peacetime army. They worked from seven to five each day
with weekends off at Saturday noon. You don't even have to wear a
uniform off duty. Of course, the pay isn't too good, but there's plenty
of room for advancement and it's a well established firm. Now if I take
medicine I undoubtedly won't get there in five years because the
war won't last that long. In peacetime it would be ten years plus a
year of internship plus two or three years of setting up a practice
before I could get married; I could get hooked, though, on my pay
after graduating from West Point—not that I see that that is any
criteria. Anyways I still love you. Think it over and tell me what you
think.

    Love Carl

Aug 15, 1943
Saturday

    Hi Mom!
    I'm writing this letter in a 1935 Chevrolet traveling on a
typical Texas highway, so you'll have to excuse the hydrographical
appearance.
    I've been waiting to write this letter until I received yours in
response to the one I wrote about A.S.T.P. and West Point, and I still
haven't but anyways. (It may take a little concentration figure out that
last sentence.)
    I understand that the first sergeant never handed in my name,
and it's now too late. (That's the way the army is run) I'm not sure
because he's on furlough right now.

I'm hitch-hiking now from Waco to Dallas. I called up Betty K in Waco and have a date all fixed up. She sent me her picture. Not bad at all—but not too good either. But with no date in three months I should be choosey?

Time has been going very fast lately. Days are cooler, work is more interesting, and the guys I go with are swell. I really feel like an old soldier now. Got my bathing suit and fudge. Love Carl

———

Carl takes a slightly different tone when writing a similar letter to his brother.

———

Saturday AUG 15, 1943

Dear Fred,

Right now I'm between Waco and Dallas in a 1935 Chevy on a typical Texas highway. That explains the handwriting. I'm going to Dallas for my first date in three months. The party of the second part is Betty K, Helen Kaven's [Carl's cousin, the daughter of Elizabeth Kaven] roommate's sister (at Wisconsin). She goes to Texas A & M and of course she's an ΑΕΦ—I still remember my alphabet.

I've been writing to her and she sends me her picture. Has possibilities. Did the family tell you about Mugsey in Muskoka? The mater, determined to strike up a romance, got her to write to me and we've been corresponding since. Seems really O.K. Sent me some pictures, one in a two piece bathing suit and a pin-up girl pose (flat on her back) which she did justice to.

I'm starting to get a kick out of the army. We haven't had hardly any more hikes these last four weeks (although we're going to finish up our basic in a week with a hundred mile one). Things have been more interesting with tactical maneuvering, night problems, and convoy work. I drove a half-track the other evening. Remember the ones that passed through Canton all the time? That's our basic weapon, with a .75 mounted on it. Pretty nice to drive. By the way, it is now Wednesday evening, and this is the first time I've had to myself since the weekend.

That date I mentioned earlier turned out next to perfection. She's one of those girls that you have to put in your application for three weeks ahead of time in school if you want a date. (Lucky for me there's a war going on—ha.) Perfect dancer, wonderful personality, very good-looking, good sense of humor *AND* she has a car. Called her up and she picked me up at the U.S.O. We went to the Plantation Club—open air night club and about the best in Dallas. Good orchestra and full moon. And now I am back in the woods.

I think I'll get called to A.S.T.P. in about two weeks now. Who knows, maybe I'll be sent to Ohio State. Boy, am I an optimist!

So how are things going with you? Did you get your uniform yet?

Yesterday marked the end of three months of the soldier's life (Only three more months and then I'll just have to visit for the duration, as one of the guys said.) Only three more months and I'll be eligible for a furlough—and then probably six more and I'll get one. Have you been home on a weekend yet? Or are you studying like you should? Write soon.

Love Carl

August 19, 1943
Wednesday

Dear Mother,

You make me feel like a heel, writing all those letters when I haven't been sending very much at all. But you make me feel very good too—so keep it up. Please understand that my time is very limited. It's practically a matter of choosing between going out on weekends or writing letters. The last two weekends I've been going out so I haven't been writing much. But after two in a row, both my budget and my body are tired—so I'll stay in this coming week-end. About two out of three evenings, when we're supposed to be on our own time, are taken up by something or other. F'rinstance Monday night they picked twenty-five of us to learn to drive half-tracks. They're the armored trucks with wheels on the front and tracks on back, that pass through Canton all the time, with a .75 mounted on it. They're pretty nice to drive and it looked good to see "Diebold Safe & Lock" stamped on them with "Canton, Ohio" below. By the way, are they still passing through? I mean the one with tracks, not the four wheeled ones. I am very interested in knowing if they're still making them. They are being replaced with a new (restricted) vehicle and I'd like to know if they have stopped making half-tracks yet. You'd better ask Pop.

Tuesday evening we had range shooting for those that didn't qualify before. Remember I told you I missed it by three points? We fired from four different positions at 200 and 300 yards. Out of a possible 210 we had to get 140 to qualify—I got 164 so I was quite happy about the situation. We used Springfield instead of Enfields, which may account for a lot of that. The Springfield, which is a 1903 model, is supposed to be the best army rifle in the world—including Garands. Seems funny, doesn't it? But it is more accurate than the Enfield, a 1917 model. Ask L.B.L. [Leo Lavin] about it—he should still remember. And when you're asking him questions ask him his estimation of the percentage of meat sold in the black market. I'd like to know.[15]

Those half-tracks have the same gear shift as the big Sugardale trucks, so I guess I got some good out of my work there. They weigh twice as much, though.

One week from tomorrow we go out to a dam near here, where we will stay in pup tents for three days, and which will end our basic. It's a regular park there with swimming, etc. Shortly after that I imagine I'll get shipped someplace to a S.T.A.R. unit.

Of course I won't know for sure until about 12 hours before I go, but you can always piece together all the rumors you hear and get a fairly accurate picture. You don't understand what the word "rumor" means until you get in the army. Write soon. Love Carl

———

August 24, 1943
Saturday

Dear Mom,

First of all, as for the ambiguity I was referring to West Point when I said I didn't think the 1st sergeant had turned in my name. As I said, he is on furlough so I can't ask him about it. The acting serg. says he thinks it was turned in.

As for A.S.T.P., I can't get into that until basic is finished, one
week from today. Then we start a 65 mile hike to our advanced training.
Don't know if we'll be called before or after that hike. There is nothing I
can accomplish by "pushing" it, except make myself obnoxious.

Now for my date with Betty. The reason I hitch hiked is because
it is the fastest and also the cleanest way of getting from Waco to
Dallas. I have never heard of anyone yet that took along a change of
clothes on a weekend pass. I showered and washed several times at
the U.S.O. so don't worry about my being clean. My manners were
exemplary. My God, woman, stop worrying! I'll admit that I did
commit one or two social faux pas in my first year at dance class. But
since then I *have* made a few improvements. I think the last time you
saw me on a date was when you drove me. Try to remember that I am
not a kid anymore. That old maternal instinct wants to remember me
as one, but it's wrong. I will not be treated as a kid anymore. I am
capable of handling my own affairs and forming my own opinions and
judgments and I intend to do so.

Anyways, that date was a perfect one. She picked me up in
her car at the U.S.O. and we went to the Plantations Club, the best
night club in Dallas. An open air one, with a full moon and a good
orchestra. She is a perfect dancer, wonderful conversationalist, good
looking, etc. So all in all I had a perfect time.

Could you send me some caramels or some salt water taffy? Or
some nuts? Just giving suggestions. How about sending me some
lollypops—no kidding. There are six of us here who like them, in
spite of the fact that we're big, husky, fearless T.D.s.

Well, s'all for now. Take it easy. I still love you - Carl

August 25, 1943
Sunday

Dear Mother,

I just went over your letter again and I realize that there were a
few things I left out of mine.

I got entirely rid of my poison ivy about two weeks after I got it. I
still haven't had my picture taken—and I don't know how or when I
can get one. We're supposed to have a company picture taken pretty

soon. So I'll send you a copy and you can see both what I and my environment look like. O.K.?

I won't say anything more about what you said concerning my not knowing how to act. But I did become annoyed all over again by just rereading it. My God, Mom!

The other A.S.T.P. interviews come at the S.T.A.R. center. I don't believe I mentioned that.

That's good news about Fred. I guess he really decided to work. I should talk.

Love Carl

P.S. I'm hungry.

August 27, 1943
Wednesday

Dear Mom,

I'm on guard duty right now, and it has come at rather an opportune time. Yesterday we had that twenty four hour problem I told you about and, since we went on guard at 18:30, we didn't have to go and got the whole day off. Proof that there's good in everything.

You'd better not expect much mail from me in the next week and a half as I doubt that I'll have much opportunity to write any. It finishes our basic and we're going to pretty damn busy. I'll let you know just as soon as I hear anything, though. I've noticed in quite a few of the magazines lately that they've shown the M-7 Assault Gun, nicknamed "the Priest," as a Tank Destroyer. It has an 105mm howitzer mounted on it and the T.D.s use only flat trajectory weapons, mainly the 75mm and the three inch. Just thought I'd clear it up for the record.

How has the heat been in Canton lately? Those very hot days here all over with, I hope. It only gets up to around 105 now instead of 115. There might not seem to be much difference between 105 and 115, but believe me, there is.

I read in the *Sunday Rep* about that tornado you had. Why didn't you say anything about it? According to the paper the path of the storm was just about directly over the plant. Was there any damage done to it?

From all the trouble Spitzy seems to be having I guess that old
age is really leaping up on her. Tsk, tsk.

We are out at McCannon Dam right now—about fifty miles from
camp and where we will remain until Saturday. This is a sort of
half-vacation for us. We just got done with two hours of swimming
in the Colorado River—about three miles wide here, and blue and
wonderful after three months of dust. The scenery around here is
rocky like Canada, only more so. More like the movie *Texas*.

So—let me know how things are going on at home.

Love and kisses Carl

———

Tuesday 9/1/43

Dear Mommy,

Remember that hike I was telling you about? Well, we're having
it. They were sweet enough to cut it down to 45 miles, which we are
taking in easy stages. Today we hiked about 15 miles—or rather this
morning we did. This afternoon we're resting up.

However, they've got me down here at the battalion Command
Post as a runner and in that capacity I've gone another three miles so
far.

But this is really more of a vacation to us than work. We only
work four or five hours a day and have the rest of the time free. Of
course whenever I mention free time, you've got to subtract 1/4 to 1/3
of it for details.

Tsk, tsk— where did you ever get such a metaphor: "…when
your mother flutters around her chicks like a wet hen." Sounds like
something from the *New Yorker*.

That good news you were waiting for hasn't shown up yet. But
don't worry, there are about 30 or 40 men in the battalion who are
trying to get in so I don't think they'll forget about us. The army
always takes two or three weeks longer than is necessary in things
like this. It didn't take me three and a half months to learn that.

The STAR unit is a sort of induction center for the ASTP and
works the same as the induction center.

How are you getting along with the new gas rationing? Has it
curtailed your Jewish Center Activities any? Are you taking good care
of the Chevy for me?

I just got a letter from Fred. He seems to be pretty happy and
getting along well. He wrote me all about his campus life and he's
happy about the whole thing.

By the tone of your letter you seemed to be rather happy too. I
hope you stay that way.

I suppose that there's a slight possibility that I might get a
furlough before A.S.T.P. but don't count on it at all. I'm not.

Still happy and healthy.

Load of love Carl

———

September 7, 1943

Dear Mother,

After that hike we were supposed to move right into the barracks
at Camp Hood, but the battalion that was supposed to move out to
give us room couldn't get transportation. So we have been living in
our pup tents like babes in the wilderness for over a week thus far. It's
rained five out of the last six nights, mostly combined with a 20 to 30
mile wind, which was not too conducive to drowsiness.

———

Thurs Sept 9 '43

Had to cut short this because I was called out for a dramatic
turn. I was one of 15 men from my company picked to see it. It was
a demonstration of the firepower of our infantry battalion (The T.D.s
and the infantry work together). There were about 3000 men watching
all together. They had all guns going at once, arcing tracers at night.
Most impressive. The .30 caliber machine gun crossfire was one
solid stream of flame. Impossible for any living thing to get through,
apparently.

Still waiting for A.S.T.P. and still waiting for our battalion to move into Camp Hood. A few more weeks of this animal living and I'll become entirely untamed.

They had a few of us out driving half-tracks today. Went over quite rough country and through woods. Boy, did I have fun! See, that wild driving I did in the old Plymouth really stood me in good stead.[16]

I got those two boxes of candy you sent. Very good and very much appreciated.

What's happening to those *Sunday Reps* you were sending? Haven't received one for three weeks. And do me another favor, please. Send me the *Sat. Eve. Post*. Get a subscription. Haven't been getting very many letters from home lately. Keep me posted on all that's going on, willya huh? Goodbye mom and Love Carl

———

September 13, 1943
Sunday

Hi, Babe [Mom]!

Back to civilization! We moved into Camp Hood (*not* North Camp Hood) yesterday and got set up in our barracks. After two weeks of pup tents, dirty clothes, walking 300 yards to wash, and going to bed with the sun this place is heaven. Cots, electric lights, floors—I can't get over it!

I had a lot of fun coming down. I believe I told you I've been assigned as a driver, didn't I? (Anyways, I was. That's why I had that training on driving half-tracks.) Well, one of the M-10s had to be repaired (same as an M-4 medium tank but has an open turret and a 3 inch gun) so it was driven down here earlier yesterday and another guy and I went along as assistant drivers. I climbed on top of the back end of the gun and found that because of the recoil mechanism it is just the same width as a horse. So I rode the whole ten miles horseback. No kidding, it felt exactly the same as one, especially in going over ruts and ditches where it was the same as a bucking horse. It certainly reminded me of home and those times I used to go riding with the kids.

I finally heard the good news. I leave for ASTP this Thursday. I haven't received any official notice as yet but have received the info

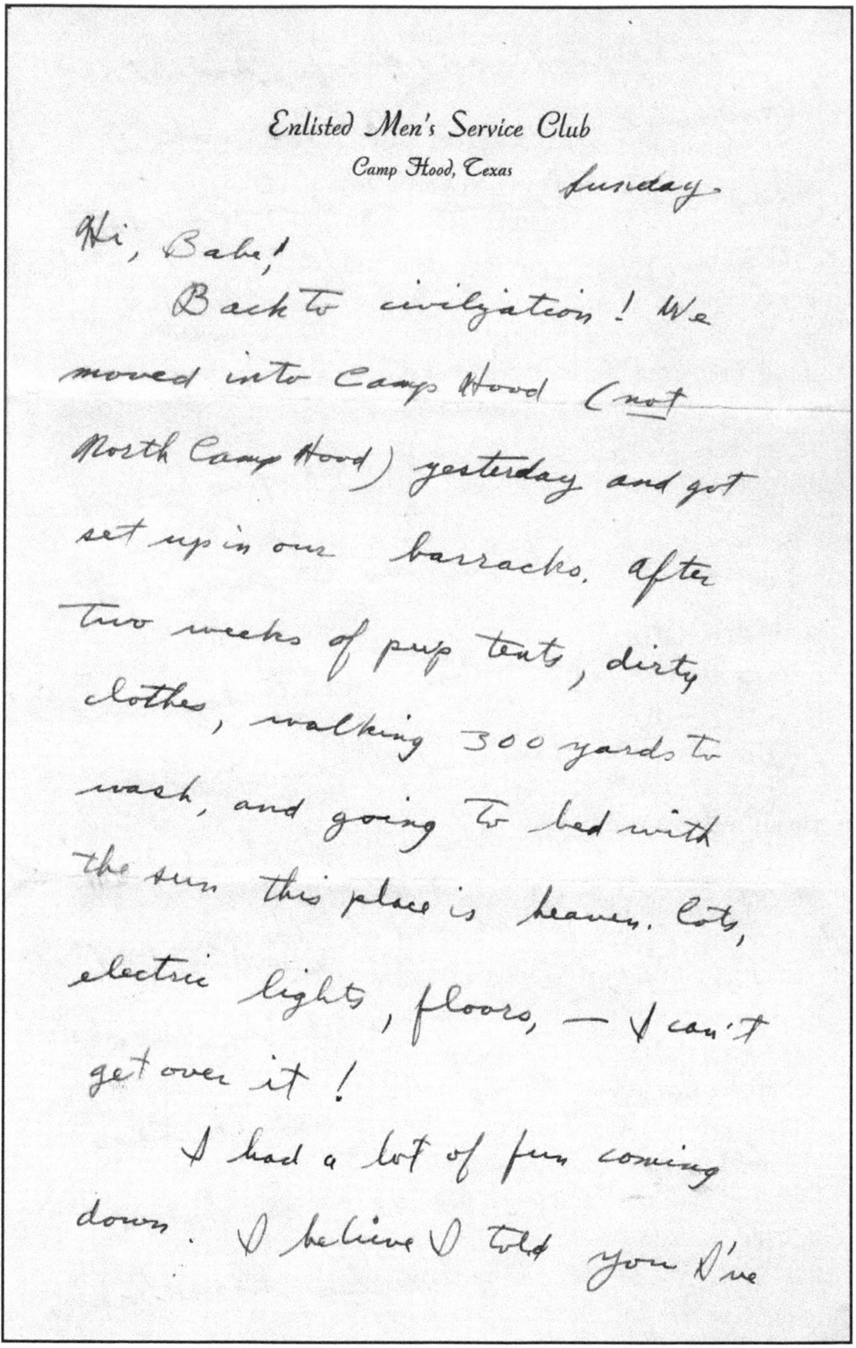

Enlisted Men's Service Club
Camp Hood, Texas   Sunday

Hi, Babe!
        Back to civilization! We
moved into Camp Hood (not
North Camp Hood) yesterday and got
set up in our barracks. After
two weeks of pup tents, dirty
clothes, walking 300 yards to
wash, and going to bed with
the sun this place is heaven. Cots,
electric lights, floors, — I can't
get over it!
        I had a lot of fun coming
down. I believe I told you I've

Figure 2-2. Enlisted Men's Service Club letterhead, Camp Hood, Texas, September 13, 1943. *Author collection.*

from what you might term "generally reliable sources" or, as it is
expressed in the army, a shit-house rumor. But from my four month
experience with army rumors, I can term this one as correct.

How is everything going on the home front? Anything happening
lately?

Keep your chins up –Love Carl

———

Camp Maxey Service Club[17]
October 12, 1943

Hi, Maw,

Well, I have been here a week and I guess I should have written
you before and I still don't know where I'll be sent. There is, however,
a very nasty as well as persistent rumor that our group will end up in
Baylor University, which is right in the middle of Waco, which is just
thirty miles from Camp Hood. I can think of no more horrible a fate.
But if that's where they want me that's where I'll go. I'll probably find
out this week.

Now tell me all about Chicago. Did either the American Meat
Packers' Association or the Exalted Order of the Hadassah reach any
decision? Did you see that play about the Russians?[18] Did you have
fun? Did anything exciting happen? Tell me what.

I got a three day pass this week-end for Yom Kippur.[19] I spent them
in Dallas. Had a pretty good time there, too. Stayed with some very nice
people that I got through the Jewish center. They had a lot of people
around both nights and we all had quite a gay little time of it. Went to two
dances at the center which were enjoyable. Found the best steak place in
Dallas. In fact I did about everything but go to temple. Tsk, tsk.

About all I'm doing here at Camp Maxey is taking it easy and
resting up for my coming college days. Of course, a few things do pop
up now and then to interrupt, such as the ten mile hike we had today
and K.P. duties.

Did Fred find out yet whether or not he's going to be staying in
Miami for another semester? Tell him he's owed me a letter for a
month now. I ran into a guy in Dallas who was a Frosh at Miami with
me and was at Camp Wise with Fred. I forget his name, though. He's
been in about seven months. I told him all about Fred.

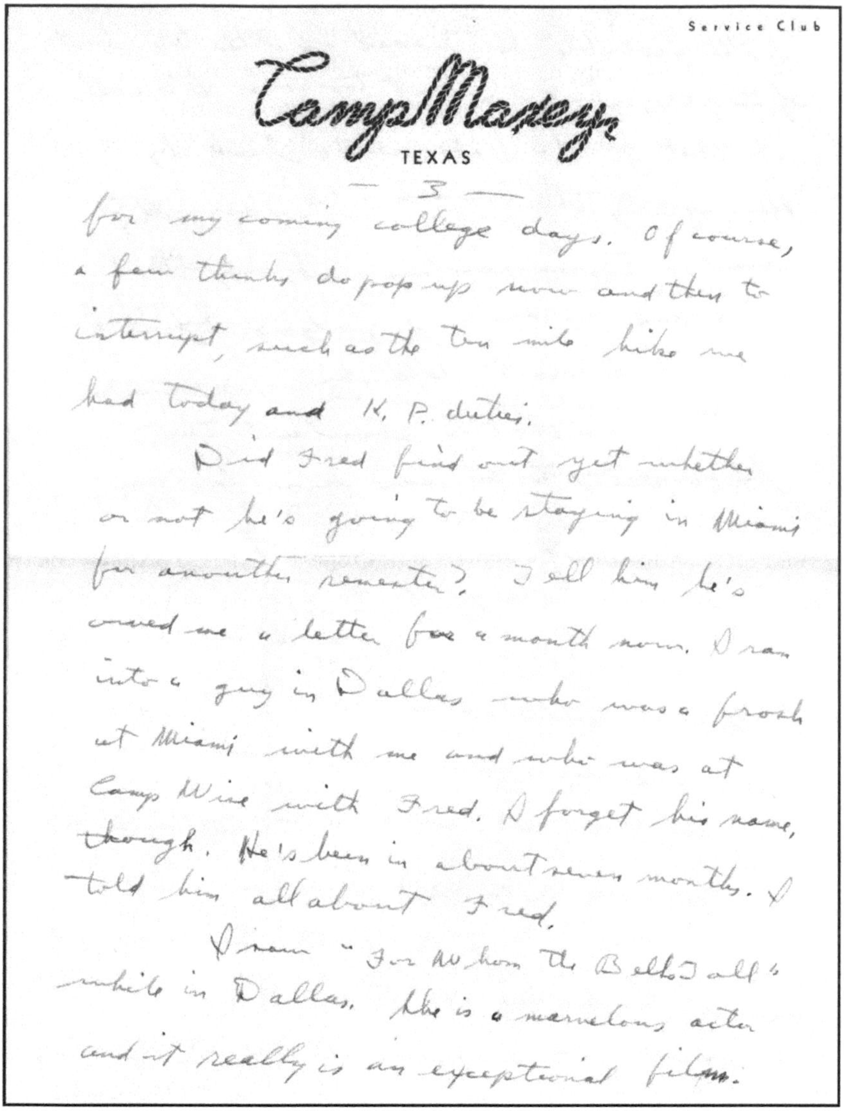

48

Figure 2-3. Camp Maxey Service Club letterhead, Texas, October 12, 1943. *Author collection.*

I saw *For Whom the Bell Tolls* while in Dallas. She is a marvelous actor and it really is an exceptional film.[20] It'll probably be named one of the ten best of the year, but I'm not too sure I'd call it that good. I also read a book by Hemingway this week—*A Farewell to Arms*—disappointing. The only thing I've read by him and judging by this one book I don't like him.

And that's about all that's happened to me since you last saw me.
Write soon.

Lots of love –Carl

———

Oct 25, 1943
Sunday

Hello Mother,

Glad to hear that both you and the tonsil are better. You still
haven't told me whether the latter has been removed or not. Has it?
And you didn't say whether it was serious or dangerous or not. Was
it? If it was, I presume that now it isn't. Yes? Good.

Stop worrying about my hair, woman. I haven't been able to find
any barber who could pamper and coax it. But it is now at the place
where I have to comb it, and a semblance of a wave is reappearing. At
the latest sounding for depth it was "mark one—and—a—half." I'm
expecting a "mark twain" at any time.[21]

Is Fred home yet? If so, hello, Alfie. Do you know what's going
to happen to you? I suppose you're in the same boat that I'm in (or
perhaps I should say you're in the same M-10 tank destroyer I'm in.)

For about two weeks there hasn't been a single shipment out
of here. While we were here the previous three weeks about twenty
shipping numbers went out and they stopped one number short of
mine, or rather ours; "ours" meaning the guys that came in with me
from 665 and came into Ft. Hayes with me.

But anyways a brief analysis of all the latest latrine-grams
(rumors) reveals that this week they will start sending us out once
more (Ohio State, Purdue, Brooklyn, West Coast, to name a few
locales).

I would like to have seen that first snow you wrote about. Howz
the weather now? Many blizzards? It's pretty cold down here now,
about like it was up there when I was on the furlough. We have three
field ranges to a barracks and they keep us nice and cozy. In fact one
of them is beside my bunk and same is gradually taking on a fairly
charred appearance. We're getting into the rainy season now. And
when it rains here I mean the drops come down. Last night while in
Paree (Paris, Texas to you—comparable to Alliance) it started to rain.

50   Two minutes later the streets were flooded. Of course, this wouldn't be something to write home about except that this was the first I've seen in three months that didn't come out of a Lister bag.[22]

Well, take care of yourself and don't neglect to have your tonsils taken out if they need it.

We just had our monthly examination for venereal diseases. I passed with flying colors. Thot you might be interested. Still pure as driven snow.

     'Bye—Love Carl

Camp Maxey, Texas
Friday Oct, 29

Dear Mom,

At last, at long final last, the jolly news has come! I've found out where and when I'll be going! I'm going to Queens College in Queens, N.Y. So it's not such a bad deal. I've never seen the big city yet. And this will be my chance. From what I've been able to gather from the guys from N.Y. I'm pretty lucky in getting Queens. It's got a campus, unlike the other city schools there, and is supposed to be a rather good school and not one of these real tough ones.

I'd guess I'd have a little trouble coming home on week-ends, but it'll be pretty good for the seven day furlough, which I have only three months to wait for now. Who knows, maybe I can get home for Xmas or New Years.

I don't know which way the train will go—but if it goes through Chicago I imagine it will also go through Canton—which it probably won't. If it does, however, I'll call you from somewhere and I can see you and pop for ten minutes. Maybe you can get on and ride to the next stop and we can have twenty minutes together, but that probably won't work because you won't have any way of getting back and also it most likely will be a troop train and civies won't be allowed on it.[23]

I may not even be allowed to get off of it so I may not even be able to call you. Soooo, don't stay at home all week just to wait for a phone call.

By the way, are any of your activities going to take you to N.Y. again? Come on up, I'll show you around.

But enuf of that. Where is Fred now? Back at dear old Miami?
How did he enjoy his furlough? What did he do? Has anything
exciting happened in Canton lately?

The Houston Symphony Orchestra played here a few days ago.
I enjoyed it very much—for the laughs. I thought Texas had become
civilized but I found out how wrong I was. The Houston Orchestra
is supposed to be the best in Texas and Texas is quite proud of it, of
course, as they are of everything having to do with said state. Well,
do you remember how the Canton Symphony sounded a few years ago
when they were going strong? That is a favorable comparison with
the Houston Symphony. They played Tch's 5th, some Strauss, some
Mozart, Templeton's parody of Mozart (not bad) and finished up with
the "Red, White, and Blue" and "Deep in the Heart of Texas." More
fun.

Keep your chins up—howz your throat?

Lots of love —son Carl

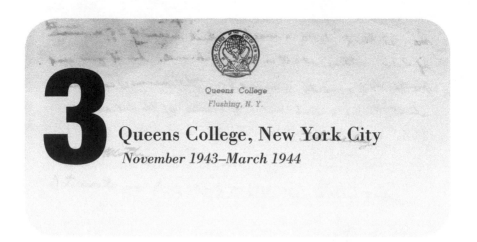

3 Queens College, New York City

November 1943–March 1944

Carl was out of the infantry and assigned to the Army Specialized Training Program (ASTP) at Queens College in New York City. America was at war and Carl was going back to school.

The ASTP came about because of politics. A majority of undergraduate students had been males, so the colleges were depleted when they were called into the army. The colleges brought political pressure to bear to use the colleges in training, and as a result the army started the ASTP.

Anyone with more than a 115 IQ could get in. There was no military training, just academic work. It was taking basic college classes extra fast. And it was generally believed that if you got into the ASTP you were assured of becoming an officer.

The program was a blessing for Carl. He no longer was in the infantry. He was in an academic setting in New York City, an exciting, expensive city that Carl could occasionally explore. An Emerald City.

It was wartime, but sometimes you wouldn't know it from Carl's letters. Carl was horseback riding, ringing in the New Year at Times Square, dancing at the Stage Door Canteen, hopping on the Staten Island Ferry, and even taking in Broadway. And he wasn't doing it alone.

Carl was falling in love, with a girl and a city. And he was on the verge of becoming an officer. It was almost as if Carl had won the lottery.

Almost.

Queens College opened in 1937, though many of the Spanish tile–roofed stucco buildings had been built in the 1900s and 1920s. Its position on a hill provided a clear view of the Manhattan skyline from the far-end of the campus.[1]

The first ASTP unit came to the Queens College campus in the summer of 1943, and the appearance of all 345 ASTP men there was a welcome sight for the 1,625 civilian students.[2]

The ASTP students were still in the army, meaning they wore uniforms to class, received their same service pay and had to follow all army rules and regulations. Basically, ASTPers had "approximately 59 hours of supervised activity a week."[3] Though it could differ, it typically meant that from Monday to Friday ASTPers around the country arose to Reveille at 6:30 a.m. and ended their day on campus with Taps at 10:30 p.m. On the weekend they were required to wake at 6:30 a.m. on Saturday as well as attend classes from 1:20 to 3:20 p.m. After that, the students' schedule freed up until 6:30 p.m. the next day, Sunday.[4]

———

Carl joined the program as a replacement. He would move into the recreation building, with army bunks taking over the gym floor. With him were several hundred enlisted men from across the United States.[5]

A student by the name of Anna Lee Kram captured the campus scene with her poem "Forward, Cupid—Hut!":

> They came in August,
> A.S.T.P.
> Marching and drilling,
> (Gosh, it was thrilling!)
> Olive, drab, spilling
> From out building C.
> Girls went wacky
> Over khaki
> Preened and primped,
> Homework skimped
> Soldiers to vamp us
> On the campus.
> Classes cut.
> Forward, hut!
> Alas! The Dean's Office says
> "—Eyes on your books.
> Be efficient and curt,

54

Don't talk, smile, or flirt;
The war effort's hurt
By a coed's coy looks."
AFTERTHOUGHT
But never mind the ruling,
girls,
Lay aside your fears.
Just leave the maneuvers to
the F.A.L.
And the plans to the engineers.[6]

———

Nov 19 1943
Thursday

Dear Mother,

Yes, the work is pretty hard here. I'm taking 27 hours (average in a college is about 17) and taking 18 weeks work in each subject in 12 weeks. Only free time is one hour each evening and 24 hours each weekend. Besides we still have a lot of military stuff and gym. They're trying to make this a second West Point. 30% flunked out last period.

But the work is very interesting, and the time goes rapidly because you're always busy.

Yes, I could use some money. We weren't paid this month yet and the cost of living is damn high in N.Y.

Went to the Stage Door Canteen two nights.[7] Place is just like the movie but smaller and more crowded. They have a lot of talent, but I didn't see any famous names. Have 20 mins. of dancing and 10 mins. of some kind of entertainment. Very good. About all the hostesses are your girls that belong to the actors union but not too bright lights. They are really something to talk to, and good dancers. So there you have the Stage Door Canteen. Anything else you want to know about N.Y.?

Saw Radio City, Empire State Bldg. at night, *Arsenic and Old Lace*, Times Square, and lots of people.[8]

This letter probably has a slightly scribbled effect to it because I'm writing while running between two classes at opp. ends of the campus.

Where's my watch?! Did you get the socks yet? Send my gym shoes also, please, if you can find them.

Love Carl

—

During Carl's stay in New York City, the city and its famous lights would show the strains of war. To protect the city from the threat of enemy raids, the neon signs of Broadway disappeared, top floors of skyscrapers went dark, cab headlights were covered, even the glow from the *New York Times*'s news ticker faded away.[9]

Downtown in Manhattan, the United States Courthouse had its "gold-leafed roof" painted black.[10]

And in the harbor, the Statue of Liberty saw her lamp go from the gleam of "13,000-watt lamps" to the dim of two "200-watt bulbs."[11]

But even with less light, and the fear and the sacrifices that come with an international war, New York City life and culture carried on.

An illustrated "Camel" man blew smoke rings out of an elongated Times Square billboard. *Oklahoma!* began delighting crowds at the St. James Theater in March 1943. A variety of sports were still played inside the older incarnation of Madison Garden. And day baseball continued at the Polo Grounds, Ebbets Field, and Yankee Stadium.[12]

With limited free time, Carl and his fellow ASTPers still were able to enjoy New York City and all the activities it had to offer.

Affordable entertainment was never lacking in Gotham, but it didn't hurt to be in uniform. Some events were free to servicemen—and many were under a single dollar.[13]

—

November 22
Monday

Dear Mother,

First of all, you'd better be expecting very few letters from me from now on, because that's what you'll be getting. I just don't have the time. I'll try to write at least one a week, but I may not be able to. But don't let that stop you, please; I still have time to read them. Try to send them longer between ends and shorter between times, willya?

Thanks for the fifteen. It'll come in pretty handy. The cost of living in a big town and all that, you know. I hope to God that by this time you've sent my gym shoes. Have you? By the way, see if you can find some of my leather gloves around there will you? Dress [dress gloves]. Tell me if you can't and I'll buy some here.

I called Helen [Helen Kaven Stein, the daughter of Leo Lavin's elder sister Elizabeth Kaven, making Helen Carl's cousin, living in New York] a few days ago, but won't be able to see her til she gets back. You worry too much, woman.

You were right about *Arsenic and Old Lace* not being a particularly good play—but it wasn't a particularly bad one either. As you said, you have to get tickets to the good plays about a month in advance and the only time I'll be able to see them will be Saturday night, because most of them don't have Sunday matinees. We saw *Artists and Models* yesterday afternoon, which is really good.[14] It's a yearly review musical, like the follies and I was surprised to see that it was as good as it was. Ethel Merman was there watching it, too. I passed her in the aisle and she seemed happy, so if she likes it why shouldn't I?

We ate in Jack Dempsey's which was noticeable for the number of times Jack Dempsey's name appears in print around the place and the excellence of the food.[15] It costs no more than the places in Canton and you get better food. Amazing.

Saturday night four of us Jewish guys went to a sort of meeting and party combined. The head of the Jamaica Jewish Center wants to open it as a U.S.O. for the Queens College soldiers and we are to help him out in what the boys want.

So I had a busy week-end. What about broadcasts? The socks are perfect. Thanks again.

Much love —Carl

Rationing and sacrificing were also part of the New York landscape.[16] Citizens throughout the nation were asked to reduce the use of certain household staples and consumables, or live without them altogether. The war effort and the stability of the American economy would "require the abandonment not only of luxuries but of many other creature comforts," said President Roosevelt.[17]

Items that Americans couldn't buy included new cars, tires, and type- 57
writers. Men had to do without trouser cuffs on new pants. New bicycles
were out of the question. Appliances, jewelry, silks, toys, nylon, phono-
graph records, and metals would be more difficult to come by. Noted the
Office for Emergency Management: "Enough steel goes into a washing
machine to make six 3-inch shells for a 75-mm. field howitzer." Also becoming scarcer were razors, leather goods, Vitamin A preparations, wool-
ens, sporting goods, and coffee. Sugar, gasoline, and electrical power would
all eventually have to be shared or rationed.[18] The shortages went from the
material to the personal noted Queens College student Kathie McDermott in October 1943:

> 1940 – no running board.
> 1941 – no gears.
> 1942 – no car.
> 1943 – no driver.[19]

Nov 26 1943
Thursday

Dear Mother,
I've been leading a pretty busy life lately so haven't had time to
write. This is Thanksgiving but we had a full schedule of classes today
anyways. We're supposed to have a big turkey dinner tonight though.
By the way, how was the family Thanksgiving? Tell me all about it.
Did I tell you I received all the stuff you sent me? The socks are
really swell; they're just what I needed. The watch, however, wasn't
repaired. In fact it was in worse condition than when I left it at home.
I wore it for two hours and the minute hand fell off. I found out it
hadn't been put on correctly, got it fixed, wore it two hours more, and
it stopped completely and firmly refused to cooperate further. So now
it's back getting repaired again. But the fudge was damn good so I'll
excuse you.
And, oh yes—the $20. That came in quite handy also. It lasted
me one weekend. I spent $10 for a pair of pants and $6 for tickets to
see *Ziegfeld Follies*[20] last Saturday night and *Something for the Boys*
in two weeks.[21]

Two weeks ago three other Jewish guys and I were invited to what we thought was a party but turned out to be a committee meeting. We are now half of a committee that's supposed to be running a sort of canteen Sunday afternoons at the Jamaica Jewish Center for the Queens College A.S.T.s. Last Sunday it was singularly unsuccessful, with 50 girls and 12 boys. But we're putting on a renewed campaign for this Sunday. You should see the Jamaica center. All new in what I guess is a Cretian style of architecture. It has rich furnishings, a swimming pool, bowling alley, beautiful main hall, and is about as big as the Masonic Lodge in Canton, but much nicer. If you want more members for the Canton Center I can tell you how to get them. Just build a place like this one here.

I read about the Massillon game in Sunday's *Cleveland Plain Dealer* which I got down-town. Tough. It seemed to be a pretty good game, though. I've been getting pretty much practice in football myself. We have six hours of physical a week and I've been spending them playing football, not tackle. Swell weather for it.[22]

You said you saw *Angel Street*[23] in Cleveland. How was it? Is it worth my seeing? It's been running here for about two years. The only time I can see any plays is Saturday night because most of them don't have Sunday matinees. We get off from 330 Saturday to 730 Sunday evening.

I got a short letter from Fred before he went to Chicago. Said he would write a longer one. Chicago is supposed to be the best town in the country for service men, so he should be pretty happy.

I don't think I'll be able to get home for Xmas. It comes on a Saturday and all we get off is from Friday night at 5:30 to Sunday night at 7:30. By train I could get home at 8:30 A.M. Saturday and have to leave at about 5:00 A.M. Sunday. By plane I could get home at 9 P.M. Fri. and would leave at 3:30 P.M. Sunday. I put my name in for a plane reservation but they're all filled up and no one will be likely to cancel their reservations. And by train it is hardly worth it. So it looks like I'll be spending Xmas in New York.

My grades are O.K. so far. Don't worry. I'm well above the average. Most of the guys have had just about the same amount of schooling that I have.

Bye now and write soon. Love —Carl

ASTP academic standards were demanding. Courses were condensed and packed with information. It turned out that Carl's mathematics professor had given the same course every year for thirty years and now had to give it in half the time—which he did by talking twice as fast. What the professor was used to giving in four hours, now he gave in two. Perhaps the double-pace of the Lehman High math teacher was good preparation.

—

To Mrs. William Lavin
December 2, 1943

Dear Aunt Ceal (or isn't that the way you spell it?) [Celia was the wife of Leo's younger brother William],

Hi. You must have been partly psychic when you started to knit that sweater. Anyways, you sent it at a most apropos time—the coming of winter and my coming to Queen's College. The students here seem to be quite proud of the fact that it is "the coldest spot in New York." It's located right on top of a hill and there's always a stiff wind blowing.

It's a very beautiful sweater, and I still don't see how you did it or found the time to do it, but unfortunately it's so cold that I have to cover it up with about all the other clothes I wear and so the world at large has no chance for appreciation.

But really, I do appreciate it and I think it was swell of you to do that for me.

With love –Carl

—

Dec. 6, 1943

Dear Mom,

I've been pretty busy—Which brings up the sordid subject of lucre, or money as it is often called. Last weekend cost me about $15.00 (Bought myself gloves, pigskin, and a pair of shoes, which probably aren't too good for seven bucks but have held together so far, and went horseback riding.) I think it would be a very good idea if you'd send me about $20 each month. Better send it by money order since it's almost impossible to cash checks here and we're never off during bank hours, and you also better send it around the middle of the month since we get paid the first. O.K.? I knew you'd agree.

How was the Cleveland Orchestra? I'm afraid my intellectual entertainments have been sadly neglected since coming to N.Y. We only have time for a little, and the animal in me is always satisfied before the mental. However, surprisingly enough, all the musicals seem to have at least one ballet number in them so it's not too bad.

Last weekend I went to two dances, one party, and had a date horse-back riding as I said before. I am meeting quite a few nice girls, and all wealthy which may interest the old man.

Lots of love –Carl

According to an ASTP historian:

> ASTP enrollment peaked in mid-December at just over 140,000 men. By that time many college administrators, having damned the Army for six months for every problem imaginable, were finally saying the program was actually going pretty well. They especially liked the young ASTP scholars themselves, One called them "alert, bright, capable, attentive"; another praised them as among "the most earnest groups of young men it has ever been my pleasure to be associated with"; yet another added that they "work much harder than our civilian students and like it."[24]

Dec. 13, 1943

Hi, Folks,

I suppose you want to hear a report on Helen and Jim [Stein, cousins]—so here it is—they've got a very nice home and a very nice car. Betsy is a beautiful baby, too. So, they should be happy. Jim was in bed with the grippe for three days but got out Sunday and seems to be O.K. Helen looks pretty thin, but I guess she always has. We had lamb, which was pretty good. I'm going back for dinner in two weeks again, when Aunt Betty [Elizabeth Kaven, Helen's mother] will be there.[25]

That was a very pleasant surprise, having you call. I still don't think that was three minutes, though. Is Fred coming home for Xmas? And do you know yet when you'll be coming up here? I believe I'll be coming home for a week around the 30th of January. Already I'm half way through one term and it seems that I just got here.

How is the financial situation coming? Unfortunately, my liquid assessments at this period are at the ebb tide stage. I hope you didn't take my request for pecuniary assistance too lightly. As a matter of fact, I have a date this coming Saturday, which has a high priority. Saw Ethel Merman in *Something for the Boys* Sat. Pretty good but I was so sleepy as a result of giving my blood to the Red Cross that I heard more of it than I saw. After that night I didn't feel any different, thought. It was rather interesting and I got a good meal of sandwiches out of it.

We've been having a little bit of excitement around here lately. The civilian coordinator of A.S.T.P. at Queens had become very unpopular with the boys, as a result of a few minor incidents, and one day about a week ago he was found hung in effigy with a knife in his back (the dummy's back—not his). It was in most of the N.Y. papers and we were restricted for a month for showing "lack of discipline," but the major later relented and we weren't restricted at all—only scared. We promised to be good boys. And then we also had a small flu epidemic here, but it's all over now and I'm left unfazed.[26]

I received the fudge in good condition and taste. Thank you very much. You still make the best fudge I've ever eaten, mother.

Do me a favor, willya? Get me a subscription to the *Sunday Rep.* And this time please get a subscription. Don't send it yourself. I'd really like to have it and it'd only take about a day to get here.

All for now—by with love –Carl

———

December 16, 1943

Dear Mom,
First of all, here's your answers.
(1) Yes, the army gave me an overcoat seven months ago which weighs about eight pounds and should protect from anything from a king-sized hurricane to absolute zero. (2) The shirt situation is very

well taken care of. I can wear either wool or cotton and have two of each. (3) Since I can't find any answer to the question of who washes my socks, I decided to let you worry about it. Did you get them yet? (4) I haven't the slightest intention of catching cold. We had trouble with flu around here, but it has gone away (5) There's absolutely nothing I can think of that I need, except money. Oh, yes—you might send me a bag the size of a bag wrapped around 50 pounds of sugar that I can use for laundry. Just a *small* one, anyhow.

Howz the weather at home now? Do you know, it hasn't snowed here once yet. But this school is located right on top of a hill and is supposed to be the coldest spot in Queens, which isn't much of a distinction one way or another. Don't we get a hell of a wind here. In fact, after standing here for fifty years all the buildings have developed a 20% list to leeward.

And on that note of whimsy we close this day's report on Queens College.

With love –Carl.

Jan 4, 1944
Tuesday

Dear Mom,

Am now at the local hamburg stand at 10:30 and bed check is at 11:00 so this will be a short letter, of necessity.

I'm still taking Edith out—the girl I told you about. We ate downtown in a Chinese restaurant, spent a couple hours looking through Greenwich Village, took a ferryboat ride to Staten Island and back, spent 12:00 in Times Square (crowded) and called it an evening.

Took her out Sat. and Sun. too and I'll probably continue to do so for a long time. May be falling in love with her—can't tell yet. (something for you to worry about)

'Night and Love Carl

Dear Mother,

I don't know how I'll be able to see Fred if the only time he gets off is on weekends. If I went directly from here to Chicago I wouldn't get there til Sunday night—and if I came directly back to N.Y. at the end of the furlough, from Chicago I'd have to leave Saturday evening. Does he have Sat. afternoon off too? I'll write him and we'll see what the score is.

The $10 you sent me was a very sweet gesture—but hardly anything more. I finally broke down and bought myself a hat and a scarf which came to a total of $9.50. I'm going to have to buy a train ticket which will cost $15.00. It costs me from 75 cents to a dollar a day to keep living. The evening meal here is like your ten dollars—only a gesture—and laundry and dry-cleaning run me at least $1.50 a week, which means $25 a month if I did nothing at all on the week-ends. So if you send me the $25 a month I asked for, that means I can spend about $5.00 a week-end. Because of the hat and the ticket and the rest of this month's $25, I think it'd be an awfully good idea if you'd send me 35 or 40 bucks in a big hurry.

The reason I haven't been writing so much lately is that for the past two weeks I've been doing what I should do before what I want to do and after I do what I should do (my lessons) there isn't enough time to do what I want to do (write letters). For a while there I was doing what I wanted to do first, and that's when you were getting a lot of letters. But for some strange reason I became conscientious again—not so many letters.

By the way, did you ever get my subscription to the *Sunday Repository*? I don't think so—I've never received it. 'Smatter?

Well, in spite of all your faults, I still love you. Keep your chin up. Love –Carl

P.S. I still need $40.00!

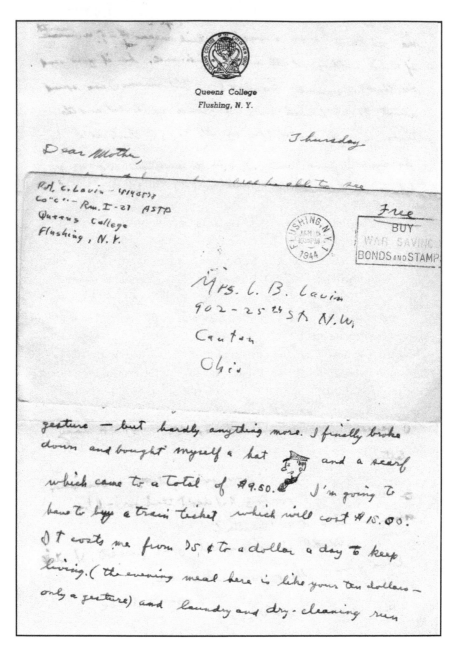

Figure 3-1. Queens College letterhead and envelope, Flushing, New York, January 6, 1944. *Author collection.*

Jan 28, 1944
Thursday

Dear Mother,

I'm going to leave here Sunday morning at 8:00—decided it is
the best time. However, the train doesn't go to Canton, only Alliance.
So I'll get in Alliance at 7:03 Sunday nite! I'll take a bus to Canton
from there, don't bother to drive all the way over to get me. If you did
you'd probably end up having a three hour wait or something.

We finished all our finals Monday, but still haven't found out
about them. We won't know our grades for a month or so yet. I did find
out about three, though—Math, English, and Geography. In Math I
got about the fourth highest grade in our class and I'll get an A in the
course. In the English test I got the highest grade in the whole unit,
but I'll probably get a B in the course because I didn't do too well
in Speech. In Geography I got one of the highest grades in class, but
don't know what I'll get—probably miss an A though.

I think I did pretty well on the other tests, too. Happy?

Be seeing you soon, with Love Carl

———

Feb 11, 1944
Thursday

Dear Mother,

We'll be taking those aptitude tests for medical school I was
telling you about, in a few days now. I'll tell you more as soon as I
learn. We still haven't received last semester's grades yet, by the way.

The Astor Hotel is on Broadway between *44th* and *45th* St, not
41st. That was definitely established by me when I stood across the
street from it and read the street signs. So that would be the best
location for you in N.Y. You might tell Sam N. that, but maybe you'd
better not if he's getting those tickets. How are they coming along,
anyhow?

Happy Valentine's Day! [drawing of heart] (It's this Monday.)

I took my watch into a jewelers here, and he fixed it in 15
minutes and wouldn't even let me pay for it. Works swell, too. Maybe
you'd better send your repairing to me to be done after this.

66   Did you ever find that paper for those extra ration points I brought home?[27]

Keep the home fires burning.

Love, Carl

———

16 February 1944

Dear Mom,

I received your little valentine and got a laugh out of it. Very cute. Where did you get the idea?

We took those medical aptitude tests yesterday. I believe I did pretty well in it, but that doesn't mean much since they only take about 5 or 10%. If I passed it I'll go before a board in about a month for an interview, but I won't find out their decision until the end of this term, so I've got a wait of about 10 weeks before I can find out whether the army wants to make me a doctor or not.

How is your back? Have you decided yet what you're going to do about it? Did you go try those treatments yet?

They still haven't told us our 1st term grades, by the way.

How are your plans for coming to N.Y. developing? Any notable changes, additions, or subtractions? Did Fred find out yet whether he gets that furlough or not? He's owed me a letter now for quite some time. Bawl him out for me, willya?

Well that's about all from here except that I'm still going with Edith and I still like her more each time I see her.

Write. With love Carl

———

ASTP was supposed to last a regular school year, but it would last only five months for Carl. By that time the army was in Africa fighting Rommel, and quite a few Americans were in combat. Adding to this manpower shortage, a large-scale invasion was in the works.[28]

The hue and cry went up: Why are some of our guys getting killed in the deserts of Africa while others are going to college?[29]

First came the rumors.[30] Then came the news: the army was drastically cutting the program nationwide, recalling all men not in the advanced

courses. About 8 out of every 10 men, or approximately 120,000 soldiers
total, were returning to active duty.[31]

Included was one Carl Lavin.

—

Queens College
Feb 28, 1944
Friday nite

Dear Mom,

I was impressed by the beauty of your logic in giving the reason
why you sent ten instead of twenty. However, I didn't need the other
ten since I still haven't bought that shirt yet. But I will buy it.

I was also impressed by the volume of good advice you two
have been piling on me. I realize what you say is true and I have not
stopped studying. If my telling you so does not convince you, perhaps
this will: after considering all the rumors and reports, and knowing
how the army works, I think I can say that we probably will remain
here until the end of the term, or at least until we can get a term's
credit. The chances are that we'll be here until the middle of April, at
least. Therefore I haven't stopped studying. Also—therefore, I think
you'd better keep your plans of coming up here as you were, or as
they were rather.

I've been living from day to day just waiting for the food you said
you were sending—but no package. What happened?

I received the tickets for *Othello*.[32] Thanks, and thank W for me,
willya? Did he, by any chance, get any of the other ones I wanted?
Did he get any more tickets for you?

Have you had those pictures taken yet that you said you were
going to? If not, why don't you? Take some snapshots of yourselves if
nothing else. I'd like to have some decent pictures; the ones I have
aren't very good.

'Bye—lots of love –Carl

—

March 6, 1944

>   Dear Mother,
>   Your ten arrived in good condition but the box is still wandering around somewhere between us. It probably came over the weekend and I'll get it today. Thanks.
>   You still haven't said anything about coming to N.Y. How do your plans stand? And how about that date for Fred. By the way, I haven't heard from Fred in a month now. Tell him to write me. Are you going up to see him get his commission [as Ensign]? It sounds rather silly, and I know it's a long way to go, but it would make him happy if you were there.
>   Well, write and tell me what's going on, willya? As far as I'm concerned, the situation is exactly what it was a week ago, nobody knows nothin'. Yesterday I had a talk with Capt. H for about an hour and a half. Seems to be a pretty nice guy, but he can't help me at all. He has the job of getting aviation cadets and, since I can't get into that, he can't help me any. The representative for Canton district of his firm was here also. I forget his name but you know who I mean. He says he's the one responsible for my lifting around those 100 lb. cases of M.F.B. back in the shipping room. But I got a free meal out of his expense account.
>   I didn't sleep over at Edith's yesterday. We had our yearly physical exam Sunday and had to get up at 5:15 in the morning for reveille. By the way, I am deeply in love with Edith—thot you'd like to know. Bye—write—with love –Carl.

On March 15, the entire unit at Queens College was "inactivated." A farewell dinner was held March 20.[33]

Carl, with new orders, left New York a few days later. All that remained of ASTP unit 3222 at Queens College were memories and the group's mascot, a cat named Queenie.[34]

A letter from Carl's girlfriend, Edith:

Jamaica, NY
March 18, 1944

Dear Mrs. Lavin,

I'm sorry that the "fortunes of war" are such that we won't have
the opportunity of meeting.

Carl had spoken so fondly of his family so often that I was really
looking forward to seeing you all. Well, some other time perhaps. My
thanks to you anyway for your thoughtful invitation.

It was fun having Carl here, Mrs. Lavin, and if he enjoyed
being here as much as we enjoyed having him—no other thanks are
necessary.

Carl tells me that you and Mr. Lavin are celebrating an
anniversary. My sincere hope that it will be a happy one and that your
next anniversary will be even happier for having both your sons with
you.

Sincerely, Edith

Mar 23, 1944
Wednesday

Dear Mom,

We move out this evening, but no one knows where or when.
The best rumors center around Louisiana—but. Anyways, I'll let you
know when I get there. It'll probably be at least three days. That's
about all I can tell you about what's going to happen to me. I've never
been so much in the dark in the army before. All we can do is wait
and see.

I'm certainly going to hate to leave this place. Even discounting
Edith I've still had a better time here than any like period in my life.
I've never felt before that I was actually learning something, but I felt
that here. I've never known a group of guys that I enjoyed being part
of as much as these, and in fact everyone feels that way. We had a
farewell banquet Monday night, and you never saw such an exhibition
of picture taking, autograph trading, and fare-thee-well trading.

All I hope is that we all get somewhere together. By the way, should I send Edith's parents something to thank them? If so, what?

What do you think of this picture of her? I took it; she's better looking than this. Did you and dad get your pictures taken yet? I wish you would, really.

By the time you answer this I suppose you will have heard from Fred what's going to happen to him?

Well, keep looking out the window. Maybe I'll pass through Canton again.

With love Carl

P.S.—I'm sending some stuff home in packages. Keep it, mom. Carl

—

When the army ended the lion's share of the ASTP program, all of the affected men were assigned to the infantry. For Carl, it was the 69th Division, based in southern Mississippi.[35]

For a New York minute, Carl had a girl, a great education, a path to officership, and all the Big Apple trimmings. But that was not to be Carl's future. His fate was bullets over Broadway.

4 Mississippi
March–October 1944

      After spending months at college, enjoying Edith's company and experiencing New York City as best he could, Carl was back on the parade grounds. He was posted to Camp Shelby near Hattiesburg, Mississippi, where spring brought pleasant weather but summer could unleash wilting temperatures in the 90s.

      Not only was school over for Carl and the other ASTPers, but ending as well was the path to officership, the camaraderie of the classroom, and the safety of academia. The students had been told they were the nation's smartest soldiers, specially selected for advancement, but instead of becoming officers, Carl and the rest of the ASTP bunch were being sent back to the regular army without anything to show for it. There were no extra stripes, promotions, or fast tracks. Worse, through their ASTP participation they had foregone the normal military training and advancement that would have been available to them. And to add the misery, they were late in joining already established units, with settled leadership and friendships.[1]

      At one time, Camp Shelby was the busiest US training facility during World War II. With an official capacity of 84,000, Camp Shelby found itself with a population of over 100,000 at least twice during the war. At Camp Shelby, Carl was assigned to the 69th Infantry Division and became a rifleman. General Patton noted that riflemen "inflicted 37% of casualties on the enemy, but took 92 per cent of the formation's losses."[2]

      Now placed with a combat unit for a second time, Carl rekindled his thoughts as to how he could take his leave from it. If the system had an opening, Carl would try to find it.

72 And, to Carl's consternation, Dorothy would pursue her motherly designs as well.

—

Mar 25, 1944
Friday nite

Hi, Mom,

Just arrived here, but haven't gotten assigned permanently yet, so I don't know my address as yet. But it'll be on this envelope. So far all I know is that I'll be in the 69th Division here at Camp Shelby Mississippi. I'll be in either the tank destroyers or the infantry; I hope the former but I'm afraid it'll be the latter. We're all getting split up, so I don't know who, if, or how many of the guys from Queens will be in my company.

We're only 130 miles from New Orleans, Ma. Don't we have a lot of relatives there? Give me the addresses of someone I'd like to see, willya? I don't know I'll have a chance to see them or not, though, because we're going out on maneuvers in three weeks.

You should see the weather down here now. We couldn't ask for any better spring weather. The temperature is around 70 and everything is green and blooming. Of course, everything is also getting washed away by the floods, but we're discounting that.

Well, write as soon as you receive this and let me know what you know, and what Fred knows.

Love—Carl

—

Leo, who served stateside during World War I as a Supply Corps Sergeant, passes on some sound advice to Carl: See if you can stay out of the infantry.

—

Apr 2 1944
Sunday

Dear Pop,

I told some of the guys about the advice you gave me. It got quite a laugh. When I learned they were closing ASTP I said that the last thing I wanted to get into was the infantry. If there were any possible way of getting into anything else I assure you I would take them. But there isn't—you can't even volunteer for the paratroopers anymore. If anything does come up in the future I intend to do what I can to help myself. You needn't worry about that. Incidentally, about a third of my company is made up of former ASTP men, so that I still have the kind of guys to go around with that I did back at school. I'm really very lucky in that respect. Everybody from Queens came into this division with me, and quite a few into my regiment so that I'm continuously running into them. (It comes in quite handy at times. In the evenings, there are always long lines waiting to see the movies and it's nice to know that no matter which one you go to, you'll find someone that'll let you get in line beside him.) Three of the guys from Queens are in my company and in my barracks. My friend, George, is in the next company to mine, so we get to see quite a bit of each other.

I can't exactly say I like the place, but at least it's tolerable. We've been having all you could ask for in the way of perfect spring weather, the food is the best I've had since I entered the army, the training has been easy and even interesting at times, and I've become closely acquainted with some of the guys in our company. For the first five or six days it was pretty hard though. I was really homesick for New York I guess. And then it was raining continuously and they were giving us some training that I've had at least three different times before and that is very uncomfortable physically.[3]

I spent the last three days going through Combat in Cities, the Infiltration Course, and the Close Combat Course. This is the one you probably heard about, where you crawl under machine gun fire and through barbed wire, while they set off charges around you and you fire at targets that pop up. It wasn't as dangerous as that sounds—everything is well-controlled—and besides I'm all through with it now. Before I went over these courses I didn't think I'd like them very well, but it turned out to be a lot of fun. The only trouble was that it was kind of dirty. Every time a charge would go off near you, you'd get covered with mud and water. It was worth it, though, to see the looks on other guys' faces when that stuff was coming down on them.

Love Carl

Apr 6 1944
Thursday

Hello, Mom,

Today is a day of grace for us. They worked us all last Sunday, so they gave us today as a substitute. The only trouble is that there's absolutely nothing to do.

I still don't have anything new to report on what's going to happen to me. It seems to be pretty definite that we'll go out on bivouac on the 17th, though.[4] There's a rumor circulating that those of us here that had basic training in something other than the infantry will be returned to their respective branches. I hope it's true; I can't exactly say I like the Tank Destroyers, but I didn't dislike it as much as the infantry.

However the training here is still almost interesting. Most of the men are old-timers and so our training is advanced and specialized. I now know the proper method of loading and securing equipment on railroad flat-cars, the habits and habitat of the anopheles mosquito (malaria), the German army's methods of training, how to lay mortar positions, and a few dozen different ways of killing a man. Well, they may come in handy in civilian life. You never can tell what'll happen.

I still haven't been outside this camp since I came. And I don't think I will, either. You have to go clear to New Orleans to get to anything decent, and that takes up half a week-end.

We spent Monday on the rifle range and it was quite enjoyable. Things here aren't nearly as strict as they were back in Camp Hood, and another guy from Queens and I got together and had a lot of fun. We worked our way into taking charge of part of the ammunition and gave ourselves about twice as much as we were supposed to get. Then we ran it all off in the practice rounds. We used the M-1 rifle, the Garand that you've heard about, and it's a marvelous weapon. Except for the fact that it's not made of very good steel it's one of the best rifles ever made. It hasn't got very much kick to it. In fact it's possible to fire it by just holding it in the hands from the waist. (I tried it.)

I received the box of fruit candy that you or Sugardale sent me. It wasn't bad, but don't you think it's a little late for Valentines? Anyways the boys and I appreciate it.

Tell Fred to write, willya? And write yourself. Love –Carl

P.S.—Probably get a furlough in about four months. Oh, well.

—

Many of the guys on the firing range put wadding in their ears to protect their hearing. Not Carl. He was too proud to do such a thing as stuff his ears. It was a foolish decision he would pay for later. As he reached middle age, he developed hearing loss in his right ear, the ear closest to his weapon.

—

Apr 10 1944
Sunday

Dear Mom,

This is an emergency. Send me ten dollars right now, will you please? You see, we get paid the first of every month, but since we left Queens at about that time we didn't get paid then. They told us we'd get paid the tenth and since the "cost of living" is very low here I figured I could last that long. Since we were getting paid tomorrow I decided to go into town last night and borrowed five to do it. Well, today they told us we wouldn't get paid until the 20th so that leaves me with ten days to go on a capital of minus four dollars.

It isn't really a life or death matter, but ten would help out.

I hate to tell you this, but I have once more taken the fatal step; I got a G.I. haircut.

Nice and cool and I don't have to comb it. But don't worry, by the time I get a furlough it'll probably be down to my shoulders.

I got a letter from Fred Friday. He seems to be enjoying things pretty well. He's probably left for Hawaii by this time.

We're going to start getting a five weeks basic course starting Monday. The "we" referring to the ASTs. The only thing I haven't had is bayonet drill out of all the things they're going to teach us. Oh well, there're worse ways of spending five weeks. Thanx. Love –Carl

—

After being commissioned as an ensign, Fred was sent to Hawaii and was waiting for a ship assignment when he was given his first job: He had

76 to act as a sort of a foil for the shore patrol. His job was to walk down the street with the shore patrol discretely following. They would then pick up any sailor who failed to salute. As this included "old salts" as well as men returning directly from combat, it left Fred feeling distinctly uncomfortable.

Apr 11 1944
Monday

Dear Mom,

I received the wallet you sent me today. Thanks very much. It is really "just what I need" as you noticed when I was home. A nice one, too. But more than the wallet even, I think I'll appreciate the pictures you said you were sending. Have you sent them yet?

I got another package today. For some reason or other the Jewish War Veterans of Canton decided to send me a package of pin-up girls. Very sweet of them. But they're behind times. The magazines say that the army doesn't like pin-ups any more.

Did I tell you in the letter I wrote yesterday that I tried to go to New Orleans last week-end? Anyways I did. Try, that is—I didn't succeed. Travel conditions are worse here than in any camp I've been in. I'll make one more attempt in a few weeks; give 'em one more chance. If I do get there I'll try to look up what's-their-names.[5] Nothing new going on here. So—goodbye.

Love, Carl

Apr 13 1944
Wednesday

Dear Mother,

Your timing was perfect. I received both your letter and the package on my birthday. Thanks very much. I appreciate it.

Yes, I heard from New Orleans. I got a letter yesterday from Mrs. Marcus [Leo's cousin][6] which was very nice. She has a daughter of 18. Invited me to stay any week-end at her house. Of course, now my only

problem is how to get there. I think I told you of my attempt to get to
New Orleans last week-end didn't I?

Lights out now—so goodbye, Love Carl

Apr 16 1944
Sunday

Dear Mom,

Received your ten and on behalf of the boys in the hutment may I express my thanks?[7] Also received the letter the Old Man wrote me. It arrived at the right psychological moment. I was going to write and thank the [cousins] Marcus' and the Panglin's (they both asked me to stay with them) but I was going to put it off for a few days. So with your prompting, Pop, I wrote them both last night. Told them I couldn't accept since I'd never know in advance when I'd be able to make it. (the odds are about four to one against my getting out of here and making it there on any given week-end) but I'd look them up to see them when I do get to New Orleans.

I think I told you they're giving us basic all over again (short course) didn't I? Well, we're starting to take those damned long hikes all over again, which is the part of the army I hate most. (For someone who doesn't like to go on marches, I haven't got myself a very good position, have I?) Almost a tenth of the guys fell out of the one we had yesterday—pretty fast cadence. I was pretty surprised, and pleased, to learn that there aren't very many guys that can take it as well as I can. I'll be damned if I know how I got into that condition, but it's a nice condition to be in.

I'm going to try to get transferred to the anti-tank company of the regiment. I think I may be able to do it. In that company you ride wherever you go—you don't walk.

Learned yesterday that all that stuff about moving from Shelby was just stuff. We'll be here indefinitely.

'Bye now—love Carl

Apr 18 1944
Monday

Dear Mom,

O.K.—I'm ready for those pictures—let's have them. Are you and Daddy getting some made together? I think it's a great idea, personally.

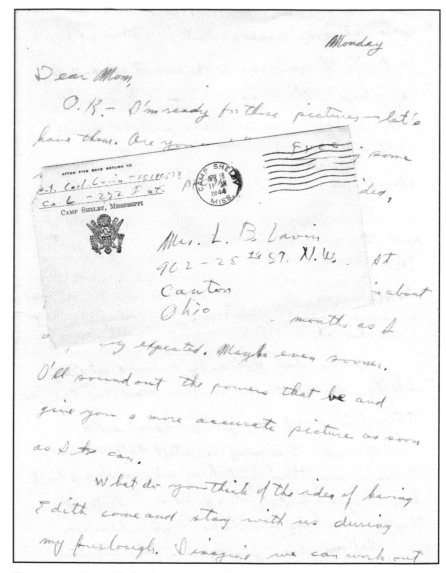

Figure 4-1. Camp Shelby letter and envelope, Mississippi, April 18, 1944. *Author collection.*

I've got some pretty good news. It looks like I'll be getting a furlough in about six weeks instead of four months as I originally expected. Maybe even sooner. I'll sound out the powers that be and give you a more accurate picture as soon as I can.

What do you think of the idea of having Edith come and stay with us during my furlough? I imagine we can work out some sleeping arrangement or other. (In fact if things come to the worst she and I can sleep in the same room—but I don't suppose either you or she would agree to that.) I haven't said anything to her about coming to Canton yet.

Spring has officially arrived at Camp Shelby. We went into cotton uniforms today. A terrific cold snap is expected by all concerned. The army is still determined to make something out of me physically. I don't know yet whether it's good or bad. But they're working us like—ah—beavers.

Let me hear from you. Let me know of all the excitement of and in Canton.

Love –Carl

—

Dorothy Lavin was in contact with her congressman, Rep. Henderson Carson[8] (R-OH, 1893–1971), in an extensive effort to attain some type of consideration for Carl. This type of constituent request was frequent during wartime and when you add to this the fact that Carson was in his first term in Congress as well as a member of the minority party it should not be surprising that her efforts were not particularly fruitful.

—

Apr 18 1944
Friday,

Hello, Mom,

I'm still very dubious about what Carson can do. If you're going to get some good out of him, why not have him get me into an O.C.S. or some special training of some kind? That metabolism stuff sounds like a lot of bunk to me, but if a chance comes for a transfer, I'd welcome it.

Whatever happened to those pictures you were going to send me? I'm still waiting for them. By the way, physically I'm better off and can take more than about half the guys here. I'm disgustingly healthy. It'd be pretty much of a joke if I got out of here because of a physical disability. You know my metabolism is normal.

It's late mother, so good night.

Love –Carl

A letter from Edith:

Brooklyn NY
May 2, 1944

Dear Mrs. Lavin,

When I received Carl's letter asking me to come to Canton during the time he's home on furlough, I was hesitant, naturally, about accepting—though there's nothing I wanted more—not knowing what his family thought of the idea. When your warm-hearted and thoughtful invitation came it was very sweet of you to ask me, Mrs. Lavin, especially when I know you and Mr. Lavin would much prefer having Carl to yourselves, for the short time he's home, to sharing him with anyone.

Because I do want to meet all of you and because, needless to say, I want very much to see Carl, I'm going to be as selfish as you've been unselfish, and accept. I'd love to come—thank you.

I know I'll have a wonderful time—being with Carl and his family is guarantee of that.

Sincerely, Edith

May 4 1944
Wednesday

Hello Mother,

First I want to thank you for writing to Edith and I know you would write her as hospitable a letter as you could. You didn't have to assure me of that. I have confidence in your judgment (even if you don't in mine—but wait 'til you see her.)

Yes, she goes to school, but she gets out on the seventh of June and I won't get my furlough until about the middle or end of it, as near as I can tell.

I don't believe any harm can come from writing to Carson, don't worry about that. But, by the way, has any good come from it yet? I mean, if he wants to make me an officer I won't object.

The watch hasn't come yet, but I'll start thanking you for it anyways. I do appreciate all the trouble you went to get it. It's coming at an opportune moment, since the crystal fell out of mine a few days ago and I haven't been able to have it fixed yet. I'll send it back. There's nothing wrong with it but the crystal and it'd be a good idea to have it fixed and cleaned when you receive it. By the way, take it anywhere but to C's.[9]

Those cartoons you're sending me are really very good. No, I don't see them in any other papers, so please keep it up, please.

Yesterday we got back from a four-day bivouac out by the rifle range. We shot the carbine and the rifle for record. I presume you'll be proud to know your soldier scored "expert" (highest you can get) on the rifle and "sharpshooter" (above average) on the carbine. Scored a 45 out of 45 on rapid fire at 300 yards, and I think I was the only one in the company to do it. That should prove to you, pop, that I can think and act quickly.

Only about five more weeks and I'll be seeing you, I hope.

Until then—love Carl

———

May 10 1944
Tuesday

Hello, Mom,

Received the watch! It's really wonderful! Although I didn't ask for the sweep second hand, it's exactly what I wanted! Thank you very much.

I'll tell you in a week how it runs, but I'm pretty sure that you couldn't ask for anything better.

About two weeks ago I told you I was getting my furlough in six weeks, remember. Well, now I'm getting it in seven weeks. (not even holding my own.) That's as definite as anything can be in the army (which it can't.) That is, the orders for my furlough are definite; the time isn't. There are forty-five guys ahead of me, and they're sending new men out as the old ones return, so the time is rather indefinite. But I think we can figure on about the last of June.

Tonight at two o'clock we go out on a twenty-five mile hike, with full field pack and gun, of course. The infantry's got something new out called an expert infantryman's badge and you have to pass a lot of physical and mental tests to get it.[10] So this is supposed to be the toughest physical part. Probably by tomorrow I'll be about two inches shorter after being pounded into the ground for eight hours and having my feet worn away for ditto time by all that weight.

Well, I'll let you know what's happening and what's happened, when it does. Same from you?

Bye now—with love Carl

May 12, 1944

Mother's Day Card

"A tender greeting
Filled with loving cheer
To tell you, Mother,
How very dear
You are to me
On Mother's Day
And all the year!"

And a hand-written note:

I hope that it does, Mother! You are, believe me, although I'm afraid I don't show it very often. With love –Carl

Figure 4-2. Mother's Day card, May 12, 1944. *Author collection.*

Separate letter

Thursday

You asked whether I liked fudge or something else. Maw, that's not a very hard choice. There isn't anything I'd rather have than fudge, than your fudge, rather.

I wish you'd forget about trying to get me out of this because of any physical reasons. If Carson has any pull, push him into getting me into O.C.S. but he'd have to have more than pull for that, he'd have to have a prime mover.

Remember I told you I was trying to get a position as a driver? Well—that's out. I am now working on something new and 100% better—battalion intelligence. It means interesting (comparatively speaking, of course) work and a chance to use more brain and less brawn. About 50% more men volunteered than there are room for so I won't know for a while whether I'm one of the fortunate or not.

Yesterday morning we finished that 25 mile hike I told you about. You should have seen everybody hobble, crawl, limp, or what-have-you around the company area all day yesterday—it was like a slapstick comedy. But my God, were my feet tender! And did I wake up stiff this morning! Ah, the rugged life! Nothing like it, thank God! But—didn't hurt me, I guess.

Bye Love –Carl

The Lavins' house in Canton contained two bedrooms, one for Dorothy and Leo and one for the boys. A houseguest in that home meant that Carl would sleep on a couch or on the back porch, and the guest would take the boys' room. In May 1944, Dorothy and Leo decided to purchase a larger house about six blocks away.

—

May 16 1944
Monday

Dear Mother,

Today in the 69th Division, of which I have the somewhat dubious honor of being a part, is celebrating its first birthday. So, after a parade this morning, we are having the rest of the day off. Personally, I think it would have been a nice gesture on the part of the general had he waited two more days to hold this celebration, for then both the 69th and myself could have celebrated our first year in the army, together. Yep, two more days and I'll be practically an old army man. But the general is a stubborn man.

Since this is my first typing endeavor in about a year, you'll have to overlook my mistakes and you'll have quite a few of them to overlook.

The watch is completely good, except for one thing. It really works automatically; I haven't had to wind it since I got it. But it gains about a minute and a half, or two, a day. By the way, in case you're wondering why my old watch hasn't arrived yet, here's the reason, I haven't sent it yet. But I will as soon as I get a chance.

If I ever manage to get out of this place over a week-end, I'll call you some Sunday morning (It takes at least six hours to get a call through from camp.) So far, I've been able to get out on exactly one week-end out of eight, what with the transportation the way it is, which is negligible, and the detail list the way it is, which is almost all-inclusive. If I get a chance on other than a week-end I'll try to call you then, too. But don't worry if you learn that I've called when you weren't home some time. If anything important ever turns up I'll let you know by telegraph, not by phone.

Incidentally, what kind of sleeping arrangements are you figuring on when Edith and I get there? It's going to be a little difficult for you, I guess. I hope all this isn't going to trouble you too much, but it means quite a lot to me. I may as well warn you now, Mom, we aren't going to get much sleep during those seven days and it won't do you any good to try and get us to. Also you might notify the Lavin family and friends that any glimpses they get of me beyond the absolute minimum will be purely coincidental.

Just got your letter. Was surprised to hear you're really intending to sell the house now. But your plan seems to be a very good one. All I want is that you keep it until after my furlough, which you said you are doing.

Goodbye for now—Love Carl

May 19 1944
Thursday

Mother,

Friend Carson must really be something, after all. I've never seen anything move so fast in the army before. And somebody must have thrown a scare into somebody. Yesterday I was called in out of the field (orders were marked "emergency"!) and sent to the hospital. There two majors and a lieutenant colonel worked on me. While this was going on there were majors and captains out in the field questioning my squad leader, platoon leader, first sergeant, and C.O. about my physical condition.

They put my hands and feet in ice water, asked me question after question and I'm afraid they arrived at the conclusion that I am healthy. They aren't done yet, though. Today they tried to give me a metabolism shot, which didn't take. (Remember when I tried to take one before?) But they're going to try again tomorrow.

Yes, I've done everything and said everything I can. Don't worry about that. I'll tell you what happens as soon as it does.

But if Carson can do all that, why don't you put his powers to work along a more helpful line? Maybe he can get me transferred into something requires more brain work. Some kind of specialized job. If he wants to know if I've any experience in anything he mentions within reason, say yes. It's surprising what you can bluff through in the army.

Have you heard again from Fred lately? Let me know.
Meantime—Lots of love –Carl

———

May 26 1944
Thursday

Dear Mom,

I'm afraid your hopes that the army will make a neat, punctual
person out of me are due for disappointment. Every soldier's first
post-war plans include such things as getting a rifle and throwing dirt
on it, never walking in step, never hanging any clothes up, sleeping
until two every day, and never walking more than twenty consecutive
steps at a time. In other words, to do just the opposite of what he's
been doing under compulsion.[11] This may explain daddy's behavior.[12]
Maybe if he'd never been in the army he'd be happy in sleeping
normal hours. But the stigma of regimentation has probably lasted all
this time and so he can't bear to sleep as everybody else does. So it'll
be the same for Fred and me.

That telephone talk was pretty nice. Shame I didn't get a chance
to talk to pop. But one of these months maybe I'll get into town again,
and there'll be another chance. After I talked to you, I called up
some people that A wrote me the address of. Her roommate's family,
in fact. They invited me out there, along with the guy I came in with,
for Sunday dinner (which was the reason I called them up—don't
worry, I was very diplomatic—"Oh, no, I couldn't think of imposing
on you like that, and besides I came in with a friend.") So we went
out there and had a wonderful time, surprisingly enough. We spent
the whole afternoon and evening with them. Met about all the family
relatives and friends, as they'd drop in and we went for a ride in the
car and called on several people. Everyone we met was very nice and
treated us wonderfully. It was a week-end just like one back home—
everything peaceful and quiet and civilized. Nothing to remind us
of the army. There was a fifteen year old daughter—quite pretty and
smart—which added to the amusement. We helped her with her
homework after supper. (They insisted on supper—what could we
do?) By the way, don't worry about the watch being fast. (sent the
old one back on Tuesday—get it yet?) the mother works in a jewelry

store—or owns it—father is dead—and so she is having it fixed for me. I'm sure they'll do a good job. Simple to do anyway.

Have you gotten any kind of report on my "condition" yet? Keep me posted. Oh, and keep sending those cartoons, please. They're excellent.

And by now it's only five more weeks. I hope.

Love and kisses, Carl

Jun 1 1944
Wednesday

Hi, Mom,

Glad to hear that your finish in the Hadassah was such a climactical one.[13] But why quit? How are you going to spend all your time now? It seems to me that these activities need you, and you need them.

A new order came down on furlough. No one gets one until six months after his last one. Which means that it'll be the beginning of August for me, instead of July as I thought. That's eight weeks away. I'm not even holding my own. (a month ago I thought I'd have one in seven weeks.)

Yes, I told them about those operations.[14] But naturally they don't mean anything. How could they?

Oh, by the way, the length of the furlough was also changed—but this one for the better. Now it is ten days plus traveling time. Which I can make eleven days at home. That'll be almost twice as long as any furlough I've had so far.

Lights out now—so 'Bye—With love –Carl

A letter from Edith:

Jamaica NY
June 3, 1944

Dear Mrs. Lavin

Now that the inevitable "eleventh hour" rush of end term work is over, I can do what I meant to do long before this, write and say hello.

88

Friday was my last day of class. (A good thing too that the end of the semester came when it did! For several weeks now I've been letting a bad case of Spring Fever and an awful lot of daydreaming about Canton of course play havoc with my powers of concentration—and, probably, with my grades.) I've still a few exams threatening me, but they'll be over soon and then I can really let go and relax.

Speaking of relaxing, I'm afraid I'm not going to give you a chance to, am I? Carl told me you're very active in organization work. Mother's interested in the same type of thing and knowing June is one of her busiest months, I imagine you'll be pretty rushed yourself these next few weeks. Then, instead of having a chance to recuperate you're going to have to be bothered with a houseguest. (I might have said this before Mrs. Lavin but I mean it, truly. I hope you and Mr. Lavin won't feel you must put yourselves out to entertain me. I'll feel very badly if you do.)

I agree it was thoughtful of the Army to postpone Carl's furlough till I finished school. Thoughtful as far as my studies were concerned, that is. As far as my feelings were concerned, however, I'm not so sure.

According to Carl, the Army intends to keep the exact date of his furlough a closely guarded secret—until just a few days before it comes through. At least so for a while yet, I won't be able to make definite plans. As soon as I can though, I'll write.

Say hello to Mr. Lavin for me won't you.

And one thing more, thank you for taking time out to write. It meant a great deal to me.

'Bye Edith

The United States and Allies launched the liberation of Europe—D-Day—on June 6, changing the pace of the war and Carl's narrative. As one historian wrote, "The 8,230 U.S. casualties on D-Day included the first of almost 400,000 men who would be wounded in the European theatre, the first of 7,000 amputations, the first of 89,000 fractures."[15]

Carl and the other soldiers had no doubt they would soon be going into combat. But Carl was still at Shelby for three more months after D-Day. He kept wondering why he was just getting the same training over and over and over again. When was he going overseas? Why was he still here? The whole division was on the sidelines, and he wanted in.

Jun 8 1944
Sunday

Dear Mother,

Today we came out into the woods. We're on bivouac for an indefinite time. I don't know why, but I always get a big kick out of camping out. The woods here are very much like those that I was in on that trip throughout the West, and it reminds me of it. I used to be thrilled by it then, and I still am.[16] You get the impression that you are a part of all the perfect beauty.

Tuesday night

Pardon the interruption—but had to go to bed Sunday because we got up at 4:30 Monday for a 36 hour problem, which we just finished. It was pretty tough, especially with only 3 hours of sleep Monday night. And, tomorrow we start out at 3:30 in the morning on a 15 mile hike. They're really sticking it to us. I guess they figure now that the fight is on we ought to suffer along with the rest of the boys. By the way, the only way we get any news our here is fifth hand. Do me a favor willya? Send me all the maps pertaining to the fronts (all of them) from the newspapers, along with the captions. Don't forget now, please.

I got the picture, mom. It's not too bad, but I think you're a lot better looking than that. But it is a very nice picture. Thanks. By the picture you're getting into the benign stage and passing from the vibrant one.

Well behave yourself –Carl

Jun 13 1944
Sunday

Dear Mom,

Sorry I haven't written much lately, but they've really been rushing and pushing it out of us. In fact, I brought a new *Life* magazine out with me, I've been here eight days and today was the first day I've opened the cover.

We go out tomorrow on a five day problem, so I won't be writing much for a while again.

If I go to West Point, I sign up for a seven year stay in the army. Don't think I'd like that.

No, it doesn't make me particularly happy to have the army call me physically perfect. I didn't have to have them to tell me that. I thought what you did was a bad idea when you started it, and I still do. If Carson can do anything, O.K., but let's at least be sensible about it.

While I'm on bivouac, I'd really appreciate it if you'd send me some food. Could really use it out here.

Have to get up five hours from now, so—Good night.

With love Carl

P.S.—That fudge you promised would be quite nice.

———

Fred's second job in the navy was even stranger. Still awaiting assignment to his ship, Fred said that his job after working with the shore patrol to arrest sailors who failed to salute was to help run some sort of semiofficial brothel. He wasn't clear in his own mind what it was, except that it was a brothel and operated with full awareness of the navy. His job was simply to check the ID cards and orders of the clientele. So the brothel itself was not a problem, but sailors without proper papers were.[17]

Given that Carl got to go to college and Broadway shows while Fred was checking IDs at a brothel, it should be no surprise that Carl was the better correspondent.

———

Jun 16 1944
Thur.

Dear Mom,

Received two letters from Fred in two days—he got my letter after he sent the first one. He didn't tell me anything you don't already know about him.

We've been out on bivouac now for 11 days and getting damned sick of it. Saturday, we go back to garrison for a while. It'll feel awfully good to put on clean clothes, take a shower, eat a candy bar,

sleep in a cot, and generally enjoy such forms of civilization as an
army camp has to offer.

It's raining now, and the only thing between me and the elements
is a rather scrawny pine tree—so you'll probably get this in a pretty
beat-up shape.

Did I tell you it's getting a little tougher down here. If I didn't,
it is. (In fact, even if I did, it still is.) Had three guys sick from heat
exhaustion in our platoon alone today—30 men.

I'll write a long letter Saturday when we get back, if I'm in
condition to—

Meanwhile—love Carl

After a year, pretty much everybody was promoted to Private First
Class. There wasn't any salary difference to speak of. Carl started in 1942 at
$21 a month and by the time he was discharged in 1946 it was somewhere
in the $30 range.

Rick Atkinson relates slightly different salary numbers, perhaps including a combat pay differential: "A private earned $50 a month, a staff
sergeant $96. And a valiant GI awarded the Medal of Honor would receive
an extra $2 each month."[18]

Jun 18 1944
Sunday

Dear Mother,

So you've taken the final plunge—sold the old Lavin homestead.
I can understand your crying, Ma, it seems a little sad to me, too.
Maybe you shouldn't have sold it. Kept it for a summer home, or art
gallery, or night club, or something.

Have you decided yet where we're building? Let me know.
And what's all this about plans for adding onto the Beef House [at
Sugardale]. Let's have 'em, Pop, get specific, what, where, how much,
and when? Tell me just what you're thinking about or have decided on
so far. The facts—maybe you can send them in code if it's too much
or a secret—don't worry—nobody will see them.

Yesterday we came back from two weeks in the field. Can you imagine wearing the same clothes for two weeks, not bathing during that time, and working hard in temperature over 90 every day of that time? Yes, we were kind of dirty—and the smell! Remind me to join the navy for the next war. Last night I slept nine hours—and did that feel good! First time since we'd left that I had more than six hours sleep—except for one night. The night before we'd slept from twelve to one (and I don't mean thirteen hours) got up, and hiked ten miles, made an assault, dug in, withdrew to an assembly area, and dug in again. So we were tired.

As I told you, I'm the B.A.R. man for our squad. Which is probably why I'm a Private First Class now. If Daddy doesn't know, a BAR is a Browning Automatic Rifle—weighs twelve pounds more than a rifle—has a faster rate of fire than a machine gun— shoots a 20-round magazine. Right now that 12 extra pounds is the outstanding factor; overseas, it'll be the automatic part. Anyways, as beat up as the others are, I'm just twelve pounds more beat up. Ah, well, c'est la guerre, or something.

Although the men do all the work on these problems, it's only the officers who get anything out of it. We know what to do, because our jobs are relatively simple, but the officers learn a lot of things—such as what things to watch to keep a maneuver from getting snafued, (surely—even you must know by this time, if only the civilian translation. By the way, it is a marvelously apropos word.) How fast and far men can go over various terrains and in various situations, how to think when things go wrong—and a thousand other things. Well, they're learning, God bless you, but I only wish someone would think of some way to make the officers pay for their mistakes, instead of us. If he does something wrong, it means we have to march harder and longer and sleep less to make up for it. If he's fairly smart and his superior officer not too good, he can get out of being blamed for making a mistake. I imagine you know pretty well what I mean, Pop, passing the buck—excuses—it's all through the army just as you have it. Only because of its size, so much more.

If there's anything else you want to know about the army, or rather, anything you want to know, just leave out the else, just ask me. Glad to oblige with facts or comment.

Let me in on any new building projects up there and keep me informed on the present ones.

A BAR was similar to a rifle except for its twenty-round magazine and automatic fire. It was an easy weapon to operate, but for one fact. It was very, very heavy. It weighed more than twice as much as a rifle and Carl not only carried that but also carried twelve magazines. Each magazine weighed about two pounds, so altogether Carl must have carried close to 50 pounds of extra weight. Measurements of two GIs from the Korean War showed that one BAR man carried a total weight of 80 pounds and one carried a total weight of 110 pounds.[19]

The particular model Carl was handed was a Model 1919, which indicates when it was designed, one year after the close of World War I.

The BAR had a simple purpose: to throw down a great amount of fire. It was comparable to spraying a water hose. And if there was an occasion that called for a spray, that automatic gun could do it. A BAR was capable of firing 650 rounds of 30-caliber rifle ammunition per minute.

The army selected Carl to operate the BAR not because he passed a special test or showed a particular aptitude or anything like that. It was because he was six foot two and could carry the thing. The big kids were invariably assigned the BAR while everyone else in the squad was handed a semiautomatic M1. Unlike the German rifles, GIs didn't need to manually cock the M1 after each shot. One pull of the M1 trigger sent out one shot.

The BAR was no M1. It was bulky and required its operator not only to clean it often but also to carry those dozen magazines.

Carl was very much aware of the difference in weight, and perhaps a little proud of it, though sometimes he wished he had an M1. There were two reasons for this. First, a working BAR sounded like a machine gun and that attracted German fire.

Second, the weight of the BAR prevented a soldier from running full-speed. If the situation called for an all-out sprint, the best Carl could ever do was a kind of fast shuffle. An M1 didn't make you a target. An M1 didn't slow you down when the situation required you to run like hell.

Military historian John McManus summarized: "The BAR . . . was heavy and deadly. It dated back to World War I, so it was not exactly state of the art, but it provided something that American small units were sadly lacking—mobile firepower. Because American infantry did not have an effective light machine gun at their disposal, the BAR was the next best thing, and it worked splendidly."[20]

—

Jun 18 1944
Sunday

Dear Mother,

I got the fudge today. Thanks very much, ma. I still insist you make the best fudge I know of. I could say more, but I don't want to spoil you.

And now I'm going to ask for something else. I've been meaning to ask you for a long time, but always forget. Do you think you can get me some good wool socks, long? Mine are all pretty well beat up by now, and they're impossible to get down here. Even if you can't get good ones, then just get socks. Those brown socks you got me last year were marvelous, if you could work something like that. But just the bare remnants are still in service now. Make it a half dozen, willya please?

Hope you've stopped sending me clippings, and thanks for them when you were. In camp we can get the daily papers.

Nothing but the same old grind. Oh, tomorrow I'm one of a group putting on a squad demonstration, so maybe the army considers me somewhat of a soldier.

Love and more love —Carl

—

Jun 30 1944
Thursday

Hi, Folks,

I've got a couple of things to tell you, both pretty big and nice.

1st – Infantry O.C.S. has been enlarged and we can apply to it once more. I've applied. Now, the chances of my getting in are about 100 to one against me. Over half of our company applied, and this undoubtedly is true for the whole division, since it is greatly made up of former A.S.T.s. So only about 1% of the men applying will be taken, probably. The fact that I've been in the infantry only three months, and have no rating will hinder me considerably. But still, it's something to hope for, and work for.

2nd – I'll probably get my furlough on or about the 15th of July! This just came out, and is an order. But of course, it could easily be changed in the next minute. I'll let you know.

Anyways, send me some money, please. I think twenty will be enough. Don't send it in a check or money order. Make it in at least two, or perhaps four, different letters with the money divided up evenly among them in bills.

That lot sounds very good. I don't think you could have gotten a better location than you did. (Have you got it yet?) You'll probably be bubbling over with excitement and happiness for the next four years, mom. You sounded pretty happy in your last letter.

Lots of love –Carl

Jul 1 1944
Friday

Dear Mom,

Wrote to tell you never mind about sending me the money. (Nope, nope, furlough hasn't been cancelled. I wouldn't be this calm if it had.) You see, we get paid today, and for some reason the records were mixed up and no one had any bond deductions taken out this month. So I've got about twenty dollars extra now.

Do me a favor will you? I'd like to have a Penn. R.R. schedule. Can't get it here. I've been busy figuring out train schedules. Or if you can't get one down here in time, perhaps you can tell me what I need to know. Here's the facts. I'll get off at 4:30 P.M. on whatever day it is. I can get a train at 11:50 that arrives in Cincinnati the next night at 9:40. From there I can get a N.Y. Central that leaves at 11:50 and arrives in Cleveland the next morning at 6:50. (No nearer stops to Canton than Cleveland). Or, I can get a train there that leaves at 8:30 and arrives in Chicago at 9:30 the next night. Now, the problem is, is there a train from Chi to Canton that I could catch that would save me some time? I don't know how long it would take by bus from Cleveland. There's also the fact that the Southern R.R. (the one to Cinci) has very poor trains, while the Ill. Central (the one to Chi.) is supposed to be pretty good. Also the run from Cinci to Cleveland is quite bad, while the Penn. R.R. (from Chi to Canton) isn't bad at all.

You'd better do the looking-in-to the bus and the Penn R.R.
schedules, Pop. Not that I don't trust your judgment, Ma, but I'm
afraid the timetable might get you a bit confused. And with that great
responsibility on your shoulders—I leave you—with love

   Carl

Jul 2 1944
Saturday

   Dear Mother,
   I'm writing with a good deal of trepidation. Three letters in three
days, I mean. Some one's going to be sorry for it; either you two, from
advanced shock, or me, because I've got you spoiled now and you'll
be expecting this sort of thing from now on.
   But a couple of things led me to it. First of all was your
wondering whether I still feel the same towards Edith. Well, I do. You
know how I like to write letters; well, we average six letters a week
to each other, and keeping that up for three months must indicate
something. Listen, I've just been living these three months since I've
seen her so I could see her again. I don't know if I can explain it any
better, but I love her, and I'm going to continue to love her for a long,
long time. And I know she loves me. The only way I could keep her
from coming down here to visit me was to tell here I'd never know
when I'd be out on bivouac. (The reason I didn't want her down is this
is such a hell-hole around here. Just like you read about, the army
towns.) Hope that convinces you. But you'll see for yourselves.
   Secondly, about 40 men are shipping out of our company this
week. This will forward the number of men who will leave on furlough
around the 15th, since it's done on a percentage of the company
strength. If I'm unlucky, it'll be another two weeks.
   Thirdly, I received the socks. Thanks very much. You're "right on
the ball."
   Love −Carl

Jul 9 1944
Sunday

Dear Mom,

Well, all I can say is that I'm fairly certain I'll get my furlough
on either the 14th or the 15th. If I do I'll probably be home at 7:50 in
the morning of the 15th or 16th. I'll call you up from Chicago in the
evening and let you know. I want to spend as much time with Edith
as possible, so I told her to get to Canton before I do. I'm going to
telegraph her as soon as I leave camp, which will give her a whole
day in which to leave. She probably will feel a little shy about getting
there and meeting you before I arrive, so I don't know just when she
will. Anyways, she'll let you know so you can meet her, or we can, if
she gets in after I do.

You know, the last time I was at the dentist's was about six
months ago. So maybe you'd better make an appointment for me.

Oh! And please do not accept any invitations of any kind for me.
If it's something that you feel I just have to attend, tell them you don't
know when I'm coming home and that I'll call them up when I get
there.

I hope the gas and food situation are both pretty satisfactory, for,
I warn you, I'm going to take full advantage of both of them. I believe
this is going to be my last furlough before going overseas, and I'm
going to be pretty selfish about things. Hope you understand.

Well, be seeing you with love –Carl

P.S.—did I tell you I got the fudge? Well, I did. Thanks, very,
very much—Love

———

A letter from Edith:

Jamaica NY
July 27 1944

Dear Mr. and Mrs. Lavin,

It's difficult for me to put my thanks for your hospitality into
words but I'm sure you know how I feel—how much I appreciate
everything you've done for me.

I enjoyed meeting the family—their friendliness made me feel very much at home. I enjoyed your food—it was delicious. And most of all, or course, I enjoyed being with your son—he's wonderful, really.

Thank you.

Edith

He's wonderful, really. Really? Several decades later, Dorothy gently chastised her son Carl over his behavior during this visit by Edith. "You didn't speak two words to her during the entire visit," Dorothy said. Carl, somewhat embarrassed, conceded the point. By way of explanation, he related that they had been in love but that it had apparently cooled over time, and seeing her face-to-face made him realize he was, in fact, no longer in love. Yet there was no way for him to tell her it was over. And he believed he was shipping out to the front soon in any event. So it seems the expedient step was simply to ignore her. Though Carl would make mention of Edith again, their relationship faded with time.

There was an odd discussion on the train back to Camp Shelby. "There was one guy I remember getting in an argument with. He was claiming that no Jewish soldiers were anywhere except in the quartermaster corps or they were cooks or they were truck drivers . . . worked it out so they were never in the infantry. I said, 'What the hell do you think I'm doing here?'

He said, 'What does your father do?' I said, 'Well, he's president of a company with about 200 employees.' He said, 'Well, I'm surprised you're here.' 'Here I am.'"[21]

Back at Camp Shelby, Carl still had the opportunity for the long-planned weekend in New Orleans.

Postcard – Cotillion Lounge, Jung Hotel, New Orleans

Aug 11 1944

Dear Folks –

I'm sending you this card because this is the only place I didn't
go to in N.O. Therefore, total costs are 33 cents and goodwill. Paid
$8.00 this year. Need $20. Please send. Love $on

——

August 20, 1944

Dear Folks,

This is just to let you know I'm still alive and healthy, since
nothing of interest has happened since I last wrote.

Well how do you like it up there this year? Anything changed?
Let me hear all about everything.

Terribly sorry to hear about Spitzy, but frankly it doesn't bother
me too much. I think it would have been quite a blow, though, had
she died about six or seven years ago. Ten years have been a pretty
long time, though. I think I'll be shipped out of here around the first
and I hope I'm right. I'm getting sick of this place and damned sick
of learning the same thing over and over. I'm glad of one thing; all
of us ASTs who came in here together are (supposedly) shipping out
together. The guys here that I go around with are, to me, better than
those any other place I've been—Queens, Camp Maxey, Camp Hood,
or Miami. You know, I've enjoyed my companions more at each place
I've gone to since I left home. But I don't think its them—I think it's
me—I'll always be grateful to the army for that one thing above all
others: I've been thrust in with new groups of people so often that I've
learned (and am learning) the best way of getting along with people.

Well, until the next time—With love –Carl

P.S.—Received the 20—thanks a lot. Came in very handy—Did
I tell you I also received the fudge and cheese? I think I did so thanks
again. Have you heard any more from Fred?

Love Carl

——

Aug 23 1944
Tuesday

Hi, Pop,

Just now I'm down at the dispensary waiting for all the companies in the regiment to go through sick call so I can see about my glasses. Broke 'em. So I confiscated this pad, although the medics don't know about it.

Received your letter yesterday. After a long and intensive study I even managed to decipher a few phrases. First of all, P.O.R. means Port of Replacement. It's the same as P.O.B. except that complete units are sent to P.O.B. while individuals are sent to P.O.R. It means that if I do see combat it'll be as a replacement in an already experienced outfit, which is the healthiest way of fighting a war.

And as for my being a Lavin, I agree with you. Of the four of us who went down to N.O. I was the only one who didn't either pass out, get sick, or appear in an M.P. report. I was the restraining influence, but without too much restraint.

Well, write and keep on writing and let me hear all about the wonders of Canada.

Love Carl

30 August 1944

Hi, Family,

Hope this gets to you in time before you leave. Well, how was it? Did the vacation measure up to expectations? I hope so.

Yes, I'm still here. The date of our shipping has been advanced to the fifth. About O.C.S., I doubt if I'll get into it because of the fact that I will be shipping. I thought things were moving pretty slowly so I inquired and found out a lot of procrastination was going on at the company headquarters. So I started goading and am continuing to goad. You see, papers have to go back and forth about a dozen times before one even gets to the interviewing board. So there are a lot of chances to procrastinate. It now looks like a neck and neck race as to whether the interview or the shipping comes first. One will rule out the other.

I just finished three days of tests—and passed, and am now an "Expert Infantryman" which means I can wear a blue medal and get $5 more a month. The tests covered everything. Really very inclusive. Bayonet, grenade, field proficiency, rifle accuracy, first aid, physical fitness, endurance, military appearance and courtesy, and so on, ad infinitum. Only about a third of those who took it passed. Maybe I was meant to be a professional soldier.

Love –Carl

Sep 10 1944
Saturday

Dear Folks,

Well, I've got some news for you. It's not what I would consider too good news, but I guess you would. Orders came out that no more men would be sent out of this division for shipment. That means I won't be going overseas for quite some time at least. And it kind of looks like I'm not going over to fight at all, maybe we'll be sent to some other camp in a month or some, to take some other kind of training, which may very well be (post-war) occupational work. That's an awful lot of conjecture to swallow at one letter.

Anyways, occupational duty is one thing I do not want. I can't picture myself spending three or four years at a German crossroads, opening and closing a gate three or four times a day.

But now I'm fairly certain of getting a chance to go before the O.C.S. board. That should happen within a week or so. Don't worry, I'll let you know as soon as it does. By the way, I hope you realize that my chances right now of becoming an officer are about three to one against, counting the board, shipments and especially O.C.S. itself. (about half of those accepted are flunked out.) So I don't want you to mention my application to anyone, understand? I imagine you've already considered this yourselves, but if you haven't please do. Once the bars are tacked on, it'll be time enough to let people know I've been to O.C.S.

Give me Fred's new address when you get it please.

'Bye Love –Carl

Sep 17 1944

Dear Folks,

Nope, nothing to report. All I'm doing is waiting, but impatiently. The status, as of my last letter is still quo.

Tomorrow we go out on bivouac again, probably for a couple weeks. And on bivouac one is quite apt to get hungry. So—please?

Haven't heard from you in some time. How come? And I still don't know if Fred is in the country or no. Is he?

Happy New Year![22] It's here again, and I'll have to admit I'm glad to see it because it means an extra pass for me. Last year it enabled me to go to Dallas from the STAR center. I didn't quite know if I wanted it then because of trying to get in to ASTP, and now I don't quite know if I want it because of trying to get into OCS. But I'll find out how things stand, and I imagine I'll make New Orleans.

I'll let you know as soon as I learn anything at all. Until then –
Love Carl

Vicinity of Sept 21 about Friday I think

Dear Folks,

This is only a token letter—just to let you know that I'm still alive and kicking (mostly kicking, being the good soldier that I am) because out here in the field there isn't much time or opportunity to write any other kind of letter. Still healthy, still fairly happy, still waiting for the O.C.S. Bored, bored.

Didn't I tell you what I did in Mobile? I thought I had. Well first I called her up and reserved her the evening, along with a girl for one of my friends.[23] She picked me up at the bus station in her car—a real live car—that alone, down here, would make an evening an historical occasion. We drove, both the other guy and I taking turns, out of town to a dance place—thence to an eatery—and thence home. And it was a pretty nice evening—good dancer, good personality, good time.

But right now I'd settle for a good shower. Smell? I wouldn't be surprised if you could smell me in this letter.

All for now—Love –Carl

—

September 27, 1944

Hi Folks,

Today is Yom Kippur, and I got a day and a half off again. I attended services last night at a Reform Temple. The rabbi was a rather young man, and sincere in what he was saying. I think it's been a long time since I've gone to Temple and listened to what was being said, if I ever did, but last night I heard everything and was interested in it.

I am glad that I went.

I hope you had an enjoyable a time during the holidays as I have had. As I told you, we've been in the field and these two chances to rest and enjoy have been grand, to me.

I imagine that it was so obvious to me that I never gave to you the reason for my not appearing before the O.C.S. board. It's simply that the board hasn't met since my papers went through regiment. And there's no way for me to find out when it will meet, since the board itself probably doesn't know at this time.

What's happened by now concerning the house? As I recall, weren't you supposed to have moved out by this time?

Tell me what's going on. Take care of yourselves.

Love –Carl

—

15 Oct '44

Dear Dad,

Yes. I'm back in camp once more. Civilization, comparative. Wasn't too bad in the field. Got cold the last four or five nights, though. In fact it was so cold that it was uncomfortable under four blankets and a canvas wearing all our clothes. The last night another guy and I decided to stay warm so we dug a hole two and a half feet deep by seven by four, filled it with six inches of pine needles, our four blankets and one tent half, and put logs over the top and covered

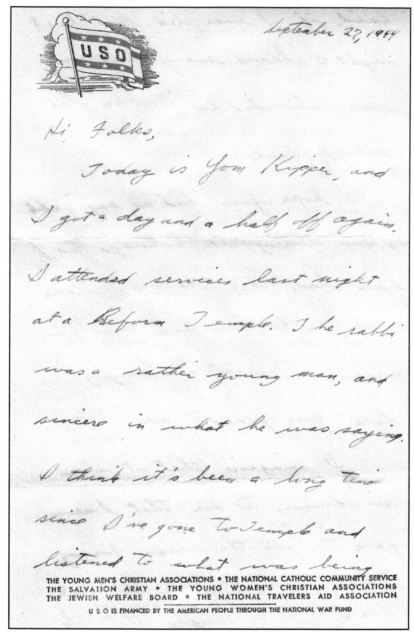

USO

September 27, 1944

Hi Folks,

Today is Yom Kippur, and I got a day and a half off again. I attended services last night at a Reform Temple. The rabbi was a rather young man, and sincere in what he was saying. I think it's been a long time since I've gone to Temple and listened to what was being

THE YOUNG MEN'S CHRISTIAN ASSOCIATIONS • THE NATIONAL CATHOLIC COMMUNITY SERVICE
THE SALVATION ARMY • THE YOUNG WOMEN'S CHRISTIAN ASSOCIATIONS
THE JEWISH WELFARE BOARD • THE NATIONAL TRAVELERS AID ASSOCIATION
U S O IS FINANCED BY THE AMERICAN PEOPLE THROUGH THE NATIONAL WAR FUND

Figure 4-3. USO letterhead, September 27, 1944. *Author collection.*

them with the other tent half, and dirt and pine needles. Well, it took us two hours to do it but by God, we were warm that night.

You know, from the letter you just wrote me it doesn't look like you read that one letter of mine very well. As I told you, the O.C.S.

board hasn't met since I turned my papers in. When and if it does meet I'll go before it. Now if you can get the divisional commander to hold a meeting of the board you can help me out. But that's the only way any one could possibly help me. Probably the O.C.S. quota has been reduced and that's why there have been no board meetings lately. So I guess you'd have to go first to the war department and convince them they need more officers before the commander would hold a meeting.

But, Pop, I appreciate your desire to do something to help me. And if you've got the time to come down here I'd love to see you. In fact, all three of you could spend a vacation in New Orleans, which incidentally is a good place to spend one—excellent facilities—and I'd probably get a three day pass to spend with you.

But it's not too good of an idea, since you'd have to get here within a month. The division is supposed to ship to another camp in about that time.

Is Fred home now? Hope nothing went wrong with his leave.

Let's hear from you a little more often. Love –Carl

—

17 October 1944

Dear Family,

First, I want to thank y'all for the packages. They were well received and greatly appreciated and quite timely. So thanks very much. Aunt Dodo[24] also sent me a package. Box of cookies, not home-made. Yes, I thanked her.

Sure wish I would be home with all three of you now. I thought for a time that I might be getting a furlough now, but found out that I won't. Oh, well, enjoy yourselves.

There's one thing I wish you'd get for me, Ma, and that's two or three strong metal glass [eyeglass] cases. I'm always crushing them (leading the rugged life, y'know) and I have no way of getting new ones.

Let's hear from all of you. Love Carl

—

Dear Folks,

I'm going to try to call you tonite, but in case I can't get you, I'll write what I want to say here.

I think I told you the furloughs were cancelled, but in case I didn't, they are. And we'll be moving to another camp some time sooner or later, so don't come down here.

Have you had that pair of shoes repaired that I left at home? Let me know if you have, and if you haven't please do so right away as these I have here are pretty well shot and there's no decent place here to get them repaired. But whatever you do, don't send those shoes to me until I say so, O.K.?

I received the twenty. Thanks very much. Unfortunately they've put us on a seven days a week training schedule so I have yet to enjoy that pass (week-end) I was looking for.

I'm going to go now, and see if I can talk to you. It is now 9:30 Sunday night.

Love, Carl

P.S.—Come to think of it that's a bad time, isn't it? Oh, well it'll take a couple of hours for the call to get through. Carl.

———

Calls from the base would soon no longer be a concern. Less than two weeks later, the 69th Division would be sent up north to begin their journey from New York Harbor to Britain. The trip from Camp Shelby to Britain was described by Lt. John F. Higgins:

> More than 2.6 million men passed through the New York—New Jersey piers. . . . The men received their final inoculations at the staging area and they prepared for the worst at sea, taking part in drills that had them scrambling down ropes to lifeboats resting in a pool of water. . . . Within 12 hours of the order to move out and head for the piers, the GIs were put on "Alert." They removed their division patches to preserve troop-movement security and their helmets were chalked with a letter and a number indicating their seats in the trains taking them directly to the docks. . . .

But where were we going? The Pullman porter knew, but like all railroad employees, he was the vaguest source of information, and there remained only the usual unimpeachable channels of latrine rumors. It wasn't long, however, before word started spreading from car to car that we were doing the "Jersey Bounce!" The Yankees in the crowd started immediately to expound on the merits of New Jersey, with assurances to all who had never been there that they were now to see how the "other half" lived. It was true. We were on the way to Camp Kilmer, near New Brunswick, and the prospect was thrilling to those lucky individuals who happened to live in the vicinity. The trip was pleasant, with the usual troop train diversions. Some played cards, others sat and talked; some just sat. The food was good, and the Pullman bunks were clean and comfortable.

The first group of the regiment arrived at Kilmer early the morning of 2 November, and all during the day, the balance of the command arrived. To the accompaniment of some lively music, we marched to the two-story barracks that were to be our home for the next few days. Almost immediately began the overseas orientation schedule, and it was amazing to note the efficiency with which the many details were accomplished. Remember the cargo nets, the lifeboat drill, the lectures on censorship, the procedure in case of capture, the introduction to the Army's new type of gas mask, etc.? Or who will forget that physical exam, where they passed you by an electric bulb, and if they couldn't see through you, the seal of approval was put on your forehead, the equivalent of a free ticket for an ocean trip.

Of the many good features of Kilmer, its most appealing was its proximity to New York, just 20-odd miles away. Remember those passes to the big city? Times Square, the Village, the Music Hall, and the way you skidded through the gates in Penn Station for that 5 a.m. train back to Kilmer. . . . There was so much to do and so little time in which to do it. . . . Take a last look; pour down that last scotch and soda. . . . It may be a long time. It was even harder for those who had been able to get home and had to say the last farewell when the last pass neared its expiration hour. But this was what we had been training for.

On 14 November, we again boarded a train, but this time it was a very short trip; in fact so short that it almost wasn't worthwhile to get out of the GI harness, since they were soon lining us up to get off. Next a ferry ride, but without the familiar atmosphere of the accordion player and considerably less comfortable. Across the river, amid much speculation as to where we were headed, we finally pulled in at Pier 44, where they added insult to injury by having a band play "Somebody Else Is Taking My Place." The Red Cross was on hand to pass out coffee and sinkers to those who still had strength enough to hold up the cup. Beside us was a large ocean liner, dark and gray in the night. It was at this time that all who had the hot tip on the "Queen Mary" paid off their bets, and we all struggled up the gangplank of the MS *John Ericsson.* . . . our home for several days. The ship was spacious and well planned as a trooper, so that there was no confusion as the men were rapidly assigned to their quarters.[25]

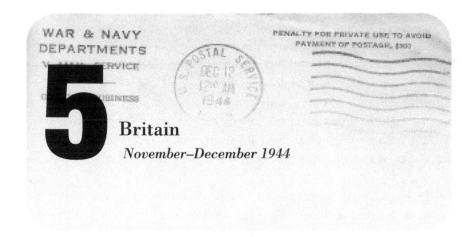

5 Britain

November–December 1944

In November 1944, Carl crossed the Atlantic, some five months after D-Day.

Carl embarked on the MS *John Ericsson*, formerly the Swedish liner *Kungsholm*. This prewar luxury liner was about thirty years old with six or seven decks. Berths now took the place of bunks, and there were lots of them. About 1,500 to 2,000 troops, almost one regiment of the 69th division, embarked—many more than the number of passengers when it was a luxury liner.

The metal-framed berths were suspended on chains and stacked five high. The accommodations were so cramped that Carl could not lie on his side; he had to sleep either on his back or stomach. If he turned, his shoulder would touch the person above.

The ship did not sail in a large convoy because a convoy could only travel at the speed of the slowest ship, 11 knots or so. Carl's ship, in a small group, could double that speed.

Lieutenant Higgins provided some color:

> Once assigned and quickly oriented to the need of wear-
> ing lifejackets, we put the weary bones to bed on canvas cots,
> which were in four tiers and strung in every possible place. It
> was not until 0600 the next morning that we set sail, and in the
> gray mist of early morning, we saw the familiar and beloved
> skyline of New York drop from view. Through the Narrows,
> and out into open water, where we were soon joined by many
> other ships that were to be in our convoy. One had only to
> look around at these vessels to be impressed with the stupen-

dous shipping problem that war presented and be struck with the efficiency with which the problem was being met.

Those of us who had been landlubbers all our life were soon tossing coins to decide which was port and which was starboard, and trying hard not to look too lost when someone said something about the 'Liberty two points off the port bow.' It wasn't long before the gulls began to drop back, and we came to realize that the ocean was a pretty large place.[1]

During the trip, there wasn't much to do for the GIs, most of whom had never been to sea before. The ship was manned by Merchant Marines, and US Navy personnel oversaw the deck guns and the depth charges. Carl's job was to help a group of fifteen to twenty soldiers clean up the mess hall, two decks below sea level, and to punch meal cards, ensuring no soldier doubled up on food.

The Atlantic was stormy throughout the trip and many GIs were seasick, so they passed their meal cards to friends looking for a second round of food. Carl, not one to deny another man some extra portions, looked the other way and punched the cards.

One noontime, Carl was mopping up the mess hall with other soldiers. Their task wasn't exactly hard work. The GIs were at the instructions of some of the Merchant Marines, and they were all having fun, tossing around buckets of water and then sweeping them up. All of a sudden there was a big explosion. The GIs could hear and feel it. They were under the water line when the ship shook. The first explosion was followed by a second "kaboom" and then a third.

Instantly, a couple of the GIs broke for the stairway. The rest of the squad more or less grabbed the Merchant Marines and fired off questions: "What's happening? What's going on? Have we been torpedoed? Are we sinking? Have we been hit? What is this?"

And the Mariners said, "No, no, no, don't worry. Don't worry. That's just the guys up on deck shooting off depth charges, and you heard three depth charges going off.

"They just picked up something on sonar. Usually it's a whale or it's a school of fish swimming very tightly together so that they make an echo. It's hardly ever a submarine."

The GIs were just starting to feel a little bit reassured when suddenly the ship started to tilt, the entire deck was listing to the right. Again, a great unease took hold of the GIs and they encircled the sailors once more.

"What is this? What is this?" they asked. "Have we been hit? Are we sinking? Why the tilt? Why the tilt? My God, what's going on?"

"Ahh. . . . Don't worry. Don't worry," the Mariners said. "That's just 2,000 GIs all running to the starboard rail to see what's going on. Don't worry; we'll become right very quickly because the officers will order them back."

Sure enough, within thirty seconds the ship gradually started to right itself and soon it become square again.

As Higgins related, "several depth charges were dropped by the escorting naval vessels, shaking our ship considerably and making the men in the lower deck compartments wonder if their nickname, 'Torpedo Junction,' might not be too far from the truth."[2]

The rest of the sea passage was quick. The liner made it safely to England in five or six more days, maybe ten days in all.

Higgins captured the disembarkation:

> They say that England has two seasons, winter and August. We missed August. It was cold as we debarked at Southampton on 27 November to entrain for our billet area. After being served some very welcome coffee and doughnuts by the Red Cross, we helped each other get through the narrow doors of the railroad coaches, and were carried about 15 miles inland to Winchester, the ancient capital of England. Winchester, rich in story and legend, where the statue of King Alfred looks down the crooked, winding streets, and the solemn majesty of Winchester Cathedral stands quiet guard over the city, able to tell so many stories of the changes it has seen in man's life.
>
> Most of the regiment was billeted in Winchester Barracks, in the middle of the city, and here one got his first taste of British military tradition on noticing that over each door was inscribed the name of some famous battle in which the Hampshire Regiment had participated. After we cleaned up and got the chill out of the buildings, they turned out to be quite comfortable. The 3rd Battalion went to nearby Arlysford [Alresford] and there received their billets in its vicinity. Headquarters and I Company were at Armsworth House, Companies K and L were at Bighton, and M Company stayed at Bishop's Sutton.[3]

From November until December, Carl was in a camp in southern England near Southampton.

The war was progressing. The American and British forces were advancing rather rapidly across France in the fall and had almost reached the German border. Some people thought the Allies would be in Berlin by Christmas.

When Carl landed in England, he expected to go across the Channel and be put into combat any day. But it didn't happen.

It was mystifying to Carl that he wasn't mobilized on D-Day, and it was just as mystifying that he was held back in England. Maybe General Eisenhower wanted to have some men in reserve, Carl thought.

It was never explained, though. Soldiers were just there, staying put. Whatever the reason, it proved sound. Eisenhower's decision to hold troops in reserve was to be critical in just a few weeks.

⸺

28 Nov '44

Hello, Folks,

Since you last heard from me things have been fairly interesting, approximately comfortable, slightly educational, and generally different.

On the ship the one thing that was surprising was that it was quite warm all the way over. Never even had to wear a jacket on deck. We were lucky in having a very good ship—used to be a luxury liner on the Swedish-American Line—complete with swimming pool and mahogany paneling. It's supposed to be one of the smoothest riding troop-ships in the country. Well, I'd hate to be on one of the rougher ones.

It was a rather rough voyage. Didn't exactly get sea-sick, but I wasn't hungry on two or three days' occasions. And that was really too bad because our company was given the pleasure of furnishing the K.P.s for the entire ship on the way over. So when I felt like eating, I had all I wanted and what I wanted. Managed to get myself sort of an executive job, for K.P., namely punching mess cards. Don't imagine I can tell you how many times I punched a hole because then you'd probably be able to figure out something or other, but I've got a callous on the palm of my right hand.

About the time England came into sight it started raining and getting cold. The weather is exactly as you would expect it to be. English.

Candy is very hard to get here, so please send me some, and often. You'll probably have to show this request to the Post Office.

Love to all of you, Carl

———

Britain
November 29, 1944

Dear Family,

Hello again. We're not doing a damn thing now so I've plenty of time. So I'll be writing you quite frequently for awhile. Hope it encourages you to do the same thing. And I hope that when I stop writing quite so often that that doesn't discourage you, see?

Received the letter today, mom, that you wrote after you talked to me—the first one since I left the States. I enjoyed it quite a bit. I hope you won't worry too much but I suppose you will anyway.

Sorry I can't exactly write you a newsy letter, because just about everything I consider newsy, the army considers verboten.

But anyways, today I finally got a look at England. In other words, it was a clear day. And this really is a lovely country. Because of all that moisture the colors in the fields look like they're always lush or should be. I'm pretty sure I'm going to enjoy England.

From what little I've experienced of it, it's O.K. It's mostly like I imagined it to be—I was a little impressed though, at the fact that it actually is a foreign country. You don't really quite expect it to be.

I think it's good that you're enjoying yourself along with the rest of Canton's "society." I don't see anything wrong with giving parties or dinners. I don't see how it helps the war any to sit at home.

Tell me what you hear from Fred and send him my address and have him write me, please? I suppose by now you know where he's stationed. It looks like the main shortages for me are going to be almost entirely in the edible line. So please send me a package of food about every four or five days, willya? And please don't make it one of those great big packages. Just something small like a box of candy and a few boxes of cookies. And place an emphasis on candy bars—caramels, things like that—gum, too. And I wish you'd enclose in your letters some clippings from the *Repository*. Things local, you know. I can read the British papers.

Still feeling healthy. Hope you are, too. Love, Carl

———

November 29 1944
To: Ens. Alfred B. Lavin

Dear Fred,

Got your letter today that you wrote the 26th of Nov. and the reason I didn't write is that I didn't get your address while I was in the states.

Try sending some V-mail to me.[4] They seem to get here quicker than air-mail and next time please lets have a bit more quantity per epistle. But on second thought you can't exactly fulfill both these qualifications at once, can you? Oh, well.

There's not much to tell you since I wrote. I had a pass to a small town that is world-known for something I won't tell you about and didn't even see it anyways.

By the time you get this I suppose you won't even be in Ill [Illinois]. Are you completely well yet?

Sympathy with you in having to have a date with A instead of K. "Mentally void" is about as accurate a description of her as you could give. Tough.

I keep running into guys I know from Miami and Lehman and guys that know people from same. So far, no one you'd know too. Write.

———

1st December 1944

Dear Folks,

Finally got out of camp and to a small town, near. The people are surprisingly friendly and don't have as much of an accent as I'd been led to expect. The country is compact, clean, quaint, and surprising. There's a village every two or three miles, and little roads and lanes cut in and wind around all over the place. And everything has been sitting around so long its part of the ground, and is kept clean by all the drizzle and rain. One more thing is the war, superimposed on, and incongruent with, all of this. That's a very personal impression of England, and a very first one. Love –Carl

—

Higgins described the environs:

> You will recall the many points of interest in and about Win-
> chester. The Cathedral, built in 1079, the church of St. Cross,
> the Guildhall, King Arthur's Roundtable, the Westgate, etc. It
> was an interesting and informative insight into British history
> and tradition. Remember too the pubs, the "alf & alf," fish and
> chips, and last but not least those passes to London. Many last-
> ing friendships were made in England during the seven weeks
> we stayed there. Much was done toward working out a more
> thorough understanding between Americans and Britons. Who
> could help but marvel at the courage and tenacity of these
> people upon seeing the havoc wrought in London and other
> cities by air raids and V-bombings?[5]

Carl was not unlike most American soldiers, who liked and respected the British people. Military historian Peter Schrijvers explained:

> What the Americans came to admire the most in the Brit-
> ish . . . was that the restraint which seemed to pervade their
> whole being made them carry the many burdens of war with
> an unbending will and perfect dignity. Over and over again,
> GIs described the British civilians as uncomplaining, patient,
> disciplined, persevering, stout hearted, and brave. They thought
> British imperturbability beyond description and agreed it was
> their gift for understatement, more than anything else, that
> made them both an amazing breed and a great people.[6]

—

December 3, 1944

Dear Folks,

The next time I write I'll tell you what London looks like. There were just a few passes available so we drew cards for them, and I got a king. Ray! [Hoo-ray!] And I've now learned all about English money. We played black-jack with it last night for the purpose of learning just that. It worked very well, and I was 18/9, pronounced "18 and 9" and meaning 18 shillings and 9 pence—1 and 3 less than a pound. You could call it 3 crown, 3 shil, and 9; or 9 florins and 9; or any number of things ad nauseam.

Went to a tea-house about a mile from camp yesterday. A very small sign outside that you'd almost have to be looking for to see, and an atmosphere inside that makes everyone speak in whispers, and only three spoons, so the customers have to trade them around, and self-service which includes cleaning up the dirty dishes, and modest prices. Love –Carl

Wednesday 6 December, 1944

Hello Folks,

Well I did get that pass to London after all. Just returned last night. And here's what I did:

Got up at 4:00 A.M. Monday morning to go in trucks a distance of 20 miles so we could catch the train. I suppose you've heard how the coaches over here are built. Even the third class ones are separated into compartments, and each compartment has its own door to the platform. These trains are considerably more comfortable than ours— little noise and rattle, and almost no sway.

Reached London with quite a confused air, not knowing or being with anyone that knew what was what. But we got to our room, which had been arranged for us, near Russell Square, after a certain amount of confusion. It was somewhat on the order of a garret, but warm and clean. Half of the building is demolished, but not the half we stayed in. It was done before—by a bomb, I presume.

From there we went to Piccadilly Circus, which is sort of the center of things. You see, London is not like New York with a Times

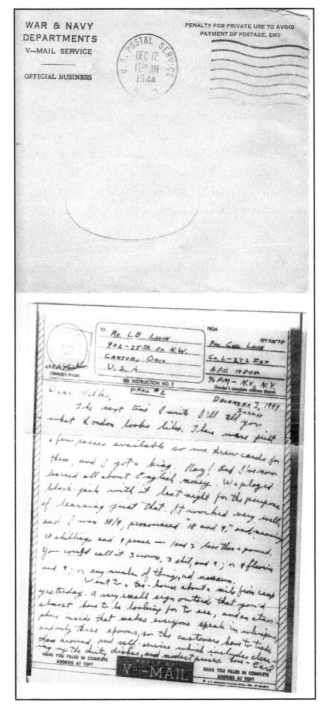

Figure 5-1. V-mail, December 3, 1944. *Author collection.*

Square from which everything radiates; it's more on the order of Chicago, with a large conglomerate downtown district. There are four or five main squares or circles or circuses which are the centers of unofficial sections. Pica, you might say, is the main one. Anyways, we went there.

We went to the Rainbow Club, the main Red Cross club, to get ourselves oriented, which we did, approximately. We went to a show in the afternoon, *Strike Me Again*, a musical comedy with Sid Fields, one of the big comedians. It's very similar to New York musicals, although not quite so lavish in costuming and scenery. The jokes and acts were no subtler nor no cruder than New York, but a bit different, of course.

Anyways, we did enjoy it, which is more than I can say for some I saw in N.Y., although some of that enjoyment may have come from the difference itself. I was surprised at one thing—how very similar the dance routines are to N.Y.'s. They were a mixture of jitterbug and ballet mainly, and pretty good. They can and do jitterbug here just as well as what I've seen in the states.

In the evening I went to a couple of dances. First, to one in this Rainbow Club, where I met one of the nicest girls I've yet met in the army—but couldn't get her address, and then to a public dance hall where my friend and I took out two English MPs, female. I'll have to continue this tomorrow because the mail goes out right now. Happy Birthday Mom—Love again –Carl

---

7 December 1944

Hello, Parents,

In case you haven't yet received the letter I wrote yesterday, I was telling you about my two day pass in London and got through the first day of it.

Now continue with the story:

The next morning we decided we want to see something of London. So we went down to the Westminster Square district, where the houses of Parliament and the governmental offices and Downing Street are. And of course, Westminster Abbey. Whitehall Ave., sort of the 5th Ave of the government, lies between Westminster and

Trafalgar Sq. and we walked it. But I'm getting ahead of myself. First
we went in and through Westminster Abbey. You've seen pictures
of it many times, so I don't have to tell you what it's like. But the
impressive point about it is the great high arches inside. And the
many famous monuments and graves inside. Chaucer, Dickens,
Kipling, Pitt, Disraeli, Darwin, the unknown soldier, and about 400
others; doubtlessly the four hundred other, Generals, Lords, and
writers, you know.

Then we walked up Whitehall. You get the impression that you're
looking at the outside of big things. Canes, perfectly tailored coats,
and spats, walk around you. Long black cars enter and leave guarded
gates. We went past a Museum of War and went in. It turned out to be
just an ordinary museum of war, and after a while we started to leave.
But I noticed a sign by a door, "Through this hall passed Charles I
just before he was executed." We looked around and found out that
the building was the headquarters hall of the old Whitehall Palace.
I believe it was the Palace before Buckingham was built. And the
scaffold was built outside the first window on the second floor (which
the English, incidentally, would call the first floor) which was the
main banquet hall. We stood where he hung after.

After that, to New Oxford Street, a kind of small shopping
district. Finally went into a tiny picture shop, as all shops in
London—in England, in fact—are tiny, where I bought a pretty good
water-color copy. Right now I'm trying to send it to you. Don't know
if I can or not because they've got some sort of rule or other about
sending pictures home, but I'll see what I can do.

And then it was about time to catch the train back, so we went
to a cinema. Saw *Summer Storm* which wasn't bad in case you've not
seen it yet.[7] There was an alert about half way through the picture,
which didn't bother anything—only eight or ten people left—but
when we got out to take the "tube," or "underground" to the train
station, guess what—it wasn't running. So we had a bit of excitement
scurrying around trying to get there. Finally got a bus just in time.

And that is what I and another guy did in London. But there's still
a bit more to tell you about. The people, the meals, the underground.
Well I'll have to make another letter out of that. This one is getting
pretty long by this time. But in a general summing up—I love
the place. I'd like to come here after the war for some time. It's a
wonderful place, mainly because the people are wonderful, I imagine.

That'll take care of London for the present. When am I going to start receiving letters from you? I've only had one since I arrived. And incidentally, I'm still pretty much in need of food. So please keep on sending the packages. Let me know what you hear from Fred and what's going on in Canton.

Lots of love —Carl

———

December 16 saw the start of the German offensive in the Ardennes, which became known as the Battle of the Bulge. In launching their offensive, the Germans sought to go all the way to the Belgian coast, cutting off the northern part of the American and British forces to separate and annihilate them. Carl learned of the attack through *Stars and Stripes*, the US Army paper, which Carl considered "about as good as the average American paper."

With the Allies trying to contain the ballooning expanse of German forces, the Bulge became the largest battle in the history of the US Army—with hundreds of thousands of soldiers on each side clashing and killing for weeks.

———

19 December 1944

Dear Folks,

I got the letter today that you sent Nov 24. I think I'll start getting them quicker, though, after Xmas. I hope your pal in the post office has been helping you out in the sending of packages, because I haven't made many requests, only general ones. So from now on, I'll be a bit more definite. And no—don't send any cigarettes; I still don't smoke.

By the time you receive this I imagine something will have happened to Grandpa one way or the other. Has it?

Oh yes—notice that my A.P.O. has been changed again. It's 417 again, what it was in Shelby. If you want to send a cable to me, address it like this: PFC Carl Lavin, 15140578 AMOWEV and nothing else.

Hope you're still healthy and happy, like me—have you done anything about the house? Take care of yourselves. Love —Carl

P.S. Will you send me a pair of light wool gloves and some candy bars and nuts please —Carl

---

19 December 1944

Dear Family,

Got a letter from Fred today, but it's been some time since I've heard from you. I'll probably get twenty all at once. Try sending some of them V-mail, a lot of guys seem to be getting them more quickly than air-mail. Anyways I hope you're still writing regularly and still sending food regularly.

Had a pass into a small town near here yesterday, which naturally I can't tell you about. But it's world-famous for something that naturally I can't tell you about. But then, I didn't see that thing anyways—so, naturally, I can't tell you about it.

Boy, would you mind getting clippings out of the *Rep* and sending it to me? Things I'd be interested in—sports accounts and write-ups and stuff like that? You wouldn't? Good.

By the time you get this, it should be fairly evident of how long things are going to last in Germany. As a result of the present German offensive I mean. Well, we'll see if I'm right. Goodbye for now. Please send me some fudge and cookies, Mom.

Lots of love   Carl

Britain
21 December, 1944

Got the letter today that you sent Nov. 20th, Ma—the one in which you told of Dad's train wreck and Fred's date trouble.

That was pretty lucky, Pop, and I must say you showed an admirable amount of foresight being in one of the three cars that weren't derailed out of eighteen.[8]

Got a letter from Fred two days ago in which he told me about that date with A. Sympathized with him in my answer.

I'm sure you've been wondering what kind of a time I've been having over here, it's been rather pleasant. We're having no difficult training, we've got sufficient warmth, food and shelter (factors I never realized the importance of, until I went through some bivouac and maneuvers) and an emphasis is being placed on athletics now to keep us properly tempered and contented. In fact today had quite an interesting little football game (non-tackle)[9] with another company, which we lost 7-6, but shouldn't have. Out of it, I got a lot of fun and a few bruises.

And for Xmas there's going to be a Company party. In town and complete with girls. I'm telling you, this is getting to be a second A.S.T.P., almost. Of course we do a lot more than just loll around, but not much.

The main trouble is that candy, cookies, et cetera are rationed so strictly that I can buy as much now in a week as I used to get in a day.

In other words, please send me a box of candy.

With love —Carl

———

December 22 1944

Dear Mom and Dad,

Well so far I haven't been getting very many letters from you but pretty soon now I expect to be receiving answers to letters I've written from here.

There isn't anything much I can tell you about what we are doing or what training we are getting or anything like that and since I don't have any letters to answer questions from, that only leaves me two subjects: London and packages.

I've covered London about as well as I can, Dad. Did I tell you, though, the easiest way to get around is by subway? I have one more subway stop than bus stop, and perfect interchangeability and all buses and trams are much easier and quicker than taxis to catch. And if you say "you" for "one" and "I am done" for "I am finished" no one understands you. And the enunciation of a Britisher is fascinating to listen to. And I have quickly become at home with British money. It isn't confusing, only different.

As far as packages, please send me some food. And will you get me a good pen knife and three pairs of cotton shorts size 32. See what you can do please. Love – 'Bye Carl

———

Carl's grandfather Harry Lavin passed away on November 26, 1944, age 74, after a lengthy period of declining health.[10]

———

December 25, '44

Dear Mom and Dad,

That was a beautiful letter that you wrote, Mother. Thank you for it. I don't know if I'm really sorry to hear of Grandpa's death or not, because it was his time. I did always hold a great deal of respect for him. He lived a life.

In honor of today, the camp had quite a few kids in from the neighborhood and is giving them a real treat. Most of them are permanent or temporary war orphans, and not used to or expecting very much. So they're truly appreciative, but also very polite. And now they're having the time of their life, running all over the place wearing our equipment. About all you can see of some of them is a helmet, a pair of shoes, and a field jacket.

It's not a white xmas, though I still have yet to see my first English snow. But at least there are the kids, and the spirit, and also the turkey.

You know, I don't believe I've ever told you about our housing, have I? Well, we live in Mission Huts. If that means nothing to you, they're nothing but cylinders made of corrugated iron with bunks inside. The floor is of concrete and there's a stove in it. We sleep in double-deck bunks. So altogether it's comfortable enough and warm enough, as long as somebody feels like going to the coal pile.

Let's keep hearing from you—Love –Carl

P.S.—Send me a box of candy, please. Love –Carl

———

The Battle of the Bulge was an exchange of extraordinary firepower, a battle of wills, in the worst of winter conditions among hilly and wooded terrain.

Nine days after the German offensive started it was Christmas Day and Carl's company was having a noontime Christmas banquet. All the Jewish guys, including Carl, had traded their KP assignments to help serve. Halfway into the meal an announcement came over the loudspeaker system. The men were immediately ordered to report to their barracks, where they would receive further instructions. At the barracks, the GIs were then told to pack up their duffle bags and be ready for departure in fifteen minutes. And in fifteen minutes, the men were on trucks barreling towards Southampton. The GIs were going to cross the channel. Their turn had come.

Wrote Higgins: "On Christmas Day, we received a rush call to furnish riflemen as replacements for the forces in the Ardennes. Eight hundred and thirty-one men were sent to the front, which was saddening to those who remained behind while all this was going on across the Channel."[11]

That Christmas day over a quarter of the men from three of the 69th's infantry regiments were reassigned to other fighting divisions in the European theater. According to historian Peter Mansoor, from May 1943 to the end of 1944, the 69th Division was stripped of 1,366 officers and 22,235 enlisted men, earning the 69th "the dubious distinction of being the most stripped unit in the Army of the United States."[12]

A few hundred miles away in the forests of Belgium, Company L of the 335th Infantry encountered their most ferocious moment of combat: "completely surrounded by the enemy December 24 and 25. All its commissioned officers were killed or wounded." A tech sergeant became temporary commanding officer of the company, which eventually made it to safety.[13]

Company L needed replacements.[14] Carl was going to the front.

Harry Lavin (in vest, fifth from left) and Wurstmeisters, early 1920s. *Used by permission of McKinley Presidential Library & Museum, Canton, Ohio.*

Fred and Carl, 1928. *Author collection.*

Extended Lavin family, early 1930s. Fred appears somewhat pensive, Carl and
Leo seem self-confident, and the only person in the photo not looking at the
camera is Dorothy. Back row, left to right: Fred, Arthur, Elizabeth Kaven, Carl,
Leo, Cele, Lou Kaven, Bill Kaven. Besides Fred and Carl, Bill Kaven was the
only other family member of military age during the war and saw combat in
Europe as a navigator for the Army Air Corps. Front row, left to right: Dorothy,
Helen Kaven (Stein), Ben, Harry, Marilyn, Mary, William, David, Dodo. *Author
collection.*

Late 1930s, and Leo is happy. *Author collection.*

Carl's 1942 Lehman High yearbook photo. *Author collection.*

Carl in his uniform, Camp Hood, Texas, July 1943. "From those pictures you'd get the impression that being in the war was really rather jolly, everyone's so smiling and jaunty" (Fussell, *Wartime*, 145). *Author collection.*

Home leave before shipping to Britain. Carl, looking purposeful, is wearing his 69th Division patch. *Author collection.*

PART II

In the War

A Note on US Army Organization

Carl Lavin served in combat in the 84th Infantry Division. During World War II such a division had approximately 14,000 men at full strength. During combat operations, division strength was closer to 10,000 men.

The main components of the division were three infantry regiments and the division artillery. Each regiment contained approximately 3,000 men. Carl served in the 335th Regiment.

Each regiment comprised three battalions and some special companies. Carl served in the 3rd Battalion. Each battalion had some 850 men.

Each battalion comprised five companies and Carl served in Company L. A company had something like 180 men.

A company was made up of four platoons of about 40 men each. A platoon was made up of three squads of 12 men each. Carl served in the Third Platoon.

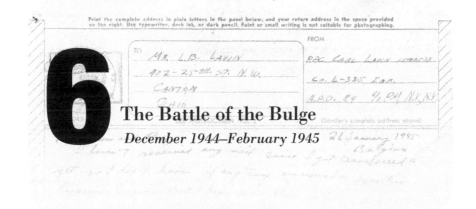

6

The Battle of the Bulge
December 1944–February 1945

"Nobody gets out of a rifle company. It's a door that only
opens one way, in. You leave when they carry you out,
if you're unlucky, dead, or if you're lucky, wounded. But
nobody just walks away. That was the unwritten law."

–Infantryman Charles Felix[1]

In December 1944, the fate of the Western Front hung
on the Battle of the Bulge. If Hitler could smash through to the Atlantic
coast as he did in 1940, the entire Allied offensive would be halted. If the
Allies could hold their ground, they knew that eventually their superiority
in manpower and material would prevail.

The setting of the battle was the Ardennes, a geographical nightmare
for the forces who faced off in Belgium. For combatants, it was an obstacle
course of forests, ravines, winding paths, and small villages that became
even more troublesome when cold weather was added to the mix.[2]

Summed up by John Eisenhower, "It was the biggest single battle ever
fought by the United States Army. More than 600,000 GIs were directly
involved, another 400,000 had supporting roles. That was more men than
the entire U.S. Army of 1941. About 20,000 GIs were killed in the Ardennes, another 20,000 captured, and 40,000 wounded. This was more
casualties than the total number of men in the Army of Northern Virginia
at Gettysburg. The Americans lost nearly 800 tanks, more than there had
been in the entire U.S. Army in 1941."[3]

On Christmas Day 1944, Carl boarded an LCT (Landing Craft Tank),
a huge open-aired shoebox, with seventy to eighty other men. They

crossed the Channel, making the thirty-mile journey from Southampton to Le Havre, France, in about two hours.

Upon landing in Le Havre, Carl was told to put his duffle bag in a truck, which would take it to a temporary camp. Carl was ordered to make sure the duffle bag was properly tagged and labeled because he was told it would be waiting for him when he needed it. Carl never saw that duffel bag again, but it didn't matter much. All it contained was extra clothing and a toilet kit.

When you're in combat, you don't worry about looks, smell, or a change of clothes. You wear the same clothes for weeks and weeks—and that's if you're lucky.

Historian Michael Doubler described the replacement process:

> The typical replacement set foot in the ETO through one of the entry depots at Le Havre or Marseilles. There he had a stop of several hours or an overnight rest while awaiting transportation to another depot further inland. At intermediate depots troops received individual weapons and equipment, clerks updated personnel records, and instructors gave lectures and classes. Replacements finally reached army depots where they underwent administrative processing before loading on trucks for the final leg of their trip to the front. Replacements ended their odyssey through the human pipeline under a variety of conditions. The lucky ones joined divisions in rest areas where they had a chance to become part of their unit before going into combat, while others went directly onto the firing line with little knowledge of their location, unit, or mission.[4]

Carl was in this second group. Once in France, Carl was assigned to the 84th Division and placed on a train headed to the front in Belgium. During the two-day trip in an old boxcar, a small knothole in one of the car's walls helped pass the time.[5]

The knothole—with the help of the French winter sun and the speed of the train—became the eye of a pinhole camera, capturing the scenery outside and projecting it inside the train. Carl sat back and watched the world go by. It was all beautiful and quite clear. But just like a real pinhole camera, the images were inverted. The world was upside down.

Fitting into that upside down world was the replacement system. Many historians have criticized the manner in which the army of the

United States integrated its replacements during World War II. Steven Ambrose, one of the great champions of the American army in Europe, went so far as to write, "Had the Germans been given a free hand to devise a replacement system for ETO, one that would do the Americans the most harm and least good, they could not have done a better job."[6]

Military theorist and historian Martin van Creveld's assessment of the personnel replacement system was even harsher: "Perhaps more than any other single factor, it was this system that was responsible for the weaknesses displayed by the U.S. Army during World War II."[7]

Chief among the problems of the replacement system was that the new GIs would likely face some tough entry conditions, including the cold-shoulder treatment from fellow soldiers who had already been in the fight.

Perhaps with a tinge of guilt, one of the "old-timers" with the 84th recalled the frosty reception given to reinforcements:

> I think infantry replacement must have been the dirtiest job in
> the whole war. When we went over we went over with people
> we had trained with and people we'd gone to town with and
> got drunk with and all that. So we knew all the people we
> were with. In our first attack, our company went from 160 men
> on the line down to about 40 in three days. When we pulled
> back off the line and when I say pulled back we were about a
> half-mile or less from the front line. We were in a shell-torn vil-
> lage and within range of shells, but we got replacements in and
> mostly we didn't welcome them in, introduce them and tell
> them what they were going to run into, we just kind of ignored
> them and stayed with our own—the people we knew and the
> replacements were assigned to a squad so they knew their squad
> leader, maybe, but most of them, people I talked to, didn't even
> know what company they were in, they didn't know what
> Division they were in, they hardly knew anything about where
> they were. They were just bewildered sheep when they came to
> us and if they stayed around long enough, then they got to be
> part of the company and we got to know them like we had the
> other fellows, but until then, as I say, they were just lost and we
> didn't do a hell of a lot to help them out, because we were too
> worried about ourselves.[8]

The good news was that the United States could mobilize large numbers of troops quickly, but the bad news was that the process was poorly designed and the replacement GIs paid the price. Carl's new home, the 84th, was created during World War I and initially composed of National Guard units from Kentucky, Indiana, and Illinois.[9]

The 84th Division took the name of the "Lincoln Division" because Abraham Lincoln had roots in all three states. Lincoln was born in Kentucky, raised in Indiana, and found his adult footing in Illinois. The Division's insignia was rather simple, an ax and a split rail in honor of Lincoln's early job and nickname. For that reason, the 84th also became known as the "Railsplitter" Division.[10]

The Germans, though, were not as enthralled with American history and simply called the Railsplitters "hatchet men."[11] During the early days of fighting in the Bulge, "hatchet men" probably wasn't the most apt description for the 84th. The Germans, it seemed, were doing a lot of the chopping. The 84th only arrived in Europe in November 1944 and had lost 1,250 men in its first month of combat.[12]

In one instance alone, during a multiday battle at Verdenne, Belgium, that began on Christmas Eve 1944, the 84th captured 592 German soldiers. However, in doing so, they lost 582 of their own men, of whom 112 were killed.[13]

With losses of almost 6 percent of the entire division, Carl's Christmas Day mobilization should be no surprise. Casualties were mounting and riflemen in particular were in short supply. He was needed at the front.[14]

The trouble was that the front didn't exist.

The Germans' quick thrust caused great confusion. Allied troops were routed to new positions with unclear boundaries and thrown into a storm of violence:

The first thing the commander of the division, Major General Alexander Bolling, encountered were rumors: Germans in American uniforms and vehicles were roaming behind friendly lines, German paratroopers were in the rear, American supply dumps had been captured. The veracity of these rumors was in question, but Bolling did know two things: strong German forces had pushed the First US Army line back forty miles, and the Germans were headed in his direction.[15]

Part of the confusion was by design: Hitler had indeed sent German troops behind enemy lines disguised as US soldiers. This plan, under the code name Operation Greif ("Condor") resulted in some two thousand German soldiers wearing US Army uniforms and using captured jeeps and other US army equipment, along with some disguised German tanks, crossing enemy lines. Once they infiltrated the US lines, these commandos could commit sabotage, change road signs, and otherwise harm the war effort.[16]

In retrospect, the damage inflicted by Operation Greif was lethal but not pervasive, with scattered encounters with the infiltrators. However, during the Battle of the Bulge there was a widespread view among the GIs that German infiltrators could be anywhere. Units quickly adopted security measures, challenging other soldiers by asking them about popular culture, matters that the infiltrators would be unlikely to know. "Who was Mickey Mouse's girlfriend?" became the challenge called out by Carl and his platoon. During the battle, it was deadly serious, a question that could get you shot if answered incorrectly. Every GI knew of incidents where US troops had been killed by these false troops. In subsequent weeks as the war improved and the unit was moving quickly, "Who was Mickey Mouse's girlfriend?" became an ironic comment, a joke, or a universal statement of meaninglessness.[17]

The 84th was a perfect example of how a division adapted to the ever-changing currents of war in the European theater. Noted Mansoor:

> The 84th Infantry Division was fighting with the Ninth U.S. Army in Germany on 19 December; two days later it was positioned seventy-five miles away near Marche in the direct path of the German advance toward the Meuse River. Hitler and his commanders had not counted on such a swift reaction to their winter counteroffensive. . . .
>
> With its flanks in the air for three days, the 84th Infantry Division was an island in the midst of attacking forces from the 2d and 116th Panzer Divisions. Its orders were to hold the Hotton-Marche highway "at all costs." This was a tall order for an infantry division extended over a multi-mile front.[18]

One 84th GI wrote: "Foxholes were 150 yards apart over a six mile line. As the men waited for the inevitable attack, there was an understandable loneliness, accentuated by the overpowering silence of tall hills and thick pine forests."[19]

By December 26, the German offensive was ten days old and starting to reach its peak, but as John Eisenhower wrote, "Hitler thought that Antwerp could still be taken. But he had now specified two requisites for victory: one was the capture of Bastogne, the other the destruction of all Allied forces on the northern front between the Ourthe and Meuse rivers—in other words, the US 84th Infantry and 2nd Armored divisions."[20]

Mansoor provided additional details:

> Stopping the German drive was one thing: eliminating the Bulge was something altogether different. While the Third U.S. Army attacked north from Bastogne, Major General J. Lawton Collin's VII Corps attacked south toward Houffalize with the 83d and 84th Infantry Divisions and the 2d and 3d Armored Divisions. The terrain and weather placed the onus of the counterattack on the infantry. The terrain was vintage Ardennes: hilly, wooded, with a poor road network connecting isolated villages. The weather was some of the worst Europe had to offer in over half a century. Snow, sleet, and rain pelted the soldiers. Roads turned into ice rinks, and tanks and vehicles constantly slid off them and blocked columns. Infantry trudged to their objectives through knee-deep snow. Starting on 3 January 1945, when the counter-attack began, it snowed every day for a week. Two of the snowstorms were bona fide blizzards. Temperatures hovered near zero degrees Fahrenheit.[21]

Corporal Perry Wolff from the 334th Regiment expounded upon these difficulties:

> It was an impossible problem for the infantryman. Even with the best of care he stood a good chance of frostbite. Too much clothing would restrict him in an attack; too little would freeze him in the preparation. Physical exertion would make him sweat; rest would freeze the perspiration. Dry socks were passed out in chow lines and men wore a pair around the neck to keep them dry with body heat. Overcoats were discarded for many layers of clothing. Typically, a man wore two or three wool undershirts, a wool sweater, two shirts, and a combat jacket. Some men preferred two combat jackets, one to wear normally, the other to be wrapped around the feet in stationary positions. Men let their hair grow long and slept with helmets on to gain the last possible heat.[22]

There was at least one small and cruel way in which the weather was   139
an advantage. Fritz Kraemer from the 84th's intelligence section marched
German POWs "in the snow, had them take off their shoes and stand there
til they were ready to talk—which proved to be but a few minutes."[23]

The 84th's offensive began on January 3 with battles for the villages of
Beffe (January 4) and Magoster (January 4), Devantave (January 6), Doch-
amps (January 7), Samree (January 10), and Berismenil (January 13, 335th
Regiment, 2nd Battalion).[24]

—

5 January 1945

Hello, Folks,

I suppose by this time you've guessed why I haven't written to
you in two weeks. But I don't think you've guessed, and neither would
I have, that I've been transferred to another division—the 84th.
About all I can tell you is that I am on the other side of the Channel,
but I can't mention the country yet.

Remember what kind of grades I used to get in French? And how
long ago I took it? Well in spite of all that I can actually make myself
understood in the language, and can understand it when the native
speaks it, too. I was greatly surprised to find that out, believe me. And
by now I'm sort of one of the unofficial interpreters of the group. If
Miss Vogelgesang could only see me now!

From now on, at least for a while, I won't have many opportunities
to write to you. So don't start worrying because I don't. It may be two
or three weeks between letters. But please continue writing to me as
regularly as you can. And I can still use what candy you'll send me.
Love —Carl

—

10 January, 1945

Hello, Folks,

I can't tell you where I am now, but if you've read the papers
closely enough, you've already found out. It was announced two days
ago that the 84th Division is part of the 1st Army and is fighting on

the northern part of the German salient. I'd be willing to bet that by the time you get this letter, however, we'll be about on the border of Germany again.

The people of Belgium all seem to be what you would call "very nice people." The children are almost all quite well behaved. They don't beg of us as the French did. But I believe Belgium at least the southern part was much less harmed by the war than was most of France.[25] The populace appears healthy and the children strong. All the farms have livestock on them and as many, I should judge, as in normal times. And there is almost no physical destruction of the land around here, as there was in France.

Almost everyone around here speaks both French and Flemish, the language of the Netherlands, although French is more the language of the large towns. Incidentally, it is interesting that they speak a dialect of both languages, not the original tongue.

When they transferred me out of the 69th they split us up, and since then they've split us up quite a few times; with the result that I'm with only a very few of my original company, and none that I know well. Believe it or not, but I've been feeling homesick for the old company.

I can't tell you much of the trip over to Belgium from England. But, as you'd know, we sailed from one Channel port to another, which ones I can't say. We came in an L.C.T., which is quite a nice hunk of a ship, and the crossing was exceptionally smooth. We crossed France in the old 40 and 8's of World War One fame, with American locomotives.[26] There were 34 of us in our car, which made it too crowded for everyone to lie down. We were on them for more than two days, which would've made things a little cramped had it not been that we had a chance to jump off and look around in almost every town we entered. There were always plenty of people to trade almost everything for cigarettes and chocolate. We got some amazingly good cognac for 10 packs, which we probably could have gotten for 6.

Some of the people must be making a good thing out of the war. I saw the best fur coats and sheerest silk stockings I've seen in a long time and this was in a small village too.

The one thing that surprised me most about the Continental institutions was the extent to which the natives accept the normal activities of nature. One of the soldiers was squatting over a hole, which, incidentally, is the commonest method of elimination disposal in use in the army, as well as a very good one, when a peasant walked up to him and introduced in turn, himself, his wife, and his three daughters in the teens. And it is not too uncommon to see a woman on the side of the road lifting aside her skirt with one hand and waving to a passing truck-load of G.I.s with the other. Do you know what they use for toilet paper here?[27] Well, I'll tell you—a can of whitewash applied to the walls of the lavatory every few months.[28] It's amazing in its simplicity, no?

Lots of love –Carl

P.S.—Send me a package of food please. Hope you are not spending your time worrying about me. Love –Carl Write!

———

Addressed to Ens. Alfred B. Lavin

Jan 10, 1945

Dear Fred,
I have been transferred out of my old division as a replacement into the 84th which is in Belgium now working against the northern part of the German salient. I haven't been assigned to a company yet and am sitting here five miles behind the lines doing little but trying to keep warm and pulling guard duty every other night.
I'll be assigned and sent up in a day or two, but meanwhile I'm sleeping in a barn and eating warm meals so I'm comfortable enough so far.
One nice thing about war is that no one gives much of a damn about anything and there's no chicken found around.[29] And there's so much that's new and different, like money and equipment from six different countries that it's rather interesting here. But of course having separated from the old company makes up for all of that. And those of us who were separated are being split up into various units so we won't even be together.
Anyways, I'm getting a good chance to practice my French, which I can actually make use of. Write –Carl

———

11 January 1945

> Hi, Family,
>
> Just a quickie to let you know what company I've been assigned to. The army has apparently decided that I've become a true soldier, disliking change from my accustomed habits, because I'm not only in a Company "L" again, but also in a third platoon. Well I'm happy to have found a home after spending all this time wandering over Europe and it is a pretty good home too—pretty good guys.
>
> Let's hear from you. Let me know what's goings on back on the home front. Any good scandals or fires or news? And where is Fred now?
>
> Until next time – Love Carl

On the first day of the Allied offensive, January 3, 1945, snow fell and fell and continued throughout the week, sometimes bringing with it temperatures as low as 13°F and limiting vision to 40 yards or less.[30]

The division history goes on to note:

> In this cold and snow, the problem of taking cover was supreme. It took a good two hours to get through the frozen crust of earth. Riflemen reported that it took them as long as five hours to dig down as far as 3 feet. Not only was digging a foxhole a job in which a whole day's energies could be consumed but it was practically impossible to dig a good one at least 5 feet down. When the freeze came, rest went. In that terrible cold, there was only one thing worse than not sleeping—and that was sleeping. The quickest way to freeze is to lie still. Men went to sleep in overcoats—when they had them—and woke up encased in icy boards. It was practically impossible to bring up rations and supplies in anything but half-trucks. Water froze in canteens. Frostbite was as dangerous as all the Germans and their guns put together.[31]

Said Schrijvers, "It was no wonder that a soldier of the 84th Infantry Division called Belgium 'the coldest place on earth.'"[32]

Cold weather gear was modest for the GIs. They had a jacket and an overcoat and boots. Carl wore two pair of socks. And there were galoshes

that could go over the boots. That was it. All of that would keep a soldier
perfectly warm, for about twenty minutes.

Mansoor noted that "Half of the division's casualties in the Bulge were due to sickness and trench foot."[33]

——

19 January 1945

Dear Folks,

Don't know why I'm writing. There isn't a thing to say. Our company still hasn't gone up to the front since I've been in it. We're waiting here in a burned and bombed out village, doing little but getting acquainted and trying to keep warm.

If you don't hear from me for a long period of time, I don't want you to start worrying, because if I was a casualty, you'll hear through the War Department long before you'd ever suspect it by the absence of my letters.

Hope everything is going O.K. with you. Keep writing and keep [illegible] me [illegible], and of course, keep sending me food please.

So long, with love –Carl

——

Carl's company went into combat.

He was trucked to the nearby lines at night and walked some distance in full field pack with other GIs. On Carl were food, water, an entrenching tool, a pocketknife, and his BAR.

"On occasion, new men were fed into units actively locked in battle," said Mansoor. "Sent in by night and placed in among dark forms who occupied grave-like holes ... they could hardly have known where they were ... sometimes a new man did die before dawn and none around knew him by sight or name ... without the sustaining strength of unit pride or comradeship, he had started battle reduced to the final resources with which every man ends it, himself, alone."[34]

Most of the men that night were experienced, having already seen combat. Only ten to twenty of the men were replacements—though everyone was expecting to be shelled.[35]

Carl quickly learned the thing to do was copy the other soldiers. When the shelling began, the men around him hit the ground. Carl followed suit, but instead of facing fright, he was initially excited by the experience. Winston Churchill once famously said there is nothing more exhilarating than being shot at without effect. That was the feeling Carl had—at the beginning.[36]

There was a belief that if a new person could make it through the first forty-eight hours, his chances of surviving increased significantly. It was the inexperienced guys who weren't alert. Soldiers had to take cover, quickly. They had to react to four threats: rifle shots, machine gun fire, mortar shells, and incoming artillery. Being instantly alert to each distinct sound of danger was the most important thing in the world. That's what Carl and other men learned during their first forty-eight hours of combat. Or did not.

Both rifle and machine gun fire have a very flat trajectory, but the German machine gun is scarier, Carl noted, "because the sound is so distinctive, like a *rrrrrip*, the sound of cloth tearing magnified a hundred times." The response to both is the same. GIs didn't get any warning here because German machine gun bullets traveled faster than sound. But rifle and machine gun fire gave away the general location of the enemy. In this situation, when attacked, soldiers took cover and fired back.

"The crack of small-arms fire, on the other hand, sounded like 'static on a forgotten radio during an electrical storm,'" wrote Schrijvers. "It could not compare with the artillery's pandemonium, but was no less threatening."[37]

Mortar shells go almost straight up and straight down, so soldiers can't place them with their ears. The shelling usually comes in a series. Throw shells up very quickly and move a few notches. With mortar shells, there's a line, meaning GIs could see them going off maybe one a second, left to right or right to left. What was frightening was if the line was aimed right at them.

Schrijvers explained why this was a particularly nerve-wracking experience: "German mortars taxed the American soldiers in quite a different way. Their projectiles, some of them as large as 120 mm, were silent until right before they hit; even then they only made the slight sound of 'a sighing yawn.' It was the sneakiness of these weapons that made them dangerous and mentally destructive. Moreover, they were known to be deadly accurate. As a result, some GIs found them worse than regular artillery, and not a few combat soldiers snapped under the sustained mortar barrages."[38]

When artillery is shot in a soldier's direction, the sound comes before the explosion. There are slightly different sounds to an artillery shell that is going overhead compared to one that's going to fall short, or compared to

one that is going to land nearby. Three different sounds. A GI had to listen
very, very carefully to determine which was which, and maybe it would be
halfway between the sound of passing him and the sound of landing close
to his feet. Of this, Schrijvers said:

> What struck most fear into the hearts of the Americans, how-
> ever, was the tremendous accuracy of the German artillery. The
> 88 mm piece in particular was the most dreaded of all German
> weapons and Mauldin dubbed it 'the terror of every dogface.'
> The gun became notorious. It had been designed to be ef-
> fective against aircraft, armor, and personnel. Its high muzzle
> velocity eliminated the familiar long, moaning whistle of the
> other shells. Instead, it merely triggered a short, sharp sound
> 'like the scream of a madwoman' that barely left time to drop
> to the ground.[39]

84th Division Sergeant Ed Stewart recalled a soldier's feelings about
the sound of the 88 mm:

> It has a screaming sound . . . and at first it's absolutely fright-
> ening, it's a nightmare. It puts you into another nightmarish
> existence. I eventually get accustomed to it and begin to make
> judgments about it. Is it coming in close? Is it going to go far
> or what? And you begin to be able to estimate pretty much
> where it's going to hit. . . . The sound itself is replaced by the
> need to make a judgment about it. So it hit here, you know the
> pattern of the firing. It comes in threes. And then it's fifty yards
> out, it's twenty-five, well how about the third one? So then you
> become preoccupied with that. You almost begin to like the
> sound because this gives you some information of what you
> might do, or what's going to happen.[40]

Several different times a group of three, four, or five guys all heard the
sound, each looked at each other's faces and had to make a decision within
half a second whether to hit the ground or not. A GI couldn't just hit the
ground with every shell. Each time was more exhausting than the last. And
if it wasn't necessary, soldiers didn't want to do it. The decision to fall or
continue standing was made only by looking into each other's eyes and
reading each other's faces. It was a real trust exercise.

The Germans preferred to attack during the day. There was hardly any action at night, perhaps one or two minor occasions. At night, the main threat was the possibility of infiltration, of the enemy trying to sneak in between foxholes.

A German attack would begin with an hour's worth of artillery. US attacks were similar. So each side knew what the other side was up to. The advance was not really a charge, but a cautious move, picking your way, hoping the artillery did a lot of damage.

During a heavy artillery bombardment, Carl's entire unit took cover in their foxholes and kept their heads down. During one barrage, a GI appeared by the side of Carl's foxhole. The GI had no rifle. He was standing straight up and holding his helmet in front of him. Blood was running down the side of his head from a shrapnel wound. He said, "I'm going back," in a way that was half an emphatic statement and half asking permission to go to the rear and get treatment. He wanted verification. Carl quickly yelled back, "OK, go on back—but not like that! Don't stand up! Get down! Get down!"

The GI proceeded to walk on back to the rear, standing up, while the artillery barrage continued. He made no attempt to take cover or protect himself in any basic way. It was as though he was saying, "I've finally got a legitimate excuse to get out of here and I don't have to follow your silly rules any more." Carl kept yelling at him to take cover and so did other guys in nearby foxholes who could see what was happening. But the wounded man just ignored his comrades and kept on walking steadily to the rear, upright. He was half out of his wits, but made it safely back.

A US Army platoon is traditionally made up of forty men, including three squads of twelve as well as a few specialists, mortarmen, scouts, and radiomen. But most of the time Carl's platoon was less than half strength because they kept taking casualties. So instead of having three twelve-man squads, Carl's platoon had two squads of eight or nine men each. Every week to ten days they would get another batch of replacements, but never fast enough. They took casualties faster than replacements were assigned to them.

During Carl's first thirty days with the 84th, the platoon lost twenty of its forty members, putting Carl in the top half of seniority of the platoon in less than a month.

In the total of five months of combat, only about 15 percent of Carl's original company was still there. The rest were casualties, more wounded than killed. Replacements were injured or killed, and those who replaced them were injured or killed. New soldiers kept coming and coming and so did the casualties.

If you count all of the people who came in, the company had a 150 percent casualty rate. So it was in the Battle of the Bulge that Carl encountered the first time he should have been killed. Actually, it was one long "time" composed of many incidents from the end of December 1944 to the end of February 1945.

———

At night, two guys paired off and huddled in a very small foxhole. They'd dig the foxhole with a step in it so the one taking duty could sit. The other guy could lie down.

Digging in frozen earth wasn't easy. What the GIs hated more than anything was when they had to move position.

The situation may call for them to relocate. Maybe a change happened on the flank. So they had to move to straighten the line. And they had to dig a new hole.

All Carl had to dig with was this almost-toy shovel with a two-foot wooden handle. It was half a hoe, half a shovel. Mechanically, it was built so a GI could adjust the spade part so it was in line with the handle like a shovel, or put it at 90 degrees and use it like a hoe.

A soldier would use the hoe on the frozen earth. Carl would pound and pound and pound away and eventually he would just bend the point of the spade hoe. But if he pounded long enough, eventually he broke through one spot. He'd then hollow out the hole with his knife, carving pieces an inch and a half thick and helping to dislodge them with a stomp of his foot. That was how to dig a foxhole. It was just lousy, lousy work. A foxhole that took forty-five minutes to dig in November took five hours to dig in January.[41]

Carl felt vulnerable while digging, but the foxhole served as great protection, a secure place to shoot and take cover. If soldiers were being shelled or hit with a rifle or a machine gun, the trench was their security. A shell could land very close to the GIs, even four feet away, and if they were in their hole, they were going to be ok. And that's what happened. The soldiers got shelled and they survived in their foxholes.

Schrijvers discussed how important ground cover was to the infantry:

> Foot soldiers always stayed close to the soil. They ran heads
> down, they stooped, they crouched. When enemy salvos re-
> sounded, they instinctively dropped to the ground and flat-
> tened themselves, pressing cheeks, knees, and ankles against the
> earth, burrowing into the sand with belly and thighs. Under
> fire, the slightest hole, depression, or crevice beckoned, and
> infantrymen considered tank ruts or ditches the next best thing
> to pillboxes. When bedding down, or during other long halts,
> soldiers simply disappeared beneath the earth. Day after day, GIs
> hurriedly dug holes, using shovels and picks, entrenching tools,
> helmets, and bare hands. They excavated slit trenches to lie
> down in, foxholes to sit or stand in. When the advance bogged
> down completely and enemy fire intensified, the men con-
> structed dugouts for the long haul. Such underground shelters
> could look like veritable homes, with roofs of corrugated steel
> camouflaged with sod, floors covered with mattresses and rugs,
> and walls with stoves and chimneys. When the GIs were not
> digging holes, they were enlarging them, strengthening them,
> improving them.[42]

It was the squad sergeant's job to go out to check the foxholes during the night. The job was very dangerous. Everyone was listening for a noise in the dark. Every once in a while someone would get jumpy and let off a shot.

On patrol, the squad sergeant would advance and whisper the soldier's name. Soldiers were supposed to reply, "Halt. Who's there? Advance and be recognized." That was the official way. Each day there would be a new password and countersign and GIs were serious about using them.

There was one particular guy, a replacement in Carl's squad, who was just a nervous wreck. After a day or two of combat his hands were shaking and he couldn't control himself. The term used then was "battle fatigue." The new guy got battle fatigue after having just barely been in combat. He was very nervous, and he couldn't stop himself from crying. He was also jumpy and accidentally let off a couple of shots at night at the sergeant who was making his rounds.

Not surprisingly, the replacement was soon replaced—yanked back from the line. "I can't stand it. I just can't take it anymore," the soldier said, half-screaming, hysterical. "I can't stand it. I can't stand it."[43]

———

Many military historians view it as a mistake of the Allies that they were not prepared for the Battle of the Bulge. The general sense was that it was a major blunder on the part of America and Britain to be caught by surprise by the German offensive.

John Eisenhower placed the blame squarely: "There is no gainsaying that Allied intelligence failed regarding German intentions in the Ardennes; despite all the claims made by individual intelligence officers, there is little to support the contention that the Allied High Command was adequately warned."[44] The Germans must have been accumulating forces for quite some time, and they had to be massed and ready to strike. The Allies controlled the air by this time, as the German air fleet had pretty well been wiped out. Yet the Allies were still unprepared and taken by surprise.

One simple example of unpreparedness: American GIs had green field uniforms, while the Germans had white covers or white uniforms for the snow. One American commander ordered his unit to wear their white long johns over their uniform to provide some camouflage, a point noted with amusement in the official history.[45]

———

The Battle of the Bulge was a story of endurance, faith, and inner courage as soldiers faced miserable conditions and very tough odds. The American forces were getting outright pasted, shellacked, during the first few weeks. But the GIs stood their ground. It wasn't heroism in the traditional sense. It was the heroism of hanging on. And that was the key to winning the Bulge: The GIs held fast in difficult circumstances. They hung on, so reinforcements could arrive and turn the tide.

The German army suffered anywhere from eighty thousand to one hundred thousand casualties, and they were never on the offensive again.[46] Mansoor described the battle as a tipping point: "The Normandy campaign and the Battle of the Bulge were the two most critical tests of the Army of the United States in World War II. One was a great offensive victory, the other a defensive triumph . . . . More than any other event in World War II, the Battle of the Bulge would test the combat effectiveness of the ground divisions of the Army of the United States against a capable opponent on nearly equal terms."[47]

—

For the men of the 84th Division, the Bulge was officially wiped out on January 16 at 9:45 a.m. when the First and Third armies met near the village of Engreux by the Ourthe River.[48] Although Germany was no longer capable of another major offensive, the German military remained highly lethal.

Going from the defensive to the offensive was a psychological swing in the Allies' favor, but it did not lessen the ferocity of combat. The 84th was afforded a five-day rest, then was tasked with curving north and the 335th was sent to clear the enemy from Gouvy and Ourthe.[49]

Theodore Draper described the ensuing clash:

> Men (in the division) died, dug for cover, ducked 88's, bandaged up buddies if they could, the same way. It was still cold. The snow was 3 or 4 feet deep. Vehicles still could not get off the roads without staying off permanently. There were many bridges in our new zone and all were down. Tanks, heavy machine guns, artillery, and rockets were still at the enemy's disposal. As far as the man in the line is concerned, war is funny that way. There are big objectives which make big headlines that are relatively easy to take. And there are little objectives which nobody notices that have to be bought with blood yard by yard. For the man in the line, the big battle is the little one.[50]

The Bulge was over, but the danger was not. On the front, Carl was usually cold and hungry. With replenishments coming every few days or so, food and ammunition were not keeping up with needs, nor were replacements keeping up with fatalities.[51] And Carl was saddled with a twelve-pound piece of metal that was a lightning rod for any German soldier who could draw a bead on him.

Things did not look good. Carl started to write this all down, but what good would it have done to tell his parents? If he made it, all of his problems didn't matter. If he didn't make it, they mattered less. And what kind of son complains about the wartime situation to his parents?

Also, US Army censorship forbade any discussion of the imminence of death. So Carl reached out the only way he could: He wrote nice, upbeat letters home, telling his parents how important they were to him, and how he loved them. Carl would deal with the bad news on his own. He would face his mortality and get on with it.

Paul Fussell described this process as one "of slow dawning and dreadful realization," which took place in three stages:

> 1. It *can't* happen to me. I am too clever / agile / well-trained / good-looking - beloved / tightly laced, etc. This persuasion gradually erodes to
>
> 2. It *can* happen to me, and I'd better be more careful. I can avoid the danger by watching more prudently the way I take cover / dig in / expose my position by firing my weapon / keep extra alert at all times, etc. This conviction attenuates in turn to the perception that death and injury are matters more of luck than skill, making inevitable the third stage of awareness:
>
> 3. It is *going to* happen to me, and only my not being there is going to prevent it.[52]

Carl's first two letters after fighting in the Ardennes were both dated January 26. While dates can be wrong or overlap, the letters taken together exhibit the highs and lows a soldier can feel in a single day.

The first note is written after a moment of great personal peril. Carl is attempting to reach his family, but forbidden from expressing himself directly. Yet, he wanted his parents to know that if this were his last correspondence they were ever to receive from him, love for them was in his heart.

No teenager would normally write this sort of letter to his parents. This is the type of letter you write when you are facing death. The kind of letter you want to leave behind to console your parents.[53]

26 January 1945
Belgium

Dear Mom and Pop,

I haven't received any mail since I got transferred yet so I don't know if anything unusual or exciting has happened to you. But I hope everything is O.K.

I'm warm and comfortable now, and sitting here in front of a fire. And this is one of times when I fall into sympathy with home.

I don't think I ever realized or appreciated before how lucky I am. You know, the four of us make a grand family. There's nothing material we don't have that we could want, and socially, too. I wish I could be aware of this when we're all together. I imagine you feel pretty much the same way, don't you? Well, maybe we will appreciate it after this.

My thanks for being such grand parents, with my love.

Be seeing you –Carl

―――

But shortly after that letter was posted, Carl's fortunes returned. We assume it was the arrival of replacements, fully loaded with food and ammunition. With his second January 26 letter, Carl's morale was restored and he was no longer in jeopardy.

―――

26 January 1945
Belgium

Hello, Folks,

Still hale and hearty as of today. Hope you can say the same.

And I'm glad to be able to report to you that I've decided that war is a lot more enjoyable than I'd expected it to be. First of all, I'm lucky that I haven't yet been in a situation where I've been physically uncomfortable for more than a day or two at a stretch. That is one of the most important factors. As long as you've got the necessities—as long as you can be dry and warm every so often—then it's O.K.

As for the danger—it hasn't bothered me so far. That which I've been afraid of coming up against, and still am, now that I'm experiencing it, is first the discomfort, secondly the inconvenience, and lastly the danger—you just can't convince me that anything is going to happen to me.

But what's nice about it is that fairly often we get chances to
spend a night or two in a town. We patch up the holes in a room
or two, look around for a stove and some straw, or maybe some
mattresses; get a pig or maybe a couple of chickens, and generally get
comfortable. It's amazing what improvisation can accomplish.

Well, by for now. Love –Carl

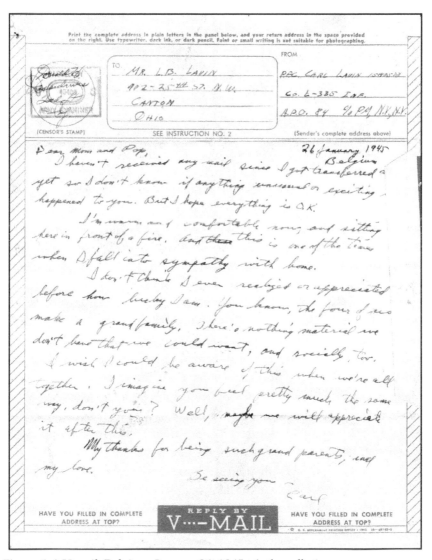

Figure 6-1. V-mail, Belgium, January 26, 1945. *Author collection.*

As the Battle of the Bulge drew to a close, Carl's company was less than half strength. They had lots of casualties and very little sleep at night. The GIs would alternate sleep with their foxhole buddy every two hours. One took the 10 p.m. to 12 a.m. shift, the other 12 a.m. to 2 a.m., and so on. Those were long, long, long hours. One soldier was awake and the other guy was trying to sleep in ten-degree temperatures while breathing through a slit in a poncho.

During the daytime, the men stayed in the trenches if they were on duty. If not, the GIs could get out and gather around a bonfire. Half the guys were in their holes. The rest were building small bonfires or milling about exhausted.

One day, Carl was tending the bonfire for his platoon when the lieutenant approached, passing by and loudly saying to a sergeant: "Sergeant, put together a detail and take these prisoners back to battalion headquarters and be back here in twenty minutes."

Carl's company had four prisoners at the time. When the lieutenant came by and made his announcement, every American soldier knew exactly what he was saying. They knew darn well it would probably take a couple of hours to get to battalion headquarters and back. They also knew he was saying it loudly and clearly because a lot of the Germans could understand English. He didn't want to alert the Germans. They would understand the whole story. The platoon all understood the command: Take them in the woods and shoot them. The prisoners would have endangered the unit as no men could be spared to guard them.

Carl had no training or instructions on how to handle POWs. He couldn't even say "Put up your hands" in German. But Carl knew right from wrong, and he was disgusted that the lieutenant would give that order and shocked that no one else seemed to be bothered by it. This was something you'd expect Germans to do, Carl thought. You don't expect Americans to do it. And all the Americans knew the Germans had actually done it. Six weeks earlier, on December 17, the Malmedy Massacre had taken place with the murder of more than eighty American POWs. Widely reported, it jolted the American public and military alike.[54]

The sergeant heard the lieutenant's order and obeyed. He wasn't surprised at all. He must have been told quietly ahead of the announcement.

Carl looked at the lieutenant. His mouth kind of dropped. He wanted to say something but couldn't think of what to say. He was exhausted and not able to think. The lieutenant saw Carl's mouth agape and shot back a real hard look, meaning, very clearly, "Shut up. Don't say a word. Do you

want to endanger your own men? You're not going to stop me. Just shut
up."

So Carl did just that. He didn't say a word.

The sergeant was selecting his detail. Carl told himself that if he was selected he wasn't going to shoot. The sergeant half understood that. Carl stepped aside and the sergeant picked out four other GIs who marched off with the prisoners.

The sergeant and the GIs returned in twenty minutes' time. The POWs were nowhere to be seen.

Carl soon walked up to one of the men and asked what had happened.

"Did you guys do it?" he asked.

"Yeah, we did it," the GI said.

"How did you work it?"

"Took them by surprise," said the GI. "We signaled each other by tapping on the shoulders. We went through a narrow path through the trees. We gradually dropped back and pretty soon the Germans were all walking ahead of us.

"We're all behind them. The sergeant silently let us know with taps and motions. We all got ready and fired and it was over in a few seconds."

For sixty years after the war, Carl would only discuss this tragedy with his wife. In his eighties, he shared it with his children, still haunted by the moment. You just don't shoot prisoners—no matter the argument. Carl was troubled throughout his life by this injustice.[55]

———

Carl's best friend in Company L, third platoon of the 84th, was Paul. He was from Greensburg, Indiana, near the Ohio border.

Just before Carl joined the squad, Paul had been slightly wounded. A bullet grazed his shoulder. It drew blood but Paul refused to tell his sergeant about it. All the soldiers were telling him to see a doctor, but Paul shrugged off their suggestions, saying it was just a slight wound. Finally, word got to the sergeant who ordered him to go for medical treatment.

Paul recovered, returning to the company three or four weeks later. Carl heard a lot about Paul before he came back. Paul was religious, dignified, a Catholic man whom everybody admired. All the soldiers talked about him. The widespread praise struck Carl as sort of strange. Then he met Paul. Carl took an instant liking to him. Paul was very outgoing and fun to talk to. He even showed Carl his scar. The two became fast friends.

Paul was also tall, strong, and kind. He was always helping other people. When the company was on a heavy march and some guys were overloaded and couldn't quite make it, Paul would carry their rifles or any extra weight. That was unusual. Not many guys did that. Paul commonly did.

After learning his own killed POWs, Carl talked with Paul to make sense of the brutality.

"Americans don't do that. We don't do that," said Carl.

"Yes," said Paul. "But what can you and I do about it?"

———

Unfortunately, crimes involving POWs were not uncommon. Enemy soldiers "were not always killed out of blind revenge," Schrijvers explained. "Sometimes the GIs eliminated them merely because they formed a practical nuisance. Armored spearheading forces rarely had the time or means to bother with POWs at all. The job was left to the infantrymen, who had to walk them to improvised pens several miles to the rear. But, during battle, caring for POWs often proved to be too much of a burden for them as well."[56]

Sometimes it was blind revenge. Schrijvers added that "Men of the 84th Infantry Division managed to subdue a tank operator only after he had already killed two of the POWs they were herding to the rear. He turned out to have just arrived from the Bulge's Verdenne pocket, where he had lost too many good friends."[57]

———

29 January, 1945
Belgium

Dear Folks,

Right now I'm back in a rest area for a few days, generally enjoying things and taking them easy. Six of us are billeted in a house here.[58] We're pretty fortunate in that we've got a radio and two daughters, nineteen and twenty. You probably haven't got the correct conception of a rural European house (we're in a small village) because I know I didn't. They're built to last, in the first place. They're generally anywhere from twenty to a hundred years old and it's impossible to tell one of the former from one of the latter except by looking at the date. They're of stone, a foot and a half or two feet thick and the barn is part of the same building. There's a coal stove in the kitchen, which is also the living room and dining room, and for us, the bedroom, since it is the only heated room in the house. There is a pump or a well or two in the village and a reasonable bucket under the toilet seat, which is exposed to the temperature but not to the neighbors. Imagine it's like life in the States in the eighties with the addition of electricity. Went to a dance last night. Quite an impressive affair.

Bye –Love, Carl

---

30 January 1945
Belgium

Dear Mom and Pop,

Let's see now—what is there to tell you about? This is really becoming difficult, writing when there is nothing I'm allowed to say, and there's no questions I can answer—mainly because I'm still waiting for my mail to catch up with me.

How about the weather? They've got the damnedest winter weather over here. Ever since the first snow, which landed about a month ago, the ground has been covered. The stuff won't melt and every time it snows again it gets deeper, and more annoying. At this point it's about two feet deep, not counting drifts. How I could have used some of this back home before! Just perfect for skiing and sleighing.

This country around here is about half pine-forest, and this with the snow makes striking scenes and compositions. It's magnificent scenery, although it's a bit difficult to appreciate when one is living and dwelling in it.

Don't worry about me, folks. I'm watching my feet especially and so far the cold has not affected them. I can take care of myself—don't worry.

Lots of love –Carl

158   31 January 1945
         Belgium

         Dear Mother and Dad,
         I'm still here, taking a rest.
         The only trouble is that out of the eight guys in the house now,
         I'm the only one who has even a smattering of French. And it's a
         wearying job to carry on conversations between seven GIs and two
         girls plus the parents and all the neighbors who drop in and insist on
         keeping us informed of all the village gossip. And me sweating and
         straining to get each idea across! I wish I'd studied my French either
         a hell of a lot more, or a hell of a lot less!
         We had a company party last night and a dance two nights ago.
         They weren't bad, but they made me long for those dances and parties
         I used to go to back in high school. The Belgian country girls are a
         pretty poor substitute for whatever we had back there.
         Well, I hope you're still writing to me often, and I hope you're
         still sending me packages. You know, about the only thing I really
         need is candy—and I hope that is about the only thing that you've
         been sending.
         Take care of yourselves, now—Love –Carl

There was a practical reason why many of Carl's letters ended with a
request for specific items. Schrijvers noted,

> European deprivation eventually forced many GIs to turn to
> the home front for more and better food than they could find
> in their rations. Because of the chronic shipping shortages,
> American postal services required evidence of a serviceman's
> request for a package. As a result, the GIs regularly put post-
> scripts in their letters with detailed descriptions of the kinds of
> food they wanted their families to mail to them. They stressed
> they should send only small packages because they had to
> throw away what they could not carry or immediately eat, and
> asked them to include only food that did not spoil easily such
> as canned products, dried fruits, and hard candy. They begged
> their families to be sure not to mail anything that resembled
> what was in the rations: no crackers, no Spam, not even Life

Savers. Although restrained by rationing practices themselves, 159
relatives and friends in America were able to ship tons of food
products to their boys in the front lines of the kind to make
Europeans mouths water: from sausage and fried chicken to sar-
dines, from tomato juice to soaps, from apricots and grapefruit
juice to honey and jellies, and from doughnuts and fruitcakes to
Aunt Jemima pancake flour. The combat soldiers craved sweets
more than anything else and so their families also sent them
Three Musketeers, Babe Ruths, marshmallows, Hershey silver
bells, and chocolate-covered peanuts.[59]

2 February '45

Dear Folks,
Yes, still waiting here in a rest area. They've got the damnedest
weather here I've seen. For a month the temperature has been below
freezing and the snow has been piling higher and higher as a result
and now we've had 48 hours of steady warm winds and the two feet of
snow melted—just like that.
And now its spring outside—everything green and muddy with a
fringe of snow still around the fields. It looks nice from here—inside
a house—but I don't think I'll appreciate it quite so much in a little
while.
Our "mama" here—there's always a "mama" and a "papa"
in every European house we stay in—made us a couple of apple
pies last night, along with her bread. And I don't know whether it's
because it's been so long since I've had a pie or not, but anyways that
was about the best-tasting pie I've ever had. These people treat us
pretty nice.
So long –Carl

Procuring an apple pie might have been easier than one would guess.
Men of the 84th Infantry Division worked out an exchange rate with
Belgian housewives during a rest period at Nonceveux: one warm apple
pie, without sugar, for one pack of cigarettes.[60]

—

By February 3, Carl and the 84th were back in Germany. Their task was to hold the line from Himmerich to Linnich before a planned crossing on the Roer River on February 21, an attack formally known as Operation Grenade.[61]

After coming out of the Ardennes, the 84th was a fighting group, with confidence restored.[62]

—

3 February 1945

Hello, Family,

Well, as usual, there's nothing I have to say, or can say. Can't tell you what country I'm in or what I'm doing in it, or how long I'll be in it—etc, etc. So the weather is fine right now. All the snow's melted and the sun's shining away. I understand that you're having a pretty hard winter back in the States. Hope it's better by the time you get this. I never realized before just what bad weather means—I never depended on it before, never had my comfort affected by it, good or bad.

Have you gotten hold of an apartment yet? Or have any new developments come out on the new house? I hope I start getting mail soon. I'm really getting left out on what's going on back there. And where is Fred by now? I suppose he'll be going back out to sea pretty soon?

I haven't been getting any packages lately, either, of course. But don't let that discourage you now. Please keep sending me stuff like candy and fudge and gum, willya?

Well, behave yourselves—Love to you Carl

—

Summing up the 84th's six-week experience in the Ardennes, Draper said:

> None of those who were in it will never forget the Ardennes.
> If we came through, by far the largest credit must go to the
> men who shouldered rifles and carried machine guns and

mortars in the freezing weather, plunged through knee–deep and waist-high snow, dug foxholes in ground as hard as steel, stormed hill after hill in the face of perfect enemy observation, and cleaned out woods as dark as night in the middle of the day. That is not the whole story but it is the best part of it.[63]

In Belgium when spring arrived a few months later, locals noted that the returning swallows were disoriented when they found "not a barn standing in which to build their nests."[64]

7

The Battle of the Roer
February–March 1945

There was a brief break in the fighting as the Battle of the Bulge ended. At such breaks, Carl was occasionally able to get away from the front. Superiors relieved a battalion or maybe a company at a time. Another company would fill in the spot.

These breaks would mean either a stay in military barracks or in private home for a few days at a time and that happened on two or three different occasions. Living in barracks instead of a foxhole meant having a shower and getting a change of clothes. It wasn't very distinctive but soldiers were able to get a night's sleep and a blanket and a bunk. That's mainly what it was. Carl and his company ate food in a mess hall instead of K-Rations, and slept in a bunk instead of frozen mud.[1]

During the pause after the Bulge, the 84th ran an "assembly line," taking units to a rest and recuperation facility near Waubach-Eygelshoven in the Netherlands, only about a mile from the German border. Carl had a long weekend in what had been a private house.[2] Just off the front-line, Carl was in the house on the ground floor cleaning his BAR when someone blew the whistle for lunch.

Upon hearing the whistle, Carl began putting the BAR back together. To make sure he had reassembled the weapon correctly, he did what he always did—slammed in a clip and fired a few rounds, forgetting for a brief moment he was not on the battlefront but on the ground floor of a house.

Carl was holding the BAR in a vertical position, which was normal for a test trigger pull, and found out he reassembled the gun correctly when bullets flew toward the second floor. Pow, pow, pow, pow. Luckily, the men who had been upstairs were now coming down the steps for lunch.

"Oh, God, is anyone still upstairs?" Carl asked. They were shocked and so was Carl. Carl couldn't stop apologizing to the group. They inspected the room above and found only bullet holes.

"Here's the table where I was just sitting," one of the men said. There was a checkerboard and chairs, now perforated with bullet-holes.

"I'm so sorry," Carl said. "I'm so sorry."

For several days thereafter there were jokes and wisecracks—"Lavin, the wild man," and such—but the incident was just plain scary. You can leave the war. But the war doesn't necessarily leave you.

Back in Germany, the 84th's objective was to hold the Linnich-Himmerich front near the Roer River before hopping over to the other side.[3] From there, they would strike toward the Rhine, moving ever closer to the industrial heart of Germany in the northeast.[4]

But the German military—frayed but still dangerous—wrenched up the plan. Several corps, including three hundred thousand men from the Ninth Army, were forced into a holding position across dozens of miles as the Germans successfully sabotaged dams and flooded the region.[5] The mission to cross the Roer was stalled.

According to Atkinson, "The Roer valley would be flooded for days by 100 million tons of water. . . . Overnight the Roer rose eight inches, and kept rising... a river usually one hundred feet wide from bank to bank now stretched a thousand yards, and in some spots more than a mile. . . . For nearly a fortnight, fifteen American divisions would wait on the west bank for the reservoirs to drain and the torrent to abate."[6]

The crossing, scripted for the early part of the month, didn't launch until February 23. Not all was lost, however, as the downtime gave the Allies plenty of hours to train and plan, to organize and scout.[7] "The 84th Infantry Division conducted six full-dress rehearsals at sites on the Wurm River near Marienberg and Suggerath. Planning focused on engineer support, coordination of fires, and traffic control. Six divisions (8th, 29th, 30th, 84th, 102d, and the 104th Infantry Divisions) were to assault across the river at night under the cover of smoke and artillery fire from two thousand guns, which would batter enemy defenses for forty-five minutes prior to H-hour."[8]

6 February 1945

Dear Mom and Dad,

One of the greatest disadvantages in writing within the constrictions of censorship is the requisite of being able to tell only of generalities—never of specific instances. That makes it easier for me, in a sense, but also less interesting for you. I can't tell you of anything I've done, or experienced, or am doing, or what I've seen, or where I've been—well you know all I can't and would like to say. So I hope you understand if my letters sometimes show the strain of being stretched to fill a page, when all I have to say could be put into two lines, in their contents.

It's amazing how much the human body can become used to. That's one thing I learned out of this. It's supposed to be a highly specialized organism, not given much to adaptability. But I disagree with that. And life means not only the ability to take punishment, for I've experienced little of that. But rather such things as becoming used to change itself. Change, differences, newness used to make a deep impression on me—but now I've had so many changes, such extensive and un-thought of ones, and had them so frequently, and so incongruously, and so unexpectedly, that now it's my accustomed way of living. In other words, I'm used to it. And there you see what I mean about generalities.[9]

Anyways, I'm feeling fine folks – Love Carl

However upbeat his letters home, Carl's postwar memories related a different set of emotions: "I remember waking up with a feeling of depression when I would wake up wherever I was.... I guess that was very normal to be depressed. [Chuckles]. Those guys were out there trying to kill me, I should feel depressed. That's normal [chuckles] to feel depressed."[10]

Kindsvatter also discussed the emotional toll of war: "Immersion in war was thus a process of discovering combat's dangers and hardships while struggling to survive and maintain a moral compass.... The average soldier emerged from the initial shock of combat a confident and effective veteran, but in time he became increasingly aware of the odds against him while suffering the physically debilitating effects of continuous combat, often in a harsh climate."[11]

———

8 February 1945

Hello, Folks,

Well today I had a bit of encouragement. One of the fellows that came into this company with me got a letter! So now maybe mine will be catching up with me one of these days. How have you been receiving my mail? Tell me how it's been coming.

I came across a remarkable coincidence the other day. I ran into one of the guys in my old company who was transferred here with me, but into another company of the battalion. He showed me his steel helmet. There were two holes in it on the right side from front to rear where a piece of shrapnel had entered and left and there was a two inch gap cut in his wool knit-cap. But his head had been scratched barely enough to draw blood. And then he called over another fellow in his company who had also been in our old company and been transferred with us. Believe it or not, but this guy also had two holes in his helmet—on the right side—from front to rear—and he also had a two-inch gash in his cap—and he also was barely scratched. And they both got it on the same engagement. Don't think it was the same shell, tho. Take it easy—Love –Carl

———

Carl also had a close call with shrapnel, but he was hit in the foot rather than the helmet. The blast happened after Carl's company had moved to a new position and he and a buddy had just started to dig a foxhole. There was some shelling going on. Not real close to them, maybe a hundred yards away.

Carl had gotten maybe two shovelfuls out when he felt a sharp pain in his foot. His immediate reaction was that his foxhole buddy was attempting to play a poorly conceived joke and kicked him too hard. Carl wheeled around, a little angry, but quickly realized his friend couldn't be the perpetrator. His buddy was at the other end of the hole, digging away.

Carl looked down and next to his foot was a rusty triangular piece of shrapnel. It was a fragment from an exploded shell that was designed to

166 break into razor-sharp shards upon impact. He could see immediately that not only was the fragment a regular shape, but that its newly created edges were clean and shiny.

The shrapnel must have hit Carl's boot flat on because it didn't cut the boot. Still, it was a powerful blow and it hurt something fierce. Carl took off his shoe to see if any bones were broken. He only received a deep bruise and went back to shoveling. Maybe he was correct in his earlier note to his Mom that he would never be wounded. This was Carl's second escape from death, for if the shrapnel had hit his midsection, that would have been it.

9 February, 1945

Dear Mom and Pop,
(How do you like my heading? Sounds nice and long, eh?)

I'm afraid that all this letter is going to do is let you know that as of the ninth day of February, in the year of Jesus Christ one thousand nine hundred forty-five, I, Carl Lavin, am of reasonably sound body and mind. That "reasonably," of course, takes into account all interesting conditions and circumstances which I have been conditioned and circumstanced to, lo, these past five months. And as a result of which, an amazingly wide latitude may be allowed without expanding the bounds of reason in defining the term "sound;" as applies to aforementioned party of the first part.

In other words, if you think I look bad, you should see what I might look like.

A sense of humor's a wonderful thing, no? If it doesn't do anything else, at least it's filled up space.

Well, behave yourselves—and keep on writing with love –Carl

11 February 1945
Sunday

Dear Dad and Mother,

Just made a startling discovery! Today is Sunday! I know because I looked at a calendar. That is, it is Sunday for you, but for me it is just one more day in February. ("almost the middle of the month now—two-and-a-half more months and maybe we'll have good weather—") That's a strange way to live, isn't it? Without Sundays.

One more reason why I wish the mail were quicker and I'd been receiving your letters before this time is that I know to what extent you worry about me, and I know that you, mother, long before this, have picked one single factor to concentrate most of your worries on. And if I knew what it is, I would try to tell you how wrong you are to fear that particular occurrence. Please do not worry too much. It doesn't help me at all; nor you either. But since they aren't, and I haven't, I can't and you will, and would anyways. Oh well.

Lots of love Carl

17 February 1945

Dear Mom and Pop,

Well, I'm finally starting to get mail once again. It still hasn't gotten up to me from the 69th but now I'm getting it direct from the States. But the only trouble is—I've still not received it from you.

I'm getting overseas and combat pay now and I don't have anything much to spend it on—so I'm sending home $25 a month. I made out an allotment to you, Dad, starting in April.

The weather has been perfect over here lately—might even say it is balmy, at times, but a rather damp balm, naturally.

Keep sending me the edibles, please—who knows—maybe I'll even start receiving it after awhile. Lots of love to you –Carl

"The US Army went to great lengths to pay its soldiers as regularly as possible, even if it meant that payment officers had to rush from foxhole to foxhole under fire," said Schrijvers:

> But money was totally out of place at the front… GIs quite often lost all of their pay in battle. . . . There were few opportunities to spend money in the combat zone anyway. . . . In more

populated areas, on the other hand, many articles were lacking or reserved for civilians with ration coupons. . . . By February 1945, between 90 and 95 per cent of the enlisted men overseas had automatic monthly deductions taken out of their pay for family support or savings. On top of the—often substantial— allotments, seven out of ten soldiers were able to send extra money home, generally by postal money order.[13]

17 February 1945

Hello, Parents,

Whopee! The day of days has arrived at long, long last! I got a letter from you! Mailed January 30. I don't know whether it's because it's been so long or if you're getting better in your letter writing ability, Mom, but that seemed to me to be about the finest letter I'd read. You wrote about it being Sunday afternoon and you and Dad and Fred lying around doing nothing—listening to the radio, playing cards. Sounded pretty swell.

I wish you wouldn't worry about me, though I know you will. Really I'm comfortable more often than not. As for "hardships" that's entirely relative, and I think as long as no lasting harm is done, there is no such thing. And lastly, I have full confidence that I will not become wounded—don't know if that'll do me any good or not—but anyways, I do hold that confidence.[12]

Missing all that precious mail, it came as quite a shock to me to hear that Fred is out of the navy now. You gave no indication of how it happened, and neither did he in the letter I just received from him, but I presume it was a result of the stomach trouble he had. I hope it isn't any worse. I'm glad he got out of it. And besides, it will make it easier for you now, too, won't it? I imagine I'll get my old mail in a few days now, and hear all about it.

Nope—I didn't receive box #6. In fact, I only got one or two—I forgot which—back in England and haven't had any since. But I'm glad to know four or five more are on the way. Something to look for. Don't let that discourage your sending some more boxes, now. Have to keep the chain going, you know. I could use some more candy, so please send it.

Have you taken any pictures lately? I wish you'd send some. And
if you haven't—why don't you?

Write often—with Love –Carl

---

18 February 1945

Dear Mother and Dad,

Things are really picking up now. Got three letters from you
today, Jan 29, 31, and Feb. 2. By your letters you all seem to be
happy and well. I'm glad to hear that, because I was wondering, as
is natural, I guess, of maybe something or other had happened in all
that time I didn't hear from you. I guess that sounds funny to you, but
still, seven weeks is a long time, and a lot of things can happen—
even in Canton. Glad to know they didn't.

The coldest weather is over now, I'm pretty sure, so please stop
worrying about my feet. I've paid very careful attention to them all
along.

I hope you continue writing as often as you can. Letters mean
quite a bit more here than they did in the States. And you, too, Pop—
how about a few lines every now and then?

How are my letters coming in? Well, behave yourselves.

Love—Carl

---

19 February 1945

Hello, folks,

Well things are really picking up now. I got sixteen letters today,
covering, sporadically, that long black period. Well, I'll try to answer
all the questions and comments in your letters, but I only got them
from the beginning and the end of January, and one from the middle
of December.

First of all, about West Point—no I definitely do not want to
apply. Why? That little phrase "eight years." I know how concerned
you are about me and how much you want me to be in a safer
position—but, eight years. Along that line, you'll probably be pleased

to know that there's a slim chance of my going to O.C.S. over here. If I do, it'll be in the near future. The chances are almost 100 to 1 against it, but it's something for you to hope for. I've already applied, passed my physical and the regimental board, but there's still the divisional board, and here's where that 100 to 1 comes in, almost all of the other applicants have had more combat and leadership experience than I. But we can still hope, if nothing else. I hope that this has put you at least a little more at ease.

I don't know why you should feel guilty about entertaining or being entertained just because of the war. I don't see how you're sacrificing yourself unnecessarily or leading a stern existence will alter anything. One scene in the movie *Mrs. Miniver* along that line made an impression on me—probably because I thought the lines were good and true.[14] England's just getting into the war and the young man is shocked because the girl still wants to attend a certain party. He says, "Is this a time for gaiety?" and she replies, "Is this a time to lose your sense of humor?" I don't know if you see what I mean, and I can easily understand your attitude. Because I see it here. When the infantry comes back off the line for a while and sees the rear echelon men with clean shaves and clean clothes, they dislike them for it, and go out of their way to show contempt for the rear echelon. Yet it would be foolish for them to remain unshaven and dirty when they have opportunities to clean themselves. (And there isn't one infantryman who wouldn't give up his pay to be in the rear echelon.) Wouldn't it?[15]

Well now I know why Fred got his discharge. Is his ulcer very serious or can it be? I'm terribly glad he got the discharge but I hope he doesn't have anything that's a great deal worse than him not getting it. Tell me exactly how it is.

So we finally got the new rabbi, eh? Where's he from and what's he like and how's he doing?

Oh yes—don't ever send me anything in a package but food. One of the guys got one today full of toilet articles—ugh!

Love Carl

Got five more letters today that you sent to Eng., and also a V-mail from you, dad. I don't suppose either you or the army postal service can keep this up for much longer, but it's nice while it lasts.

I don't quite get the idea for building that new office. Sounds like it's pretty small and noisy. What was wrong with the old one? Well, I guess you know what you're doing.

I'd have liked to have seen that record snowfall you told me about. We had pretty much over here, but not 10 inches. And here it's an irritation, but back home I remember how I used to go wild over a big snow fall. But snow seems funny now. It keeps getting warmer over here. If it'll only last! I got a kick out of your telling about daddy spinning the wheels getting the car out and the discussion on whether the smell was anti freeze or rubber. Don't know why but it made me laugh.

Yep—I guessed right—you are worried about my feet, and about my taking care of myself. Well, I've resignedly decided that nothing can be done about it—you'll just have to go on worrying. I can't stop you apparently. But if you didn't, I guess no one would. That's what you're there for. Send candy please.

Love, Carl

22 February 1945

Dear Mom and Dad,

You know, you don't know which army I'm in, and even if you did know you still couldn't tell when I'm in action and when I'm not, by reading the papers and seeing that this army is making a drive and that one is just holding. Don't try to figure out when I'm fighting and when I'm resting. You'll only trouble yourself more, and you'll probably be wrong most of the time. Don't worry, please.

It's still spring over here—Maybe we've seen the last of winter. It gets warm enough during some of the days so you can't see your breath. Help me hope it lasts.

Love to you both –Carl

After almost two weeks of waiting out the floodwaters of the Roer River, three corps, including the 84th Division, were given the go to cross in the early morning hours of February 23.

Preparatory work for Operation Grenade began February 22. Mac-Donald set the scene: "No sooner was it dark than infantrymen began moving into cellars as close as possible to the river's edge. Engineers started transporting boats and the bridging equipment to within easy carrying distance of the water. Artillerymen were careful to fire no more than normal concentrations lest the enemy discern from increased fire what was afoot."

MacDonald continued, "Beginning at 0245 on the 23rd, the massed artillery began its thunderous bombardment. Forty-five minutes later, infantrymen of six divisions lowered assault boats into the swollen Roer to do battle . . .with a treacherous current." [16]

The 84th had to cross at a destroyed highway bridge in the town of Linnich. Crossing by the bridge foundations ensured that the river would be narrow, but it limited them to a one-battalion front, thereby tripling the time it would take to move the entire division. And it seems division leadership forgot about the Venturi effect, that the current would increase as the river narrowed.

The first wave got over with relative ease but then things started to go wrong. The strong river current took the assault boats 75 yards downstream, making it difficult to recover boats and get them back to the landing site and throwing the schedule off for the second wave. Carl's battalion was trapped on the west bank, unable to assist.

Not to worry, there were contingency plans. Combat engineers were simultaneously constructing foot bridges in three separate crossing spots which would make up for the lost boats. Unfortunately, the first bridge was never even completed, as a German unit opened up with fire on the combat engineers as they were attempting to anchor the far end, rendering it unusable. The second bridge was completed and anchored successfully when an empty assault boat from another division upstream hit it and knocked it out. Shortly thereafter, the remaining bridge was hit by German artillery and also knocked out.

So the 84th Division spent most of February 23 split by the river, with the east bank without tank or tank destroyer support. The surprise was gone, the bridges were gone, and many of the boats were gone. It wasn't the Longest Day, but it was long enough. What saved the moment was that the Germans were also gone. Not completely, of course, but the other

divisions crossing the Roer were apparently successful enough that they
could keep the Germans off balance.

Carl's regiment, the 335th, was finally able to cross over a sole foot-bridge, starting at 4:15 p.m. and ending "before midnight."[17] Mansoor described the crossing: "Although the crossing did not go entirely according to plan due to the rapid current and preregistered enemy artillery fire, all divisions were able to reach the far bank and carve out bridgeheads. Enemy counterattacks were broken up by small arms and massed artillery fire. By the end of the second day of the attack, bridgehead strength equaled thirty-eight battalions of infantry, supported by armor and artillery. By 26 February enemy disorganization was complete and a breakthrough was at hand."[18]

Of the many soldiers crossing the Roer, 1,400 would be killed, injured, or go missing.[19] According to Atkinson, the casualties were "mostly engineers" working furiously to build bridges for the men, their tanks, and other vehicles crucial to the fight.[20]

The next days saw some heavy fighting as the 84th snaked north. They faced pockets of resistance that tried to stand fast with a variety of firepower.[21]

The Allies' ultimate prize was this breakthrough, the point of war when the enemy buckled and began to fade without much loss to the conquering side. This was what Hitler was trying to achieve three months earlier when he smashed into the Ardennes. Now it was the Allies' turn. The 84th thought that defining moment was in its grasp. The decision was made to put together a tank-leading task force to storm the Germans and unhinge them with other units cleaning up from behind.[22]

On February 27, the 84th won that prize and became the first Allied division to achieve a breakthrough, shattering the enemy's ability to regain its balance, morale, and lines of attack. The 84th was now moving so fast that there was no chance for the Germans to fully regroup.[23] On that one day alone, the 84th captured 1,249 prisoners—a staggering amount considering that the division rounded up only 1,503 men during four weeks in the Ardennes.[24] "Not that any particular effort was made to gather in prisoners during the breakthrough. None was necessary," explained Draper. "Hordes simply decided that the war was over for them and started marching in column to the rear. Most of these pessimistic characters were not fighting men. They were clerks, shoemakers, tailors, blacksmiths, butchers. Some were just handed rifles and told to defend a ditch which they never found. Others were caught as we overran rear echelons."[25]

"In its three-week drive to the Elbe, the 84th Division alone captured more than 60,000 POWs," noted Schrijvers. "Erecting prison pens became so time-consuming for the division that engineers came up with the idea of driving around the POWs while dropping barbed wire and posts at intervals and then supervising the Germans as they fenced themselves in."[26]

Continuing, Schrijvers described the Americans' reaction upon meeting their enemies face to face: "The GIs' scrutiny of captured German soldiers revealed that they were neither the valiant nor fiendish enemy they had pictured. The Americans were shocked to find how washed-up and burned-out the formidable German foe turned out to be. 'The alleged magnificent heroism of the German people,' concluded a relieved corporal of the 84th Division in a letter to his parents in Seattle, 'is refuted by the number of prisoners taken and the manner in which they were taken in these last few months.'"[27]

Regardless of how many surrendered, there were many other enemy soldiers who were prepared to fight to the end.

Going into combat, every GI carried one or two grenades in an open buttonhole found on their jacket collar. They would stick the grenade trigger release in the buttonhole and then as a safety measure, when they could, they would wrap a little adhesive tape around it to avoid accidental detonation.

Carl used his grenades only once or twice. On one occasion, his unit had just cleaned the Germans out of a small town and began checking houses to make sure no enemies had stayed behind. Carl came out of one house when a fellow GI came up to him. The GI said that he saw a German soldier and thought the man ducked into a cellar for cover. The GI then asked Carl what they should do about it.

Carl felt the best option was to use a grenade. Soon, Carl was standing with his back to the house right next to an open cellar window. He grabbed a grenade, and pulled the pin. A grenade's fuse is supposed to last five seconds. Carl didn't want throw it immediately because it'd be possible for your enemy to pick up the grenade and toss it right back. So Carl pulled the pin and started counting. Sweat broke out on his face as he counted. One. Two. Three. And, with that, he tossed the grenade through the window. The timing worked. The grenade blew.

Carl and the other GI went down to the basement to assess the damage. There was a lot of water because the grenade took out the water heater, but other than that, nothing. There was no one there. No one knows what happened to that German soldier.

———

Another time, a German bullet flew toward one of the guys in Carl's company and struck him right in the grenade trigger assembly on his jacket. The bullet not only dislodged the grenade from the GI's lapel, but also set off the grenade's fuse. The grenade tumbled down and exploded at stomach-level. In a split second, the soldier's face changed from the elation of not being seriously shot to the horror of realizing his grenade was going to explode and he was going to die.

———

When the GIs were going through German towns, the most common attitude from German civilians was fear. They mainly tried to avoid the GIs and stay in their homes. To keep quiet and keep out of the way.[28] The GIs had to search every room in every house. They went door to door. Looking for combat situations. Looking for the enemy.[29]

Carl typically did not get a hostile response. But it was anxiety-ridden work. "Could there be a soldier in civilian clothes?" every GI wondered.

While some German civilians wanted to extend an olive branch, the residents that Carl encountered were mostly cowed and wanted to keep out of the way. They didn't want to cause trouble. Plus, the GIs were all armed and they weren't. Nevertheless, the possibility of physical injury or worse was always there.

———

Carl was assigned an assistant BAR man, J.T. from rural Mississippi. If Carl got hit, J.T. was to take over the BAR. But until then, his job was to give Carl fire support with his rifle as well as carry extra magazines. Those extra magazines were important. When a BAR man used up a couple of clips he could hand over the empties to his assistant and get new ones so he could have a complement of full magazines.

The assistant was to be by the BAR man's side. J.T.'s main job was to be Carl's right-hand man, to stick close to Carl—but often J.T. wasn't there. J.T. sometimes would just wander off without notice and be some-where else. A head of straw.

During one house search, Carl was told by his sergeant to exit a second-floor window by jumping down to a lower level, which was covered with a slate roof. Carl must have weighed close to 250 pounds with full combat gear. He crashed through that slate roof and landed in the room below.

No real harm was done, except some of the slate splintered and Carl got a deep cut on his forearm, which left a lifelong scar. Also, Carl damaged a tendon so he wasn't able to use his trigger finger for a brief spell. Carl had to give the BAR to J.T., his supposed backup, who was not excited about his new starring role.

"No, no, I'm not the BAR man, you are," J.T. said.

Carl replied: "J.T., I have a bad cut. You take it."

Within a couple of days, the motion returned to Carl's finger. He took back the BAR from J.T., who went about his business, whatever that was.

———

During another episode, Carl and another GI were sent out to scout. They were ahead of their unit by a few hundred yards. As they approached a farm building, the men spotted a spiral staircase that led to an upper floor. Carl volunteered to run upstairs to get a better vantage point.

The staircase was old, enclosed, and made of stone. The winding structure had no windows, leaving Carl unaware as he ascended that a German patrol was suddenly approaching. The other GI saw the approach from his ground-level position and he left—without telling Carl. A few seconds later, Carl reached the second level and saw the same approaching German patrol. Carl scurried down the steps to tell his buddy that they needed to get out of there, quickly, but his friend was nowhere to be found. The GI had already hightailed it. Carl, deserted, scrambled back to the unit by himself. "Deserted me under fire," is the handwritten caption on a squad photo in Carl's scrapbook. A cowardly lion, but without redemption. This was Carl's third encounter with death, though more precisely he might have been taken prisoner.

———

Even with the follies, miscues, and individual gaffes, the firm belief was that America's victory was inevitable. The Germans were now suffering the effects of being outmanned and outgunned. The Russians were advancing fast on the eastern front and inflicting a lot of damage, killing approximately "nine times more Germans" than American and British soldiers did, according to Atkinson.[30]

The race to the Rhine would only take about eight days, and the 84th wanted to be the first division to cross it.[31] The higher-ups dashed those dreams, sending the division northward to Homberg on March 2 and putting them in a holding position for weeks.[32]

The 84th had much of which to be proud. Draper described their deeds:

> In ten days, February 23–March 4, 1945, the 84th Infantry Division advanced approximately 45 miles from Linnich on the Roer to Homberg on the Rhine.
>
> The 84th led the U.S. Ninth Army to the Rhine, its flanks almost always exposed because the flank divisions could not maintain the same pace once it achieved breakthrough. . . .
>
> The 84th Infantry Division was one of the very few divisions which fought all the way from the Roer to the Rhine without losing its momentum for a single day.[33]

5 March, 1945
Germany

Hello Parents

How are you? I suppose you've been worrying because you haven't heard from me lately. Well, I'm mighty glad to tell you I'm perfectly all right. Nothing wrong with me a good bath, bed, and barber wouldn't fix. Look at one of the characters in "up front with Mauldin" and you get a fairly good idea of what I look like.[34] But I guess the life agrees with me—I don't even have a cold.

All that time when I couldn't tell you where I was, I was in Holland. And doing nothing but sitting around in a house, eating, sleeping, and seeing a show every once in a while. The division was changed from the 1st to the 9th army for the drive and they were trying to keep it secret. That's why I couldn't tell you anything. I got the box of Hershey bars today. They'll come in mighty handy. If you'll send some more, we'll use them.

I received a lot of mail from you, also, during this time. But I always had to read them in a hurry, and couldn't carry them with me so had to burn them up. So I can't remember if there is anything you asked me to tell you about. But I do remember that it was pretty wonderful reading your letters. They were really interesting, and usually just the thing I needed when I got them. Keep telling me about all that you do and plan to do.

Got a letter from Fred today. I guess it's kind of difficult for him to get used to college again. But he seems to be fairly happy there.

Can't tell you anything of what we've done on this offensive. Guess you'll have to get all your news on what I'm doing from the papers. Hasn't been too difficult, but a bit nerve-wracking at times.

I'm tired and sleepy now—can't think. I'll write again soon, and a little more coherently. Love —Carl

———

The 335th Infantry, according to Draper, did everything from protecting roads to "mop[ping] up scattered enemy units."[35] Moving quickly, Carl's company even "took over a [working] beer hall" in a town called St. Tonis on March 2. "While the proprietor served beer, an interesting fraulein—one German word every GI was able to learn sooner or later—played the piano and sang."[36] By March 4, Company L was in Lohmannsheide "to seize a road junction."[37]

Another example of troop speed after the breakthrough: The captain of Carl's platoon wanted to look at some maps, "went into a house along the road, fortunately through the back door, and found six German officers sitting around a table in the next room. It was an enemy CP [command post]," Draper related. "[The Captain] left quietly."[38]

By the next day, March 5, Company L was at the Rhine.[39]

———

8 March 1945
Germany

Dear Mom and Dad
Not doing much just now.

Got a chance to get a little rested up—feel pretty good about this
time.

This fighting a war in Germany isn't as bad compared to what we had in Belgium.

There's a town about every half mile or so around here—when we want something we just go into the nearest house and take it. And don't be too surprised if, when I come home, I run out to the garage to look for eggs, clean room on the stove and the kitchen table by shoving everything on the floor, ransack the cellar for jams and preserves, tear out the shelves looking for bread and grease, cook myself a meal, and then jump into bed with everything on—shoes, pack, and such![40]

And can you picture me cutting a piece off a curtain to clean the pans and table with? And throwing all the garbage on the floor? Well I'm warning you now so you won't be too surprised in case I forget where I am sometimes, after I get back.

Hope everything's O.K. with you back there. Love to you. Don't forget to write often.

Love Carl

If Carl was adding color, it might not have been much of an exaggeration: "Infantrymen descended upon what was left of the towns like parasites. They ripped shutters from windows to serve as litters. They tore down curtains to use as bandages," wrote Schrijvers. "They turned billiard tables into operating surfaces. They smashed up furniture for firewood. They unhinged doors and gates and placed them over dugouts as roofs. They dragged mattresses into foxholes and cellars. Amidst all of this, the dying European communities gave off a sickening odor. It was composed of the smell of cordite, charred wood, dust, musty walls, blasted manure piles, and gasoline fumes as well as the stench of burned flesh."[41]

Carl's division "sat on the Rhine for almost a month," Draper said. "It was the first real relief for the soldiers in 15 weeks. [They] were holding a sector of the riverfront but it was relatively quiet. The Germans on the other side made themselves as scarce as possible."[42] Draper continued his description:

Approximately 30 percent of . . . two regiments on the river remained in prepared positions all the time but a system of rotation gave everyone a rest.

What does a battle-weary soldier do when he gets a chance to take it easy?

He washes. He scrubs himself, his clothes, his equipment. In combat, dirt is almost as common as danger. An outfit that is in the line under fire for three, four days, maybe a week, has other things to think about than a change of underwear. To wash, to smell of soap, is almost a symbol of peace. On the Rhine, the war was by no means over but, for a little while, the fighting was. That peace was enough for the moment. A filthy hero can go a long way from war to peace on a cake of soap.

He talks. Not that all soldiers like to speak about their experiences at the front but most do. It is always remarkable how much a man who has been scared to death can remember. It is even more remarkable how honest, absolutely honest, he can be. In a month or a year, he may unconsciously drop out of the story all the unpleasant or embarrassing details. But in the first 48 hours, just back from the line, he has an obsession to tell the truth, every terrible bit of it. He has to get it out of his system, the good and the bad, as if he had a crime on his conscience. He is not worried about being a hero. He figures he did enough just to be in it and come back.[43]

———

9 March 1945
Germany

Dear Mom and Pop,

From my hole, I can throw a stone in the Rhine. We're lined up on one side of it and the Jerries are on the other. This is what they should really call "The Watch on the Rhine."[44] It's a nice, peaceful, placid river—hardly worth fighting for, though.

As I told you I spent three weeks before this drive in a house. It was near a large city in Holland and we got quite a few chances to get there.

Before the war, Holland was a rich country. There are more modern homes and more of them than in the States. The stores and landscaping and furniture are all modern, well-planned, and have been well cared for. Of course I'm judging by only one town but that one town was amazing to me. It looked like a model community. But there is the inconsistency of an almost absolute absence of central heating and running hot water. Seems funny, doesn't it?

Love –Carl

The next letter included eight bank notes, ranging from 1920s Germany to the current Allied occupation.

11 March 1945
Germany

A—100 million Mark note, 1923

B—500,000 Mark note from "Die Rheinishche Stahlwerke" (presumably occupied Rhineland), 1923

C—Allied occupation currency—half-mark note

D—20 Mark Reichsbank note, 1910

E—5,000 Mark note, 1922

F—5 mark note, 1914

G—5 mark note, 1917

H—Allied occupation 5 franc note, 1944

Dear Mother and Dad,

Received another box of Hershey's from you today. And on behalf of the whole platoon, thanks, they really are swell.

And another letter from you, Pop! Fine work—I'm proud of you! I think I'm getting spoiled with attention, though.

What about this new Rabbi? The way you talk and from what Fred mentioned I gather that he's something pretty wonderful. Is he? Where's he from? Weren't you head of the committee that selected him, Dad?

Here's some money that will interest you. Notice how the quality of the money deteriorates with the value. That 100 mark note I'm not sure about. Does that mark the beginning of the inflation—1929? I think it does. And it's interesting to note the increase in the increase. From 100 to 5,000 is two years, to 500,000 in eight months, and to 100,000,000 in five weeks.

Figure 7-1. Banknotes Carl found from the Weimar and Imperial Germany, including a 100,000,000-mark note. *Author collection.*

And here's also a French 10 Franc note, worth 20 cents, and a 5 franc invasion note—same relative value—and a German invasion note. A mark is worth 10 cents. On the French invasion money it says "Friends of France." Don't know what it says on the German— you'll have to tell me that. But I don't imagine it's quite as amicable. I believe I'm pretty fortunate in finding such good indications and examples of inflation. It seems pretty complete to me, with those dates. I ran across a couple of cigar boxes full of it, in one of the houses we stayed in. There were stored away in a special place along with records and valuables. Can you imagine what hopes and securities, blasted, must be represented in those boxes? I imagine the owner hung on to it all these years in the wisp of the hope that one day, somehow—like those Southern families with their chests of Confederated money, and their poverty.

Isn't that peculiar? Of all the dozens of tragedies I've seen in these past weeks—the homeless, walking, lost people, the dead, the tortured, the ruined—and I'm affected by a symbol of what happened a generation ago. And another thing—I see what war does, and means, to all these other people, and I'm appalled by it. It seems so terribly wrong to me that these things should be allowed to happen— to these other people. And yet I'm not particularly impressed by the fact that my life is being pretty well upset by the war. I'm not conscious that I'm experiencing hardships. I'm sorry for them—but not for myself—and that really is peculiar—for looking at it, I should be.[45]

But of course, I don't mean I'm invincible to loss. There are times when I feel acutely the desire to be back with you again. I get deep twinges of missing you and I'm always aware of a certain longing, but I am not miserable because of it, and I'm glad of that.

One of the compensations of this is that I feel now as if I appreciate your finesses as parents and as persons. I think I was too young before to see far enough under our bickerings to find what a family we all make.

Goodnight, for now, with love —Carl

Schrijvers elaborated on the theme of money:

> The little cash the soldiers did keep for themselves was usually
> paid in the currency of the country they happened to be in.
> This further lessened the meaning of money to them. The GIs
> were bombarded with information on all kinds of foreign cur-
> rencies and exchange rates, from the farthings, threepences, and
> half crowns of the British… to the 14 different coins and bills
> of Germany. But combat soldiers never stayed long enough in
> any of Europe's countries to figure out the intricate currencies.
> Moreover, the strange designs and shapes of bills and coins gave
> foreign money an even more unreal character. The Americans
> called it "playmoney" and loved to send it home for souvenirs.
> To add to the confusion, it was not always clear to the GIs
> whether certain kinds of European money were still valid or
> not… eventually, the combat soldiers stopped bothering about
> money all together.[46]

---

13 March 1945
Germany

Dear Fred,

Well, it's a tough war. I'll have to take back my generous offer of
my last letter. They're clamping down on looting and checking every
package we send home. So we can't send anything that's not military,
and we can't send pistols.[47] So—can you use a rifle? I'm going to
try and get hold of one. It's difficult, though. They always break the
stocks of their rifles before they give up.

Still nothing to tell you. I'll write a longer letter soon and try to
give you a personal idea of what the countries are like—that's about
the only idea I can give you.

This is just to let you know that as of March the 13th 1945 I'm
hale, whole, and hearty, and kicking—mostly kicking.

Lets hear from you every once in a while—tell me what Miami
is doing and how it's getting along. Oh, yes—thanks for telling the
powers that be, down there, my present address—I presume you did.

Love –Carl

As the war progressed, GIs usually found deserted or semideserted towns. As a unit moved toward a town, the civilians mainly tried to leave and take what they could carry with them.

During active combat, there wasn't a lot of pilferage. GIs weren't out to steal money or make a profit. Though out of necessity, American soldiers would grab useful items like a piece of food, an article of clothing, a mattress, a radio, a typewriter, an iron, or the like.[48] It also wasn't uncommon to take a small trophy or token like Nazi memorabilia, a weapon, even old banknotes. They were the odd mementos of war.

13 March 1945
Germany

Dear Mom and Dad,
Your timing is getting down to perfection now. We just finished the second box of Hershey's about four hours before another box came from you—the one with the O'Henry's and nuts etc. Thanks again.
Received the letter you wrote, Dad, about Mason and the policeman, and thot it was pretty good. Remember Mr. Ginsberg from Canada? He wouldn't stay away from the police for more than ten days.
It's a little hard to get hold of stamps here. How about sending me some air-mail? Only 6 cents for one, don't forget.
I was surprised that you were so taken by that Mauldin cartoon, "wake up papa—I think we've been liberated."[49] You see, Mauldin is our great favorite over here—and out of all his cartoons I believe that that one is the greatest favorite. It's so amusing to us because it's so close to the truth—but, as I said, it's surprising that it should strike you the same way.
Love –Carl
P.S. send packages, please.

Because of army censorship, Carl could not tell his father when he was going into combat. Before he went overseas, Leo and Carl worked out a private code, so that Carl could tell Leo he was going into combat by telling Leo that he (Carl) was going to "visit Mr. Ginsberg." Carl dutifully followed instructions and the message took several weeks to get home, and then Leo's response took several weeks to get back: Who is Mr. Ginsberg and why are you telling me you are going to visit him? Leo had forgotten the very code he had helped design. Carl, of course, could not truly correct him until the war was over.[50]

———

14 March 1945
Germany

Dear Mom and Dad,

Picked this up in one of the houses. It's a page out of a German dress-pattern book, as you can see. I thought it might interest you, mother. If you ask me, most of the dresses would look sharp on 5th Avenue. Or am I wrong? And it seems to me that these patterns don't take many pains to save cloth. So you get the impression from this that these people here aren't hurting too much, that shortages aren't affecting them too severely. And that's a true impression. What I've seen here of food, clothing, and shelter differs considerably from what I'd been led to expect. Their houses are well constructed and on the whole newer than those in the States. (Incidentally, as long as I've been in Europe, including England, I haven't seen a wooden house larger than three rooms. They just build to last here. The walls are always solid, or brick or stone, and the cellars cement and are reinforced. A cellar here is as good a bomb shelter as you can get.) It's very seldom you see a shack or a really poor looking house. They're always well supplied with coal—good coal—and good bread and preserves and other foods, and there's always plenty of clothing hanging around. And I mean good clothes.

For four years I've been reading about how bad off these Germans are. How they're eating sawdust bread and getting a pair of socks and a necktie a year. And yet here you get the impression that, discounting the direct results of war, the civilians are no more affected by the war than you are back there. Well, of course that's an exaggeration—but not a very large one.

One more thing about these fashions. I'm a little surprised to
see that the ideal Kraut female has the same characteristics as the
American one. Tall, slim, narrow hips, square shoulders, and they
even emphasize them more than the artists back there. Seems funny,
doesn't it?

Figure 7-2. Fashions from Germany. *Author collection*

How fast are these free letters getting there? Tell me. Keep writing and keep sending those packages, please.

Love to you —Carl

——

16 March 1945
Germany

Dear Folks,

Got your letter telling of the new address, as you see. Hope your plans didn't go wrong and that you're really there by now. But I'm so in the habit of writing the gold old "25th St." after the good old "Mr. L.B. Lavin" that it probably be some time before I get myself regulated to the good old 31, eh? So don't wonder why about half of my letters for the next month or so carry the old address.

What all have you done to fix up the place by this time? Let's hear all about it.

Just finished eating the third package in about a week when—the fourth came. The one with the O'Henry's and the underwear, and the knife.[51] You sent it to England. Can't carry the underwear with me and I've already got a couple of knives from prisoners I searched, but thanks, anyways. The candy is very much appreciated, you know

Love —Carl

——

18 March 1945
Germany

Dear Folks,

Here's a money order for a hundred dollars, enclosed. Tell me you received it right away.

Did you ever sell that radio stock at 11 ½ as you said you were going to do? If you haven't, I wish you would sell it now, unless the market is below 10, and with the money from that, plus this $100, plus the first allotment of $25 that should come in about now buy me a $375 war bond. The difference—add or subtract—from my savings

account. O.K.? Please write me as soon as you've done that and tell
me you have.

I imagine you're wondering where I got that amount, aren't you? Well, I just got paid for the first time in three months. Since I left England I've spent about four or five dollars! There's one good thing about living this kind of a life—it doesn't cost very much.

Got another batch of back mail today. Among the letters one from your pal, Col. Estes and one from you telling about him.[52] I must say you're improving all the time—first a captain, then a congressman, and now a colonel. Go up a couple more ranks, and maybe we'll be getting somewhere. Where did he come from, anyways? I can't remember hearing you speak of him, Pop. And I think I know why he's retired. The circulatory trouble I'm supposed to have, he refers to as "respiratory."

Hate to disappoint you, but even if I did think I could get out of this because of any personal physical reason, I wouldn't. Even if you and everybody in the company thinks I'm crazy.

Well take it easy, and behave yourselves. Lots of love –Carl

18 March 1945
Germany

Dear Mother and Dad,

Well, it sounds like things are buzzing along quite cheerfully back there, by your letters.

You said you were anxiously waiting my letters written after Feb. 22—well I hope you didn't worry because of that long delay in my writing after that date. But I guess that by now you know why I don't write—because I don't have the opportunity, you realize.

That new house sounds pretty nice—but a little crowded. From all the arranging you're doing it appears that you're preparing for a long stay. I thought it was just a temporary thing.

I didn't realize that candy was so difficult to obtain back there. How about making me some fudge? Or can't you get sugar either? I'm afraid that all those boxes coming all at once, that I told you about, has spoiled me. I'm used to it now.

We took some shots a while ago—the regular army shots for various susceptibilities. And I was amazed at what babies men are. Back in the States when we took them, everybody tried to get out of it, and talked about it, and worried about it—and actually it's nothing. You'd have thought they'd be ashamed to put so much importance to so little a thing.

And then I came over here, and saw G.I.s do things like going out on a patrol with about an even chance of coming back unhurt, and not say a word about it. And then we take shots over here—and these self-same guys spend an hour complaining about it! They carry on just as those others did back there. I don't get it.

Wish I could tell you more of what I'm doing—but I can't

So—So long for now with love Carl

20 March 1945
Germany

Dear Mother and Dad,

Got another burst of correspondence from you—both of you—yesterday, which was quite cheering. Pop—you're outdoing yourself! Establishing a fine record! Also got the pair of light wool gloves you sent to England. I have used them very well, since they'll fit under G.I. gloves. And with them an old letter also sent to England in which you told me of the subscription to *Life* you got for me. Haven't gotten any yet, but magazines arrive 6 wks or two months later here. However, they're no less welcome because of that, and "Life" is difficult to come by, so that'll come in very handy—Thanks! Yes your packages arrived in pretty good condition, usually. Two of them had to be re-wrapped by the A.P.O. though.

The new rabbi sounds like he's making even more than a stir in the Canton tea-pot. Might even be a tempest, if the discussions about erecting a new temple are serious. Incidentally, I thoroughly agree with you on the foolishness of the argument of servicemen acquiring a deeper spiritual feeling and therefore our/your needing a new building. Even if they have acquired that feeling, which they have not. (I've two things I want to say and I'm digressing from the first to the second now, so may as well finish the second.) "No atheists in fox-holes" really means "No fearless men in fox-holes" and one wants the quickest straw while drowning, or believing himself to be drowning in a barrage. Religion spawned in terror has a poor chance of reaching maturity. (Incidentally, while I'm thinking of it I still haven't found a reason why I should believe the covenants I swore to in my confirmation.) My God—now I'm digressing on my digression! Well, to get back to the first point: I read in *Stars and Stripes* the other day of a congressman saying he was sick and tired of hearing the "fighting men" brought into every argument, whether it was relevant or not. I suppose he'll get jumped on for saying that—and his argument will be borne out by the arguments of those that jump!—but of course he's right, and you're right. Why must every good thing be over-worked 'til it's ludicrous and undignified? Yes—we're being inconvenienced the most and we should be considered by the nation, proportionately. But at least let the consideration be logical! How can the point of the moment fit all debates?

If I'm not careful I'll get myself excited here. Which would be a thing unnatural to me, according to you, Pop. And I think you're right.

So I'd better say good-bye for now. With plenty of love Carl

Carl always had a strong sense of Jewish identity, but he never had been very religious. There was a saying during the war that there were no atheists in foxholes, but Carl was. He was an atheist in many foxholes. While he respected others who believed in a higher power, he didn't call out to God. He never found himself praying for his safety. He didn't think God would spare him over someone else because he asked. He didn't believe God cut deals and he did not like the idea of transactional prayers. Rather than carry a Bible, Carl carried paperbacks—free Armed Services Editions.[53]

20 March 1945
Germany

Dear Mother and Dad,

This is your anniversary, isn't it? I just realized it, on hearing
the sound of the date. I guess I should have thought of it two
weeks ago, and you'll get this a little late. But anyways, I wish you
congratulations, many, many happy returns of the day, and everything
else that can possibly go with it. Here's hoping I can help you
celebrate the big one, next year.[54]

I remember once, when I was out of the hog-pens at the beef
house, one of the men told me that a hog's head was always on the
wrong end. I've also heard that Dutchmen were pig-headed. But
I never up til now knew there was any tie-up in the two sayings.
Recently, I was part of a detail handling moving civilians so they
wouldn't interfere with military traffic. And handling them was
exactly like handling hogs into pens. They had to be watched so they
wouldn't slip away, you had to tell them something four or five times
before they would do it, and my God would they argue! They'd mill
around and as soon as one would start arguing with you a dozen more
would crowd around and start stating their cases! I thought their
trying to argue in German when they saw I couldn't understand a
word of it was bad enough, but when they tried to prove their point by
showing me Nazi passes, that was too much.

Boy, these people are persistent. And it's only when they persist
to the point that they make you angry and you yell at them, that they
become quiet and obey until they get another chance to argue!

A G.I. is too easy going and soft hearted to act the part of a
conqueror. It's pretty hard to see an elderly woman pushing a heavy
cart—with all her possessions she has left in it—hungry and cold,
and have to add to her hardships. You just don't want to do it.

Well, behave yourselves. Love, Carl

25 March 1945
Germany

Dear Mom and Dad,

Got another package from you in the box of pecan bars you sent.
You're doing fine—keep it up. In fact, please consider this as another
request for some candy to you, and the post office.

I'm sending my watch home. After a year of good and faithful
service, it finally gave up. Whatever you do, don't take it to any of the
Canton jewelers to have it repaired. I think C's ruined my other one.
Please be sure that whomever you get knows his business. Or, you can
just let go til after the war, since I don't want you to send it back to
me. Keep it until I get home. You, see, we're allowed to buy personal
items, such as watches, from prisoners we take—and it is amazing
what effect a rifle has on the law of economics. So I'll probably get
hold of a fairly good watch sooner or later, with no financial hardship
attached.[55]

Don't forget to let me know as soon as my watch arrives. I insured
it for eighty dollars.

By the time you receive this letter I imagine you'll be well settled
at 31st. Well, do you still like it as well as you did at first? They
say you never find out if you like a house til six months after you've
moved into it.

Glad then you didn't throw anything of mine out when you
moved, Mother. That a girl! After all these years I've finally got you
trained.

Sorry to disappoint you, but I'm pretty certain that's not me in
that newspaper picture. At least, I can't remember ever having it
taken. Which should be fairly good proof.

Dad, what do you mean you're "only" delivering five days a
week? When I left, it was three days a week.[56] And from the tone of
your letter, things don't sound too bad at the plant. How about giving
me two or three pages on what the score has been there for the past
six months, in comparison to the last couple years, and before the
war?

Solicitation on your vice-presidency of the temple—guess you'll
have to attend now, eh? Sorry. Love –Carl

27 March 1945
Germany

Dear Folks,

Still getting old mail you sent to England. I got the letter in which
you told me of receiving that picture I sent from England. I'm glad
you mentioned it because we have to go through so many regulations
and complications to send a package. It gives me a little more
confidence in the fate of my watch. (I wrote you a letter two days ago
telling you I sent it. Get it?—the letter. I guess the watch will take
some time to arrive.)

Since we've been in the war, I've never yet felt that the end was
near. I've always believed the Germans would hold out for "quite
a while" longer. But now I don't think that any more. I'm sure that
now it's a matter of weeks—possibly even days—until the end. Well,
notice the date and see if I'm right, or not.

In the meantime—Lots of love –Carl

30 March 1945
Germany

Dear Folks,

Let's get on the ball with your letter-writing! Haven't received
one in four days now. Where's your patriotism? Well, we'll put it down
to the erratic-ness of the Army Post Office instead of you, for now. I
hope you're still writing as often as you have been.

And that leaves me devoid of subject matter. I can't write of what
I'm doing, and now I can't even write of what you're doing. Yep, it's a
tough war.

Do you remember what kind of appetite I used to have? I think
I used to eat about half as much as the average person. Well, things
are different now. In fact, I'm known as a chow-hound around here.
That's one thing I'll have to be grateful to the army for. It developed it
for me. Took a couple of years, and it was a long gradual process, but
I've got it now. I used to think I'd never get a build like you've got,
Pop—but now I don't know. I used to eat just because it was the thing

to do—but now I feel uncomfortable if I don't have something to gnaw
on every four hours.

It's been seldom that I've had the chance to sleep more than three consecutive hours since I've left England, and yet I've put on weight! And another thing—every time I go back to a rest area I get a cold, and every time we go back to the front I get rid of it!

It seems that everything I've been led to believe is contradicted over here. Of course, that's not so. In the army you incline to become disdainful of everyone in a more fortunate position than you—soldier or civilian. Here, that covers almost everybody. And as a result you actually look for contradictions—first in beliefs those others have, and then, following, in all beliefs. It's natural, even if it isn't fair.

Be good—and write.

With lots of love Carl

8

The Battle of the Rhine
April–May 1945

While Carl was in combat, the army came out with a new invention called "artificial moonlight." Searchlights played underneath the clouds about two miles back, and that would reflect a sort of moonlight ahead of the men. The effect was wonderful. Carl loved it. All the GIs loved it.

Since the light came from behind, the Germans would only see the Americans as silhouettes. The GIs would get a pretty good view. It would reflect as much light as a full moon. This innovation proved decisive at the Battle of the Rhine, where the Allies moved into the heart of Germany by capturing the last remaining bridge, at Remagen.

According to Mansoor, "Technical innovations helped defend the Remagen bridge from German attempts to destroy it. One such innovation was 'artificial moonlight,' created by bouncing searchlight beams off overhead clouds. This technique created enough ambient light to allow defending American forces to see at night. Artificial moonlight was used not just at Remagen but at many places along the front in the fall of 1944 and winter of 1945."[1]

The captured bridge over the Rhine at Remagen became a beachhead for the US forces, even after the eventual collapse of the bridge. Crossing the Rhine was a movement of enormous propaganda importance because it placed the Allies deep in Germany. Carl crossed the Rhine at Remagen, but in a boat. He was one of those wielding a paddle.

According to Draper, "The 335th 1st Battalion began to cross the Rhine at 2:15 p.m. on April 1. That night, the 335th's entire combat team went as far as Lembeck, about 15 miles from the Rhine."[2]

On crossing the Rhine, the war became one of fluidity of movement. From then on it seemed as if the proportion of Germans who wanted to

surrender, as opposed to those who wanted to keep fighting, was changing
daily. Carl's unit moved rapidly to take towns, villages, and hamlets. With
no formal opposition front, the American forces were trying to cover as
much ground as they could.

As Atkinson related, "The war had again become mobile and mecha-
nized, precisely the war for soldiers with 'machinery in their souls,' as John
Steinbeck described his fellow Americans. A war of movement, distance,
and horsepower was suited, as Time rhapsodized, to 'a people accustomed
to great spaces, to transcontinental railways, to nationwide trucking chains,
to endless roads.'"[3]

1 April 1945
Germany

Dear Mother and Dad,
Just got paid and that allotment I told you I had gotten hasn't
been taken out of my pay yet. So I sent home $50 more by PTA. Let
me know when you get it.

It's been six days now or thereabouts, that I haven't heard from
you. How'se come? There shouldn't be anything to prevent you from
writing. Well, I imagine I'll hear from you pretty soon now. And while
we're on the subject, send me another package, will you please?
Candy or fudge.

Well, now, let's see. What to tell you? I can't even think of any
more opinions of things to tell you. At the moment I'm getting along
fine—no complaints—healthy and wealthy—and enjoying life. I'm
even just getting over a cold I've had for a long time.

Behave yourselves—Love Carl

By the next day, the 335th streamed about thirty-five miles forward
to a town called Appelhulsen. Two days later, the 335th found itself at the
Weser River, over a hundred miles past the Rhine.[4]

"Politically, the problems east of the Rhine were typical of our experiences," said Draper. "By covering so much ground so quickly, we overran
hundreds of cities, town, and villages, their populations intact or swollen

with refugees and 'displaced persons,' that curious, official name for Germany's army of forced laborers."[5]

The 84th encountered resistance in and around the Weser in the form of enemy fire and improvised roadblocks.[6] Still, they were able to bridge the Weser on April 7.[7]

The 84th was bogged down for a bit both before and after the river crossing, still facing intermittent resistance, taking on soldiers, tanks, and artillery fire, and grinding forward about thirty miles to Hannover.[8]

Combat movies generally struck Carl as being pretty much off the mark, because to do a dramatic scene you need guys exposing themselves to fire, which was absolutely the opposite of how to survive combat. Soldiers live if they take cover, but cover makes for poor theatrics.

Even in his later years, if Carl watched a fictionalized battle scene in which a guy stands up in full view and fires his weapon, he'd whisper, "That just never happens." No matter the war, you try to crouch and fire from a protected position.

Carl noted that at nighttime, this rule was even more strictly observed:

> You're alone and it's night and you hear a noise near you, you get very nervous. You shouldn't shoot for the noise, but some guys were worn down enough, got scared and nervous enough, that they would shoot at night. Actually it's a very dumb thing to shoot at night at a sound because you're not going to hit whatever's making the sound, first of all, and secondly, your muzzle flash is going to reveal your own position precisely, should it be a Jerry whose sound you're hearing. You're giving yourself away and you've not got that much of a chance of hitting him. So it's a very stupid thing to do—to shoot at a sound. But a lot of stupid things were done.[9]

The war was winding down, but still care was needed, especially when a town was taken. Soldiers were required to inspect every room in every building in the town, going through houses, office buildings, and factories. Carl did his part, looking for people, looking for ammunition, looking for weapons.

Usually, two or three guys would go through a house together. You didn't want to go by yourself. There was always a little bit of a leery feeling as you went to open a door, because if someone was there and wanted to shoot you, he was in a perfect position to do it. So it was always a bit of a nervous thing going in.

If the door was locked, Carl would kick in the door. Kick it in so his foot would hit right by the door handle.

In one particular town, Carl and two others had just finished going through a house in the suburban part of town. And as they walked out a back door, they heard gunfire—an unusual sound because there hadn't been any firing for a while. It was late April, and the Germans had pretty much given up. Here we have Carl's fourth brush with death.

Carl saw two other GIs just ten yards away. They were taking aim at a group of about four German soldiers who were running across an open field into woods approximately a quarter of a mile away. This was a perfect job for a BAR man. Carl could spray bullets—giving the enemy two choices: to surrender or to be cut down by automatic fire.

Carl began moving to assist the two GIs were when he heard his sergeant's voice calling, "Lavin, Lavin."

Carl recognized the voice. So he stopped, turned around and looked behind him. But the sergeant wasn't there. Carl kept looking around. Looking. The sergeant said, "Up here. Up here."

Carl looked up higher. And from a house—next to the one Carl had just inspected—there was a window with horizontal and vertical bars in it and an arm sticking through the bars waving wildly.

Carl couldn't see through the bars, but he assumed it was his sergeant, Sergeant J, calling him.

"Come here. You'll get a good shot from here," Sergeant J said.

Carl said to him, hollering back, "The Germans are getting away."

Sergeant J said, "I know. You got a perfect shot from here. Get up here. Get up to this window. Hurry up. Bring your BAR. Get up here quick."

Carl immediately recognized this to be a bad command because of the amount of time it would take him to run to the back of the house, find the hallway, locate the stairs, and scramble up them. Carl knew by the time he joined his sergeant the Germans would be in the woods.

It would have taken two seconds to assist the riflemen, but now, as a dutiful soldier, he had to obey his sergeant. He ran to the back of the house with his BAR as fast as he could and found the sergeant firing his rifle through bars in a bathroom window.

Just as Carl stepped in the door, Sergeant J caught a bullet in the elbow and staggered back. He fell half backward toward Carl. Carl caught him the best he could and eased him to the floor.

Carl's job was now J's safety. He dragged him to the hallway in a half-sitting position to get him out of harm's way. Once there, Carl started to look at J's wounds and saw blood surging out of his elbow. An artery had been hit and it was pumping out a lot of blood. Carl could count J's pulse by watching the blood spurt.

"Never mind me," J said. "Get those Jerries."

Get those Jerries? Carl's immediate reaction was to ignore him. But Carl's job was to obey, and he did as told.

The bullets were still streaming in through the same barred window. The bottom of the window was about three feet high so Carl crouched under it. He bobbed his head up and down, trying to get a view and hoping he didn't get a bullet in the forehead. What Carl saw was startling. It was two GIs, his fellow soldiers, shooting at the window![10]

Carl darted his head up once more for confirmation's sake when he felt a million bee stings all over his face. A bullet hit one the cross-pieces of the metal bars in the window, peppering Carl's face and neck with rust and metal shards. Carl wasn't bleeding. He just experienced that heart-stopping moment when people realize they faced death from an inch away.

Still, Carl had verified the shooters and recognized them. One GI was kneeling and the other was standing. Both were shooting at Carl through that window. They must have seen J's rifle from the barred window, assumed it to be a German soldier and opened fire on the window.

Carl rushed back to J, telling him, "Hey, those are our guys. They aren't Germans. They are our guys. They thought you were Jerry."

J gave it a moment's thought, changed his priorities and said, "Get Smitty. Get Smitty."

Smitty was the squad medic. Smitty always said, "Never yell 'medic.' Make sure you yell 'Smitty' and I'll run as fast as I can to come help. I don't want to get diverted helping someone else."

Carl rushed downstairs to get Smitty, but he stopped as soon he arrived at the door. He didn't want to be shot by his own men, so he took off his helmet and full field pack. He dropped his BAR and threw down his ammunition to make himself as light as possible.

Carl bolted from the door, hoping his men recognized him before they filled him with bullet holes. And it worked. No one shot. They recognized

Carl. His helmet was off and they were all hiding in bushes around the edge of the yard.

And they started yelling, "Lavin, Lavin, get down. Get down, Jerry's in there."

Carl's yelled back, "No, there are no Jerries. That was J and me inside."

And they're yelling, "What? Are you crazy? Are you telling us that you and J were shooting at us?"

"No, no, that was J shooting over your head. J's hurt. Get Smitty. J's hurt. Get Smitty," Carl was yelling as loud as he can.

The GIs started shouting for Smitty, who decided to the fastest way to get to the scene was to jump a fence. Unfortunately, Smitty's foot caught a rail and he went sailing with his medical equipment being thrown loose. Through the air went the morphine syrettes, the sulfanilamide, the gauze bandages, the compresses, the surgical tape, the tincture of Merthiolate, aspirin, bismuth, paregoric, sodium amytal, and tags for logging morphine injections.[11] The GIs helped Smitty pick up his gear. "Come on, J's hurt," they said. "Stop fooling around. C'mon."

They raced upstairs.

Carl and the men saw blood was still pumping out of J's arm with each heartbeat. Smitty immediately pulled out a tourniquet, placed it on J's arm, and stemmed the blood loss.

Unless it was a light wound, Carl never knew for sure if a guy lived or not. Carl surmised his sergeant survived or so he hoped. The sergeant did not return to the company.[12]

———

There is something that happens after a few months of fighting: combat fatigue.

Author Paul Fussell explained: "We came to understand what more have known than spoken of, that normally each man begins with a certain full reservoir, or bank account, of bravery, but that each time it's called upon, some is expended, never to be regained. After several months it has all been expended, and it's time for your breakdown."[13] Elsewhere, he elaborated on this theme: "In war it is not just the weak soldier, or the sensitive one, or the highly imaginative or cowardly one, who will break down. Inevitably, all will break down if in combat long enough. . . . There is no such thing as 'getting used to combat.'"[14]

Mansoor added, "Combat exhaustion casualties usually fell into two broad categories. The first type occurred among new soldiers just before entry into combat or during their first five days on the front lines. . . . A second type of combat exhaustion occurred among experienced veterans who had endured continuous, severe fighting of four months or more. In the spring of 1945, First Army determined the longest any man could remain in combat and retain his wits was about 200 days."[15]

Carl was over halfway there.

The 84th came to a point where it was no longer overrunning villages and towns. It was increasingly able to tackle major cities. It came in view of Hannover, prewar home of half a million people, on April 9, and captured it the following day.

Wolff describes the 84th's capture of Hannover:

> The streets were lined with refugees and Germans cheering our troops. The SS had organized the Volkssturm resistance, and then pulled out of town, realizing the position was hopeless. The departure of the SS and the speedy drive of our Second and Third Battalions were signals to burn the Volkssturm armband, get rid of the panzerfaust, and hang the white flag from the window. We drove through the streets between five story tenement houses, alternately watching the civilians and the top story windows, which were excellent places for snipers. The First Battalion moved through the city and secured bridges for the next day's advance. RCT 334 billeted in Hannover for one night.[16]

Military historian Charles MacDonald noted how quickly the mood changed once the city was occupied: "Acres of rubble from Allied bombing and thousands of foreign laborers made overly exuberant by looted liquor posed more problems than did the Germans."[17]

9 April 1945
Deutschland

Dear Mom and Dad,

I'm writing this on a liberated German typewriter, which, as
you see, isn't in the best of condition. I don't know when I'll get the
opportunity to mail it though, since we're in action at this time. This
machine is just like an American one except that the "y" and the "z"
are exchanged, and these letters are added: ö, ä, and ü. And there's
this: $\mathcal{RM}$ instead of a dollar sign.

No, nothing's happened to me this time either, so far. In fact it's
been comparatively easy most of the time. But you get a better idea of
it from the papers than I could tell you.

Right now I'm sitting on the front porch of a house, at a chair
and table from inside. They were moved out to give us enough
sleeping room last night. It's a Spring day out here. There's a cherry
tree blossoming in front of me, and a row of them to my left. In back
of me on the road German civilians are carrying bedding and food;
slave laborers—Russians and Poles with a smattering of French,
Dutch, Belgians, and Italians—are walking to the rear, many still
wearing their original uniforms; a few prisoners are still coming by;
but dominating them all are the military vehicles taking over the
road. Groupings of Jerry equipment lie in the ditches and in the barns
where they were fired on and surrendered, or thought it over and
surrendered. And their bodies, too, lie in those places, with white
faces and huge tears and crushes. The buildings here are mostly
unharmed. The advantage, or disadvantage if you will, of a fast war.
That is, they are unharmed directly by the war. Indirectly speaking,
when we move into a house to spend the night, we really move in—
and the house moves out. But that isn't all that I see from here as I
write this. There's another side to it. In back of that cherry tree I told
you about, lies an open field. And in that open field are the bodies of
nine Americans. They were shot a day ago.

There's a description. Does that tell you what it's like for us here?
You wanted to know. But, no, I don't think that shows you. There's so
many added factors. There's the hopelessly unrelated relationship—of
objects, of course, of people. The superbly unusual becomes common.
In fact, unusualness itself is common. And you only realize it when
you sit down and think it over. You aren't aware of all this otherwise.

Maybe that helps a little more in telling you what it's like. I never
could actually tell you.[18] And I'll be eternally grateful that you'll
never know, when I see how many are affected by war, and to what

extent. We're one of the few families in the world not harmed by the war. That's pretty wonderful. I mean that. Nothing will happen to any of you now, and I know nothing will happen to me. You say I've had those last two years wasted. Well I don't agree with you, even though most of the guys here won't agree with me when I say so. I believe I've gotten out of them what I never would have otherwise. So all four of us are extremely lucky.

Lots of Love, Carl

———

According to Draper, "The chief immediate problems [in Hannover] were political, economic, and social. From a normal population of more than about 475,000, Hannover was down to about 250,000 Germans and 50–60,000 'displaced persons,' about half Westerners, including 10,000 to 20,000 Allied prisoners of war. . . . The 335th Infantry was left in Hannover as XIII Corps reserve."[19]

———

Carl turns twenty-one on April 11. Now he can vote. There's no mention of it in his letter.

11 April, 1945
Germany

Dear Mother and Dad,

Here we are again. This time I'm sitting in the office of a candy factory, which makes things nice. Everybody has bloated themselves by now, including me, of course. Oh, oh—word just came that the mail has caught up with us again and this time they brought packages too. Five sacks of it. Now I ask you, what better time since we've started this drive could we use packages, now that we're flooded with candy bars? Oh, well, c'est la guerre.

Which reminds me, we could use you over here. Did you ever try arguing when neither of you knew what the other was saying? Try it, it's a lot of fun, but rather exerting. But then, the fact that we've got weapons and these civilians haven't adds some weight to our arguments. You know, actually it's surprising how much you can make yourself understood without the aid of language. And you pick up a few phrases, which help considerably. Like the word for eggs (remember how I never used to eat eggs? It's different now. I've had eight at one sitting already, and fixed by myself, too, which makes the taste better, I believe.) and "nix vershstah," which is a universal answer and has quieting effects.[20]

Unless something surprising happens in the next ten hours, I'm going to be out five of my hard earned dollars. A while ago I made a bet that the war would be over by today. But now, from where I sit, still in the candy factory, it doesn't look as if I'm going to win.

Well, that rumor was no rumor. Two packages from you just came in. Candy and cookies. But don't worry. They won't be wasted. I'm disbursing the largesse, and no matter what you've heard, American equipment is better than Jerry and that includes edibles along with everything else from women to pistols.

Two letters from you this time but I got three a couple of days ago and one from Fred. So long with love. Carl

P.S. Here's a couple of souvenirs. The insignia is off of an officer's cap. Carl

P.P.S.—Our platoon sergeant just walked in with the most candy rations we've had in three weeks! How do they do it? This is why old soldiers get battle fatigue.

———

12 April 1945
Germany

Dear Folks,

How do you like this stationery? Pretty sharp, eh? One of the guys ran across a little print shop here. This place we're in is a paradise. I'm still talking about the candy factory I told you about yesterday. It's completely modern and completely equipped. There's a dentist office, which is now a barber shop, and a large chemical laboratory that I should say has at least five thousand dollars worth of equipment, which is now a wash-room, and there's an inter-office phone system, and showers. Oh, we're really living! Whee.

Recently I had more fun than I've had since I came over. Remember how I used to drive about five years ago when I first learned to drive? Well we got hold of three civilian cars and commenced chasing each other all over the scenery with them. Just like the good old days. Only trouble is that these little cars over here aren't made to be beaten around like that. But, anyways, we get a kick out of it.

Well, take it easy and behave yourselves.

Love to you Carl

The 84th liberated Ahlem on April 10 and Salzwedel on April 14, both satellite camps of the Neuengamme Concentration Camp complex.[21]

Draper had this to say of Salzwedel: "On the eastern edge of the town was a filthy concentration camp for 3000 women, 2700 Jewish women from Eastern Europe and 300 non-Jewish political prisoners from Western Europe. . . . Many of [the women] had come from the 'extermination camp' at Oswiecim (Auschwitz), Poland, and their sufferings had left deep marks. In Salzwedel, these women had worked in 12-hour shifts in the local munitions factory making shell casings for small arms."[22]

The 84th liberated the two camps, but it was the 333rd Regiment, not Carl's 335th. Afterwards, the captain summoned Carl. When he got to the waiting area there were three other Jewish soldiers. They all knew each other. There were just four Jews in the company.

The captain called for them because General Eisenhower passed down an order that any Jewish soldier who wanted to see a death camp could do so.[23] The army would arrange special transportation and take them there. The trip, they were told, would last a few days. They'd see a camp, get a tour, and return back to their unit afterward.

By this time, Carl had read about the death camps. The *Stars and Stripes* had written about the Americans liberating the camps. The soldiers had seen the pictures of the living skeletons and more. It was a shocking thing. The three other men accepted the offer. Carl declined, believing such inhumanity was better left unseen. For Carl, it was better to forgo the experience than to feel additional pain and horror. It was a decision he always regretted: "I would have liked to have had the experience to see it with my own eyes… see what was happening. See if there was some way I could be of help to some of these poor, suffering people."[24]

President Roosevelt passed away during his fourth term on April 12 after a stroke in Warm Springs, Georgia. He had been president since Carl was eight, making him the only president of whom Carl would have

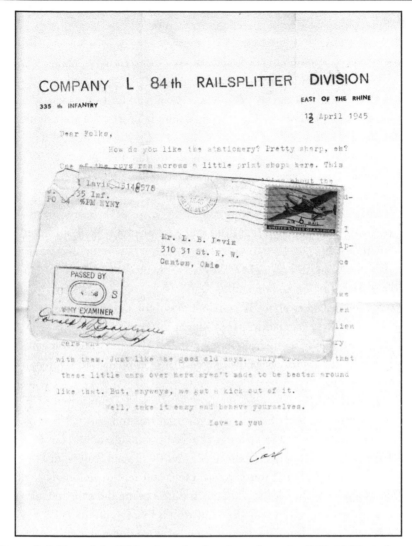

Figure 8-1. East of the Rhine letterhead and envelope, April 12, 1945. *Author collection.*

awareness. Germany's statement? "At this moment when fate has removed the greatest war criminal of all time from the earth, the turning point of this war shall be decided."[25] Vice President Harry Truman was sworn in as president the same day.

B. Sprengel & Co [Hannover chocolate company]
15 April 1945

Dear Mother and Dad,

That account of the six people in a car meant for two, as you
guessed, failed to impress me. As one example of why not you should
have seen a jeep I rode on about a week ago. On it were nine of us
plus all our equipment, plus a couple hundred pounds of general
equipment, plus a machine gun. And back in the States it was
considered heresy to ride five men in a jeep!

Did you sell my stock yet as you said you were? You say you're
sure it will get higher but that I did make a fair profit. Well, all I can
say to that is "Hah." I'd call 100% more than a fair profit, and what
makes you think it'll go higher? Of course by now it's probably up to
20 and all this sounds damn silly.

As for that story about Mr. Ginsberg and the police, you can
blame everything on Daddy.[26] He brought the thing up in the first
place in a letter he wrote from the plant. Tell him to try and remember
very hard. And if that doesn't work, wait til I get home and we'll start
all over again.

There's a slight misunderstanding as to what I meant when I
spoke of the covenants I swore to in my confirmation:

I certainly was not referring to the Ten Commandments. For I
believe in them absolutely, their need, and their good. But what I
meant was four beliefs I was supposed to swear to, the coming of
Zion, the immortality of the soul, our religion being the true one, and
one other one along the same line but which I've forgotten.

It's a shame you misunderstood me because that was really a fine
sermon you wrote me. But then it does half fit because you include
"the acceptance of the faith of your people" in it, too. And that part
I'll argue with. I see no reason why "my" people should choose truer
faiths than any other people. There are a dozen different things I can
think of to say now, but they're all insufficient in expressing what I'd
like them to. So we'd better wait until I can say it instead of write it.
Maybe that'll be better.

And good-night with Love Carl

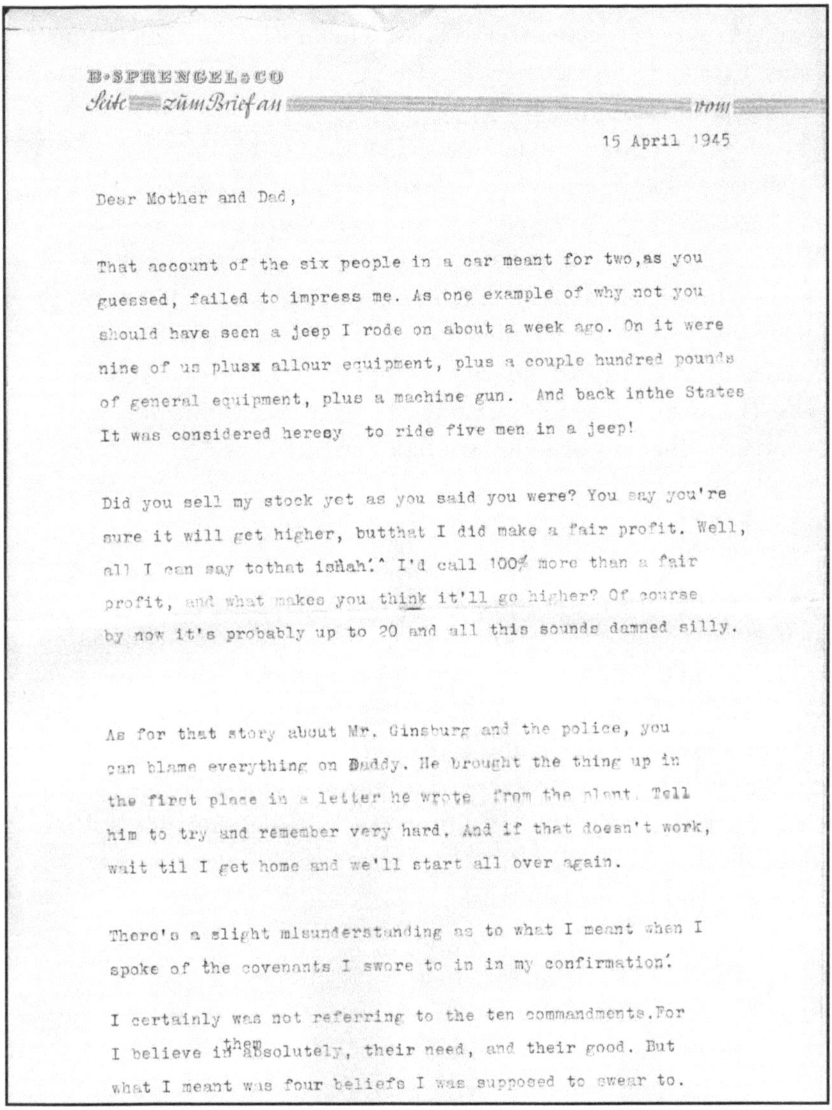

B·SPRENGEL&CO
Seite ═══ zum Brief an ═════════════════════ vom ═══

15 April 1945

Dear Mother and Dad,

That account of the six people in a car meant for two, as you
guessed, failed to impress me. As one example of why not you
should have seen a jeep I rode on about a week ago. On it were
nine of us plus allour equipment, plus a couple hundred pounds
of general equipment, plus a machine gun. And back inthe States
It was considered heresy to ride five men in a jeep!

Did you sell my stock yet as you said you were? You say you're
sure it will get higher, butthat I did make a fair profit. Well,
all I can say tothat isñah!ˆ I'd call 100% more than a fair
profit, and what makes you think it'll go higher? Of course
by now it's probably up to 20 and all this sounds damned silly.

As for that story about Mr. Ginsburg and the police, you
can blame everything on Daddy. He brought the thing up in
the first place in a letter he wrote from the plant. Tell
him to try and remember very hard. And if that doesn't work,
wait til I get home and we'll start all over again.

There's a slight misunderstanding as to what I meant when I
spoke of the covenants I swore to in in my confirmation.

I certainly was not referring to the ten commandments.For
I believe in them absolutely, their need, and their good. But
what I meant was four beliefs I was supposed to swear to.

Figure 8-2. B. Sprengel & Co. letterhead, April 15, 1945. *Author collection.*

16 April 1945
Germany

Dear Folks,
I think you're falling down on the mail a little. Where's your
patriotism?
Got a package from you yesterday. The one with cookies, raisins,
and pop-corn in it. Thank you. It was well-received. We aren't in that

candy factory any more. Also received a letter dated January 8, which must have had a difficult voyage.

Nothing new to report, except that yesterday I finally rode a motorcycle for the first time. Remember when that subject was brought up when I was in high school? Well, I still want one.[27]

You shift gears with your foot, and work the clutch with your hand. A little hard to get on to at first, as you can imagine. I don't know if they're all that way, or if they make 'em over here like they do their type-writers. I don't think they're any different, though—their cars and trucks are just the same as ours.

The weather has been wonderful lately. Here's hoping it continues. How're you doing over there? Write.

Love Carl

Draper noted that on April 16, "the division's rear echelon . . . was moving from Hannover to Salzwedel." Five days later, on April 21, the 84th launched their final combat operations, although they did not know it at the time.[28]

A few battalions, including Carl's, were "to clear the river line from Wahrenberg to Pretzetze, a distance of approximately 20 miles. . . . On the right flank, the 333rd's 3rd Battalion met very little resistance, but the 1st and the 3rd battalions from the 335th had to pay for their success."[29]

Draper takes us into the battle:

> The 335th's 3rd Battalion finished its share of the operation by 3:10 p.m. The enemy put up a fight for Gartow, a village about 2 miles from the Elbe, behind road blocks and houses. Our troops were strafed by enemy planes on the south side of the town. Some resistance was also put up in the village of Kapern. A few more villages were cleaned out on April 22 and the job was finished. The 84th's river line was 40 miles long.[30]

Carl could recount the Gartow battle decades later. It was his fifth brush with death. The war was essentially over; what was required in these final days was caution, planning, and steady progress. Yet the captain in Carl's company called a meeting to tell his GIs that he had volunteered them for a mission. The company was not at full strength and had fewer than one hundred men. The men were to take the village of Gartow from resisting German soldiers who had successfully repelled a different American company. The captain proudly told the GIs that there had been a regimental meeting at which the colonel had asked for volunteers for the Gartow mission. "I'm so proud of you," the captain said.

Carl recalled that he and all the GIs were thinking, "Why, you sorry son of a gun, you are seeking glory with our guts."[31] There was no enthusiasm this late in the war for heroics. But the order had come down, and the next day Carl and his company were sent to take the village, located a mile away from their current position. The idea was that a rapid frontal assault, without any artillery support, would allow the infantry to surprise the village defenders.

Carl's company made a stealthy, running attack across some level fields. Carl was carrying forty or fifty pounds more than anyone else and couldn't run as fast—but he was doing the best he could.

Near the village, the troops reached barbed-wire fencing, which was affixed to metal poles. The men used the poles to leap over the wire. When Carl got to the fence, he propped his BAR on the other side of the wiring, and began to climb over. But the moment he put down his weapon, all hell broke loose.

The Germans had been watching the GIs advance all along, and had previously ranged all of their weapons to the fence, knowing the GIs would have to congregate there to cross. Indeed, once the company reached the fence, they were a perfect target. The Germans let loose with machine-gun and rifle fire and some mortars. There was a tremendous amount of ammunition spent.

Carl immediately hit the ground. Because he had just placed his weapon across the fence, he was weaponless. It seemed like the entire company, except for Carl, was shooting back. Worse, the Germans could recognize the BAR and direct fire at Carl's position.

As the fighting started to shift to one side of the field, Carl was able to clear the fence, grab his gun and follow the momentum of the action, which was sending the fight to the left side of the village.

Carl was running, hitting the ground, in short spurts. The fire was so intense that GIs were scattering or falling to the ground, wounded or dead.

Moving to the left, Carl could see the GIs were seeking cover in a drainage ditch, half-filled with icy water. Carl jumped into the ditch with about a half dozen other guys from his company. They were up to their waists in icy water, but the ditch allowed them to keep their heads while taking in the situation.

Carl and the GIs were quick to observe the Germans fighting from foxholes and trenches. A few of the GIs stayed in the drainage ditch. Carl and a few others decided to follow the ditch into town. Once in Gartow, a sergeant pointed Carl to a barn-like structure and told him to see if he could find a firing position inside. Carl shot the padlock off the building and found a type of office on a second floor. That gave him the vantage point from which to shoot down on the German foxholes.

In the course of combat, Carl may have killed a dozen, or two dozen men. But Carl knew of one single death for sure at Gartow:

> I was at the second story window. I saw a German trying to cross an open field, running in the direction of where the main action was. I took a quick shot at him while he was running to try to slow him down. It works, because he hits the ground on a plain, open field.
>
> I thought that was pretty dumb, that he just lies there and doesn't move. Then I tried to decide what to do. He's mine, and I could have him if I wanted. . . . I decided that I would kill him. He's not surrendering . . . I didn't want to kill him. Do I really want to take a human life, after having shot at him, and he's just lying there?
>
> I decided, well, this is a hell of a time to start to become a conscientious objector. I finally decided that, yes, I would kill him. I'm ashamed to admit that the final reason was that this would be an opportunity to have the experience of positively killing someone and knowing that I'd killed.
>
> I wouldn't have to wonder anymore what it felt like to kill somebody. So, I did. I just shot him. . . . He never moved. I've had a queasy experience about it ever since. It's the only absolute time I ever positively knew I killed someone. . . . We had a patrol going out the next day and we went right by the guy I killed. He never moved a muscle. Head down. I picked up his head and felt brains and gore.
>
> What it really meant, the position of the head and position of his body, was that my first quick shot—where I had tried to slow him down—had actually hit him in the head. I know it had to have been my first shot because he never moved when he hit the ground. So, all the time I was trying to decide should I take this life or shouldn't I, I in fact had

already taken his life. That has stuck with me very strongly
ever since.[32]

The Germans hadn't thought about the GIs getting behind them, and they found themselves outflanked. After about twenty minutes, the remaining Germans decided to surrender. They were taking too many casualties.

That was Carl's final moment of combat. Bloody and pointless. Stupid Germans for not surrendering. Stupid captain for ordering the assault.[33]

And even seventy years later, in some corner of his mind, Carl held on to the ugly necessity of death in combat and the face of the young German soldier.

After Gartow, Carl's unit stopped at the Elbe, about fifty miles west of Berlin. Eisenhower ordered the Americans not to cross the river. That bank belonged to the Russians, who arrived there a few days later.[34]

The First and Ninth armies looked forward to seeing their Russian counterparts. Around the twenty-third, the 84th Division painted a large welcome sign—in Russian. MacDonald adds, "The division canceled all artillery fire beyond the Elbe lest it hit Russian troops, but rescinded the order when German soldiers on the east bank began blatantly to sunbathe."[35]

—

April 24 1945
Germany

Dear Folks,

Haven't written you for awhile, but I imagine by this time you know why. And there's still nothing wrong with me, so stop worrying.

Naturally, I can't tell you what we've been doing lately, but I've still got the same job, automatic rifle-man in an infantry line company, and I can tell you some of the towns I've been in before. I don't believe I ever did mention them. Remember when I was back in Holland resting? We were on the outskirts of Haarlem, then, a large town in southern Holland, quite modern and only slightly beat up. There is a rest center there—only for individuals, though, not for any unit. Guys got passes there for a day or two while on line—but which we took advantage of. Or at least the movies and donuts part of it.

Then the drive from the Roer to the Rhine, which I'll tell you about when I see you, and another rest in a suburb of Krefeld which our company had helped to take on that drive. We had to be in the outskirts of that town, because that was almost the only part of it left. I'd say the main section of town was 80 to 85 percent destroyed. The people said it was mostly done on one three hour raid two years before. And it had been a town larger than Canton.

Then we took off across the Rhine and it has been both surprisingly easy and surprisingly difficult. We did little until we hit the Weser River. And it took us awhile to go from there to Hannover. That's the place where the candy factory I told you about is located. And that town, I should say, is about 95 per cent destroyed. At that time I thought all the hard fighting was over, but I've change my mind since.

Got a package from you yesterday—box of O'Henry's. Very nice, very nice. Thank you and thank you also for the birthday present. That, I can always use, starting after a while, of course.

How about sending some free hand copies of those plans for the new part of the plant? I imagine you've got them completed by now? And for the house, too. I've got an idea for you—since you're building the plant and the house at the same time—why don't you just build them together? Dad wouldn't have so far to go to work, and I know it would make Mr. H. much happier, with your orders, Ma. You know, if you were over here, you'd probably do just that. Every barn over here is the same building as the house. They're not just connected—the only way you can tell from the outside which part of the building is barn and which house, is by the windows. And that goes for many small businesses and factories, too. But then Sugardale might be a little large to be in their same building class. Maybe you'd better not do it after all.

They're probably some other items—but I can't think of them now. Sooooo 'Bye for now, with Love Carl

———

28 April 1945
Germany

Dear Folks,
Well, the war is still going on, and I'm still in it, and I still haven't suffered any ill-effects from it, and that's about all there is to

tell you, since the mail hasn't been getting to us too well lately. How is everything going with you?

Except for the fighting part of it we're still leading a pretty pleasant life (I've lived in more houses over here than I've been in back in the States.) And it looks like it'll continue that way, with little or more of the fighting part of it in prospect.

About a week ago we picked up a couple of unofficial reinforcements for our platoon—two "Rooskies" as they call themselves, "Russians" to you. We have a couple guys that speak Russian and interpret for them. We gave one a rifle and one a Tommy-gun. They're O.K., but a little excitable. One time we were firing on several Jerries running away from us at about 700 yards and the one with the Tommy-gun ran out to help out and started madly firing away. The only trouble is that a Tommy-gun has an effective range of about 50 yards and all he was doing was ploughing up the dirt 200 yards in front of us.

They spend most of their time laughing and generally enjoying themselves. And they drink schnapps like water, which I guess it is to them, after vodka.

I went before the division O.C.S. board day before yesterday and took a complete physical exam for it. I know I passed the latter, and believe I passed the former. Anyways, I should find out in a week or two. And if I'm accepted I'll go back to France—Paris?—for the course, which is now eight weeks. Well, we'll see.

Love –Carl

P.S.—Please send another box of candy love Carl

—

30 April 1945
Germany

Dear Mom and Dad,

Got the letter from Chicago telling of your adventures there. You didn't say, but it sounds like another meat packers' convention. I hope your entire stay was as pleasant as the first part. Glad you liked *Othello* so much—I knew you would. Did José Ferrer play Iago again in Chicago?[36] He was the outstanding part in the production I saw.

About a month ago I read a condensation in the Readers Digest of the book *Report on Russia* by Somebody White (there's too many of them—I won't guarantee their first name.)[37] I think it was about the January issue—we get them kind of late—but you must have read it. Anyways, it impressed me. Now, do you remember those two Russians who are with our platoons? I told you about them a few days ago. Well I decided to question one of them in connection with that article. He is the more intelligent of the two—in fact in the States he'd pass for an outstanding college man or young executive, quite different from almost all the other Russians I've seen. First I found out as much about him from him as I could. He's 23 years old, had had 10 years of schooling and 6 months of the Red Army's West Point when war broke out and he was placed in the paratroopers. He was captured early in the war and remained a prisoner for three years until we released him. He had tried repeatedly to escape, had been whipped and spent 6 months altogether in solitary confinement. He was considered dangerous and that we could easily believe. He's quite alert, quick, and capable. (and we were beside him in action since he's been with us.)

He does not belong to the party. When I questioned him about it, he seemed to consider it (the questioning) foolish. He said that now everyone is working for one thing, and party lines made no difference. I asked him if before the war, he had read of riots and disorders and starvation among the American workers. He said that in 1932 and 3 there were riots, but he had heard of none since.

He said he had heard that the equipment we had sent to Russia had been important in defeating Germany. Thinking of what White had said of the Red Lieutenant who was ignorant of our aid in equipment, I had asked him about it. But of course, you must remember here that this man had been in Germany since 1942—not in Russia, and he had ready and accurate access to news—most freed slaves we questioned knew as much of the European battle situation at the time as we. And with this in mind I talked mostly about pre-war subjects when I could.

He was in no way subservient or over-eager to please, I should perhaps add. In fact his attitude was proud and politely unscared, almost aggressive, if anything.

I told him there is one car to every four persons in America. He said he believes that, and added that in Russia the figure is closer to one to four hundred. He readily admitted that our country is more industrialized than his, that the standard of living is higher. He has an entirely realistic view of the present and pre-war condition of Russia, and what Stalin has done for it. He knows what's going on. He realizes, although not fully, the comparison of the U.S. and the U.S.S.R. This is not to say he is cynical concerning the communists and their work and works and promises. He has faith, high faith, that they are helping Russia. He said continually—"if it were not for the war" in speaking of improvements and plans for his country. He is a patriot. He became almost angry when one of the guys asked if he thought any of the Russians would stay here after the war.

I was surprised that he didn't take politics and the party with the deadly seriousness that I had expected of Europeans. Just as we would say in explanations "There are two groups in my country— Democrats and Republicans" with a tone of voice indicating that the fact is unimportant in the greatness of America's being—just so he said there are two groups—those that belong to the party and those that do not—in his.

He's enthusiastic and optimistic concerning the future life in Russia.[38] I'm not saying that's representative of Russia's young intellectuals, because his personality is enthusiastic, and not optimistic. Make from that what you can.

One thing more—Russians, not just one Russian, mind you—are as Americans. They are more like us than any other people I've come across.[39] They're more of a peasant people, of course, and one allows for that. Out of all this: general conclusion—Government is an over-rated factor; specific conclusion—what/who the hell can you believe? But that's an exaggeration, of course.

While writing this, your letter came written on your return from Chicago. I think your compliments made me stage-struck. This letter should be much better written. Need order and coherence and timing.

I'll answer it later. Sleepy. Love Carl.

———

Adolf Hitler died on April 30, 1945, of a self-inflicted gunshot wound in Berlin. His suicide was not reported until at least May 1.

———

4 May 1945
Germany

Dear Mom and Dad,

No, I'm not in a candy factory again. Just managed to run into another typewriter, this time an old, beat-up, last-century model. Note the oil all over the paper.

A batch of your letters came in. Telling of going to Chicago and what you are doing there. So you've become a porcelain addict, Mother. Well, sounds pretty nice. I'd like to help out, but I don't think I'll be able to at present. You see, the only articles we may send home are captured military ones, with the exception of pistols. And of course all packages are censored. So maybe I'll get a chance to go to France on a furlough or something sometime, and if and when I do I'm pretty sure I can get hold of something good for you. And don't worry about the cost. Yes I imagine they would be quite expensive, but German pistols are almost literally worth their weight in silver to the rear echelon men back there. So I guess I can work something out of all that. Forgot to mention, we are allowed to send things like that from countries other than Germany, which I guess you gathered by now.

Dad, when I read what you said about Roosevelt's death being so shocking to everyone because he has come to personify the government to us, it struck me that that was the reason. And I'd never thought of that before, or heard anyone else mention it. I think you hit it.

We're back to fighting another Battle of the road-blocks, which is boring, but safe. Two of us on two hours, off six, which is considered to be a good deal. Especially since at our post there was a little shack with a stove and a bed. I said was, because this morning when we went out there on our relief all we saw was two guys with sheepish looks on their faces, and some smoldering embers. Looks kind of bad when you're standing guard and your house burns down. So on our relief we spent the two hours tearing down a nearby shack and building another one of our own. How'd you like to have your house built in two hours? I'll give you a demonstration some time. Of course, a certain amount of result is sacrificed to time.

I'll write more when I get more time. Too many guys want this machine anyways.

Until the next time, love Carl

P.S. How about another package?

———

Before the Soviets appeared on their side of the Elbe, thousands of Germans tried to come over to American territory, believing the Americans would treat them more humanely than the Russians, who had been fighting the Germans for years on the eastern front.

For several days, the Elbe's far shore was black with German uniforms, maybe three quarters of a mile deep, and there were just a few rowboats available to the surrendering forces.

On just one day, "May 2, a total of 15,954 German soldiers ferried and swam over to [the 84th's] shore," Draper wrote. "By May 8, the last day a count was made, the total number of prisoners for the Rhine-Elbe operation as a whole was 62,342. The [84th's] total number for almost six months of combat was 70,109."[40]

Indeed, the surrendering forces were so numerous that the US Army "agreed to accept surrendering Wehrmacht troops only if they brought their own food, kitchens, and medical supplies. More than seventy thousand eventually reached the west bank."[41]

———

By V-E Day (Victory in Europe Day), the fighting had already ended. There was nobody left to fight on the continent. In effect, the war had been over for some days before the announcement came.

Carl was stationed in a small village near Heidelberg. It was in a liberated zone. At that point Carl was just being moved around in trucks. From a GI's perspective, Carl typically couldn't tell what the overall situation was except from what he read in *Stars and Stripes*.

Carl could not relate this in his letters, but his company was occupying a war factory, used to produce "V Weapons," the rockets and unmanned "flying bombs" that Hitler rained on London during the final year of the war:

> In fact, we were ordered to move to a V bomb factory, which
> I remember. That's where we were—in the V bomb factory—
> when the word officially came down that the Germans had
> surrendered. It was a factory in the woods with a great number
> of small buildings. We went in the buildings and there are crude

jet airplanes with an open cockpit and just very few controls and gauges on them. They were V bombs meant for pilots, which I never, ever heard about before or since. But they were built to be piloted. They were jet bombs. I never, ever heard about them being used, but we sure saw them. We assumed they were kind of like kamikazes.[42]

When the word came down on V-E Day, there was no party. The biggest thing we did was open all the shutters and let the light shine outside after living for many, many months in blackout conditions—sheer blackout conditions. The biggest change that could be would be to let light shine out through a window, so we did. [Laughter][43]

⎯

According to army statistics, listed as "tentative," in over 150 days of combat, the 84th suffered 6,561 battle casualties, among them 1,235 men killed and 4,486 wounded. Non-battle casualties were at 3,250, for a casualty total of 9,811 men, or some 70 percent of the division.[44]

⎯

Postmark May 7

Dear Mother,

This letter I'm writing to you alone, because it's to commemorate your day.

I regret that I have to be separated from you in order to appreciate and understand just what you've done for me, Mom. But at least I do now, I believe.

Do you remember how you used to come in and sit on our beds and talk to Fred and me? I used to look forward to that, during the day. You did the most for us during those hours, you know.

And I guess you took quite a hectoring from us in return. And we've all had some rather stormy sessions. But I can't say it wasn't fun—can you?

The thing to say at this time is I'm very lucky having you for a mother. And that's what everyone says. It's hard to be impersonal about such a personal subject as a mother, but if I could be I'm

positive I'd still say just that—I'm very lucky that you're my mother.
There certainly are very few that have for mothers the intelligence,
or the discrimination, or the appreciation of the fine, or the moral
dignity, or the respect, or the any number of things that you have. So I
really do consider myself very lucky.

For all those things I mentioned in this letter, for all those more
things I've thought of and not mentioned, and for all those many more
things I've not even thought of—thank you, Mother, dear.

And many more Mothers' Days, with love, Carl

8 May 1945
Germany

Dear Mother and Dad,
Just got four letters from you, 26th to 30th, and a package. Don't
know what's in the package, since I haven't had a chance to open
it yet, but I didn't approve of what was in the letters. Wow, Mother,
why in the world did you worry because you didn't hear from me? I
thought that by this time you'd know there'd be times when it'd be
impossible for me to write to you. And that was for only a week. I
haven't written for two weeks or more on occasions already, haven't I?

If it weren't for the anxiety it caused, your worrying about things
such as poisoned candy and motorcycle rides would be really funny.
I wonder if you can see the humor in it. It's like congratulating a
musician after a concert on the way his shoes were shined. And now
that the war is over, you don't have anything to worry about, do you?
You'll probably think of something, though.

How are you coming along by this time on your dual piano stuff,
Mom? Sounds pretty nice. Looks like you're getting into the fling of
things now that most of your family's moved out.

Thanks for the five dollar bill. I got your money's worth out of
it, but probably not in the sense you expected. Everybody got a
good look at it, you see, and there was at least five dollars' worth of
morale-building as a result. Looks pretty good after this play-money
appearing currency these countries use. And I've still got the five. Do
you know what my expenses have been for the past four months? Not
counting that bet, I've spent altogether about six dollars.

Just opened the package. O'Henry's and all that gum? I mean, how'd you ever get all that? Say, it wouldn't be possible, would it, to get hold of some different kind of candy bar. I'm starting to get a little tired of them. But then, they are a lot better than nothing, I'll admit. Love –Carl

As the months went on, Carl's attitude changed from excitement—wonderful, terrific—to one of fatalism—sooner or later I'm going to get it, my turn has to come. And then the war came to an end. He didn't get it. He was still alive, and it wasn't his turn. Yet his satisfaction was quiet. The war was not over.[45]

"This is a solemn but glorious hour," Truman told the nation. "We must work to finish the war. Our victory is only half won. The West is free, but the East is still in bondage to the treacherous Japanese."[46]

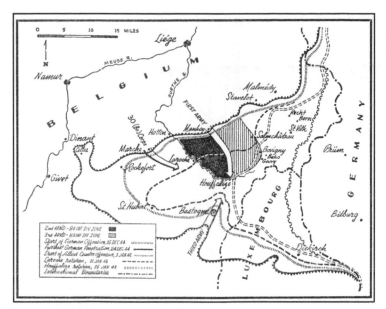

The 84th Division in the Battle of the Bulge.

Source: Draper, *84th Infantry Division*, 85.

84th Division: From the Siegfried Line to the Elbe.

Source: Draper, *84th Infantry Division*, 228.

June 1944. A happy GI wearing the only decoration worth wearing: Combat Infantryman Badge. *Author collection*.

Hannover as found by the 84th Infantry Division. Photo by Maurice Miller. *Used with permission of Mark Miller Studios.*

The 335th welcomes you to the Rhine. Photo by Maurice Miller. *Used with permission of Mark Miller Studios.*

Krefeld, Carl's final battle. Photo by Maurice Miller. *Used with permission of Mark Miller Studios.*

President Truman reviews the 84th. Photo by Maurice Miller. *Used with permission of Mark Miller Studios.*

Jack Benny entertains at a USO show. Photo by Maurice Miller. *Used with permission of Mark Miller Studios.*

PART III

After the War

9
Heidelberg and Hamelin Occupation
May–June 1945

After the intensity of war, occupation was an abrupt shift. Once boasting the strongest military in the world, Germany was reduced to a shocked, defeated nation. This former nucleus of Europe was now filled with Nazi prisoners, mangled towns, and ubiquitous US forces.

The novelist Heinrich Boll described the shattered state of postwar Germany: "Everyone possessed just their lives and, in addition, whatever fell into their hands: coal, wood, books, building materials. Everyone justifiably could have accused everyone else of theft."[1]

As writer Earl Ziemke explained, the reason for a complete occupation was simple:

> Among the various reasons for the German military resurgence after World War I, one frequently cited was the failure of the Rhineland occupation—because it affected only a small part of Germany—to bring home to the Germans the meaning of defeat. Maintained by the French and the British until 1930, the Rhineland occupation had given the Germans an object on which to focus their resentments without giving the Allies any worthwhile leverage. . . . Consequently, the World War II planners always considered a total occupation to be necessary to guarantee success in preventing a future German outburst.[2]

For the thousands of GIs stationed in Germany, their mission in Europe seemed to have ended, but the war wasn't over. Even as it was beaten back, Imperial Japan fought with ferocity. The prospect of fighting in Japan made peacetime Germany seem but a lull.

In Germany, GIs undertook basic tasks such as drill formations, guard duties, and language lessons while coping with a peacetime lassitude, and wondering what might be next for them in the Pacific:

> On V-E Day, Eisenhower had sixty-one U.S. Divisions, 1,622,000 men in Germany, and a total force in Europe numbering 3,077,000. When the shooting ended, the divisions in the field became the occupation troops, charged with maintaining law and order and establishing the Allied military presence in the defeated nation. . . . The occupation troops maintained border control stations, maintained checkpoints at road junctions and bridges, sent out roving patrols to apprehend curfew and circulation violators, and kept stationary guards at railroad bridges, Army installations, DP camps, jails, telephone exchanges, factories, and banks.[3]

The men of Company K remembered their occupation days:

> Postwar discipline—keeping two hundred healthy young GIs with time on their hands out of trouble—proved a major headache. K Company maintained a training program of sorts, and the Army set up trade schools and university classes, formed divisional baseball and football teams, and instituted liberal leave programs. But getting drunk, and brawling with civilians or rear-echelon types, remained a problem for all the companies in the division. KP duty and restriction to the company area for a week were punishment handed out for minor infractions. Digging a hole six feet square and six feet deep and then refilling it, together with forfeiture of pay, was reserved for more serious infractions.[4]

Frank Freese described occupation duty in the 84th somewhat similarly:

> Up until VJ Day we figured what we were doing was just sitting there waiting for ships to take us to Japan. But we would go around and raid towns looking for contraband or hidden

weapons or something like that which we never found, but
sometimes we would go through a town and check all the
identification cards that the Germans had to make sure there
weren't an SS or any high powered Nazi's hiding there and we
never found any of those hiding there either. Little jobs. Guard
duty sort of things. We also had athletic programs so that we
formed a swimming team and football teams and track teams.[5]

One of the most severe breaches was when soldiers violated the strict
American policy of "non-fraternization," which proscribed social contact
with German citizens: "The Germans needed to be made conscious of
their guilt and of the contempt in which they were held by the people
of the world. They needed to see the 'error of their ways' and were to be
'held at arm's length' . . . the most practical means . . . was to restrict public
contacts. The troops ought not to be billeted in German households, eat
in the same restaurant as the Germans, or attend their religious services."[6]

POWs were another matter. At the start of occupation, Carl found
himself near a temporary barbed wire enclosure set up for German prisoners of war. Several of the GIs decided just out of curiosity to go down
to look at them. Carl did, too.

One German said to Carl in English, "Why are you Americans here
anyways? This should be a European affair. Why are Americans here?"

Carl was able to say to him, "We are here because Germany declared
war on America."

He didn't believe Carl. He spoke to another German soldier. The
other German soldier explained and Carl could hear the first German say,
"Ja, Ja. The American is right." He had been unaware that his country had
started the war with the America.

Carl was assigned to a small town, which held a camp for displaced
Russians and Polish people, before moving on to Heidelberg, a beautiful
city untouched by bombs. "Having become accustomed in the Rhineland to seeing nothing but flattened cities, the Americans were surprised
to find Heidelberg completely undamaged," said Ziemke. "The university was intact, and the shops and banks stayed open while the city
changed hands."[7]

May 9 1945
Germany

Dear Mom and Dad,

To answer your letters—Yes, there is a chance I might get a picture to send you. We've been taking snapshots with liberated film and cameras. Have to send them back to some-where in rear echelon to be developed and it takes a couple months. So sometime, sooner, or later, I'll be sending you some of them, probably.

See where my old division—the 69th made the big headlines? Wrong regiment, though. Meeting the "Rooskies," I mean.[8]

See if you can find [censored] on the map.[9] You'll need a big one. It's near [censored] and on the [censored]. That's where we were a week and a half ago. Put a circle around it and I'll tell you about it when I see you.[10]

Well, Folks, keep all your chins up and take it easy. Love to you
Carl

———

Carl applied for officer's training one final time during the latter part of his combat experience. The word came down that there was Officer Candidate's School, OCS, in France, near Paris. One of Carl's officers had been a college guy and he asked, "Lavin, are you going to apply to it?" Carl did and filled out the papers.

Carl did not hear anything more about it for another couple of months. All of a sudden, the orders came down that he was to report to officers' school in Paris—just as the fighting was ending. Instead of a thirteen-week program it was a six-week program, so the soldiers were called "Six-week Wonders"—soldiers made lieutenants in six weeks.

Carl had done his best to apply to OCS at Waco, in Queens, and in Shelby. It seemed that the fourth time was the charm.

But the afternoon before Carl was supposed to travel to Paris, his company commander called him in and read him a report that OCS program had been canceled because the war in Europe was over.

The fourth time was not a charm. The fourth time was just another disappointment—but in some respects this particular setback was okay with Carl. Becoming a lieutenant meant Carl would have been more likely to move to the Pacific front and also to have a longer military obligation. Still, at the moment it was bad news.

13 May 1945
Germany

Dear Folks,

Today at this time I expected to be on my way to O.C.S., as I had told you, and had been told. However, last night they told me something else—the whole deal has been cancelled. Didn't think I wanted it very bad before, but now I realize I'd been counting on it. Or rather, counting on it as much as anyone could (count on anything) who's been in the army as long as I have.

That probably had something to do with the fact that I feel homesick now, I believe. It's a full and lovely Spring-summer day now. There are green fields and trees, a light wind, and a crystal sky. And I'm listening to music that is good on the radio. Now, that's a lot of beauty, and I should feel happy because of it. But I don't. I don't know how I feel, but homesick probably comes close to it. I guess it's just the reaction after the intensity.

We start a training schedule, which seems silly, but which is most likely what I and a great many others need right now.

I imagine you've read and heard quite a bit of speculation as to my immediate fate, haven't you? Well, I feel rather certain that I'll go back to the States, get a furlough, and go to the Pacific. [11]

And you'd better not wish me to come home soon, either. I'm sure you see why. I think the War Department will have more "battle fatigue" cases in these next few months than they've had all the rest of the way, with everybody wanting so badly to go home, and wanting so badly not to go home at the same time.

Don't expect quite as many letters from me as you've been getting. I haven't been feeling, and I don't feel now, and I don't think I will feel, much like writing. I'll admit it's selfish, but I wish you well, and I hope you do keep up your tempo, as much as you can.[12]

Love to both of you Carl

P.S.—Read where they're cutting down our rations ten per cent? Help! Send a package, please. Love Carl

"Of course I was not a Nazi, but what could I do—I was one man against ten million, so I had to play along. Let me say in all candor thank God you are here and you won and this terrible evil is over," a German POW said to Carl. Carl's conclusion? When the war was over, you couldn't find a Nazi in all of Germany. "No one is a Nazi. No one ever was," war correspondent Martha Gellhorn wrote. "It would sound better if it were set to music. Then the Germans could sing this refrain."[13]

15 May 1945
Germany

Dear Mother and Dad,

Now that the fighting is over for us, for a while, have you ever wondered just why we fought? What made us expose ourselves to, and commit, those acts of violence, when they so directly oppose our desires and instincts?[14]

Of course, we were forced to do it, had we refused, the discomfort of our punishment would have been less than the discomfort most of us experienced in battle. So it couldn't have been force. It had to be something greater.

As I see it, it was a power, of two distinct components. The one drawing; the other driving. That which drew us was an end, a goal. Freedom. I have often heard, and never believed, that men would sacrifice much for freedom. But it is true. We fought for freedom. Freedom from the army.[15]

And I'm not being facetious. In spite of the many kindnesses of the copy-writers, we are men and not Gods. Consider what freedom of the army means to us; freedom of decision, of leisure, of vocation, of respect. Those are the only Four Freedoms we have been deprived of, and therefore the primary ones to consider. That is what we fought for.

I said we are men and not Gods. We are also men and not animals. And it is because that second power, the one which drives, exists within us. It's a finer one. In fact, it's even too fine to see, and I don't know what it is. But Pride and Duty and Dignity have a lot to do with it. Whatever it is, it has us get up and run forward when we know the chances are we'll get hit if we do. After it is over we wouldn't do it again for any amount of money, but at the time that it is necessary most of us will do it. Most of us are what they call heroes.

Incidentally, most of us are cowards, too. It depends on what most of the other men are, upon the occasion. That's one fact neither of these arguments takes into account. So we did what we did also because everyone else was doing it and we were expected to do it too.[16]

That is why we fought. I started to say that about a week or so ago, but had a little trouble putting it down. Still sounds kind of sluggish to me.[17]

Yes, I really could use some reading material. Good literature is difficult to get hold of here. So I'd be very pleased to get your Olympic Yankee or anything else you've got hanging around loose.[18] You know what I like.

And while you're doing some sending, why not include a package of candy? It could be used.

One of the guys in the platoon got a letter saying he was seen in a March of Time in the drive from the Roer to the Rhine walking along the road.[19] Well, if he was, which he probably wasn't, so was I, although I also probably wasn't. Verschtay? Or something.

Take care of yourselves. Love Carl

———

At a Displaced Person's camp:
17 May 1945
Germany

Dear Mother and Dad,

Yesterday was as interesting as any I've enjoyed for quite some time. I attended a Polish peasant dance, discussed the modern dances and the Russian occupation of Latvia with two ladies from Riga, argued the merits of capitalism, French composers, and everything else from propaganda to army uniforms with a concert violinist from Poland, and gave a lecture on the wonders of America to a very attentive audience. An informal lecture, I'd better add.

I had about a two-hour conversation with the violinist. First I learned his story. He was taken by the Russians in 1939 and placed in a labor battalion. When Germany invaded Russia he was captured again, at the defensive line protecting Moscow, and again put to work, this time in a factory in Poland. He remained there until the Russian drive through Poland, when the Germans brought him back to this place.

He's now thirty-nine. He used to play first violin in one of the best symphonic orchestras in Poland. He speaks Polish, Russian, and German well, French fairly well, and English—wellll?—period. He has a strong face and a strong build.

He has an unusual mind. While talking with him, I taught him five or six words, which he used after in the conversation correctly and continuously. He asked me if he could get a better pair of pants, and when I said a soldier might go with him to take a pair away from some German, he was horrified. He said, smilingly, that he is not a "gangster." He wanted to go to America and asked insistently about his chances for getting a position there. For his experiences he has no feeling of bitterness or retribution. He didn't consider the past, only the future. He said that, although he had not played in four years, he could practice two hours a day for two weeks and regain his form.

Those figures seemed a little suspicious to me, and that is what prompted the discussion on composers. I asked what pieces he knows. Well, I think he was telling the truth. Anyways, he knows a hell of a lot more about the subject than I. I said there have been no good American composers. He agreed with me. I said there have been no good English composers. He agreed with me. I said there have been no good French composers. We had an argument. Naturally, I lost. By the way, have you ever heard of an American named Engal, or something like that?[20]

We talked of many things after that. When I say, "We talked," I mean we communicated. I never realized before I came here what a great convenience speech is in conversation! Some key words that he didn't know in English, I did know in French or German, which I have gathered a smattering of by now. Gestures, expressions, and tones contributed as much as words. But we were at least one step above the usual. Neither of us drew pictures.

Finally we got around to communism, which it turned out, he is a bug on. He believes the Third World War will be between the United States and Russia during this century. "Russia most grand (largest) communist state. America most grand capitalist state. Fight." (The only long English words he knows are words like communist and capitalist and dictatorship.) He says there are ten million communists in the States, besides twelve million Negroes, who are oppressed and therefore favorable to Communism.

Capital creates war because it gains by it, he says. Labor is weakened through losing men to the army, and capital is strengthened through increased profits. Germany attacked Poland because Germany is a capitalistic country, which must create a large army during depression, and must fight to maintain that army. I asked why we had not fought in 1930 when we had a depression, but had later, when business was very good. It was because we had no army in 1930. I was a little disappointed in his logic, but it shows he is an ardent believer. And I was delighted to learn that. I'd thought they had passed out of style among the intellectuals here fifteen years ago.

One thing was peculiar. I answered every one of his arguments—I won't waste space saying how, you can easily imagine—but after none of my answers except the one I've already mentioned did he say anything more pertaining to them. He didn't say yes or no. He neither agreed nor argued further. He just went on to another point. So maybe you wouldn't call him an intellectual after all. He has a retentive mind. He doesn't seem to be an original thinker. He gives the impression of having read some Marx, liked the idea, and memorized the arguments.

I said communism might be good if combined with democracy, without mentioning Russia. He said Russia could not survive without a dictatorship because it has too many people and covers too large an area. This was a little too ardent for me and ended the discussion.

Incidentally, as far as distinctions other than party are concerned, Russia is truly democratic. All men really are equal. You'd never hear of one Russian saying to another, "Some of my best friends are Mongolians." I'm not positive, but I think the same is true of religion that is of color.

I interviewed the two ladies of Riga through my violinist. In fact, he was the one that brought them into the scene. They're the only three in this camp that don't carry a rural atmosphere with them, literally. I asked them why they didn't go to the dance the Poles were having, and which I'll tell you about if I can keep up the pace. The dances they know, it turned out, are the Rumba, the Tango, The English Waltz, The Boston Waltz, the Fox-trot, the Lambeth Walk, and the Charleston. I asked what the difference is between

240   the English and the Boston Waltz. There isn't any. You figure it out. Then I managed to get a demonstration of the Charleston. It was, unmistakably, the Charleston. But it presented a rather peculiar picture being done by a middle-aged Latvian on the Cobble-stoned streets of a German farm village.

Oh, yes—the dance. Well, my friend, the Communist, told me they were playing two types of music, waltz and polka. But the polkas seemed to be in three-four time and they beat a drum during the waltzes. So at any given time I could not have said which was being played, had I been asked. Moreover, I couldn't even tell when one number had stopped and another started, except by the pauses. And the dancers looked like the musicians, a drummer and an accordionist, sounded. It was another combination of a polka and a fast waltz. Whenever someone felt like it, he'd take off and stamp his feet for a measure or two, his partner following or not, as she wished. Each couple had a different speed, and changed its rate continuously but still keeping time. You figure that one out, too. All of a sudden, someone would get an idea and everybody would join hands, or go through some other procedure on the order of a square dance. All in all, it looked to be interesting, but exerting.

The accepted manner of requesting one of the sweet little things for the pleasure of a scuffle is to walk up to her and clap your hands silently two or three times. If I had had a little to drink I would have tried it. But I hadn't, so I didn't.

Did I say I didn't feel like writing? Well, that was a couple of days ago. Until the next time Love Carl

———

20 May 1945

Dear Folks,

Notice the envelope? No censor's stamp. At least, I hope not. They've stopped having our officers censor all our letters, but they're still carrying on spot checking at the base censor's.

Enclosed find one map, of sorts. That is a record of my activities here in the war. Keep it for me, will you please? Here is my itinerary, as well as I can remember.[21]

Jan 17 to 28 – slow, straight, cross country drive against the
Bulge. Woods, heavy snow, and cold.

Jan 28? to Feb 3? – Rest in small villages near Liège. Billeted
in house with family, two daughters.

Feb 3? To Feb 23? – Billeted in suburb of Haarlem with
family. Two daughters. Good looking town.

Feb 23? To March 13? – crossing of Roer and drive to Rhine.
Heavy fighting first part; heavy walking last part.

c. March 13? To April 1 – rest in Krefeld, in home.

3. and 4. April 1 to May ? (8) – from Rhine to Elbe. On
trucks, sporadic fighting. Action crossing Weser and at
Schnackenburg (apr. 22) on Elbe. One week in candy factory
in Hannover. Week in V-bomb plant and DP camp on Elbe.

d. May 10? To May 17? – in small town with Russian and
Polish DP [Displaced Persons] camp.

e. May 17? To present – guarding hospital in Heidelberg

This is really the best deal I've had so far. Seven of us are on
our own guarding a hospital for German P.W.s. Well, they all know
they're better off in the hospital than at any other place they could
go, so there is not much for us to do. We stay at a room of one of
the other hospitals (the town is full of them) across the street. What
a life. Everything but breakfast in bed. We don't even wash our
own dishes or clothes. In fact, we don't even have to draw our own
baths. Surprisingly enough, the place isn't nearly filled to capacity.
So there's always plenty of nurses running around loose. A couple
of Russian medical officers, who had been captured, have the next
room. Both very young. They spend their evening with us and a good
part of the day. For that matter, I think about half the hospital staff
does, too.

I'll tell you all about this one Russian in another letter. Had
a couple long talks with him. Like all Russians, he seems to be
bubbling over with pep and good humor. You get a kick out of them.

You said we might start in on the house next spring. Meaning
a year from now? I think I read something about the government
allowing some homes to be built now. Any thing in that? Anything for
us?

Request: Please send me a box of candy, assorted things, if you can. And put some of the old magazines you've got around the house in with it, will you please?

And as for *Life* Mag—just rip the bottom of this page off and send it to them –

Dear *Life* Magazine,

Long time no see. Where have you been, you old rascal? Oh, you want to be coaxed?

On my honor as a PFC I do hereby swear, affirm, and insist that this is a bona fide request for a periodical receiving of your espewing. Please espew to: PFC Carl Lavin, 15140578 – Co, L – 335 INF., APO 84 c/o PM NY, NY

So you were surprised to hear that I'd been in action?[22] Well, I was surprised to be in action. It was April 22. And that was the last. Isn't that a silly time to be in action? The war is 99 44/100 over, and those Jerries decide to fight. And the peculiar thing about it is that that was the most difficult of all the fights that I've been through. It's an impossibility for me to give you an idea or any kind of description of it in writing. But I will tell you of it when I get home. Out of our platoon of about 30, five men temporarily lost control of themselves as a result. And I know that I practically approached that myself. I never want to go through another day like that as long as I live. Anyways, we captured the town. I'll tell you about it when I see you.

You asked what the fellows are like that I'm with. Well, I think they're pretty swell. There's no one that thinks as I do or has had the education I've had, but I don't mind that very much. That's one good thing, at least, I've received from the army. It's taught me, in all the transfers I've had, how to get along very well.

You know that story about the two travelers asking a native what the people are like in his town? He asked each of them what they were like in their towns—one said they were good and kind; the other said they were mean and evil. He told them both that the people in his town were just the same as the ones they knew before. I try to remember that and act accordingly.

Oh yes—I've got 42 points, 5 which might as well be two as far as my immediate future is concerned.[23] What do I think? Here for about three months. Then U.S., furlough, and Pacific. Keep writing with love –Carl

Rumors and second-hand stories abounded. Carl knew a guy who knew a guy who had been assigned to guard imprisoned Nazi leader Rudolph Hess. This GI, a rather large man, did so by handcuffing himself to Hess. This all worked out fine until Hess decided to commit suicide, and jumped off a landing of a stairwell to dash his brains out. Of course the GI was handcuffed to him and taken down as well. The GI ended up in the hospital with some broken bones, or so the story went. Hess survived, too.

24 May 1945
Germany

Dear Folks,

Of late we've been spending most of our time skipping around Germany. We stay in one place four or five days, and then move to another twenty or fifty or a hundred miles away. But at least it's an interesting life. Usually, we are put out to guard something or other, and so aren't very closely watched and get off on our own when off duty.

You of course know of the army's non-fraternization policy.[24] Well it's an almost total flop. It's mostly a joke. But I imagine it's a little more strictly observed among headquarters personnel and others near the higher ranking officers than it is among us.

The night before last while we were guarding another hospital, I spent about three hours talking with the doctor in charge, or perhaps I should say "interviewing" him, for that's what it mostly was. He was a Captain in the German Army Medical Corps until he was wounded in Russia. He's a young man, and probably typical of the upper class of Germany. He has a pleasant face and personality. He was an athlete, in the European sense, in school. Used to spend his vacations in Austria, skiing and hiking. He even bears a slight saber scar on his forehead which he called my attention to, apropos of something or other. His wife attended an English boarding school. He speaks English and French.

He has a correct and realistic idea of world events and affairs. He is a lover of his country, and a Nazi to that degree.

He said Hitler was good for Germany in that he brought order out of chaos. He said Hitler was right in removing the Jews from "control." It's wrong for so few to control so many, he said. I asked how they had gained control—he said by them sticking together. On the years since the last war many Polish Jews had entered the country with long beards and skull caps. And so it was all right for Hitler to remove control from their hands, but he added that it never should have been done so brutally and cruelly. Power should have been taken away, but that was all. Before we talked about the Jews, he asked me my religion and I told him. I think he would have said the same thing anyways, from what I have seen of him, but I'm not positive.

He saw nothing wrong with Germany's taking of Austria, because the Austrians are the same people. But the Czechs aren't, and there was no excuse for marching into Czechoslovakia, even though it was a danger spot for Germany because Russia might gain control of it.

He said Hitler had done many wrong things, such as his attack on all religions, his suppression of all organizations and fraternities not connected with the party, his handling of the war. Except for those things I've mentioned all that he said was just what you might expect of an intelligent, loyal German.

We talked generally for quite a bit of the time. It was very interesting, very. I hadn't known before that all dancing had been banned in Germany. And I hadn't realized how great was the German fear of Russia. He, like many of these people, told me he thinks we will fight Russia in the next year or so. He says Germany would join us and fight again if we would. It is a belief based on hope— desperate hope—the last hope. They see Russia as a Frankenstein's monster. It's a fear beyond reason. They believe any story of the Russian soldiers that they hear.

One story he told me that there is almost universal raping of German women by the Russian soldiers. He said he had talked to many wounded Jerries from the Russian front who had gotten back to his hospital and they had told him this. He said he even believes probably that they are doing it on orders from Moscow, so as to destroy the German race.

Do you remember the ex-Russian medical officer I told you about recently? I talked quite a bit with him, too, as I said. And he said he was surprised at the laxity of the American officers as to fraternization, looting, etc. He said in the Russian army such things were simply not tolerated. So there you have it. Two sources as identical as they could be. And opposite stories. Of course, neither saw it—both got it from others who had seen it.

I think I've been unnaturally fortunate in having the opportunity to talk with those two men. If I had been allowed to pick out only one man in all Russia and one in all Germany by which to judge the countries, their people, their lives, their beliefs, and to compare them, I couldn't have made a better choice in either case. Both are young and were interested in talking with me, both observant, both intelligent, both alert, both of the one strata, both good-humored. Both could come to America and become quickly successful.[25]

And their comparisons and differences must therefore be those of their countries—and nothing, or almost nothing, else. The Russian is the more exuberant of the two, the informed one. The German is more cultured and worldly. The German is more careful in his dress and manners, the Russian more humane. And that's about all.

Germany has a background of culture and Russia does not. That's the difference. And along that line, I believe that the difference between Germany and America is just the same. "What are the Germans like?" A lot of people in the States must ask. Meaning, how do they differ from us. If I were asked that I would answer, they differ mainly in that they are Europeans, and we are Americans. The Old World and the New World. I always thought the term "New World" referred only to time. But it actually is just that. Europe is one place, America another.[26]

I saw that difference in England, in France, Belgium, Holland, and now in Germany. England actually is closer to Germany than she is to us. And we're closer to Russia. We're both young and hearty as nations or as civilizations without that inheritance of traditions and culture.

And that is almost the only difference I see between Germany and the United States. They have a certain amount of smugness that you won't find among other nations, excepting perhaps, ours which has more of a cockiness. But I must add, that amount is much less than I had been led to expect. Their soldiers are certainly no less brave than ours; they have every bit as much ingenuity (I wonder who ever coined "Yankee ingenuity?" If I could manufacture and employ all the clever gadgets and ideas I've seen here and in England I'd be a millionaire.)

In other words, I think those who say the German people must be punished for Nazism might with the same amount of reasonableness insist that the American people must be punished for the depression of the 1930s. I think that if every German had been replaced over here by an American in 1933 Hitler would still have come to power, and later would have armed the Sudetenland, and later would have done all those things he had done.

It may be difficult to make a democracy out of Germany—but I insist that difficulty will be only because of circumstances, not people. If the waters are even and untroubled and the ship carries enough weight the mass of people on the top deck will sail, but if it shoves off from shore while the currents are still strong and storms imminent, it will capsize for certain, and the engine crew will be above water and all the passengers below. (That's a rather ponderous metaphor—got myself caught in an undertow and couldn't get out.)

And if that is true it follows that what has happened in this country can also happen in ours. "It can happen here." And so easily I read recently a review of a new book—I forget its name—that shows just how easily. Have you read it?

The war has been an easy excuse—indeed, a reason—for the great increase in federal power, in executive power. It seems to me it has grown out of proportion, though. Truman must have performed his greatest function by his act of replacing Roosevelt. At this time we need a weak president—not a strong one. And that isn't the only reason we need one—congress should write America's part in this peace—not the president. Wilson had too much greatness in him in the last war, and Roosevelt in this, to do that writing.

My time in the army has given me a great fear of militarism. It's a terrible thing for one man to have power over another. And so I may be unreasonably wary in what I have said about it. (Incidentally, I'm glad to say that although I have accepted the army physically—I have not mentally. I honestly do not have respect for authority which is not common no matter what man may say.) well, s'nuff – Love Carl

How big a flop was nonfraternization? Carl relates:

Non-fraternization meant different things to different people. 247
Once during this period, we were called upon to inspect every
German house in this small town. We were called upon to
inspect the houses because we were looking for Nazis . . . was
the official word. So we got up real early and at 4 or 5 o'clock
in the morning went banging on doors to inspect houses. We
were assigned to various houses, and two or three guys would
go through a house. The funny part about that was that going
through one of the houses, one of the guys saw a picture of our
lieutenant on the bureau of a dresser. [Laughter]. So, we weren't
supposed to fraternize, but here one of our officers [chuckles]
obviously had a German girlfriend. That was funny. I don't
think we had a feeling of hatred toward the German people.[28]

———

27 May 1945
Hamelin Germany

Dear Mom and Dad,
    This is the city with the rats and the piper. Pardon me, it's the one
without the rats and the piper. And the story must be true, because
since I've been here I haven't seen a rat or piper. Some kids running
around though, so someone must have exaggerated somewhere.
    Last night I went to a dance given by Stateless DP's [Displaced
Persons] supposedly, but which was attended by about every recorded
nationality. And it was a bit of a contrast to the Polish dance I told
you about. (Oh, before I go any further—I did attend that Polish
dance the next night—and determined to try it. Under the influence
of nothing but curiosity I asked one of the more slender ones for
the pleasure. I picked a slow polka. Found out on closer study my
previous report was without sufficient background experience. The
pieces *are* different and *do have* different rates.
    Well, the first half of the dance was pretty sloppy—she wouldn't
do what I did. I tried to do what everybody else did. And then I
must have worn her down slightly, for holding her as hard as I could
I managed to make her follow. We didn't do too badly then. But
at the end my right arm was dead from the effort. And sore from

pressing against such an unyielding substance.) These women were mostly German, and the musicians quite good—they had a piano and two six-stringed things they called piccolos—and the music international, and therefore more than half American. Other than folk music, American songs are in the majority among all these European nationals. It was good to hear those old good pieces again.

I danced with only two different women, but both were excellent. Few things have more forcibly reminded me what I did back there than dancing with them—if I didn't look or smell too carefully. Even got a round of applause at the end of one dance. This quite honestly surprised me—I was enjoying it so much I didn't realize everyone was watching us—and quite naturally pleased me.

I don't believe I told you that a couple of days ago in Hildesheim, I was in prison, did I? It was my own doing. I walked in and I was. I didn't say I was inspecting it, but I didn't dispel their assumptions. It is nothing but an ordinary civil city jail—or else I never would have been able to enter. It is what I should judge to be a model prison. Clean, not crowded, and the inmates were being sufficiently fed. The only men in it (it was about half-filled) were mild offenders. One that I talked with spoke good English. He said he had come to the authorities shortly after the German surrender, told them he had worked in the Japanese embassy and was prepared to give useful information. He also wanted a traveling pass to go to his wife. That was three weeks ago, and he still doesn't know why he's in jail. An American told him two weeks ago he would be free in a week.

I nodded sagely like they do in the movies in such cases, and left him. He looked like he might have been one of their doormen or chauffeurs.

Most of the inmates were D.P.s who were most likely in for short times for looting or having riots.

The prison official's offices were practically as spartan as the cells, the kitchen was clear, and everything looked very nice, as far as I could see.

Sorry to hear the meat situation is so bad. As far as I can gather from the *Stars and Stripes* it will be at the least six months before it improves. Right? Let me know, will you please?

And please send me a package of food again.

Love to you –Carl

Schützengilde Hameln e.V. [Hamelin Shooting Club]
27 May 1945

Dear Mom and Dad,
Here's a few cards I picked up in an album in the house we're
staying in now.
The one of the freight cars, which I think shows French P.W.s in
the last war—or maybe it's German soldiers in France. I'm sending
because the closed cars are identical with the ones we came across
France in. You can't see it, but they have signs on them saying 40
men or eight horses.
I don't think I've ever been in Gutersloh, but I'm sending that
picture because it's as typical a one as I could find of a German small
town, where we've done most of our fighting.
Got the package of different things you sent. Thank you, ma'am.
The packets of soap and cocoa are a good idea.
That trip to Cleveland which you've taken by now sounds
pretty lovely. Was it? And how successful was yours to Washington,
Pop. Speaking by my two years of personal experience with the
government, I'd venture to guess it wasn't.
Off to take a look at the town now. I'll tell you about it next time.
Lots of Love Carl

Schützengilde Hameln e.V.
To Alfred B. Lavin
1 June 1945

Dear Fred,
From all I can gather you should be home about the time this
letter gets there. Right? What are you doing with yourself now?
Me, I'm just kind of browsing around the country. We've been
in Hamelin now for over a week. Expect to go somewhere around
Munich in about four or five days.

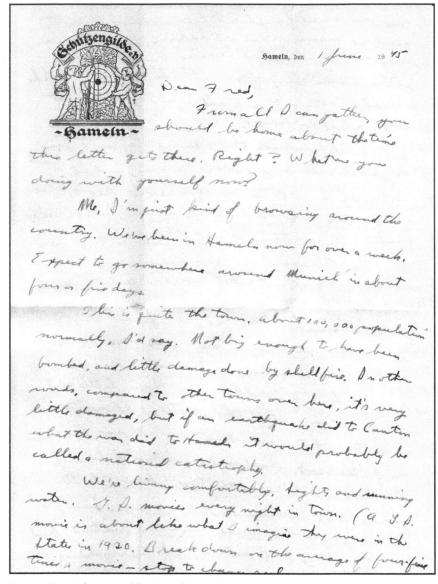

Figure 9-1. Schützengilde Hameln. *Author collection.*

This is quite the town. About 100,000 population normally, I'd say. Not big enough to have been bombed, and little damage done by shell fire. In other words, compared to other towns over here, it's very little damaged, but if an earthquake did to Canton what the war did to Hamelin, it would probably be called a national catastrophe.

We're living comfortably. Lights and running water. G.I. movies every night in town. (A G.I. movie is about what I imagine they were in the States in 1920. Break down on the average of four-five times a movie—stop to change reel—poor sound—etc.) And we know of a place where we can get pretty good ice cream. We've got radios. And for them as want them, plenty of females. And not too bad, either. Over here, there's all the difference in the world between the city gals and the country gals. But they're still not for me.

The powers that be are trying to give us basic training all over again, which naturally is not too well received. And naturally, a little friction arises, with us, naturally getting most of the fric.

Rumors keep on persisting themselves to the effect that we'll be home in July. And, really, it looks as if there is a pretty good chance of that.

Do you remember some family from Los Angeles visiting us ten or twelve years ago? Some kind of relations.[29] Had a little girl with them. Well that little girl wrote me a letter that I got about a month ago. Reminded me of the visit. And sent a picture of herself, you, and me taken at the time. She's a little young but I answered it anyways. Just got another letter, with another picture. And now, according to the picture, she is very nice. Good build, pretty face. So I'm going to keep on writing. Maybe I'll have a date with her before I take off for the Pacific. Who knows?

From all the dates you've been having it sounds like times back in the States are pretty good. Well, I hope to get in on some of it. But I'm not counting on it. At least, I'm trying not to count on it.

How's the plant getting along? From all the stories, there must be about enough meat in it to fill up a medium-sized home refrigerator. But with all the building plans afoot, it can't be too bad. Are you going to the U. of Chicago for that time-study course, or what are you doing now?

Are there any of your contemporaries in town? Or any of mine?

I can look out the window at the chow line as I write, and right now the line is just about through. So – Be seeing you Carl

10 Mannheim, Gmund, and Lauda Occupation

June–September 1945

        The US occupation force was regularly shifted to different locales. First, the soldiers had to be moved from where they were fighting when the war ended to occupy the rest of Germany, a process that took several weeks as it also involved disarming German troops in Norway, Denmark, and elsewhere. Then the GIs were shifted again to respect the various occupation zones of Britain, France, the Soviet Union, and the United States. Although agreement on these zones had been reached at the Yalta Conference in February 1945, they were not fully implemented until the Potsdam Conference that commenced in July 1945. Finally, the American troops underwent a series of shifts as the ongoing return of troops meant the remaining units had greater geographical responsibility.

        As part of the first phase, to allow the Allies to occupy all of Germany, on June 4, Carl and other men in the 84th were trucked to western Germany, near the French border. Though there were diversions enough for the troops during peacetime occupation, the likelihood of combat in the Pacific anchored the mood of the men.

———

5 June 1945
Mannheim, Ger.

        Dear Family,
        Yesterday we pulled in here, after a nice long truck ride. We're in a small town about five miles south of Mannheim, which is about

forty miles south of Frankfurt and about thirty miles north-east of the easternmost point of France.

That room sounds very nice, the way you've got it fixed up. We can be like the president now, and have a rose room.

Things still look like we're headed for the States. That is, for a while, you understand. There's no doubt in my mind that I'm going to the Pacific. If the war is over within six or seven months I don't think I'll see any action though. I'll probably be in the States for a few months before taking off.

I don't know just where Fred is now, but if he's home, "Happy Birthday Fred." This should hit you just about in time. Did it? I see by the "Greetings to the Miami Men in the Armed Services" that you've been discharged. How'd they find out, so quick?

We came down here most of the way on Autobahns, or super-highways. They're good roads, all right. Four and six lanes, separated in two, with most crossings bridged. Compared to the twistings of the other roads, they are excellent. But they still have too many curves and steep grades to be called real super-highways.

Well, 'Bye now. Love Carl

———

Eisenhower lifted the ban on fraternization with children on June 11.[1] Carl related his encounter with a former Hitler Youth:

> And there was no obvious ill-will from the German civilians. We were their masters. We were in control. It was an attitude of respect that they had toward us. I remember one funny incident in this period. I happened to be talking to a young boy. He was twelve or thirteen years old, I guess. In my few words of German, I remember asking him had he been in the Hitler Youth. 'Ya, Ya,' he'd been in the Hitler Youth. I tried to ask him in my very few words of German, what did you do? What did they train you to do? There are two words that are very much alike. One is Schizen and one is Schiezen. One means 'to shoot,' and the other means 'to shit.' I don't remember which is which anymore. I didn't at the time. I thought I was asking him, 'Did they teach you how to shoot?' [Chuckles]. I was trying to ask that question, but that's not what I said. What I said was, in German, 'Did they teach you how to shit?' [Laughter]. He looked at me.

[Laughter]. I realized I had the wrong word. To this day, I don't remember which word means which.[2]

———

12 June 1945
Gmund, Ger.

Dear Mother and Dad,

Here I am again. And I'm still here. I've been doing a little investigating of the town since my last letter. Found a watch factory, which doesn't have any watches, but which is big and modern, and which I enjoyed going through. Found an old old tower to a church, without the church. That has walls eight feet thick and a hundred and fifty feet high. I climbed up it and found a family living at the top. Quite a romantic setting in which to raise children.

I also find out there is a riding stable around here, taken over by corps special services. I'm going to make an attempt to sandwich in a couple rides between the majors and colonels. And I found out something else. Apparently war is healthy for me.

There's a scale at that bath house I told you about. And I weigh 167 now, stripped. I can't exactly remember, but I think that's about ten pounds more than I weighed when I came over. When I get back I'm going to have a pretty hard time convincing anyone that it's been rough over here, aren't I?

Things are a little quieter now than they were about our going back to the States so soon. Which, of course, doesn't mean much one way of the other. But I'll have to admit it's a little more comfortable over here than it is in the Pacific. I'm content to hang around for awhile.

We're a hundred and sixty miles away from division, so mail isn't coming through very well now. Haven't heard from you for a week. Hope everything is going all right back there. Love Carl

P.S.—(six hours later) Correction on that last paragraph. Just got two letters, one from each of you. I enjoyed your letter, Pop—write some more, why don't you? And I especially liked yours, Mother, from Hamilton, telling of many things I remember.[3] I didn't yet get your letter telling of the graduation.

You say Fred seems to be nervous and high-strung. I was sorry to read that. You said before that after he had rested a while after his discharge he was feeling better. What's the matter?[4]

Well, I went riding. This afternoon, since I started this letter. And it was delightful. The horses are German army horses, and responsive. Some of the best riding horses I've seen. The town is in a valley circled by high hills, and I rode up in the hills. So, I'm going to go every day now, if I can. With the swimming, I'm going to have a real schedule worked out for myself pretty soon.

Well, love again —Carl

———

16 June 1945
Gmund, Ger.

Dear Folks,

I just got that tracing of the plans for the new part of the plant. You know, it actually gave me a thrill to look at it. I can kind of see, now, why it would cost that much. I had no idea before that it would be that size. From what I can tell it seems to be well planned. One big packing and assembly room is very good. And I notice that there should be no congestion of movement of the various products through their various sections of the plant right into that room. That's very good. One thing, though. It seems to me that pretty much floor space is devoted to sausage. Is a room that large needed for the mixing and cutting machines? And for the stuffing? Couldn't you combine these two in one room?

The cutting and boning room and the packing room seem large to me, too. But I imagine you're allowing for future expansion, yes?

What is that little room off the shipping office labeled casings? I can't quite get that. And that garage and loading court—is that space to be partly roofed, or entirely roofed, or not roofed at all?

Those rooms marked new freezer and boiler room confuse me a little. There's no space between the present furnace room and freezer, is there? Are you going to move the furnace, or what?

Is there to be more than one floor to all this new part? I can see there must be for the office part, but what about the rest? Good place for additional deep freeze rooms.

Oh, yes—how does that refrigerated shipping dock work? The end certainly isn't open, is it? Are those to be swinging doors right at the end of the dock?

I don't see any receiving dock. You know, that always caused trouble, receiving in the shipping room. A good place for it would be just north of the lobby, with an elevator. The basement of the office section would be a store room.

That all sounds like pretty much criticism, but really I'm very much pleased with it.

If you propose to build part of it now and the remainder later, which sections will it be? And what will the cost be? Give me an idea of the financial standing and recent figures, will you? Make it in percentage comparison to the '42–'43 average, which I have an idea of.

Hey! I just noticed April 24, 1944 on that tracing. How'd that get there?

Nothing still has happened around this neck of the woods. But it still looks like I'll be home in July.

Things are getting happier around here all the time. A Red Cross canteen has opened in town. Shows have been coming around lately, too. Night before last there was a French show. The girls were just above average burlesque dancers with clothes, but the comedians were excellent. Pantomimes. Last night it was Russian. Their orchestra played popular Russian music mostly. What you'd call Jazz with a heavy Russian accent. Their dancers, of course, were wonderful. They also had a Polish girl dancer. There was a Polish girl doing a Spanish dance to a Russian orchestra playing German and French instruments before an American audience. And it was good.

I went riding again the other day—for two and a half hours. Felt pretty good. The only trouble was that the cinch strap wasn't put on tight enough—I found out while at a full gallop. The saddle started slipping to the right. By the time I reached a forty-five degree angle I decided the situation was becoming embarrassing. So I jumped. Here my skiing experience came in handy. I tried to lean as you do when falling on skis and I did. Luckily it was on nice soft grass too. So my only injury was a grass-stained suit. One of the guys fixed the saddle, and I went merrily on my way. That's my second fall. The first one was the first time I tried to jump—up in Canada. One more and I'll be qualified.[5]

I found a photographer's shop that's still in business. Two days from now, theoretically, I'll get the pictures. That is, if he doesn't go out of business in one day. Judging by the pictures he has on display and by the way he went about taking mine, he's a true craftsman.

Until then, then – Love Carl

———

19 June 1945
Gmund Germany

Dear Mom and Dad,

Well, I thought I'd have my picture from the photographer's yesterday, but all I got was the promise that it'd be ready in two more days. Now that, of course, can go on indefinitely. But we'll see, tomorrow.

This is going to have to be a short letter, since I need some sleep. The social whirl is getting me. This place is getting to be like a resort. On a typical day I'll go horse back riding for a couple of hours, and then a shower and a swim. A few pauses at the red cross canteen for doughnuts—and coffee, if I drank coffee—maybe an hour or so, browsing through the library. In the evening there's usually a show and always a movie.[6] Tomorrow night there's a dance. If I get thirsty, there's a G.I. bar that has variety and quality and quantity for ten cents a drink.

Sounds pretty nice, eh? Well it's really not quite that nice, but it's the most pleasant place I've been since we left the States.

Before I forget, please tell the *Canton Record* and the *Stark Jewish News* my present address. Yes, I know it'll probably be changed soon, but it's a lot better if they go to two different places rather than four. Got my first copy of *Life* yesterday. Beginning of April on the date, which is pretty good. It'll get better, in time, later. Thanks.

Do you read the ninth army is going home? I hadn't heard that, but it doubtlessly means the army headquarters. First place, they can't move that many men all at once; second place, any unit designation larger than a division can only be considered as being very temporary in its components now; third place, the 84th division is, for the present, in the 7th army and the VI corps. In other words,

258   don't rely on anything you hear pertaining to me in anything other than division, and even that is far from conclusive, since men are being shifted every which way now.

And don't let anything you hear stop you writing. Mail is being transferred more rapidly now than it was during the war. And packages too. I haven't gotten any for a long time. Please send me something, willya? More tomorrow.

Love Carl

20 June 1945
Gmund, Ger.

Dear Mom and Dad,

Well, here—obviously—it is at last (the photo). And this is final proof that the war hasn't had any affect on me so far. I don't look very much more weather-beaten, do I?

I think we'll move out of here in a few days—so maybe things are beginning to happen now. We'll see.

Keep the home fires burning, eh? Love –Carl

P.S.—I'm a little surprised at your optimism, Mother. I'm referring to your comments on the progress of world conditions. It seems to me the U.N.O. so far is even quite a bit behind Geneva of the last war. Then, there was at least a semblance of world equality. Now, it's the top powers will do the saying, and no questions will be asked about it. You say you'd have hated to have lived earlier in history. Why? Seems to me early Greece and middle Rome were pretty nice places. They had at least as much civilization and as fair laws as we. There has been no improvement in 5000 years. Why should there be now, in five? Politics follows human nature, and human nature changes biologically and not educationally.

To that let me add, so you won't get the wrong idea, that I feel freedom is the most precious right of the human race.

Love again –Carl

24 June 1945
Gmund, Germany

Dear Family,

I'm not sure whether that's the proper heading or not, not being positive of all of your whereabouts. But I gather you're all there still under one roof. I guess you haven't been hearing very much from me lately, have you? I'm sorry for that, but you must know that there is little to hear about. The latest word is that we'll stay over here about two more months before going back to the States. Which is all right with me. As far as pleasantness in the army goes, this is a pleasant place.

If we do stay here that long I imagine I'll have a chance to attend one of the schools that are going to open over here. That is, I'll have the possibility of going, but by no means the probability. So don't expect anything. However, I do intend to do all I can do change that possibility into a probability.

Incidentally, there's an added chance of my going back to the States. Separate from my unit, that is. I read in the S&S [*Stars and Stripes*] where they're going to take men from over here for OCS in the States. And that might include me whether I wanted it to or not. But I guess I'd want it to. Well, we'll see what happens, and what can be made to happen.

Last night I saw *The Keys of the Kingdom*.[7] I imagine it will be named one of the ten best of the year, won't it? And yet look at how much it could be improved. In comparison to the average picture, it is outstanding. But in comparison to what might be created with the talent and energy that is used, it is a failure. Hollywood is still a couple of decades behind Broadway. However, it may be that I have an unfair impression of the noble industry. Someone possibly has the idea that GI audience is even more mentally juvenile than the Bijou audience, and has selected our cinema entertainment accordingly. But I doubt that much trouble would be taken.

Tell me if you get the picture I sent in my last letter, please. And, until the next time, Love and kisses Carl

26 June 1945
Gmund, Germany

Dear Folks,

I received the book and also the package of food that you sent me. And thank you very much for both. Your selection in both cases was excellent. I'll save the reading of the book til some time when we move away from here. There is a good little library here at corps headquarters, which even includes *Yankee from Olympus* and I may as well save that for when I can't get any other good reading. By the way, I've been getting the Sunday edition of the *New York Times* lately. You didn't send that, did you? Seems to me I faintly remember getting a card from ZBT national headquarters a long time ago saying they were going to send me that. Do you still get it at home? I remember when we used to. Anyways I'm glad I'm getting it. For quality of writing it certainly outshines almost all other newspapers. One thing I can't understand about it though is how it can have one part of it so slip-shod when the rest of it is so good. I'm referring to what they call the *Times* Magazine. Generally the only thing decent about it besides the subject matter is the photography. Agree?

I think the spirit of the wanderer has overcome me since I've been over here. Any time now that I stay in any one place for any length of time I became restless. And that goes for here, too, nice as it is.

Keep on writing, whether you believe I'm on my way home or not. Love Carl

—

2 July 1945
Somewhere in Germany (no, the war hasn't started again—I just don't know the name of this place—It's near Mannheim)

Dear Family,

Our company is back with the rest of the division now. And tomorrow we start what will amount to taking basic training all over again. We'll probably learn how to shoot a rifle and throw a grenade. C'est la guerre.

When in Gmund I was reading Durant's *Story of Philosophy*.[8]
We pulled out, however, at about the time I had it half-way finished.
It covers the greater philosophers of the Occident, tells of their lives
and, mainly, their ideas. I was impressed by Spinoza more than any
other man I read about. His religion especially comes closer to what
I have wanted and have never been able to express than any other
beliefs I have encountered. Durant also told of his connection with
his age and subsequent philosophers. But what I should like to know,
and which he didn't tell of, is how is he now considered. Mother, can
you give me an idea of that? Perhaps Rabbi Lieberman—that's his
name, isn't it—wouldn't mind telling you what he thinks of him, if
you wouldn't mind discussing it with him some time when you have
the opportunity. From what I gather, he is a literary person and a
liberal. So he should be the correct one to answer that. And I'd like
him to speak as a rabbi. You see what I mean and why I say that,
don't you?[9]

The latest rumor, and it's going thick and fast, is that we'll be
over here 'til December. Yes, I said December. So you see, there's
quite a fluctuation in the time element, but the nice part about it is
the consistency of the locale element. All the rumors say we're going
from here to the States first.

Behave yourselves—love Carl

5 July 1945
Mannheim, Ger.

Dear Family,

I was very surprised to hear of the hospitalization of the female
member of the group. I hadn't suspected anything because the mail
service has been erratic latterly. I imagine it wasn't quite as cheerful
to take as you implied in your letter, Mother. But I'm glad that the
letter did sound cheerful. I guess everything's all right now, eh? I
remember all the trouble you had and all the treatments you took.
I certainly hope the operation will take care of all that for you now.
And I guess you do too. Well, good luck and good health on your
recovery, and I hope that by the time you get this those wishes will be
unnecessary.[10]

I don't quite see how the plant is getting along as you say, or at least I can't reconcile that with what I've been reading about the food condition over there. And by the way, how are you eating personally? Any steaks? Oh, and while we're on the subject of food, why didn't we ever have pork chops at home? That's about the only pork I've learned to like in the army, besides ham and bacon of course, which aren't like what "Mother used to make" by any means. But I think we ought to include pork chops on the home menu. Here's something else: did you ever mix peanut butter and jelly to make a spread? It's marvelous.[11] And fried onions with bread crumbs. I think we used to have that once in a while, though. But to get back, just how is the feed condition? And just how is everything else? Anything changed since I was there that I won't have gathered from the papers.

Have you finally decided to take up golf again? Or not? Sounds like a pretty good idea. How about swimming? Supposed to be the best exercise, you know. By the way, planning any excursions to Canada this summer? But I guess I throw those plans awry, huh. If it's any help, you'll know at least three weeks ahead when I'm coming home. You see, we first go to a sort of redeployment pool, and it'll probably be over a month from the time I hit there to the time I hit the Shores of Liberty. And I'll let you know as soon as I do hit.

Well, take it easy – Love Carl

P.S. Send me a package, please

8 July 1945
Friedrichsfeld

Dear Family,

I've been reading in the *Stars and Stripes* of all these resignations, cabinet and otherwise, in the government lately.[12] But it doesn't give any indication of the reasons. And it'll be a couple of months before I find out from the magazines. So you tell me, please, what seems to be the general idea.

How are you getting along by now, Mother? All better by now, I hope. Tell me how you're getting along.

I really have no reason for writing tonight. There's nothing I have to tell you. Perhaps you'd be interested in knowing just what the artillery situation was, that you had no doubt heard about last winter. Well there very definitely was a shortage of ammunition. I say this from my own experience and from talking with quite a few different artillery men. And I want you to realize that I don't have an adequate sense of proportion. Now it's true that we did have a marked superiority over the Germans as far as volume of artillery was concerned, but it was by no means what you would fathom from the news releases. And we did not have as much as we should have had. You see, it takes a terrific amount to be effective. Dropping twenty or thirty shells into a small village that is moderately well held is practically the same as dropping no shells at all. And sometimes worse. And we were in too many battles where they had inadequate previous shelling, and often no shelling, though there was no excuse or reason, save lack of ammunition, for it. But, as I said, we did have the Jerries outgunned. In quantity, that is; we were about even in quality I'd say, although some won't agree with me. The fault? Supply, I'm pretty certain. Space was taken up for less important material. That particular one (fault) won't happen again.

As far as I could see, there was only one other comparable mistake in the running of the war, over here. And that one was much more inexcusable. In fact, I don't even see how it was possible. That was our ignorance of the imminence of the Ardennes offensive.[13] How at least fifteen divisions could be moved towards one relative place without our suspecting anything when we have complete control of the air as well as other supposedly effective means of acquiring intelligence, is really more than I can see.

However, those are the only two objections I have to the fighting part of our conduct of the war. As a whole I think it was handled quite a bit better than could reasonably be expected. There was truth in the objections given to our tanks, but there was also truth in the answers given to those objections, and I think they, the answers, carried the greater weight. And of other material, they had certain minor advantages of design which were well compensated by those which we had, and which were again, and much better, compensated by our advantages in amounts. It's not realized generally how much better our rifle is than theirs, and just how important, at least to the infantry, that fact is. I know more than one who is alive now because he had in his hands a rifle that was semi-automatic, at the time it had to be.

This has nothing to do with the previous subject, but there's another factor that is not generally realized as much as it should be, even in the army, and that's the power of the bazooka. The infantryman is in terror of the tank, and that's unfortunate, for the tankman is in terror of the infantry. If any weapon has changed tactics in this war, it is the bazooka. It has taken the tank from a first to a third rate place. Now it's just one more supporting weapon. After we took one town three tanks moved in (incidentally, that's what usually happened when you read the tanks led an attack upon such-and-such) and parked around the square. We saw one Jerry sneak into a cellar of one of the houses around the square with a bazooka. We threw in some grenades but weren't sure we had him, so we told one of the tankers to fire a shot into the cellar, and told him why. All he had to do was swing his turret and fire his gun, but instead he yelled to the other two tanks and all three took off like rabbits to the other end of the village. Well, we didn't exactly approve of their actions, but I guess if I had have been him I'd have probably done the same. Anyways it shows what I mean.

Well I hope this talking shop hasn't bored you. Write. Love and kisses Carl

P.S. Send a package of food, please. Love Carl

Following the June relaxation of nonfraternization regarding children, Eisenhower announced an additional relaxation in July: "In view of the rapid progress which has been made in carrying out Allied de-Nazification policies . . . it is believed desirable and timely to permit personnel of my command to engage in conversation with adult Germans on the streets and in public places."[14] The division newsletter, the *Railsplitter*, made sure to qualify this statement: "You CANNOT shake hands with Germans, visit with them in their homes, attend dances or social events, drink with them, or engage in games or sports with Germans."[15]

Carl took the nonfraternization rule seriously, and never willfully broke it. He never had a German girlfriend. Still, there were casual moments. He said: "I remember being on guard duty in one town. It was summer by now, after the fighting. A group of Germans were having a picnic in someone's back yard. They had the neighbors gathered, and there were a group of maybe eight or ten of them . . . men and women sitting around singing 'Lili Marlene,' and singing rather beautifully. I remember

walking over to them and telling them I thought their singing was beauti- 265
ful. I don't think we had any great feeling against the German civilians."[16]

15 July 1945
Friedrichsfeld

Dear Folks,

I suppose you, too, read the report of the scheduled return of
divisions to the States? If you didn't, the 84th is not to go back
until after the end of the year. Rationally, I was pleased to learn it;
emotionally, I was disappointed. For it means that it'll most likely be
ten to twelve months until I see action again, and I believe there is
better than an even chance of the war being over by then.

And since I'll be over here so long I'll have a good chance of
getting into the educational program, because it should get under way
by then. I say—it *should*.

Right now, we're really not doing much of anything, just enough
to pass the time. We usually have some kind of training in the
morning, and spend the afternoon at sports or a movies or some such
thing.[17]

Went swimming the other day. Only drawback was that I had no
swimming suit. So I had to use a pair of shorts, which you know, have
a high embarrass potential. But a lot of other guys had to do the same,
so it wasn't too bad. By the by, how about including a bathing suit in
the next package?

These people over here are fiends for getting a sun-tan. They go
after it with a vengeance, and little else, if you see what I mean, and
the women go in for strenuous beach athletics. True Valkyrites, or
however it's spelled.

Another guy and I got hold of a two man kayak, which was our
first experience with the thing. It has a foot controlled rudder, which I
ruddered. I always got mixed up on which foot to push, which brought
on certain complications, added to by the fact we were on a river. The
most interesting complication was my getting us mixed up with the
river ferry. It was really nothing, but the two-man ferry crew got all
excited. I gathered we had disrupted the entire German transportation

system. They were probably afraid of the consequences if anything happened to two American soldiers in connection with them.

I got letters from all three of you lately, which made me very happy. Now keep it up. I'm not getting enough mail from you, I don't think. Fred, you said you took out J. G. I thot she was married?

Please don't forget to keep sending me packages. And I could use some more books, too, if you don't mind.

Be seeing you, sometime. Love Carl

18 July 1945
Same place, Ger

Dear Mother, Dad, and Fred,

Apparently my experience hasn't made me quite as rough as I thought. Your account, Mother, of your hemorrhage made me feel a bit sick while reading it. But your cheerfulness greatly eased my worry, which I presume was its purpose. You have more physical courage than I thought, Mother, and I got the letter that you wrote two days later, at the same time.

What was the purpose of the alcohol injection in the first place?

The tale of the doctor's saying you were all right because your ears were still pink was to me a little more forceful than I think you intended. Because it made me think of the ears of the dead I've seen. That's what is unhuman about the dead—their faces, especially their ears, are white. They don't look like they're made of flesh any more, but rather of white wax. That's one thing you never quite get used to. It's startling every time you see it. They don't look like people any more.

Of course, that's not all the dead, just those that have no blood in them.

I got a letter from Uncle Bill [Leo's brother] today that was really very nice. Say—send me the addresses of the relatives, will you? I think I ought to drop a few lines around. Uncle B congratulated me for helping to win the war! Told me Marilyn's [daughter of Arthur, Leo's other brother, making her Carl's first cousin] his secretary now, and various other things.

Did I tell you that I'm corresponding with [a distant relative] from California? I don't remember if I did or not (tell you). Says her grandmother is corres. with you. Visited us about twelve years ago. What's the relationship? She's 17 and quite good looking. I'm being a bad boy by teasing her without her being aware of it. Intelligent but a bit naïve.

Things are just dawdling along here. Even the rumors sound bored, and boring. But this is the way to fight a war.

Love to you Carl

———

In late July, US Forces formally assumed control over the American Zone:

> To help launch formal control over the American Zone, U.S. Forces launched a check and search operation code-named Tallyho. The objectives were to check the credentials of all persons in the zone, civilian or military; to search all premises for prohibited articles, such as firearms and stolen U.S. government property; and to search for evidence of black-marketeering. Staged in secret, to the extent that an operation employing 163,000 troops in the Western Military District alone could be kept a secret. . . . Of the 83,000 Germans arrested, 77,000 were held for nothing more than improper identification papers.[18]

Tallyho also had the advantage of heightening security in Germany for the Potsdam Conference, which brought Truman, Churchill, and Stalin to Germany from July 17 to August 2. In the middle of the conference, Churchill had to return to Britain to fight for reelection, and that gave President Truman a few days' break to allow him to fly down to Weinheim and review the 84th Division. Not irrelevant to the presidential planning process, we can suppose, was the fact that President Truman's cousin, General Louis Truman, served as 84th Division Chief of Staff.[19] "Accompanied by Secretary of State Byrnes, Eisenhower, and other high-ranking officials, Truman drove between miles of Railsplitters lining the roads and reviewed a special honor guard of Missourians."[20]

———

27 July, 1945
Mannheim, Ger.

Dear Family,

First of all, before I forget, although I don't quite see how I
could, I'm hungry. Please send me something to eat! And enclose a
lot of those noodle soup preparations you've sent before, please. And
anything you can think of off-hand. You might even get some of the
neighbors to help you think of things.

I suppose you read of Truman's reviewing the division? The
standing joke of the day was that he'd better not run for re-election,
because he'd already lost twelve thousand votes. It was a hot day
yesterday. My impression of him was that he looked just like his
picture, but a breath more distinguished. Eisenhower and Byrnes
were along too, and a dozen car-loads of mainly civilian court-
followers. I'm afraid Harry was the only one I recognized, though. He
was standing in an open car, which I don't think I would have done,
were I him. But I'm willing to bet it made a greater impression on
Germany than anything else we've done since the war. Hitler used to
ride around in a closed armored car, you know.

I've got about a half dozen nuts in the fire at the present time,
one of which is beginning to acquire a certain amount of warmth. I'm
going to a one week's school taking instruction training, and its being
well taught, too, by an ex college teacher. I'm going to teach some
subject, which I suspect, but am not as yet sure, is English. A very
dry thing to teach, but it will get me out of training and thus serve its
main purpose. That's what I'll probably do. What I might do instead is
go to some school somewhere in this hemisphere (50-50), or get a job
on a corps newspaper (doubtful), or get assigned to OCS in the States
(doubtful), or some other things. I can't quite make up my mind about
OCS. I'll have to reapply again in order to get any real action on it. If
I'd get accepted, I'd be sent right away, and get a furlough—probably
short—first. But then, it would also probably hasten my going to
the Pacific. And there's many more divergent and interdependent
possibilities and probabilities that it's rather hard to decide. However,
probably the strongest factor is that I believe I was made to be a
member of the ruling class and I'm pretty tired of being a member of
the working class. So-o-o-o.

Didn't tell you where I'm supposed to do that teaching, did I?
Well, under the Army Educational Program all units of battalion size
are going to have their own schools, with the instructors as well as
the students from the individual units. And from my long intimate
observation of the infantry, I'm very much afraid my students will
be on the educational level of the fifth grade. But it will fulfill the
previously mentioned main objective, and perhaps give me a little
useful experience.[21]

Glad to hear you're getting along as well, Ma. You seem to be
quite successful in your attempt to enjoy ill health. And, Fred, what's
this with the young Miss G.?

Well, behave yourselves, all. Lots of love Carl

———

After Potsdam, the four Allied Occupation Zones were established.
"The area of Germany remaining under U.S. military control was about
the size of the state of Kentucky. . . . The withdrawal into the zone had reduced the U.S.-administered area by more than two-thirds and the number of people by at least as much."[22]

———

There was no USO entertainment for Carl before V-E Day, but after
the war there were regular programs.[23] In one instance, Jack Benny and
Ingrid Bergman came and entertained the troops. Carl made a great big
point to go see them.

The performance was set in a dramatic outdoor amphitheater on top
of a high hill. It looked like it was designed by one of Hitler's architects. It
was something designed for grand glory but it was an open-air amphitheater. Carl got a seat right up front. Jack Benny and Ingrid Bergman were
just wonderful. Carl could still remember a routine over sixty years later.

Bergman was rather tall, and she played a comic scene with Benny
where they were supposed lovers, having to separate because of the war.
Bergman was saying to Benny, "Oh I admire your strength. You can leave
me and go do your duty and I'm just crushed by your departure. But
you've got this great strength of character." And she's continuing, "You're
too strong for me," and shaking him. "You're too strong for me." He's
wobbling. She's beating up Benny, despite her words. Supposedly, she was
shaking his shoulders so hard she was forcing him to the ground. It went

on. The audience, anywhere from six thousand to eight thousand men, were roaring with laughter. It was just very funny stuff.

Bergman was a true professional. Carl never thought of her as being a comedienne, but she was a consummate actress. She could play any role. It was one of the funniest things he had ever seen.

There were monthly USO shows when the war was over, but, as shown by his August 2 letter below, no one else made as big an impression on Carl.[24]

———

2 August 1945
Mannheim

Dear Mother, Dad, and Fred,

Well, after reading for two years about all the movie and other stars that I've been seeing, at last I am prepared to cease calling the army a liar, at least in that one particular. Last night our division had a display of Jack Benny, Ingrid Bergman, Larry Adler, and Martha Tilton.[25] And I'll have to admit that it was quite a satisfactory display. I was never too crazy about Benny in the movies or the radio. But here on the stage he gave one of the best presentations I've seen in a long time. He just kept everybody laughing.

Bergman gave with a little drama from *Joan of Arc*, which she says she is going to appear in in New York soon. And she did a little bit of a take-off from *Casablanca* with Benny, in which she didn't do too badly. She appeared a bit larger, ganglier, and fresher than she does on the screen. She was enjoyed, too.

Larry Adler was just the same as when I saw him at Miami three winters ago. Musically, that is—he's got a grand stage presence now. And Martha Tilton, who in case you don't know, used to be quite a popular singer in her time, is unfortunately a little past that time. But I sat far enough away from her that that didn't make any difference as concerned her looks, and she had such a marvelous control that her voice quality really didn't make any difference either.

So a good time was had by all. However, I still haven't mentioned the most impressive portion of the show. And that was the stadium in which it was held. It's on top of a fifteen-hundred foot hill beside the Rhine. Entirely wooded, the hill I mean. And the stadium is actually

an amphitheater, recently and well built, as so many things here are.
A perfect blending. You know, I'm surprised that the Germans are not better known than they are for architecture in their public buildings. They get a beauty of simplicity and sweep that you see so seldom in ours. And their houses, or rather their housing, really beats ours. You just don't see slum districts. And you don't see houses made of wood here. I'm pretty certain Hitler is responsible for that housing, because of the great amount of homes recently built.

Incidentally, the difference between these houses and ours is, mainly, that central heating and running hot water are virtually unheard-of and they make their walls about twice as thick as ours and they make them solid. If these houses were built like ours there would be more dead people in this world than there are now, including me I think.

I wish to report that I have not reached the final step of my transition from immaturity. I went to the dentist the other day on my own volition. He filled two teeth for me, and I think he did it in four minutes flat. Made me realize some of the advantage of free enterprise and competition. I made a resolve some time ago never to go to an army dentist. But it had been a year since I'd gone to G, or whatever his name is, and I didn't see an immediate chances of seeing him again. One of the patients had his jacket on when it was his turn to attend the sacrificial chair, but the high priest told him to take it off because he'd be pretty warm in there.

I'm going to ask you for some feed again. For just one reason. I'm hungry. I'm not exactly starving, but we're getting fed less than we think we should.

Oh, yes, I should also mention I saw Billy Conn perform.[26] This was a week and a half ago. We had division boxing matches first, and then he put on an exhibition with a couple of good fighters. Went two rounds with each, and although he obviously is not in condition with a bit of a belly and two hundred pounds it was still easy to see why he has the reputation he has. I've never seen a man of that size move as fast—he looked like a lightweight—and at the end of the four rounds he was as fresh as he was at the beginning. But of course he's the first big time boxer I've ever seen, so perhaps I'm not the proper one to judge.

Nothing has borne fruit as yet, but I've got a little added zest to life now, waiting and working on developments. Something new has just come up, but it'd take a couple of pages to explain, and besides it's not very important. Let you know anything that happens. Something has to come through, by the law of averages if nothing else.

With love Carl

———

In a July 2 letter, Carl had asked his mother if she could talk to the family rabbi, George Lieberman, about the Dutch philosopher Baruch Spinoza. Dorothy mentioned this to the rabbi, who then wrote Carl.

———

August 6, 1945

Dear Carl Lavin—

Although we have never met, your name, of course, did not escape me. I draw to you in kinship of spirit and I look forward to your return home so that amidst friendship and mutuality, we may share together ideas and views on problems and questions knocking upon our minds.

Both my wife and I feel at home with your parents. It was your Father who enticed me to come to Canton. During our stay our paths with them have crossed frequently and it is a delight to be with them and your brother.

A few days ago your Mother spoke to me of your interest in Spinoza. I think it is remarkable that in your present setting you could snatch the time and the mood for one of the immortal intellects in history. I can well understand how absorbing you found his life story, his encounter with the authorities, his excommunication, and above all, his structure of ideas. I can well remember how he fired my curiosity in my college days.

The study of Spinoza is an inexhaustible subject. There are vast libraries that have collected a wealth of literature on him. In every country there is a Spinoza Society. The great and the near-great in philosophy have been influenced by him.

I am sending you, herewith enclosed, some material which may clarify some of your queries as well as may bring to you additional facts of information. The material comes from several sources. Of

course it is not a detailed analysis of Spinoza's life and philosophy
but it may serve as a good summary and a key to further study.

I salute you for your pursuit of knowledge at a distance from the
classroom and the library. I am now the more eager to know you; and
I hope that events will soon lead you home in safety and in peace.

Cordially yours,
Rabbi George B. Lieberman, Litt. D.

The United States dropped an atomic bomb on Hiroshima on August
6 and one on Nagasaki August 9.

---

12 August 45
Mannheim

Dear Family,

I know, I haven't been doing enough writing lately, and I am
sorry. Being a good soldier I can only say, "No excuses, sir."

Yes, I'm still in Mannheim. Or, rather, just outside it. No I don't
remember Dr. G, but if you do and if he is curious to know what his
home town is like, tell him the only thing he'd now recognize is the
big round monument in the park as you come in from Heidelberg, and
the new, modernistic building with the theatre near it.

Yesterday I went to Heidelberg with some other guys. Got tired
of waiting for a pass, so we used initiative instead. And I'm certainly
glad we did. I'm almost willing to guarantee it is the largest unharmed
town in Germany. It was almost like being back home.

The store windows looked the same, the girls looked if not smart
at least urban. It's the location of 7th Army headquarters, so there
were all kinds of American girls there, and all sorts and amounts of
entertainment.

This was the first town I'd seen here yet that had stores selling
anything besides food. So I thought of you and your figurines, Mother.
And I found two places that sold them.

Of all the forms of art I think I can safely say that that with
which I am the least familiar is porcelain figurines. But anyways, I
got something. I don't think it's anything very good, but I do think it

is worth more than I paid for it, which was $32.50. A German woman was in the shop at the time, and she paid the same prices that the G.I.s were paying, and as I told you, we're gypping the Germans in our monetary exchanges 4 to 1. Or, at least, were, three months ago. It's probably 3 to 1 now. Of course, that woman could have been a plant, but I don't think so.

Anyways, you tell me what you think the price is worth over there, mom. After you see it, tell me if you want any more. And I'm afraid you'll have to send me the money, according to what you want me to spend on the basis of what I spent for this one and what it is worth. But I *do not* want you to send the money for this piece. I want this to be a gift to you and Dad.

It's supposed to be an antique, 150 years old. And I imagine there's a story behind it. But I couldn't find out what it is. I forgot the name of the manufacturer, but the trade-mark looks like this [circle segmented into six pie-slices] in blue. It's the figurine of a man in tattered clothes reaching inside his coat for what you take to be a gun.

I looked for pairs, but there weren't any good ones. The problem now is to send it home in one piece.

With it I'm sending a silver bracelet I got in Gmund, which is the silver capital of Germany, for cigarettes. Hope you like it.

While in Heidelberg, we saw the movie, *Wilson*.[27] My faith in Hollywood has been partially restored. It was a little cloying at first and tiring at last, and the photography didn't quite match up to the excellence of everything else. But I was greatly impressed by it.

I remember your telling me about Wilson once, Mother, and your sentiments exactly paralleled the producer's, as I recall. I guess he really was a hero, huh?

I get a typewriter so often because I have the fortune to be in a very good squad. We've acquired a radio and a typewriter and have been carrying them around with us for months. Not necessarily the original ones. It is hard to explain just how these things happen, but your possessions over here exist in a state of flux. It doesn't have the static quality that it had over there.

In combat it (the state) had its epitome, of course. I think I possessed five different watches in three months, and countless knives, combs, pens, and other personal items. They just come and go. If you lose or break a watch, you ask somebody if he has an

extra one, or you try a little harder to be the first to search the next
prisoner.[28]

I used to average one new piece of silverware a day. You see, you
live constantly in a state of preparedness to leave the place at which
you are for another place at which someone thinks you should be.
So meals were quite often rather exciting affairs, at which I seemed
always to forget my silverware. Oh, yes, it really was silver, too.
Nothing but the best would do for us.

But I'm getting slightly off the course. I was talking about the
equipment of our squad. In our heyday we had two radios, two
typewriters, an iron, and an electric stove. This is all since the end of
the war, of course.

But now it's extremely difficult to acquire things. In May we
could just walk into a house and take a radio or a mattress. But by
now the people have wised up, and they know who to tell about it. So,
in the course of events, and as exports exceed imports, our resources,
our standard of living, and our material wealth decline, until now we
have but a radio and a typewriter. But that is still more than any other
squad in the company has. We've been able to keep our standard of
living higher than everyone else in the company, that is, not counting
company headquarters. And *that* is how I get a typewriter so often.

Yes, that is what I wanted you to do—edit my letters to show
what's-his-name of the *Rep*. Just pick out the parts you think he
should see. But I still doubt that he'll have much interest in using
them. And if he's looking for something factual, I'm afraid there's
very little new I can tell him. The only thing I found out that I hadn't
seen in the news was what I've already told you about seeing the V-1
bombs with controls and cockpits for a suicide pilot. Just recently,
I saw an article on the Jap Baka-bomb saying that the suicide pilot
in it was the one innovation, or improvement, they had made in the
German's V-bombs.

As I write this, the latest news is that we are waiting for the Japs'
reply to our reply to their surrender terms.

The general reaction is pretty similar to that at the close of the
European war. They're each just as close to us at the time of their
happenings. In degree, but not in kind, of course.

In a few days I begin my job of instructing in English Grammar.
It should be quite easy, especially since there will be two of us to

each class. The classes will be two hours a day, three days a week. I'm going to take a subject, too, probably German.

Did you see that movie about Ernie Pyle yet?[29] If so I think I'd better warn you that although it is an honest attempt and gets a little closer to honesty than any other movie, it still is mainly Hollywood. We saw some news-reels of the fighting on Okinawa a while ago. Now that is the closest to it I've ever seen in the pictures. If you want a good idea of what it is like, look at them.

Sorry, but I lost that letter with the addresses of the relatives. Would you mind very much sending them again? And that's about enough for today except, Love –Carl

———

14 August 1945
Mannheim

Dear Mother, Dad, and Fred,

First of all, a correction in yesterday's letter: I have found the letter in which you sent me the addresses of the relatives. So never mind sending them again.

I'm beginning to wonder a little about the thickness of the bathing trunks myself. For over a week now it's been much too cold for swimming. But I still don't think the season is over here. The latitude is quite a bit higher than there, and the weather is according. It never has been one of those oppressively hot days here. The nights were always cool enough for the use of a blanket. You might say the season is just hot enough for swimming.

When you say you can't imagine me as a teacher, I don't know whether to take that as a compliment or an insult. Well, I start my new profession tomorrow morning. We'll see.

Request: for another package of food, please.

Love –Carl

P.S.—War still not over as of this evening. Waiting impatiently. Afraid it might carry on for months. –Carl

———

About two months after V-E Day Carl was told was he was going to be shipped back to the States, go by train across the country, and be loaded on a ship across the Pacific so he could be in on the invasion of Japan. The whole division was going to be sent—everybody. The generals wanted more manpower.

Carl was expecting to go fairly soon, when Hiroshima occurred. And he understood immediately that this was going to be the end of the war.

Carl's feeling and that of the other GIs was, "We're going to live after all." Before Hiroshima, Carl had expected to die in battle, so V-J Day was a moment of intense relief for him—more important than V-E Day.

There are some who felt that Truman made an inhumane decision to drop the atom bomb. But not Carl. He felt Truman saved his life and the lives of so many other people as well. Still, the advent of the bomb troubled him.

V-J was the afternoon of August 15 in Japan, or the morning of August 15 in Europe.

———

16 August 1945
Mannheim

Dear Family,
I take back what I said about V-J being received the same as V-E. Yesterday it was received, and what a difference! The only way you could tell it was over here was that the lights were turned back on. But yesterday was different. Half the company was rolling around the streets drunk and automatic rifles were sending off bursts every five minutes. All the old air-raid sirens were getting work-outs.

The Germans didn't quite know what to make of it at first, until they found out.

I feel greatly relieved now that the acceptance has been announced. I won't feel completely relieved, though, until we complete our occupation and their disarmament.

About as well as I can judge, I think it'll be three or four months until I get to the States. I won't even try to guess about when I'll get my discharge.

About all I can do is wait and see.

You say everyone over there is so excited about the atomic bomb. I suppose it was a great factor in Japan's decision to capitulate, but it seems pitiful that a thing of such awfulness has come to be. Among us, it appeared to cause more sobriety and fear than it did jubilation.

It's like that story "The Monkey's Paw" in which the man's wishes for ten thousand dollars is fulfilled, when his son, who is insured for that amount, is killed.[30]

So it helped win the war. But at what price? Of course, that's just looking at it one-sidedly, and being aware of cause and not effect. For even if *we* had not invented it, still *someone* would have, and almost as soon.

No, they're not starving us, don't worry. But I would really use a little addition to my daily food supply. And all donations will be gratefully accepted.

Until the next time, Love, Carl

18 Aug 45
Same place

Dear Folks,

By now you should be in Muskoka, eh? I wish you had told me earlier when you were leaving. You'll probably have left for home again before even this letter arrives. But I'll give it a try anyways.

Believe it or not, I still can't get used to there being no war. I realized that when I became aware that I continually get surprised that our training is being cut out and being converted to peace-time production. I've sort of become used to those lectures on the same old subjects. After you hear them ten or fifteen times they become old friends, and it's a little sad to see them depart so abruptly.

I don't know if I can give you a conception of them. But can you imagine a lecture covering something that every single person in the audience has heard at least ten times, and everyone openly admitting that they have, instructors, audience, and everyone concerned. It's just one more example of the ludicrousness of the army, and it's accepted as such. There's so many of them, you know. But accepting them is the only thing you can do. And you see the same thing all the way up the chain of command. But each step up they seem just a little less silly, because the familiarity lessens and the purposes in each become more apparent. In other words, the point of vision

progressively grows toward the aim and away from the result as you
climb the chain.

And that is, unfortunately, necessary, because the army is a
monarchy and is large. And there is one more reason why I hate and
fear government other than democratic. I soberly believe that for the
rest of my life whenever I have a discussion to make I shall always
ask myself the question, "How will this affect my personal freedom?"
The idea of another man's having power over me is repulsive to me. I
couldn't stand it if one did.

Of course, the army is not like that. When I first came in,
however, I found that it was, to me. But that was basic training and
I didn't have the knowledge or the experience or the confidence I
have now. Now I follow orders because of the thoughtfulness for those
that give them. I'm not kidding. If my platoon sergeant tells me to do
something I know it's because someone told him, and if I failed to
do it he would suffer for it more than I would. I would be physically
punished, but he would be mentally punished. And if 30 other men in
the platoon did the same, each of them would suffer hardly at all, but
he would suffer 30 times as much.

Everyone has to follow rules, and that's why no one has power
over me.

And if the man over me helps me to push my rules to their
very limit, he is an excellent officer and I may or may not show my
gratitude by helping *him* out in the eyes of his superior. If he makes
me abide strictly by the rules he is a poor officer and I certainly do
all I can to make him look bad in the eyes of his superior. But since
I must follow the rules so closely that is very hard for me to do. And
the chances are that he will look better to his superior than the officer
who considered his men above himself. And it takes a great deal more
energy as well as courage to be a good officer. And that is why most
officers are not liked.

But when they get to be a colonel or thereabouts, all the officers
under them are the strict type—we say they're "bucking," trying to
make a good impression regardless of the harm it may do to those
under them—and so they can afford to let down themselves and
become easy, and popular, and still get good work done.

And that's the way another phase of the army works. Which I
think has taken us away from the subject. Which was?—oh yes, no
one really has power, complete power, over anyone else.

When I have the patience to go about it the right way I can usually get my superiors to see things my way.

Unless I get unreasonable of course. And, if you'll pardon my immodesty, I think I can safely say I am well above the average in getting away with things. All it takes is a little ingenuity and a lot of confidence.

And while I'm being so good to myself, I may as well tell you of something else. This was one of the nicest things that ever happened to me: A couple of weeks ago, there was an opening in our squad for a sergeant by way of transfer. The platoon sergeant came around and told us who was getting the job—a guy in the platoon but not in the squad. Well the boys didn't go for this too well. They thought there were others who deserved it more. And since I'm one of the ones who have been in the squad the longest they went down and told him they thought I ought to have this job. And they raised a big enough stink around the company so that the next day it was given to me. Now I don't know if you know it or not, but such things just aren't done in the army. I was very honestly surprised.

Now don't go around telling everyone I'm a sergeant, because I am not. Most likely no more ratings will be given out.

But what's really nice about the job is that instead of the squad being my responsibility, because of what they did I'm really their responsibility. So the reason I gave before for obeying orders in most cases—thoughtfulness for your "superior"—in my case is doubly strong. In the two weeks I haven't had a bit of trouble, except with the platoon sergeant, and then very little. Meanwhile, I'm getting interesting experience and one more excuse for getting out of doing things.

About all I do now is see shows and attend German classes. It's been too cold lately to go swimming. My English classes have so far been cancelled by V-J Day celebrations.

Only pulled guard once in six weeks, and KP only once, for two hours, and that because I was caught missing reveille. You see, the squad leaders make reports of the men present and absent in formation, and when the squad leader isn't there to make the report things get a little too obvious. You should see some of the side looks I get when I report "All present or accounted for" with about three men standing beside me!

To forestall any lectures on "duty" and "responsibility" from you, may I say that I have never taken the army or the war seriously, or thought either worthy of my serious consideration. I've tried to always maintain myself above them. I consider them quite beneath me.

There have been only three things—no, four—I've been serious about in the army. They are: certain courses in A.S.T.P., some of the men I've met, ping-pong games, and the times my life has been closely and seriously threatened.

Now let's see you tell me as much about yourselves and Muskoka. Love –Carl

P.S.—have you been getting $25.00 a month class B allotment since I've been over?[31] –Carl

—

[Written in German]
20 Aug

Dear Mother, Dad, Fred,

Guten auben. Wie geht es iheuer/euer? Drise Woche werde ich zur Schule gehen rum Deutsche sprechen.

Vorgestern Mittag gehe ich in das Stadium nach Heidelberg um zu haven Shep Fields und sein Orchester von den Vereinigten Station. Die musick was nicht voryuglich.

Icden abend gehe Ich in ein Kino.

Ich habe kein arbeitet. Befinder sie driesen Brief furgut? Machten sie nacht ein Buch haben um dieses urteil zu ubersetzen?

Mit Liebe, Die Jungen –Karl

[Translation]

Good evening. How are you? This week I went to school to learn how to speak German.

Yesterday noon I went to the Stadium in Heidelberg to see Shep Fields and his orchestra from the United States.[32] The music was not excellent.

This evening I went to a movie.

I don't have any work. Did you forget to send a letter? Didn't they make a book to give advice on translation? With love, the boy –Carl

—

To the Arthur Lavins
23 August 1945

Mannheim

Dear Uncle Babe [Leo's brother Arthur, as the youngest sibling,
carried the nickname 'Babe' his entire life] and Ménage,

First, I want to thank you for your letter. It gave me a kind of little
extra added spark when I read it!

I'm glad to hear everything's going so well with your portion of
the Lavins. And now that the Japs have sued for peace I guess they
must be going quite a bit better. Or do you suppose the draft might
still coast along for enough to get Ben? I very sincerely hope not. Is
he still going to Oberlin? From all I've ever heard, it's a fortunate
place to go.

I'm not really located in Mannheim. It's more of an
approximation—I'm near it. Incidentally, there's little you can say
of the city that isn't an approximation. And it itself isn't even an
approximation of a city. All it looks like is what the other large cities
of Germany look like. But luckily Heidelberg is only two miles away
from us, and that, I believe, is the largest untouched town in the
country. And, being the locale of the 7th Army headquarters, it has
many other attractions, such as theatres, a Red Cross that serves
cokes (!), and shops that sell things.

And I've also been lucky personally, in that I've acquired an
almost perfect excuse for getting out of things other people don't seem
to think I should get out of, such as details. And that excuse is that
I've been given the job of instructor in our local battalion school.
Even though I'm teaching such an un-Godly subject as English, it's
still quite interesting. I only do that three mornings a week and the
rest of my time is practically my own. The millennium has arrived!

But I'm still anxiously awaiting that long voyage home. Latest
odds favor four to five months. Now you hear "I'll be Home for
Christmas" sung with a shade less cynicism and a touch more of
hope.

Be seeing you—Love Carl

Dear Folks,

For the past month or so I've been doing, you know, exactly
nothing. I've got just exactly enough now to keep me occupied, and
no more. I don't get any details—K.P., guard, etc., and all I do is
attend two formations a day, take German three days a week, and
teach English three.

(If you wonder why I'm taking German, it's because that is the
only subject being offered that I could possibly be interested in. This
is just on a battalion basis, remember.)

Yes, those English classes I told you about have finally gotten
started. And I'm surprised to find that it's rather interesting to teach
even such a dull subject as that.

And just about every night, I go to Heidelberg or Mannheim, or
one of the smaller towns around here, to see a movie. Around once
a week there's some kind of a stage show, good or bad, but seldom
different.

Heidelberg has the greater of the attractions, though, in the
Cokes of unlimited numbers the Red Cross there has. And its theatres
are the most modern and comfortable. In fact the three or four of
them the army's taken over have got Canton's beat. And the film is
35mm, and the sound is good, and there are two projectors instead of
one, and they don't break down. If you'll go back in your memory far
enough I'm sure you'll see the importance of that.

And there also is Heidelberg Castle, which I was surprised to
learn is much more famous around here than the University.[33]

Yesterday we went on a tour of the castle. It's a magnificent thing.
The fulfillment of all those childhood dreams of old castles, only
bigger than I ever imagined. Most of it was built in the earlier part of
the sixteenth century. Was for a time the capital of the Holy Roman
Empire. It was destroyed by the French in 1789, if I remember what
was said, in the War of Secession, which brought back a faint tinge
of memory of my history. Some of the walls are over 20 feet thick and
perhaps 300 feet high.

One portion was completely rebuilt about forty years ago, and the
furnishing replaced, or restored, or only repaired. There was some
artistry in it that's excellent, mainly the wood carvings and inlays in

the doorways. And some of the original statuary was there too, and it also seemed good to me, although a little too Nordic.

Guides were there who took parties of a dozen or so around the buildings. The same ones who had been there before the war. Ours certainly knew what he was talking about. Or at least no one stumped him with a question.

One of the members of our party was a middle aged woman who is with the USO. I imagine she is the head of one of the troupes. At first I guessed she had formerly been an instructor of dramatics at an Eastern girl's school. She has one of the most cultured and well-trained voices I've heard. And she knew all about the castle, and its art work, and Heidelberg, and the "Student Prince" and the Red Lion, which, she informed me, upon my inquiring, was the famous hang-out of the university students. And she had seen so many castles on her previous tours of the Continent that she really couldn't remember if she had seen this one before or not. And I informed her, upon her inquiry, that no, I hadn't had the opportunity to see the Luxemburg Castle. She was often making worldly, culturally, clever remarks like a character in one of those plays. And, owing mostly to that beautiful voice, did it well enough.

She almost gave the impression of being the real sure-stuff big-time, but unfortunately tried too hard. Now, I don't mean that she was ludicrous. Not at all. She was almost fascinating. And with that voice she could have gotten away with twice as much. I don't know which I got more fun out of—her or the castle.

By now you are back from Muskoka, Yes? Zo—How Vas? But I imagine you've already told me. Well, anyways, I *hope* it was good.

How about a package, please? I still haven't received those packages you told me about, by the way. Do I still have to ask for them before the PO will let you send them?

It's well over a year since I last saw you. That's a long time, isn't it? But yet it doesn't seem so long to me. (I imagine it must seem a bit longer to you?) Of all my time in the army, those months I've spent overseas have seemed the shortest. That's because, up to now at least, there's been no opportunity for a pattern to settle. Things have been so different—different from before, and different from each other—and sudden, and intense, and unpredictable. I guess "hard" and "fast" go together. And I'll just bet it's something upon which I'll look back with nostalgia and longing, from time to time.

Nope, I'm not receiving *Life* mag. regularly. It's coming in spurts.
Two spurts, to be exact.

Industrial engineering. I'm a little hazy as to definition, but eager.
Send along some terminology and information, will you, please?
And yes, I would greatly appreciate it if you would send prospects
of the various mounts and founts of learning, on the order of Chi,
Harvard, Michigan, etc. How do you, the government, and my bonds
stand on the economical side of aforementioned M and F of L's? And
incidentally, have you been getting $25 every month since I've been
over? I should have about $700 from that and my bonds since I've
joined the ranks, yes?

Dad, from what I was able to gather from the mass of
hieroglyphics, masquerading as a letter, you sent recently: I think
I've become more realistic in this past year. God knows, it would take
an angel not to. That's probably another way of saying I've grown up
more quickly than I would have otherwise. You seem to be worried
that I may have acquired some emotional entanglements. Well, let me
assure you—I haven't. If you still mean Edith—no worry. I intend to
see her whenever I get the chance, but that's all.[34]

I'm still trying to get into one of the schools over here, but so far,
no good.

I think now I *may* be home in four months. Nice hope, anyways.
Write—Love –Carl

———

31 August

Dear Mother, Dad, and Fred,
Got your first letters from Muskoka the other day. And I am
certainly happy to hear you're enjoying it, or should I say, did enjoy
it. It really sounds as if you did. I get a kick out of reading those
letters.

Nice that the ex Miss G. is getting along so famously. But she
seems to be prone to exaggeration, or lack of memory. She'd owed
me a letter for about three months and so I wrote her and asked how
come, had she gotten married? Which she answered yes, and, in all
fairness, rather nicely. So I saw no reason to answer that.

Received a package from you yesterday, the first of the present
series. And I must commend you on your selection. Very good. And

yes, a definite yes. I can use some canned stuff. And soup. Thanks much.

Actually went swimming two days ago, the first time in over a month. It's rained here about twenty-five days out of the last thirty, with a temperature to match. The bathing suit didn't quite get here yet and I'm anxiously awaiting. I'd like to christen it at least, after your trouble. Did it ever warm up enough while you were in Muskoka for you to swim?

Did you get a letter from me while you were up there? I only sent one; you told me you were going too late for me to send any more, and I think there's a good chance that one got there too late to catch you.

Gee, I wish I could have been up there with you! I think it's been four or five years since I've seen it, and you know how distance makes the sight grow lovelier. By now the place appears to me as at least a second or third heaven, if not a seventh.

Things are in pretty much of a turmoil just about now. Rumors, reports, discussions, etc. are thundering by at a rate and a volume not previously attained in the recordings of mankind. About all I can tell you that will still be a fact when you read it is that with the points counted since May 12, I have a not so grand total of sixty (60) points. Which stands a fairly good chance of getting me back in October. And which might get me back in January or even March. A word of encouragement: everyone above 65 has been alerted in the company and almost everyone about 75 has been transferred to a division scheduled to sail in September. They seem to be sticking pretty closely now to the point system.

Did you get the figurine yet? Most likely not. It took me about two weeks to finally get it sent out after I got it. And things like that take quite a long time in transit, you know.

We're moving in a few days to another part of the country. Nothing to do with redeployment. Some general just got restless. Too bad. I doubt we'll find another place in Germany as nice as the Mannheim, Heidelberg circuit. But I might as well see the country, while I'm seeing it.

Take it easy. Lots of love Carl

AMERICAN RED CROSS

31 August

Dear Mother, Dad, and Fred,

Got your first letters from Muskoka
the other day. And I am certainly happy
to hear you're enjoying it , or I should
say, did enjoy it. It really sounds as if
you did. I got a kick out of reading those
letters.

Nice that the ex Miss G. is getting
along so famously. But she seems to be
prone to exaggeration, or lack of memory.
She'd owed me a letter for about three mon
ths and so I wrote her and asked how come,
had she gotten married? Which she answered
yes, and, in all fairness, rather nicely.
So I saw no reason to answer that.

Received a package from you yesterd
ay, the first of the present series. And I
must commend you on the selection,Very
good. And yes, a definite yes, I can use s
some canned stuff. And soup. Thanks much.

Actually went swimming two day ago, i
the first time in over a month. It's raine
d here about twenty-five days out of the
last thirty, with a temperature to match.
The bathing suit didn't quite get here yet
and I'm anxiously awaiting. I'd like to
cristin it at least, after your trouble.Di
d it ever warm up enough while you were in
Muskoka for you to swim?

Did you get a letter from me while
you were upth ere? I only sent one; you
told me you were going too late for me to
send any more, and I think there's a good
chanc that one got there too late to
catch you.

Gee, I wish I could have been up
there with you! I think it's been four or
five years since I've seen it, and you
know how distance makes the sight grow lov
lier. By now the place appears to me as at
least a second or third heaven, if not a s
seventh.

FORM 539 A

Figure 10-1. American Red Cross letterhead, August 31, 1945. *Author collection.*

6 September 1945
Lauda, Germany

Dear Family,

Yep, moved again. This time about eighty miles east, the wrong
way. Our regiment has taken over the area formerly occupied by a
division that has now shipped out. We're out in the sticks now, but the
town of Bad Hergentin, or something, is nearby, and that's supposed
to be another one of those resort towns. No matter where you go you
run into them. I think all the Germans ever used to do for a vacation
was to go to the opposite end of the country from which they live and
find a resort. And like all other such towns this one has got some kind
of a big headquarters in it, which means it will be a pretty nice place
in which to enjoy yourself.

I'm supposed to get a pass to go back to Heidelberg tomorrow for
the New Year's services. If I'm lucky I'll get it for all three days. But I
don't really expect to be that lucky. I'll attend some services, but I'll
also attend some shows.

The receipt for that figurine I sent is in the box with it. It has
the name of the maker on it, which I didn't notice when I first
wrote you that letter. And yes, the bracelet is in the same package.
I should think you would be getting it pretty soon now. When I go
to Heidelberg tomorrow I'll try to remember to get the name of the
dealer from whom I bought the thing. But I don't see why you didn't
send me the name of this man who's the expert on them. I imagine it
would be the easiest for me to look him up.

A division consists of three regiments and special units; a
regiment, of three battalions and special units; a battalion of three
companies; and a company, of three platoons. Now, this school of
which I am a part is only on a battalion level. Meaning that all the
instructors and all the pupils are from the same bat. So it's nothing
very large or important, and it doesn't change my status in any
particular, except that it affords me an almost perfect excuse for
getting out of almost everything.

No, I don't have any Hyman Kaplans that I know of in my class.[35]
But I do find it quite a bit more interesting than I ever expected to,
so there must be something in it that serves as its recommendation.
I don't teach it by myself, in case I haven't told you. There are two
of us. The other guy is a New Yorker, and talks like it, which adds

a slight note of disconcertment to the class, or rather me, since the class doesn't appear to have enough discernment to be disconcerted. I'd say the educational level is the seventh grade, and the educational level somewhat lower than the rest of the infantry, which is somewhat lower than that of the rest of the branches of service of the army, which is low. One of the scholars is a first lieutenant, which gives rise in me to a bit of a battle between my senses of justice and vengeance and propriety. Settled by treating him and talking to him exactly as to everyone else.

One of us is supposed to be the primary instructor and the other kind of an assistant. But he's the aggressive type so we've ended up splitting the work and the time, which works out very well.

The weather here is still very much like what you probably had at Muskoka. The nights are cold and the days are either cold, or wet, or cold and wet, or warm. Which makes for rather comfortable living, but uncomfortable fighting, or vacationing.

I really enjoy your letters from Muskoka. You sound like you're having an enjoyable time of it. I got one today mailed the thirtieth and I suppose that will be the last one from there. Hope you found everything at home all right.

And while you're there, send me another package, will you please? And while I'm on the subject, no matter what I tell you about the imminence of my coming home, don't stop sending me packages. I don't think I could exist through another period like this again, two months without supplies. Of course, I'll admit it was my fault for telling you I was expecting to leave soon. But anyways, even if you expect me to be home the next day, don't stop sending me stuff.

And I don't expect to be home the next day. Well, Love to you
Carl

———

12 September
Lauda, Germany

Dear Folks,
Well, I feel very proud of myself now. I got that pass to Heidelberg I told you about, and while there I attended two services! They were conducted in what I imagine was the Conservative type.

About half of it was in Hebrew, with a lot of chanting, led by a series of cantors, or whatever they are. One of them had an especially good voice, and I'll have to admit it was impressive. There was an Oriental beauty in it, even if it did become a little tiresome after a while.

I got some enjoyment out of being with Jewish companions again, too. It had been a long time since I had been among Jewish humor and personality, and it made me feel rather good to hear it again. Like remeeting an old and long-lost friend.

On my return here to home base I found something else very pleasant. Three of your packages awaited me. *People on our Side* and two or more fundamental requisites.[36] And I must compliment you on the discernment of your choice in all three cases. You're getting better all the time. Thank you, ma'am.

Another pass is coming this week-end for Yom Kippur. And of course I'm going to take it. But if three years ago someone had told me that, among other things, I would ride almost two hundred miles in the back of a truck, just to attend services, I don't think I would have agreed with him. If I hadn't have been so religious this last time I would have gotten a pass to Paris. Passes came up at that time for three men in the company, and I'm at the top of the list. In fact, I've already turned down two other passes waiting for one to Paris, or London, or the Riviera. I wait a whole year to be religious, and then when I do look at the thanks I get! Just for that, I don't think I'll go next year.

Glad to hear you got back from Muskoka safe and sound and happy. I bet I can get a pretty good picture of the family spirit at about one o'clock that night. A bit strained, wasn't it? However, I'm afraid I can't sympathize too sincerely with the tribulations of your traveling conditions.

It seems there was something else I was going to say, but I can't think of it now. So,

until next time then, good-bye. With love

———

19 September 45
Lauda, Ger.

Dear Mother, Dad, and Fred,

Greetings! Life for us is kept at a high peak of interest these days. Since J-V day following the redeployment news has been comparable with following the war news before. Every day something new comes out. Sometimes favorable, usually not. There's not much use in my telling you all the latest stuff, because you probably hear everything, or at least a great deal, that we do. All the news sources naturally make a big noise of anything they hear even remotely connected with the subject, since it's the one their customers have the greatest interest in. So every day we get a story from the radio, the *Stars and Stripes*, the division paper, and Madam Rumor, all different.

And while I'm on the subject of news sources I might as well exhaust it for you. Rumors I believe I've covered sufficiently to prevent shock from exposure. So, the other three. The *Stars and Stripes* is good. Better than one could reasonably expect, in fact. Off-hand I can't think of anything else in the army that has more openness and fairness to it. If anything its spirit is anti-army. And the physical aspects are as good as most big-city dailies. Its letters column is its most popular and famous feature, and it actually seems to get things accomplished.

The division paper, known as the *Railsplitter* because that's supposed to be the 84th's nick-name, because it was originally an Indiana division and Lincoln is from Indiana I think, is just about what you expect. On the order of the *Stark Jewish News*. Which reminds me, do me a favor willya please, and tell the SJN my present address? And also reminds me, yes, I did get a laugh out of that article you sent me from it, but I can't quite see why you singled out that particular one? It appeared to me to be quite typical. However I will admit that that ultra-swanky northwest residential section is a new high for Mssr. W, whose inimitable style I recognize.

As for our radio, it is quite similar to yours, but without the advertisements of course. But I long ago passed the point where I cared much for anything other than music and news from the radio. I don't really know whether in the last two or three years my tastes have become more discriminating or my nerves more delicate, but there have been many things of that sort that I've noticed have affected me in that way. I trust it's part of the process of maturing.

I just had my first taste of venison a few minutes ago. The woods around here are pretty thickly populated with deer and GIs hunting them. They're not much like what you find in America, but they are deer. Most of them weigh about thirty pounds, I'd guess. But they've got huge rabbits, to make up for it. At a distance, and running away, you often mistake one for the other! And I'm not exaggerating. It tasted better than I expected. A little strong, but tender.

But ammunition is getting a little harder to get now, so I still think you ought to keep on sending packages. How about mailing one now, please?

Take care of yourselves. Love Carl

———

24 September, 1945
Lauda, Germany

Dear Family,

The big excitement of late around here is that in two days everyone with sixty-six or more points leaves for a division that is scheduled to sail the 15th of October. So, if there is no hot breath on my heels, at least there's a slight smudge on the horizon behind me. I now permit myself to entertain an intimation of a suspicion of a breath of hope that perhaps I stand a small chance of sailing in November. You may accept that statement literally, but literally. You see, I'm in the army, and all inmates of that exalted institution must continuously bear the realization and acceptance of the supreme necessity of allowing from three to five hundred percent leeway on all suppositions, guesses, reports, announcements, orders, rumors, and events. In other words, I'm kind of hoping to sail then, but don't you expect me to.

It's about time for the mail to come in. I haven't received any from you in about four or five days, so there should be some to-night. I'll finish this after I see. Bye.

Nope—Wass ist loss? (or something) which reminds me—that letter written in German that made such a big impression on you, well, if I said I was helped on it that would be an exaggeration. Most of it wasn't me.

Behave yourselves Carl

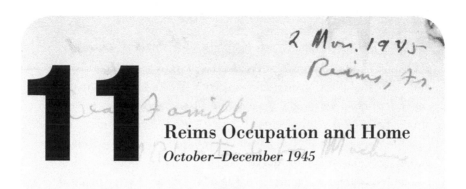

11

Reims Occupation and Home
October–December 1945

Carl was in line to go home. As part of the repatriation process, the army first transferred him to Reims, France, a "big city ... devastated by the fighting."[1]

In Reims, his superiors put him to work, manning something he had never encountered before: IBM computers. As Carl remembered it: "A few other guys in my outfit were selected to go to an IBM processing unit in Reims, France. I was assigned to this to operate IBM machines. That was okay with me. I liked the change. They were old-fashioned IBM machines with electric currents. There were punch cards. The cards would pass over a machine with ... little copper brushes. It would make contact where there was a hole."[2]

———

3 October 1945
Reims, France

Bonne Soir, Maman, Papa, et Frere,

And now, as we bid a fond and tearful adieu to beautiful, quaint old Germany, with the deep winding rivers and forbidding castles, we promise ourselves that some day, somehow, we shall once more.

Well, of course, that's a little different than the impression I got of the place. But, you know, I would like to go back some time as a tourist. Or, what I probably mean, as a sentimentalist.

What am I doing in France? Ma, I'm not on my way home. This will have no bearing one way or the other on the time it takes me to get home. I've been transferred to this outfit until that time arrives.

MRU stands for Machine Record Unit. We handle personnel cards. Or rather, we handle the machines that handle them, by means of punched and punching holes in them. You've heard of it.

The reason they picked me and forty-nine others to work on them is that our names happened to be handy to someone or other. There's no one left in the ETO [European Theater of Operations] with any experience. Any of you know anything about the things? If so, give me a few pointers; maybe I'll get to be a T/S [Technical Sergeant] before I leave.

This outfit, as near as I can figure it, is the headquarters or a headquarters of a headquarters. About as far back as you can get. The only comment I've been able to think of off-hand is that this is ONE HELL of a time to get in the rear echelon! Just missed the timing by six months or so! I'm waiting for someone from an army headquarters to give me a sneering look. (That's the way it is, you know. Just as we looked down on our company hdqs., so did our company clerks look down on battalion; bat. on regiment, and so on. These guys used to think of those in England as "rear-echelon S. of B.s").[3]

Don't know as yet just what kind of work I'm going to do. With all the redeploying going on the boys are pretty busy here. Working three 8 hour shifts seven days a week. That'll be good for me. I've been living too softly and easily these past few months. In Lauda things had retrogressed to where we literally did not do a thing we didn't want to except stand reveille. We'd sleep, eat, and spend half the day sleeping some more. The rest of the time we'd read, write, listen to the radio, hunt, play ball, or have an argument. We had quite complete and entirely competent maid service (jealous?) from the mother and 17 year old daughter whose home we were in, and who were very pleasant people.

But, as I was saying, I don't think all that laxity was too good for me, so some work will not be overly unwelcome.

One thing that I've been made aware of in my short time in France is the relationship between these people and us is more—well, strained than that of the Germans and us. The reason for that, it seems to me, is that in the latter case it is both apparent to and accepted by both parties that one is the master and the other is the vanquished. They both see the same picture. But in the other case both parties do not see the same. Most of us here I'm afraid look upon the French as almost a conquered people, although we do not of course employ that term, with us as the conquerors, and the French see us as being almost unwelcome intruders; we are undeservedly and belligerently haves, and they are righteous and equally undeservedly have-nots.

And now here is another thing I notice—I have been in France two days and can give easily an accurate description of anything about the country from its mores to its whores. I have been in Germany eight months, and it is only with difficulty that I can give a plausible account of even the simplest customs of the place. I have been in America for twenty years, and I haven't the slightest notion of how I would describe it to a foreigner.

If I have talked with a man for two minutes I can sit down and fill ten pages with description of him, and I can say just how he will act under any given circumstances. But if I have been intimate with him for many months, all I can tell is his physical appearance, and his temperament, and a lot of stories that won't add up.

From which I will not draw any conclusions, for awhile.

I meant to say this earlier: I didn't know it would take me so long to go from Germany to here or I should have warned you. That is why I haven't written, you see. A snafu came up, and it took four days longer than I had anticipated.

So how's everything by you? I won't know for ten days or so, 'til my mail starts catching up with me. Write.

Love Carl

Writing about America's general view of France, Schrijvers noted that "Throughout history, the Americans had regarded the French with a 'combination of skepticism and sentimentality.' The stunning collapse of France in 1940 and the subsequent collaboration of the Vichy government with the Nazis had clearly tipped the balance in favor of skepticism."[4]

5 Oct. 45
Reims, Fr.

Dear Family,

All this outfit is, is one big compiling and reporting office. We've got thirty or forty International Business Machines, electrical, that do all sorts of amazing and complicated things. And my job is to help make them do it. They're the same machines that insurance companies, personnel agencies, and such people use, and it parallels auditing, both theoretically and practically, I understand. So maybe I'll get a little bit of good out of it.

Eh, bien, il faut que je parte maintenant. Avec tout mon cour [Ah, well, I must go now. With all my heart] –Carl

13 Oct. 1945
Reims, Fr.

Dear Family,

Reims and I have had the opportunity by now to digest each other. Don't know how I affected Reims, but I find her at least palatable. The town was almost completely destroyed in the last war, you know, and has been rebuilt. So it looks less European than most, in that most of the buildings are not in the last stages of decay. And it has, of course, that cathedral. For what it is worth, my opinion is that it would serve as a model, the state of perfection, for all other building of its type to try to reach. I'm partial towards Gothic architecture, though, and that might account for part of the force with which I was struck upon seeing it.

I find the French women pretty (don't stop) much as I was led to expect to find them, except that I firmly do not agree that they have good taste!

Reims is crowded with GIs, which is bad, but which accounts for five Red Cross clubs, and other things of that nature, which is good.

I'm spending my time these days feeding cards into various places on various machines, and taking them out of various other places on the same various machines. I'm still learning the various varieties of these varii (well, why not?), so it still holds a certain amount of interest for me. Everybody here in the outfit has a mixture of awe and pity for us, and so doesn't expect too much of us as yet. That'll wear off soon.

One thing I've been meaning to bring up for a couple of years—I am amazed and appalled at the morals of 95% of the people, members of the army being people, and of these countries, that I've been in contact with. Question: why wasn't I aware of that? Did you want me to find out for myself?[5]

Might—with love –Carl

———

13 October 45
Reims, Fr.

Hello,

Well, your letter really did sound like you were excited over that figurine and I'm pleased that it made you that happy. I'm afraid I'm going to have to disappoint you now, though. Or whereas I could get things for 1/3 of their worth in Germany, here of course I must pay three times their value. And this town being crowded with GIs, even cigarettes and clothes are not worth very much. However, I'll see what I can do. But don't send any more money; it's likely useless.

But then I might get a furlough to England or Switzerland from here, and Switz. especially would be a good place for me to get what you wish. We'll see.

I'm having a hard time writing—I'm in the midst of a big argument—ASTP style, and it's getting hard to concentrate. All of us transferred have high IQ scores, which brings back the old ASTP atmosphere.

Love –Carl

———

20 Oct. 1945

Dear Folks,

This is just a fast one to tell you that I've got nothing to tell you.

If Sugardale ever gets to the point where it needs I.B. Machines to keep track of stuff, why then I can be Vice Pres. in Charge of Same. And by the looks of things it's likely that by the time I get out of here that'll be necessary.

One thing, though, the time passes much more quickly now that I'm doing something with it than when I wasn't.

Here's a couple pictures of "the boys," back in Lauda. I took one of them, so don't try to find me in it. Ma, those are not heavenly visitations trying to sneak in.

Love to you all Carl

———

24 October 1945
Reims, France

Dear Mother, Dad, and Fred,

First I think I'd better dispel the apparent misconception you have about my being on the verge of entering The Promised Land. I'm not. I now suspect, although not as yet expect, that it'll be about the end of year. So don't count too heavily on my reentering school at the second semester of this year.

But I also want you to continue to acquire all the dope you can that I'll be interested in concerning school. I don't suppose you could get a record from Miami omitting my second semester marks, could you? And get those from Queens, of course. I agree that it wouldn't be a good idea to send me catalogues. But could you kind of give me any synopsis (that's right, isn't it?) of the better ones, with facts, figures, and possibilities?

About Switzerland—that's one of the places you can go if you get a furlough, with a quota just like other places. At the time I left the 84th I was at the top of the list, but now I've got to work my way up again. I did have the chance to go to Switz. once back there, but, and it is a long complicated story, which I'll tell you the next time I see you, I started getting smart and finally outsmarted myself out of it, which should have taught me some kind of a lesson, but which I don't think did.

Anyways, now I'm about a hundred miles from Paris, so I'm going to take off one of these week-ends and see it, illegally, of course.

That, by the way, is how I used to make all those trips to Heidelberg and Mannheim, illegally. But I never got caught which should prove something or other.

How are things progressing in the building line? Any later developments? Keep me posted.

Have you seen the movie, *Junior Miss*? I think you'd like it.[6]

Haven't had much success in getting you a butcher, Dad. But all hope is not yet lost because there's a couple of P.W. camps around here. They're used for doing the dirty work around the post. About all I can promise is that if I do find some I won't have much trouble inducing them to go to the States later on. All I or you could do is take their word for it (their abilities), unless you intend coming over here, and as soon as they find out why I'm asking questions—well! Most of them would welcome any opportunity to come to America.

I'm somewhat happier here than I was in the discussion as far as companionship goes. They picked us for here on the basis of I.Q., so it's something like ASTP here now. But half of them have had the same military history as mine—ERC, ASTP, and infantry. In the 84th I was the only ASTP left in the platoons, and it got a little lonely at times.

For instance, I can now play bridge if I want to, and it used to be an impossibility. I'm going to see if I can't get practiced up a little for you.

We get all we want to eat here, and there's six Red Cross clubs in town, so I don't think the packages will be so necessary any more. Maybe one or two a month just to keep you in training, but no more. And please—no more peanut butter!

Here's how I'm passing my days now—work from 6 to 11 at night, eat to 12, work to 1, sleep to 12, eat to 1, pass the time, eat to 6. You'll note I get 11 hours of sleep out of that. Whenever I feel energetic I get up at 8 for breakfast, which gives me a whole morning to figure out something to do in the afternoon. Love –Carl

———

Leo's interest in finding displaced persons or German POWs to serve as butchers might not be as far-fetched as it first appears, as his father Harry did this after World War I. Harry brought to Canton some twenty butchers from Germany who were willing to leave the turmoil of Weimar Germany, and they were featured in the Sugardale ads in the 1920s as

wurstmeisters. For several years the Lavin household help was also a German immigrant, but she kept speaking to Fred and Carl in German despite
Dorothy's admonitions. When Carl signs his name as a young boy in his
Baum books, he signs it "Karl." When the boys started saying "hund" for
dog, Dorothy let the help go. Still, the dog retained the name Spitzy, for
pointer.[7]

—

28 October
Reims

Dear Folks,

Got a second twenty today. I hope you hurry up and get that letter
to stop sending me money, because there's not much I can do with all
of it. I get about ten a week selling cigarettes, and I don't have hardly
anything to spend it on.[8] As soon as it stops coming I'm going to go to
Paris, exchange it for three times its value in francs and send it back
to you. That's a nice way to do business, although not necessarily
legitimate.[9]

Here's how I got my sixty points: 35 for months in service, 10
for months overseas, and 15 for three battle stars. I should have
only 27 for months in service, but my ERC time is included, which
shows something or other about an ill wind. When we were first
asked to turn in the number of points we thought we should have I
did not include the extra eight. Then cards were made out with our
correct score checked against our service record and we were called
in to sign them. I was surprised to find I had been given eight more
points than I asked for. I asked how come and was told by a Jewish
lieutenant who probably used to be in the ERC himself that that time
counted. I knew it didn't, but I thought that would be a hell of a time
to argue, so I didn't. Division headquarters at some time somehow got
the idea that they were going to be captured, and destroyed some of
our records, mainly our regiment.[10] That figures in there somewhere
too but I'm not exactly sure where. Anyways, some guys have gone
home without being caught on their ERC time, so I guess I can do it
too. And that's how I got sixty points.

Every month now for five months I've been expecting to be home
three months later. I've just been holding my own, in other words. But

now I am glad to announce that at last I can report a slight gain on the
market. Now I expect to be home in two and a half months.

It's a shame I didn't know before I left Germany how much you
want some more figurines. It would be foolish for me even to try to
get you something here in France. I don't see now that I have much
chance of getting out of this country before I leave the ETO, but if
I do I will certainly try hard to get you as much else as I can. And
cigarettes are always good. I'm glad I never learned to smoke.

Take it easy. Love Carl

2 Nov. 1945
Reims, Fr.

Dear Famille,

MRU stands for Machine Record Unit; OIS stands for Oise
Intermediate Section (about five of them—Sections in France for
Army convenience—geographical distinction): No, this work will not
affect my departure from the ETO. There.

Last night I found out that Bob Newman was working in a
hospital only two miles from here! So today I went there and burst in
on him working in his laboratory. He was kind of surprised.

So we spent the rest of the day talking over things that people in
such circumstances talk over. The last time we'd seen each other was
when we left high-school—three and a half years ago! We'll probably
have quite a few chances to see each other before I leave, except that
he's getting a furlough to the Riviera next week and I'm getting one to
England at the end of the month—I think.

Tell Mrs. Newman he looks good, and hasn't changed, except to get
a little older—which you might expect after three and a half years.

Good luck on your recital, Mother. Hope you enjoy yourself. By
the way, how was your trip to Chicago?

Got a couple of packages the other day—slightly delayed. Thank
you.

Here's a question that came up among the bridge friends the
other day: Is a premeditated renege ethical?[11] I include the penalty in
the premeditation.

I've been playing pretty much bridge lately. Are you still fanatics back there? I expect to be in form by the time I arrive.

Behave yourselves Love –Carl

8 November 1945
Reims, France

Dear Folks,

If anything about this letter is a little hazy, a good excuse is that my mental capacities are not at their fullest at four o'clock in the morning. And what I'm doing at four o'clock in the morning is supposedly working, but actually, and obviously, writing you a letter. I'm on the graveyard shift now, from one to seven in the morning. It took a few days for me and my body to get used to it, but now I like it. I sleep in the morning, I mean the rest of the morning, mainly— and have afternoons and evenings off. Now all I need is to find some reason to *want* to have my afternoons and evenings off.

Did I tell you I got two packages together the other day? I'm not sure if I told you or not. Anyways I did get two packages the other day. And thank you for them. However, and in spite of all my past remonstrations to the contrary, I really think it would be useless for you to send any more. Not necessarily because of the imminence of my return, but mostly because we get all the food here we want— further proof that in the army the standard of living is directly proportional to distance from the front but inversely proportional to the demands on the personnel (comes the revolution!)—and there are five red cross clubs in town.

Mother, that was a beautiful letter you wrote about morals. And I agree with you and Daddy and your wisdom. When I asked you I wasn't referring specifically to sex, though. I meant all the morals. I used to think I had a fairly good idea of how most people are, but I've seen since how wrong I was. I was also surprised to see how closely high and low intelligence and high and low morals go together.

I'm glad to hear you had such a good time in South Bend. They sound like grand people. I think I'd like to meet them even though I am a little tired of meeting people. You know, every six months or so for the past three and a half years I've had to make a new circle of

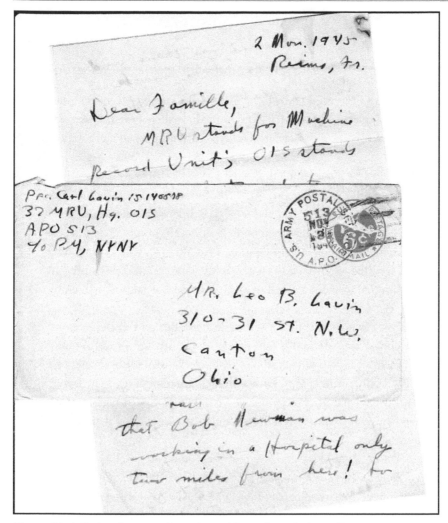

Figure 11-1. Reims letter and envelope, November. *Author collection.*

acquaintances. That's too often. Gets tiring. Anyways, hope you enjoy Chicago as well.

Every time you write me that figurine becomes more valuable. Maybe by the time I get home you can sell it and pay for the new house.

The reason I said they have pity and awe for us is that we're all front line men, and they've all been about as far back as you can get and still be on the continent.

Write soon. With love Carl

15 Nov. 1945
Reims, Fr.

Dear Family,

I haven't written lately for a very simple reason—I haven't had anything to say. The novelty of my work here has of course worn off by now, and it bores me. But fortunately I have only three more nights of it.

At last, you see, I'm going—no! no! you're wrong—I'm going on a furlough. It's to England. Paris is on the way, so I'm going to pause there for about three days, and then to London, and then Je ne sais quois. Meaning I might go on up to Edinburgh, or look over a few tourist spots, or just stay in London. I intend to stay away from here until it's time to ship out to an assembly camp. That'll probably run my furlough over time a half week or a week, but nothing will come of it.

It looks now as if I'll be sailing in the latter part of December. So keep on writing me at this address, please, until I tell you to stop.

Here's a rather sloppy photograph I took, which I believe accidentally turned out to have a shade of mediocre art to it. Agree?

I'll see what kind of porcelain I can get for you in Paris and London, by the way. I got a brooch today, a miniature. I'll shove it along at you.

Happy Thanksgiving Day, about the time you get this.

It's now three hours since I wrote that last line. The interim has been taken up by one of those ASTP discussions—arguments, this one on foreign policies and various unrelated sub-topics. Sort of semi-intellectual, I guess you might call 'em. One of the most pleasant ways I know of spending three hours.

Well, behave yourselves—Love Carl

25 Nov. 1945
London, Eng.

Dear Family,

This is a few hours after talking with you. Now perhaps I can tell you some of the things I could have said.

Of course, it was grand hearing you, and that was the main idea, the reason for the call. And of course I was much too excited to say anything, anyways.

You all sounded so well and, I don't know why, strong. It made me feel elated.

By the way, I won't be able to call you again as I said. I forgot just then that private calls can't be made from France, and I'd better get home before my turn for another furlough comes up.

Had you received the letter yet saying I was going to England? Oh, but I guess you got my cable didn't you? I'm sorry you had to wait all last night for me. I figured you must have gone somewhere for the week-end, and that there wouldn't be much chance of getting you today either, but then I thought I might as well try it. Good thing.

Officially this furlough is seven days plus travel-time. So far my travel-time has included three days in Paris, which I had to pass through anyways, but not necessarily that slowly. I take back what I said about French women having no taste. The Parisiennes aren't as bad as their country sisters. And I'll have to admit that Paris did leave an impression on me, generally good—but only because it was better than I expected it to be. Might have been better if I hadn't had London immediately after, to compare it with.[12]

I think I must have been a Londoner in my previous life. I'm practically infatuated with the place. It seems that for the first time in a year I'm back among people that have respect and decency. I also suspect the English are the most civilized peoples of any I've been in contact with, which is not entirely a compliment.

Here's something—a sign in a door leading to a private room in a public place, such as a station or theatre, always says, in America, "Keep out—Manager's Office," in Germany, "Forbidden;" in France, "Absolutely forbidden to enter;" and in England, "Private." That's about as good a mirror of national characteristics as you could find.

I sent you a figurine from Paris, Mother. I think, but I won't guarantee, that I was quite fortunate to get the price I did. Let me know about it when it arrives.

Wandered into the Louvre while in Paris. My God, what a collection. "Winged Victory," "Mona Lisa" and all that sort of stuff. I didn't even know they were in there. I can't say that I can see anything to either one of them, though, but maybe that's my fault.

My reason for coming to London was to see plays, and that's what I'm working on. So far I've seen two-thirds of *Private Lives*—argued with my conscience for ten minutes on whether I should be on time for a nine o'clock date or see the rest of the show.[13] Damn near killed me. But she was almost worth it, tell you about her later—and *Duet for Two Hands*, which is supposed to be one of the top hits of the year, but which I found dreary and implausible, and has consequently cost a portion of my former high faith in drama critics.[14] But *Private Lives* was wonderful, and I still don't know what happened in the third act. Do you know? I've been told what happened in the movie, but that didn't help much because it seems to have been only a mutilated mutant of the parent play.

Altogether, there are four Noel Coward plays going on now, so since I seem to have found a formula, I'll stick to it a little bit.

I've met and have been taking out a very fine girl. Father regular army officer. India, culture, training, correctness, Hail Britannia, class, etc—but with five years as a nurse, a great sense of humor, and a great deal of intelligence super-imposed on all that. Probably has a great deal to do with why I enjoy London so much.

Don't worry, I not bringing her home with me, Mom. They haven't been doing anything to your baby. (In case you're confused, I'm teasing you about your "What have they been doing to my baby?" attitude, which I assume you haven't grown out of yet.)

Yes, it's true that I've gained weight here. But, believe it or not, I gained it only during action, and not at all either before or after. How do you explain that? Apparently I'm a real Jew after all, and flourish only under adversity.

Well, that should be enough verbiage to last us both for a while. Write. Love Carl

———

8 December 1945
Reims, Fr.

Dear Folks,

Got the letter you wrote the 9th telling about your plans for the phone call. I see now. It was also full of your wanting me to get etchings and mezzotints. I'm terribly sorry I didn't get that before I left. You'd never mentioned before, I had no idea you wanted them, and it would have been little trouble for me to get just what you wanted in Paris, and London especially. Why didn't you tell me on the phone about etchings? All you had to do was mention it. I know nothing about mezzotints, but I certainly would have picked out some good etchings without any instructions.

You must have realized that if I were calling you from London on the 24th, I couldn't have been able to receive a letter in Reims yet that you had mailed the 9th. Awkwardly put, but you see what I mean.

If it's physically possible for me to still to get to Paris, I'll do it. But I'm pretty sure it's too late now. Tomorrow or the next day I expect to be transferred out of here to one of the redeployment camps, and the start of a long grind of processing and channeling and waiting. I don't think I'll be able to get out on a pass once I get that started.

Spent yesterday's and today's afternoons downtown to see if I could get anything decent. No dice. The only art objects left in Reims I wouldn't call art.

I'm terribly sorry mother. Would have been a good chance for me to get rid of some of my money that I don't seem to be able to do anything else with. But maybe it's still not too late. We'll see.

That question I asked about a premeditated renege being legal you answered by telling me a dozen things I was fully entirely aware of, and not replying to the question at all. An unusual circumstance that I thought made the chance worthwhile. Worked, too. That's when the question of ethics came up. See?

Remember my telling you I'd seen the first two acts of *Private Lives* and was trying to find out what happened in the third? Well, on my last day in London, in a restaurant, the lady that plays the lead in the play sat down in the same room. By the time I'd finished eating I'd gotten up enough nerve to ask her about that third act. Just as I got to her, though, I realized it really wasn't her, and I swerved off. Went out into the street, decided I'd been rationalizing, and it really was her. So I finally came back, and found out—that I *hadn't* been rationalizing. Very embarrassing. But I at least prevented myself from going through the rest of my life wondering whether it was, or whether it wasn't!

Can't give you any better estimates than the last one of when I'll reach the Promised Land. Be good. Love Carl

Reims, France
13 December 1945

Dear Mother, Dad, and Fred,

The way things look right now I can consider myself pretty fortunate, for they seem to be working out as I planned and hoped they would.

If I had not left on that furlough I would have been transferred out of here two weeks ago, because that is when the other 60 pointers were sent out. The usual procedure is to get transferred into an outfit about two weeks before its "ready date," the date it is prepared to leave a processing camp for a post. The drawback is that these processing camps are nothing but collections of tents, rather unpleasant places in which to spend two weeks.

So I took the furlough, planning to return here after the 60 pointers had been transferred out, and hoping to get transferred individually, later, and thus miss some discomfort.

And now my orders have come through. I leave tomorrow, the 14th, for an outfit that has a readiness date of the 15th. That's cutting it closer than I'd even hoped.

But don't get the idea that I'm practically on the boat. I'm not. We'll probably get to the post about the 17th, and sail about the 21st, arriving in New York around the 29th. That is, if the POE [Point of Embarkation] is Le Havre. It might be Marseilles, which would change those dates, respectively to the 19th, 23rd, and 3rd of Jan. All dates are subject to change without notice, are my own guesses, and are tentative as hell.

Incidentally, you'd better make discouraging noises at Mrs. Stone and her protégé regarding my chances for attending that New Year's affair. I won't know until the last moment of course, and it would have to be pretty unfair to somebody or other as a result. So say no.

Well, Fred, so you're now a member of the young executives' crowd? Your joining the C. of C. (J.G.) [Chamber of Commerce (Junior Grade)] startled me into the realization that everyone gets a year older every year. Congrats.

I went into Paris the day before yesterday. The Louvre was obtuse about the mezzotint angle, but I got a couple a' cute engravings. Decided I might as well be clever about it. Not exactly what you asked for ma Maman, but maybe you'll like them. I also bought and sent an ivory miniature reproduction of a Rembrandt, which, although you may not agree, I think is pretty good.

By the time you get this it will have been a month since I sent that figurine, of the first time I was in Paris. You should be receiving it soon, if you haven't already.

If I can, I'll wire my sailing date. However, I doubt that I'll be able to.

I'll write from the post. Until then –love Carl

———

Carl was shipped out of Antwerp in January 1946:

As our ship left Antwerp harbor, it scraped against a sunken ship in the harbor. We had a gash in the hull, and they told us that the watertight compartment held but we had to go at slow speed if we were to keep on going. We did. There were a lot of storms . . . a very stormy winter. We ended up taking twenty-five days to cross the Atlantic. At first we went the northern route, and that was too stormy. Then we went the southern route. We stopped at the Azores and replenished fuel and were able to buy a little food for the people. Then more storms [chuckles]. . . . We were going at slow speed. For twenty-five days, we crossed the Atlantic, my God! We finally ran out of food it was taking so long [chuckles] with so many storms. Alas, for four or five days we ate nothing but canned fruit—diced fruit—which was really funny.[15]

The one movie the ship had to show was the Humphrey Bogart movie *Sahara*. And they showed it over and over again. Decades later, watching the movie on TV, Carl could recite some of the lines from memory.

The ship docked in New York, and Carl then went to Indiantown Gap, Pennsylvania, near Harrisburg, where he was discharged.

Upon release, Carl got his final pay and went right back to Canton after demobilization.

He saw his parents. Leo was very interested in the stories that Carl would tell, asking questions and details. While talking about combat, Carl

310   started reliving some of the events and his hands started shaking, which surprised him. Dorothy could see he was getting excited.

"Lee, stop asking those questions. Look at Carl. His hands are shaking," she said, using Leo's nickname.

Carl said, "It's all right, Mother, I want to talk about it. I want to tell."

"No, no, don't. Look at your hands. Look at your hands."

This wasn't unfamiliar territory for many soldiers after the war. "War happens inside a man," Eric Sevareid concluded. "It happens to one man alone. It can never be communicated."[16]

Carl would leave it to others to communicate his story.

For now, it was good to see his parents again.

It was good to be back home.

Epilogue

It was Sunday and the two boys were playing at home. Dorothy and Leo were reading the Sunday paper and chatting. The radio provided soft music. Carl must have been six or seven, making Fred eight or nine. Suddenly Dorothy started laughing, maybe from something on the radio or from the conversation. Leo started laughing as well, which was a little unusual given his reserved temperament. Then another surprise. Leo stood up, still sort of chuckling and lifted Dorothy up in his arms, scooped her up, and he started carrying her up the stairs. Dorothy was still laughing as well but you could tell she was also a bit surprised. When they got to the landing at the top of the stairs, Dorothy told Fred and Carl, "Father and I are going to take a nap for a bit, so please don't disturb us. Use the downstairs bathroom if you need to."

It seemed ordinary enough, but most people didn't take afternoon naps, especially grown-ups. Carl asked Fred what was up, maybe mom was sick? Fred just stared silently with his lips pursed and shook his head. He wasn't going to answer. Worse, his motions indicated that he sort of knew what was going on and just did not want to share. Carl asked again, what's up with Mom and Dad? Again Fred shook his head silently. Well, something was up, that's for sure. So even ten years before the war we have the dim awareness that there is a private world of the parents, to which Carl could not be admitted. Fred was also on the outside, but he had a better seat.

Carl got it. Life is usually a story of details, of small matters. And for the GIs, that is what the war was all about. John Steinbeck explained:

> I haven't written anything about the 'Big Picture,' because I don't know anything about it. I only know what we see from our worm's-eye view, and our segment of the picture consists only of tired and dirty soldiers who are alive and don't want to die; of long darkened convoys in the middle of the night; of shocked silent men wandering back down the hill from battle; of chow lines and water tablets and foxholes and burning tanks and the rustle of high-flown shells; of jeeps and petrol dumps and smelly bedding rolls and C rations and cactus patches and blown bridges and dead mules and hospital tents and shirt collars greasy-black from months of wearing; and of laughter too, and anger and wine and lovely flowers and constant cussing. All these it is composed of; and of graves and graves and graves.[1]

Carl used the GI Bill to pay his tuition and get his degree from Miami in 1948. He met his true love, Audrey, on a blind date in Chicago and they would marry in 1953, on Washington's birthday. They were married for sixty years. In the early years of the marriage, Carl would still play football every Saturday—and without having to hide it from anyone. He played with some of the kids from 1941, those who returned.

Many decades have now passed. Carl and Audrey's four children are well into their middle years and there are nine grandchildren, some of whom are already adults, and even great-grandchildren.

Carl went back to Sugardale and succeeded Leo as president in 1963 while Fred served as vice president. Bear Stearns took the company public in 1968, with the effort led by a young Henry Kravis. Carl and Fred were forced out in a dispute with the cousins in 1969.

The company quickly became insolvent and was sold to another local firm, Superior Meats. You will still run into people who know the name, mainly because Sugardale supplied the hot dogs for the Cleveland Indians' games, a tradition that continues to this day

Canton's population peaked at about 117,000 in the 1950 census and in 2016 it had 73,000 residents. Leo died in 1974. Dorothy died in 1982. Fred just passed away at eighty-three, in 2005.

My mind goes back to the 1960s when the television featured shows about World War II, such as *Combat* and *The Gallant Men* and I recall my father's polite disdain for the shows, which puzzled me at the time. I suppose this was when I started to become aware that there might be a story behind the story. Even if the plot was yet another attempt to hit the ball bearing works at Schweinfurt, Dad would mystifyingly leave the room when these shows came on. The TV plots were generally preposterous: a beautiful young Frenchwoman, resistance fighter, stumbles across the squad of GIs. She needs to go behind enemy lines to recover some medicine for her ailing grandfather—who himself fought in the last war. The lieutenant forbids the mission because it is too dangerous. The sergeant decides to go anyway. The rest is predictable. My dad would just roll his eyes and softly tell me that would never happen. It could happen, I would protest. No, not really, that's not how it worked.

Then one day I came across the crumbling photo album from that period with the pictures of his squad. I knew from the television shows how the unit photos were supposed to appear. The members would be given nicknames stemming either from the place of origin ("Tex," "Brooklyn") or a somewhat endearing personal quality ("Einstein," "Romeo"). It was with disbelief that I looked at the squad photo and read the captions, "I.Q. 45" and "Deserted me under fire." That was not how it was supposed to be. Indeed, it would be impossible for a member of the US military to so behave. And it was a shock to read my Dad's assessments, as I had long viewed him as the least judgmental person on this planet. Apparently he saved those judgments for the privacy of his scrapbook.

There are other personal connections to the war. Hanging on a ceiling beam in my bedroom back in Canton is a gift from the head of the local Nazi party to my great-grandfather Harry from the 1930s. Of course, the United States had no formal Nazi party, but there was the German American Bund, the leading pro-Hitler and German nationalist organization that attained a degree of support during that "low, dishonest decade."

The gift is a rather ornate double-barreled shotgun. I don't know much about these things, but it looks like a nice present. My great-grandfather received it out of gratitude. In addition to hiring the *wurstmesiters* and in addition to the German household help, the Lavins had also hired a German scientist, or a lab manager.[2] The local Nazi worked for him at Sugardale as the head of the small laboratory responsible for testing for health and quality control. As the 1930s progressed, he became known for his Nazi sympathies. Many of the employees at Sugardale were from central Europe, and recent immigrants at that—countries with fine meat processing traditions, which would be likely to produce skilled butchers. These workers were increasingly aware of the Nazi's orientation and they remonstrated against the lab chief, asking my great-grandfather to fire him, solely on the basis of his political views. Harry Lavin refused, stating that no one could be more unsympathetic to the Nazis than he, a Jew, but that it would not be appropriate to fire the lab chief for his politics. The Nazi gave my great-grandfather the gift. When the war broke out and Germany declared war on the United States, the proud lab manager committed suicide.

So are we in a crab-walk of sorts? Shifting from tolerance to intolerance, seeing the same drama played out in different generations on a different stage.

This may be the most striking aspect of my father's story. There is revulsion toward the war and its horrors, but there is no bitterness toward Germany, nor any particular criticism of Germans. Even in his discussions with Nazis, Carl retained a sedate, almost journalistic detachment. Political philosopher Hannah Arendt shared the "first rule to be learned on the battlefield":"the closer you were to the enemy, the less you did hate him."[3] Carl reserved all of his criticism for people on his side, be it the US Army or members of his own family.

My dad kept at home in Canton only a few items from his youth. The stamp collection. The short stories by O. Henry, whose cell at the Ohio State Penitentiary was just a few blocks from where Carl had enlisted at Fort Hayes. And the Oz series that was the Harry Potter of its day. He also kept one of the porcelain German statuettes that he brought back for Dorothy, which she then left to him.

Of all my dad's possessions the most significant to me is a modest but sturdy bookcase against the wall of my boyhood room, built by my father, the battalion carpenter, after he came home from the war.

Carl also brought home a Luger pistol from the war. He took it from one of the Germans who crossed the Elbe in a rowboat. Audrey was concerned about the pistol when they began to have kids, and Carl agreed it was dangerous to have a gun when there were little ones running around the house. He sold it at a local pawnshop.

When I finished transcribing these letters, I sent the last group home with a note:"Dad—This is the final batch of letters I have. A sad moment because I have profoundly enjoyed having this peculiar conversation with you, if simply reading and transcribing the letters can be called a conversation. It turns out that you are a human being after all, something I had dimly suspected, but these letters stand as pretty strong proof that you had a life other than that of a father. Not sure my kids will ever encounter such evidence regarding me. Love you a lot . . . your dutiful son."

Dad's classmate at Queens ASTP, the poet Samuel Menashe, noted how we can never fully repay the debts of those who served in his poem, "The Offering." Menashe ended up at the Battle of the Bulge as well, in the 87th Division.

> Flowers, not bread
> Cast upon the water—
> The dead outlast
> Whatever we offer.[4]

Carl said it took him three to five years to get over the war. Carl was never interested in looking backward, which he explained to me when I asked him why he was not much involved in veteran's organizations. He told me that he attended one or two meetings but did not find them particularly interesting. As GI Howard Ruppel related, "I didn't want to rehash, refight, relive, recreate images, or relive memories in a social atmosphere. I sought no recognition or special attention. I didn't want to be thought of as a hero. I didn't want my past life to interfere with my future life. I wanted to get on with living, in the manner I chose."[5]

I remember Dad talking with Uncle Fred about friends who would hit the ground when they heard a car backfire or who would reflexively field strip a cigarette for years after they left the army. More than seventy years after the war, my father still remembered his serial number, and if you asked him how to break down and clean a Browning Automatic Rifle, he could take you through the hand motions with his eyes closed. Because if your weapon jams at night, you need to break it apart and reassemble it. Some things we forget and some things we remember.

In 2007, Lehman High School honored Carl as one of its distinguished alumni. The citation read in part: "After retirement, Carl volunteered overseas to advise businesses in the food industry in developing countries and in the transition in Eastern Europe. He served on the Board of Directors of the Canton Palace Theatre Association which restored the old theatre downtown. He was Vice President of The Wilderness Center, a local nature reserve. He was a volunteer for SCORE—Service Corps of Retired Executives—which provides free advice to small businesses. He was on the Board of the Canton Jewish Community Federation. And at age 79, he passed the test to join Mensa, the society for the top 2% of IQ."

To Gus, the barber at the 30th St. Barbershop, Carl was the guy who gave him a job when he got out of the army, and Gus worked at Sugardale until he used the GI Bill to go to barber's college. Fred told him that if he ever wanted his job back, it was always there for him.

Then there is the anonymous man who sent Dad $10 every month, along with an apology, because he had stolen from Dad in the 1950s and wanted to pay back the money. Dad chuckled because he sure couldn't remember any such theft, but it was nice of the man to pay the money back.

One employee at Hoovers was Ethel Goshay, who left when they closed the grenade assembly line. She helped the Lavins at their house for a number of years until her husband tragically died. Then Carl helped her get a job at Sugardale. Her granddaughter Charita Goshay is a columnist for the *Repository*. The Diebold Family no longer runs Diebold and the Hoovers no longer run Hoover. Timken is now two companies.

In his personal papers, Carl had saved all these years a Christmas card photo from Paul, his buddy from the 84th, with his family in the 1950s, showing him married with two young kids. Nice photo, taken at a beach, and full of smiles and youth. Carl and Audrey drove out to Indiana once to visit him on his farm.

Dad explained how his adult life connected with the war:

> I felt the most benefit that I got from it was living a life as a private in the Army, being at the bottom of the social barrel. I wasn't born into that, and I have not been that ever since. But knowing that I could survive and do well in a different social milieu meant something to me, and I've always understood what it's like to be at the very bottom. I've always been able to have an empathy for people at the bottom because of my spending a couple years at the bottom myself. I always felt it was good for me to have that experience.[6]

To our family, Carl was just a wonderful father and friend—nonjudgmental, easy-going, never given to anger, with family always on his mind, often thinking about his own parents and remembering growing up on 25th Street.

Even in his eighties, when Carl heard that one particular Chopin étude, he would hold his breath and wince at a special moment, recalling the precise point in the piece when his mother might possibly miss the note. Even though Dorothy would not let him play football, and even

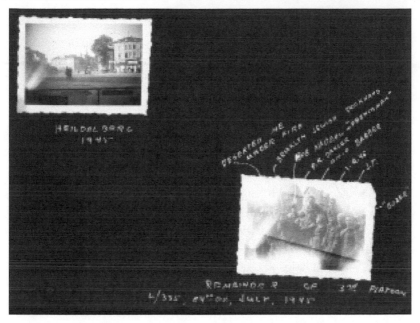

Figure E-1. Remainder of 3rd Platoon, Company L, 335th Infantry, July 1945, from Carl's scrapbook. His inscription, "deserted me under fire," was what started this book. *Author collection.*

though they argued, the sympathy of a boy listening to his mother's pained efforts still echoed in his mind so many decades later.

He would still hold his breath as she held her breath, trying to reach that note. Some things we always remember.

From Carl Lavin:

I feel a scattering of emotions when I read my letters or discuss events of seventy years ago. First of all, deep gratitude to my son for wanting to do it and for contributing so much time and effort and commitment.

Secondly, I feel sadness over the censoring of our letters home that blocked off the heart and soul of our experiences. We were repeatedly reminded by our officers to give no details as to place, actions, casualties, military gains or losses, etc. This was in case some mail would fall into the hands of the enemy. All mail was screened by our company officers.

Thirdly, I feel a sense of pride at having always been a good soldier, of doing my duty. I experienced five months of combat and was never touched although only about 15 percent company were not killed and wounded. Two or three times a month we would receive a new batch of green replacements and we had a saying, "If a new replacement makes it through his first 48 hours at the front, then he's got a chance." Reading my old letters of seventy-plus years ago has made me think and dream much more of those days and of my personal experiences. I was impossibly lucky.

Thank you for reading my letters. Keep the home fires burning, and if you have a loved one away at school or in the service, it probably wouldn't be a bad idea to send them some candy. Fudge never hurts.

Be well. And behave yourself.

—Carl H. Lavin

Carl passed away in January 2014, a few months shy of his ninetieth birthday. This book stands in testament to his service and in memory of those who served the Allied cause.

Notes

Preface

1. Ernie Pyle, *Here Is Your War* (New York: Tess Press, 2004), introduction, jacket flap.

2. Paul Fussell, *Wartime: Understanding and Behavior in the Second World War* (New York: Oxford University Press, 1990), 134.

3. Peter S. Kindsvatter, *American Soldiers: Ground Combat in the World Wars, Korea, and Vietnam* (Lawrence: University Press of Kansas, 2003), 291n30.

Introduction

1. David McCullough, *The Wright Brothers* (New York: Simon and Schuster, 2015), 1.

2. Carl's grandfather, Harry Lavin, was born in Kiev in 1870 and came to New York when he was fourteen. He moved to Akron to work in a match factory before settling in Canton to peddle produce from a wagon. Harry opened up a "butter and egg" store in 1896, made it a retail grocery in 1902, and gradually expanded into meats. By 1930, the family was largely out of the grocery business and firmly into meat processing. By 1940, Harry's Sugardale—named for its sugar-curing process—had grown to employ two hundred workers and a fleet of refrigerated trucks. Carl Lavin, in discussion with the author. Edward Thornton Heald, *The Stark County Story* (Canton, OH: The Stark County Historical Society, 1952), 3:182–84; and *The Stark County Bicentennial Story, 1776–1976* (Canton, OH: Stark Co. Bicentennial Committee, 1976), 26.

3. By age, Harry's four children were Elizabeth, married to Lou Kaven; Leo, married to Dorothy; Bill, married to Celia; and Arthur, married to Dodo. As a daughter, Elizabeth was not given any say in the business.

4. Ted Gup's moving book, *A Secret Gift*, describes the hardships in Canton at this time:

> For four years, Canton's 105,000 citizens had been battered by the Great Depression. Around town, parents were using strips of tires to extend the life of worn out shoes, the union mission was bursting with the homeless, and scrawny children in patched coats were scavenging for coal along the B&O railroad tracks. Many of those lucky enough to still have homes had sold their furniture, beds and all, and huddled together on bare floors or sat on old orange crates. . . .
>
> Newspapers, selling for three cents a copy, were shared, family to family, and read by kerosene lamp. For many, electricity was a luxury as remote as a ride on a bus or a visit to the doctor. Children went to school on empty stomachs. Many would not learn the meaning of the word *breakfast* until years later. . . . Thousands of Canton's depositors were shocked to find their bank padlocked, their savings gone. Mothers and fathers did what they could to hide their despair from their children -- and from each other. All the while the asylum, the county poorhouse, the city orphanage, and the reformatory swelled with casualties of the Hard Times. It was a landscape Dickens would have recognized. . . .
>
> By Christmas 1933, two million Americans were homeless. Tens of thousands rode the rails in search of a job. One in four Americans was out of work. In Ohio, it was worse. The jobless numbered more than one in three and in industrial centers like Canton, some put the number at 50 percent. There was no purpose in counting. There was no relief to be had.

Ted Gup, *A Secret Gift: How One Man's Kindness—and a Trove of Letters—Revealed the Hidden History of the Great Depression* (New York: Penguin, 2010), 4.

5. The 1940 Census was the first one in which a majority of American households had indoor plumbing, showing 45 percent of US households without complete indoor plumbing. No questions were asked about telephones in that census. US Census Bureau, "Historical Census of Housing Tables – Plumbing Facilities," last modified October 31, 2011, accessed November 7, 2014, http://www.census.gov/hhes/www/housing/census/historic/plumbing.html.

6. Grandfather Harry Lavin had been an active Socialist for a number of years and had run for office several times on the party ticket. Debs stayed at the Harry Lavin house the night before his speech.

7. Cabell Phillips, *The 1940s: Decade of Triumph and Trouble* (New York: Macmillan Publishing Company, 1975), 9–10.

8. Lynn Olson, *Those Angry Days: Roosevelt, Lindbergh, and America's Fight over World War II, 1939–1941* (New York: Random House, 2013), 424; and Lorraine B. Diehl, *Over Here!: New York City during World War II* (New York: Harper Collins, 2010), 62.

Chapter 1: From Canton to Miami and Enlistment

1. "The American people found common cause in the belief they were fighting a just and necessary conflict to save Western civilization. In doing so, they coalesced as never before in history." Olson, *Those Angry Days*, 436–37.

2. Paul Fussell, *Wartime: Understanding and Behavior in the Second World War* (New York: Oxford University Press, 1990), 134.

3. The essay in full:

Wars are fought on two equally important fronts, the physical and mental, although the former is often over-emphasized because it usually controls the fluctuations of the latter.

On the mental or morale front the enemy's propaganda howitzers strike our defences in three places: the Allies' trustful cooperation, their confidence of their superiority, and their trust in the abilities of their leaders.

Britain's two great losses in the past week, the capture of Singapore by the Japanese and the escape from Brest by the Germans, have greatly aided Mr. Goebbels on all three sides of the mental front. They served to disunify the Allies, as was evidenced by America's roar of disapproval over Britain's war management; they tended to make us unconfident of our own strength, for the simple reason that the battles were lost; and finally they aroused a doubt of the competency of our leaders, especially in England itself.

Actually, it is rather unreasonable of us to become so discouraged as the result of this double bad news. We have been told again and again that this will not be an easy war and that we must expect many defeats before final victory, just as we have been asked to have faith in the capacity of our leaders. our factories and soldiers, and our allies.

Naturally England as well as all the other United Nations has made and will make mistakes. But we must remember, however, in the same spirit that this is "our country, right or wrong" so are they our allies.

"Essay Contest Winners," *Canton Repository*, February 23, 1942, 5.

4. "Colored employees were first placed on the payroll on August 31, 1942. At that time most of the men in the General Labor Department were transferred to production jobs and colored men were employed to replace them. At a later date colored women were added to the General Labor Department and still later, both colored men and women were hired at random throughout the plant until approximately 300 were employed." (Total wartime employment peaked at approximately 6,500.) In the list of Hoover employees who entered military service, six of the names were Hoovers. *Hoover War History* (North Canton, 1946), 123, 169, 174; Ethel Goshay, a young African American woman, got a factory job at the Hoover plant, making hand grenades.

5. Many Canton companies were important to the war effort:

> Canton's established industries also played major roles in the country's war production. The Timken Roller Bearing Company doubled its production and turned out over 100,000 gun barrels of seamless tubing. . . . Republic Steel Corporation produced alloy steels in its Canton and Massillon plants for armor plate, ordnance, airplane bombs and submarine engines. A new type of armor plate, developed by Central Alloy Steel and Diebold working together, did much to win the war. . . . Hercules Motors Corporation was 100 per cent war production and more than 650,000 Hercules engines were produced for war purposes. The plant area at Hercules was seven times larger at the end of the war then it was at the outbreak. . . . Diebold fabricated and installed armor plate on 36,000 scout cars and manufactured a wide variety of airplane and anti-aircraft parts.

Stark County Bicentennial Story, 112.

6. Cantonians' certainty of their target-worthiness was validated in the 1949 movie *Twelve O'Clock High*, with the massive bomber raid on the German bearing facilities at Schweinfurt as the center of the plot. If that's what we would do to them, why wouldn't they do it to us? A successful 1960s television series of the same name adopted elements of the plotline.

7. "Lehman Seniors Celebrate Graduation," *Canton Repository*, June 6, 1942, 7.

8. The Enlisted Reserve Corps was the army's first attempt to get eligible young men to commit themselves to eventual army sevice while still in high school or college. Announced April 23, 1942, the plan allowed enlistees to choose between ground, service, or air forces, such a choice considered then to be the most drastic recruiting concession possible to get the eighteen- and nineteen-year-olds into

the fold. Louis E. Keefer, *Scholars in Foxholes: The Story of the Army Specialized Training Program in World War II* (Jefferson, NC: McFarland & Co., 1993), 17.

9. The Columbus Barracks were established in 1863 and were renamed Fort Rutherford B. Hayes in 1922. The most striking feature of Fort Hayes was the tall "shot tower" in the central building, where molten lead would be poured into pools of water to manufacture shot. The story might be apocryphal but the name stuck. Andrew Henderson, *Forgotten Columbus* (Charleston, SC: Arcadia Publishing, 2002). It would not have escaped a boy from Canton that Hayes served as McKinley's commanding officer during the Civil War.

10. In a letter to Leon Henderson, Administrator, Office of Price Administration, Senator Robert A. Taft argued that price controls had hurt Ohio businesses:

April 15, 1942

Dear Mr. Henderson:

I have had a number of complaints with regard to the price-fixing policies in relation to soy-bean oil, cotton-seed oil, and lard. Basically the complaints are the same—that the price of oil has been fixed without fixing the price of the raw material, with the result that the processors and dealers are compelled to take a loss.

The Ideal Packing Company, of Cincinnati, and the Sugardale Provision Company, of Canton, Ohio, complain that when the price was fixed on pork products, hogs were selling at $13.50 a hundred, and since that time they have advanced to $15.15 a hundred. . . .

It seems to me that price fixing should start with the raw material and be gradually extended to the wholesaler and retailer. I realize the handicap the Price Control Bill imposes on you through its farm provisions, but I see no reason why the price of hogs . . . should not now be fixed at the lowest price permitted by the Price Control Act, and the price of products worked out from that base. . . .

Sincerely, Robert A. Taft

Clarence E. Wunderlin, ed., *The Papers of Robert A. Taft,* Vol. 2, *1939–1944* (Kent, OH: Kent State University Press, 2001), 349–50.

11. The Canton and Massillon football rivalry is the longest-standing high school competition in the United States.

12. The banner headline of the *Canton Repository* read: "M'Kinley ends Massillon Reign 35-0" and noted that the crowd of twenty thousand saw an end to

Massillon's 52-game winning streak: "A dreary trail that for seven long years had led along the dark paths of frustration and despair wound up in the lofty peaks of unbounded joy and magnificent achievement for McKinley High School Saturday afternoon." The second article on the front page stated simply: "Allies Push Forward in Tunisia." *Canton Repository*, November 22, 1942, 1.

13. What rumors might have been circulating, we can only speculate, but rationing was implemented the next day, on December 1, 1942: "The ordinary person, the possessor of an 'A' windshield sticker, could buy four gallons a week, later reduced to three. Those able to wangle 'B' or 'C' stickers—people engaged in crucial deliveries or medical services or indispensable government work—got more gasoline." Fussell, *Wartime*, 196.

14. Hudson Bay is the eponymous name for a heavy wool blanket sold by the Hudson Bay Company.

15. Walter Havighurst, *The Miami Years, 1809–1969* (New York: Putnam, 1969), 213.

Chapter 2: Texas

1. Fussell, *Wartime*, 4, 6; Michael D. Doubler, *Closing with the Enemy: How GIs Fought the War in Europe, 1944–1945* (Lawrence: University Press of Kansas, 1994), 266; "On 1 January 1941, the authorized strength . . . stood at 356,000 troops and by 31 January 1945 the AGF achieved a troop strength of 2.7 million." Frank N. Schubert, *Mobilization: The U.S. Army in World War II, The 50th Anniversary* (Washington, DC: US Army Center of Military History, 1994), 9, 12, http://www .history.army.mil/documents/mobpam.htm.

2. "History of the Great Place," US Army, accessed November 10, 2014, pao .hood.army.mil/history.aspx; and Arnold P. Krammer, "German Prisoners of War," *Handbook of Texas Online*, http://www.tshaonline.org/handbook/online/articles /qug01, uploaded on June 15, 2010, accessed November 10, 2014.

3. Rick Atkinson, *The Guns at Last Light: The War in Western Europe, 1944–1945* (New York: Henry Holt and Co., 2013), 328.

4. Forever Yours was a chocolate bar with caramel and nougat covered in dark chocolate, now called Milky Way Midnight.

5. The emblem of the Tank Busters is a wildcat crushing a tank in its teeth with the motto of "Seek . . . Strike . . . Destroy."

6. Military historian John Keegan comments on the effect of army life on civilians, noting that it "exposed 12 million of them to a system of subordination and autocracy entirely alien to American values." Fussell, *Wartime*, 83.

7. *The Ox-Bow Incident*, starring Henry Fonda, was nominated for an Academy Award for best picture in 1944, but lost to *Casablanca*.

8. There were POW camps throughout the United States: "Prepared or not, the country suddenly found itself on the receiving end of massive waves of German and Italian prisoners of war. Texas had approximately twice as many POW camps as any other state." Krammer, "German Prisoners of War." And where there are prisoners, there are prison breaks: "Nationally, as of mid-April 1945, there had been a total of 1,583 escapes from a POW population of about 400,000." John Hammond Moore, "Hitler's Wehrmacht in Virginia, 1943–1946," *Virginia Magazine of History and Biography*, 85, no. 3 (1977) 260.

9. Peter S. Kindsvatter, *American Soldiers: Ground Combat in the World Wars, Korea, and Vietnam* (Lawrence: University Press of Kansas, 2003), 21.

10. Ibid., 301.

11. A lodge in Canada where the Lavin family took summer holidays. During the Great Depression Leo Lavin was able to rent a cabin there for $2 a week.

12. "Love-making efforts" were the parents' efforts to find dates for Carl.

13. Segregation limited the number of black soldiers who saw combat:

> Although young blacks often joined the service for the same reason as whites, seeking adventure or a career they could be proud of, in the era of segregation in America blacks also enlisted to prove that they could serve their country as effectively and loyally as whites. ...The number of black combat units formed and committed to battle during the era of segregation was relatively low because of the pervasive belief among whites that the black man was not fit to be a combat soldier. Blacks were relegated to service as support troops, often performing menial or disagreeable tasks such as stevedoring, construction, and graves registration. Those black units that did see combat in the world wars did so in no small part because black politicians, the black press, and civil rights advocates demanded a role in the fighting for black Americans.

Kindsvatter, *American Soldiers*, 267.

Black GIs and officers couldn't shake discrimination during wartime:

> [There was] nothing was more demoralizing to black GIs training at segregated camps in World War II than to see their enemy receiving better treatment from white America than they did. Lacey Wilson, a black infantry lieutenant, remembers having to go to the back door of a "whites only" train-station restaurant in Texas while German prisoners of war and their white guards ate inside: "It sickened me

so I could not eat a bite after ordering. I was a citizen soldier in the uniform of my country and I had to go through an alley to the back door while some of Hitler's storm troopers lapped up my hospitality of my country."

Ibid., 270n13.

14. One of the African American officers at that time at Camp Hood was Jackie Robinson, who would go on to break baseball's color barrier with the Brooklyn Dodgers four years later. Notably, it was at Camp Hood where Robinson was brought up on a court martial in July 1944. "By the end of the war, black infantry platoons served honorably and competently side by side with white soldiers in nearly fifty American infantry companies in Europe." Peter R. Mansoor, *The GI Offensive in Europe: The Triumph of American Infantry Divisions, 1941–1945* (Lawrence: University Press of Kansas, 1999), 236n78.

15. In March of 1943, food rationing was introduced for meat products, milk, cheese, and other foods. We have no more information on the black market, but as the family was in the meat business, they would have likely heard rumors of what black market activity there might be.

16. The story of the 100-mile-per-hour car: As a teenager in Canton, Carl sometimes ran errands for Sugardale in one of the company's four Plymouths, which were typically used by salesman making calls. Back in 1940, a sixteen-year-old being allowed to make pick-ups and deliveries in a Plymouth was like giving a kid access to a private plane. One day, Carl's high school friend asked him if the Plymouth, which had very little horsepower, could reach 100 miles per hour. Carl didn't know, but the two teenagers were determined to find out. They drove 20 miles to Green Township, which hosted the biggest hill in the area, accelerated on the decline and watched as the car hit its mark. Carl and his friend kept their test drive a secret for seventy years. It wasn't until 2009, upon bumping into each other in a restaurant, that the two friends shared their story in public. The statute of limitations had ended. The two men could no longer be reprimanded.

17. Camp Maxey is located in Paris, Texas, some 100 miles northeast of Dallas or about 250 miles from Camp Hood. Camp Maxey was the staging area for the ASTP recruits.

18. *The Russian People*, adapted for the stage by Clifford Odets from the original by Konstantin Simonov.

19. Yom Kippur is the Jewish day of fasting and atonement that follows the Jewish New Year celebrations.

20. The actor mentioned here is Ingrid Bergman, who played the female lead in *For Whom the Bell Tolls* and won an Oscar for best leading actress for the role.

21. "Mark one—and—a—half . . . mark twain" is a reference to how short his hair was. The two terms are depth soundings used by riverboat pilots on the Mississippi River, "mark twain" being twelve feet of depth and providing the source for riverboat pilot Samuel Clemens's pen name.

22. A Lister bag is a canvas bag suspended from tripod used for dispensing water in the field.

23. It appears that Carl was able to stop in Canton on his way to New York, in part because his grandmother Mary Lavin—wife of Harry and mother of Leo—passed away on November 3, 1943, at the age of seventy-six.

Chapter 3: Queens College, New York City

1. Margaret Gram, "Over There Comes Over Here," in *The People's College on the Hill: Fifty Years at Queens College, 1937–1987*, ed. Stephen Stepanchev (New York: Queens College of the City University of New York, 1989), 43–47.

2. With a shrinking student body and a more serious national climate, the lively, carefree atmosphere around the college suffered. The presence of new male blood certainly lent an air of excitement and improved parity within the co-ed population. Without the ASTP students, the ratio of female to male students hovered around a bleak 5-to-1. "Gals Outnumber Men 5-1 As Registration Drops," *Queens College Crown*, September 14, 1943, 6; "Queens Among 8 Colleges To Evolve Army Test Plan, Holloway, Young Guide Curriculum For 345 Trainees," *Queens College Crown*, September 14, 1943, 1; "Late Registration Brings Total To 1625," *Queens College Crown*, September 21, 1943, 1.

3. Army Specialized Training Division, Army Service Forces, *Essential Facts about the Army Specialized Training Program* (Washington, DC: US Government Printing Office, 1943), i.

4. Ibid., 9–10.

5. Commanding the ASTPers at Queens was Major John L. Davis, Jr. Professor. Emory Holloway was named the College Liaison and ASTP Director. Holloway was the Chair of the English department and an original member of the Queens College staff. He won the Pulitzer Prize for a 1926 biography on Walt Whitman. Gram, "Over There," 56; William Over, "Emory Holloway: Biographical Sketch," excerpted from a biographical essay, Dictionary of Literary Biography database in Gale Literature Resource Center, Adelphi University, accessed November 10, 2014, http://libraries.adelphi.edu/bar/Whitman/WhitmanIntroductionEH.htm. In a letter to Queens College Dean Margaret Kiely, Holloway described the ASTP program while laying out what was required of the civilian students:

Dear Dean Kiely:

Since Pearl Harbor Queens College students have been earnestly seeking an opportunity to help in winning the war. The coming of 345 trainees to the ASTP unit on campus gives us a very concrete opportunity to be of service. The presence of these men should be an inspiration to all of us.

Since the trainees all hope to be officers, either commissioned or non-commissioned, they are striving hard to master an extremely difficult and heavy program. From eight o'clock in the morning until five o'clock in the evening they have absolutely no free time except what they save from their lunch hour at noon and the short "breaks" between classes. They are free also on Wednesday evenings unless their privileges have been curtailed because their weekly work reports are low. We must do nothing to intrude upon their study time. Furthermore, they are being tested as potential officers and are under constant military observation. That is why they march to classes under a succession of section marchers. The correct etiquette is to step aside from the line of march of the sections and not to congregate on the steps or porches or at the entrances of the buildings into which and out of which the trainees must march in single file. By observing this courtesy we will enable the trainees in a given section to rate more highly with the military.

Marching men must keep their eyes to the front and are under orders not to acknowledge salutations from passing civilians; therefore, it is not courteous to speak to them while in formation. They may speak to civilian friends during the few minutes they are at ease while waiting to go into a classroom. They are expected to stand in their classrooms until their instructor seats them; so that it is important that the other classes evacuate the classrooms promptly. In the future each section of the trainees will march from the building and remain for five minutes at ease in the quadrangle nearest the exit, giving civilian students an opportunity to make class shifts with a minimum of confusion. One way to help the Army will be not to clog the passageways during the last five minutes of the intermission. During air raids trainee sections are under the same regulations as civilian sections.

Signs have been erected to indicate the parts of the campus and buildings which are reserved for the use of the Army. Within those areas our trainee students have a right to privacy and to quiet for study. Neither students nor faculty, male or female, should pass beyond these signs except in the case of faculty members entering on business. Trainees are held responsible if we violate this rule.

At 5:15 p.m. from Monday until Friday the Army unit has a retreat ceremony at which the flag is lowered. Civilians passing the quadrangle at that time should, of course, stand at attention when the flag is being actually lowered. This means standing erect, facing the flagpole, arms at the side, except in the case of men who are wearing hats; the latter, of course, should remove them and place them against the left breast. Military salutes, such as the trainees and the officers will be making during the actual lowering of the flag, are expected only from persons in uniform. The Army is very particular about the neatness on the parade ground. It would look upon it as a discourtesy to the flag to have this retreat ceremony on a quadrangle littered with dixie cups or other papers. We shall soon have additional receptacles in which to deposit such rubbish, but please at all times help to keep the campus and the buildings clean even though unusually crowded.

The coming of the Army means inconvenience of many kinds to us, but this is nothing in comparison to the inconvenience our trainee students have already experienced or to the greater burden they are preparing to bear for us. Queens College students have always been neat and courteous. They will not be less so when under the eyes of the highly trained military men who now share our campus life.

Sincerely yours,

/s/ EMORY HOLLOWAY

Emory Holloway to Margaret Kiely (Queens College Dean; letter contained within memo), September 16, 1943. Department of Special Collections and Archives, CUNY, Benjamin Rosenthal Library.

6. Anna Lee Kram, "Forward, Cupid—Hut!" *Queens College Crown*, October 19, 1943, 2. Sports, variety shows, assemblies, and fraternity and sorority events all lost a little luster. Even hazing seemed a bit less important. There once was a time when freshmen pledges were publicly "depantsed" for falling out of line during "Hell Week," a period of hazing for fraternity and sorority pledges. "Queens College 1937–1943," *Queens College Crown*, September 14, 1943, 2–3. Now obedient marching men in military uniform would become all the rage. Sensing an opportunity to mingle with the campus co-eds, Sgt. Rolfe Weil of ASTP's Advanced Section sought to break the ice in a campus newspaper article, which stated, "We have some 1200 girls on this campus, and about 345 young, and more or less handsome, soldiers. Now how do we get them together?" Rolfe Weil, "To the Femmes: Let's Stop Walkin' Around Each Other . . ." *Queens College Crown*, September 21, 1943, 4. By October, the campus seemed to be in full swing; while romantic intentions certainly swirled in the air (this was a college after all), the

students weren't taking wartime lightly. They were patriotic to the hilt, and did their part to show their loyalty and their support of the American cause. From selling bonds to donating valued items to volunteering their time, the college students and faculty were ever cognizant of the war and the trying times that lay ahead. "Highlights of Two Years of War at Queens College," *Queens College Crown*, December 7, 1943, 3.

7. The Canteen was a lively spot, and some of the women who frequented the canteen included then-unknowns such as Angela Lansbury and Lauren Bacall and Broadway stars such as Gertrude Lawrence and Alfred Drake:"Opening on March 2, 1942 in the basement of the forty-fourth street theatre, the Stage Door Canteen played host to an average of 3,000 Allied servicemen (but no servicewomen) seven evenings a week, between 6 o'clock and midnight. It was a gathering spot for free, world-class entertainment, food and (non-alcoholic) drink, and probably most important for a lonely GI, Sailor, or Marine, the company of a young woman for a dance and a sympathetic shoulder." Richard Goldstein, *Helluva Town: The Story of New York City during World War II* (New York: Free Press, 2010), 139, 143, 144.

8. This comedy by Joseph Kesselring would later become a movie starring Cary Grant. The cost of a matinee or evening seat for *Arsenic and Old Lace* in 1943 was 55 cents. "Open City Center of Music, Drama, Larry Milbauer," Below a Buck, *Queens College Crown*, November 23, 1943, 2.

9. Goldstein, *Helluva Town*, 183

10. Ibid.

11. Ibid.

12. Ibid., 183–87; "Servicemen were admitted free to baseball games, but they wouldn't be seeing any night games during the early war years. Night baseball at the Polo Grounds in Harlem and Ebbets Field in Flatbush (Yankee Stadium still had no lights) was banned for the 1942 and 1943 seasons." Diehl, *Over Here!*, 123, 124; "Night baseball returned on May 23, 1944, for a game at Ebbets Field." Goldstein, *Helluva Town*, 185–86.

13. Diehl, *Over Here!*, 184. The New York City Defense Recreation Committee doled out "free tickets to Broadway shows, first-run movies, sports events, broadcasts, and almost anything else" to servicemen. Bloomingdale's department store snapped free portraits for them. And the Servicemen's Recording Center provided any military man with a complimentary phonographic voice recording. ASTPers in the dancing mood could trip the light fantastic at "the Sloane House YMCA, National Catholic Community Service, the Jewish Welfare Board Club (1 East 65th Street), [and] the Carnegie Hall Recreation Center." For 55 cents, the new students could see the Ice Capades skating spectacle at Madison

Square Garden in September or for five cents less catch Sonja Henie's Stars On Ice in Rockefeller Center's Center Theatre. "Inexpensive Entertainment in the Big Town with the Accent on Recreation for ASTP'ers," Below a Buck, *Queens College Crown*, September 21, 1943, 2.

In October, they could catch John Barton walking the boards in a revival of the crowd-pleasing *Tobacco Road* at the Ritz (West 48th). "Sunday in the Park . . .," Below a Buck, *Queens College Crown*, October 19, 1943, 2.

In November, servicemen and students could devote their Tuesday evenings to a three-part poetry series, featuring such heavyweights as Langston Hughes, W. H. Auden, Horace Gregory, William Carlos Williams, James Agee, and Muriel Rukeyser reciting their verses in Room 213 at the New York Public Library. "Barn Dances and Poets Too, Bobbie Lorin," Below a Buck, *Queens College Crown*, November 9, 1943, 2.

With the clouds of war hanging over the city, New York did provide a great escape. There were the legendary nightclubs: The Stork Club, The Copa, El Morocco, and The Latin Quarter. Diehl, *Over Here!*, 185–86; and Goldstein, *Helluva Town*, 19.

Movies such as *Girl Crazy, A Guy Named Joe, The Song of Bernadette, Bathing Beauty, Two Girls and a Sailor* unspooled on the big screens in theaters with wondrous names like the Roxy and the Criterion. Servicemen and civilians alike could hear big band sounds of Benny Goodman or Guy Lombardo, or they could visit the Frick and Metropolitan museums, or they could check on the latest happenings in one of nine daily newspapers. Diehl, *Over Here!*, 185.

14. *Artists and Models* was a 1943 musical revue that closed after 27 performances. Thomas Hischak, *The Oxford Companion to the American Musical: Theatre, Film and Television* (New York: Oxford University Press, 2008), 43.

15. Jack Dempsey's, a former Times Square restaurant owned by Jack Dempsey, an American heavyweight boxing champ.

16. Diehl, *Over Here!*, 154–55.

17. Office for Emergency Management, *Guns Not Gadgets*, Arsenal of Democracy Series (Washington, DC: Department of the Interior, 1941), 2–4.

18. Ibid., 5–8, 9–10, 11.

19. Kathie McDermott, "Dust Bowl: We Just Can't Keep Up with Cupid's Peregrinations," *Queens College Crown*, October 13, 1943, 2.

20. *Ziegfeld Follies,* a Broadway revue.

21. *Something for the Boys*, a Cole Porter musical.

22. Carl is quick to reassure his mother that he is not playing tackle football.

23. By British playwright Patrick Hamilton. Better known by its movie version, *Gaslight*.

24. Quoting ASTP files: Keefer, *Scholars in Foxholes*, 70.

25. Born in 1922, cousin Bill Kaven graduated from Lehman in Fred's class, two years ahead of Carl. Although intellectually gifted (he became a professor at Cornell) he was also not a motivated student in high school and received lackluster grades in math. After placing high in the army aptitude tests, he completed training and earned his "wings" as a navigator. Proud of his accomplishment, he called on his old Lehman math teacher while on home leave. The teacher was somewhat incredulous and went into the records closet to retrieve Bill's school records. "But you never received higher than a 'C'" he exclaimed. "How can we win this war?" Bill served in southern Europe, flying supply drops to guerilla groups in Yugoslavia.

26. Presumably referring to Major Davis, ASTP commander. Not surprising given wartime censorship and morale sensitivities, there is no mention of this incident in the *Crown* or elsewhere.

27. Numerous items, such as rubber, fuel, and food, were rationed throughout the course of the war. Coupon books were awarded based on size or need.

28. "The root cause of ASTP's early 1944 curtailment was the military manpower crisis that emerged the summer and fall of 1943. Although Gen. McNair and, to some extent, Gen. Marshall, as well as many other Army Ground Forces commanders, never had much love for ASTP, their antagonism probably wouldn't have mattered much had they had as many fighting men as they wanted all along." Keefer, *Scholars in Foxholes*, 168.

29. Fatherhood continued to protect many from the draft: "By midsummer, the number of potential draftees was seriously depleted. . . . Faced with falling 446,000 men short by the end of the year, Selective Service Director Hershey on July 31 instructed local draft boards to start reclassifying fathers and to be prepared to induct them before the end of the year. Hershey's directive caused strong protests. . . . Congress agreed that fathers with bona fide family relationships would only be drafted after all nonfathers had been drafted." Keefer, *Scholars in Foxholes,* 168; "It was Senator Burton K Wheeler who kept reminding everyone that thousands of physically fit young men were wasting their time in university classrooms while others were dying on foreign soil." Ibid., 213; and Office for Emergency Management, *Guns Not Gadgets*, 2.

A February report in the Queens College student newspaper noted the decrease in the unit from 345 men to 283, followed by another piece describing how the House Military Affairs Committee was weighing what to do with the entire nationwide program. "Civilian Enrollment Increases 10%; AST Unit Loses 62 Men," *Queens College Crown*, February 15, 1944, 1; and "Major Davis Denies Rumors that ASTP Is Doomed," *Queens College Crown*, February 15, 1944, 1.

30. The *Crown*, the Queens College student newspaper, reported on the rumors that the ASTP program would be stopped:

> Reports that the Army Specialized Training Program is to be terminated have been denied by Major John Davis, commanding officer of the Queens College unit. "Such rumors," said Major Davis "are unfounded as the War Department is concerned."
>
> According to a United Press dispatch of last month, "The House military Affairs Committee may scrap their student training programs to slow down the drafting of pre-Pearl Harbor fathers by making some 200,000 younger men available for combat. One member of the Military Affairs Committee said the entire student training program 'stinks to heaven.'"

"Major Davis Denies Rumors that ASTP Is Doomed," *Queens College Crown*, February 15, 1944, 1.

31. "The rumors ended on February 18 (FRIDAY) with the Army's announcement that about eight out of ten trainees—roughly 110,000 men—would be removed from college training at the end of the terms in which they were studying." Keefer, *Scholars in Foxholes*, 171; "ASTP has been drastically reduced. One hundred and ten thousand men will be transferred from their college campuses to Army camps by April 1, announced Secretary of War Stimson last Friday [February 18th]. The remaining students will be limited to those taking advanced courses in medicine, dentistry, and engineering." "Army Training Program Sliced; Fate of Queens Unit Still Unknown," *Queens College Crown*, February 29, 1944, 1; From the files of Queens College Special Collections Department: "(MONDAY) February 21, 1944, TO THE MEMBERS OF THE ASTP STAFF: There will be an important meeting of all members of the ASTP staff at 11 o'clock in the Auditorium tomorrow morning, February 22. This may involve the canceling of some classes. I have invited President [Paul] Klapper to discuss with you the many problems arising from the sudden decision of the War Department to withdraw its unit on or before April 1. Sincerely yours, EMORY HOLLOWAY, Director, ASTP." Emory Holloway to ASTP Staff, February 21, 1944. Department of Special Collections and Archives, CUNY, Benjamin Rosenthal Library

32. The 1943 Broadway production of *Othello* at the Shubert Theater featured Paul Robeson in the title role.

33. "Queens Army Training Unit Inactivated: Men Await Orders; To Transform C, I For Student Use," *Queens College Crown*, March 21, 1944, 1.

34. Gram, "Over There," 55–56.

35. Eli Ginzberg describes the reassignment:

> Instead of being eagerly absorbed by the Ground Forces, thousands of
> these high quality men sat around for months awaiting reassignment,
> and when they arrived at their new units they were not appointed
> as noncommissioned officers. In the first place, others held these as-
> signments; and the newcomers, no matter how great their potential
> ability, did not have the specific combat training required. Many of
> them were therefore assigned as riflemen, which has led an outraged
> critic of the War Department to conclude that the disbanding of the
> ASTP was a plot to place the best brainpower in the country in the
> most vulnerable positions, where the largest number were likely to be
> killed.

Ginzberg, *The Lost Divisions* (New York: Columbia University Press, 1959), 48.

Chapter 4: Mississippi

1. "By 1944 the soldiers quickly released from ASTP and other programs were just more 'warm bodies' needed to fill gaps in the ranks. As matters stood, many qualified leaders ended up serving in their new units under less-qualified officers and noncommissioned officers. . . . One wonders how many more of these men would have assumed positions of leadership within their units if they had been assigned to combat divisions earlier in the mobilization process." Mansoor, *GI Offensive in Europe*, 43n94; As a fellow ASTPer, George Illis, 102nd Division, put it: "There is no question, if they lived long enough, the ASTP boys were superb soldiers." Keefer, *Scholars in Foxholes*, 264.

2. Max Hastings, *Armageddon: The Battle for Germany, 1944–1945* (New York: Vintage, 2005), 78.

3. "A broad consensus existed among enlisted men on the best and worst aspects of training. Soldiers felt weapons training, instruction in seeking cover and concealment, how to stay dispersed and not bunch up, and skills in digging foxholes and defensive positions helped them the most. Soldiers held the view that close order drill, military courtesy, inspections, bayonet and hand-to-hand combat drills, and chemical warfare training had little relevance to their work on the battlefield." Doubler, *Closing with the Enemy*, 249.

4. Bivouac, a temporary campsite.

5. Leo's mother, and Harry's wife, Mary, had a sister named Yetta who lived with her husband in New Orleans, so their children were Leo's cousins.

6. The boy in the household, Walter Marcus, later served as Associate Justice on the Louisiana State Supreme Court.

7. Carl was living in a long wooden structure known as a "hutment." These housed about twenty-five soldiers each. Each hutment had a stove for heat and the windows lining the structure could be raised for air circulation.

8. Carson served two terms in Congress. His greatest historical note might be that in his successful 1942 run for Congress he vanquished Jacob Coxey of the 1894 Coxey's Army in the latter's final campaign for elective office.

9. C's, a local jewelry shop in Canton.

10. The expert infantryman's badge was created in 1943 for purposes of lifting morale and possibly inspired by the German's Close Combat Badge; the badge, which contains an impression of an infantry musket, was awarded to Carl in August 1944. Paul Fussell, *The Boys' Crusade: The American Infantry in Northwestern Europe, 1944–1945*, Modern Library Chronicles, vol. 14 (New York: Modern Library, 2005), 44; and Frank C. Foster, *Complete Guide to United States Army Medals, Badges and Insignia—World War II to Present* (Fountain Inn, SC: Medals of America Press, 2004), 47.

11. "Most [GIs] were amateurs whose approach to soldiering was aggressively temporary." Atkinson, *Guns at Last Light*, 20.

12. Leo Lavin served in the army during World War I, in a noncombat position in the United States.

13. Hadassah is a Jewish-American women's group founded in 1912.

14. "Those operations" references a possible tonsillectomy and other minor childhood procedures.

15. Atkinson, *Guns at Last Light*, 85.

16. One summer during high school, Carl went on a road trip through the western United States along with other high school friends. The trip was led by his science teacher.

17. Mario Vargas Llosa uses the same situation (a military officer responsible for a brothel) in his novel, *Captain Pantoja and the Special Service*. For further information on military activity unrelated to winning the war, see the notes to the letter dated January 10, 1945, page 341, and the discussion of "chickenshit."

18. Atkinson, *Guns at Last Light*, 19.

19. Kindsvatter, *American Soldiers*, 309.

20. John McManus, *The Deadly Brotherhood: The American Combat Soldier in World War II* (Novato, CA: Presidio Press, 1998), 45.

21. Carl Lavin, interviewed by Bill Edmonds, Florida State University, Reichelt Oral History Program, June 18, 1999, 23–24. The transcript continues:

336   Interviewer: Did you ever hear any complaints that it was a Jewish war?

Lavin: No, I don't think I personally ever heard that. I've read references to that. Some people have made that statement, but I never heard it. . . . I have to say I really did not experience anti-Semitism myself.

Seemingly in contradiction, Carl would also relate that he would occasionally have similar conversations around a bonfire—at the battlefront.

22. Referring to Rosh Hashanah, the Jewish New Year.

23. Unfortunately, the context is loss to history so we do not know the background on this date or how Carl connected with her.

24. Aunt Dodo, Carl's aunt, married to Leo's brother Arthur.

25. John F. Higgins, *Trespass against Them: History of the 271st Infantry Regiment 1943–1945* (Naumburg, Ger.: privately published, 1945), 13–27, http://www.69th-infantry-division.com/histories/271.html. More information on New York area staging bases can be found in Goldstein, *Helluva Town*, 57.

Chapter 5: Britain

1. Higgins, *Trespass against Them*.
2. Ibid.
3. Ibid. He goes on to describe life on the ship:

Life aboard ship was fun, although the first few days, there were many subscribers to the idea that all the world should be land. Several green complexions and "I-don't-care-if-I-die" expressions were noted about the third day out when we hit a rough sea. A lot of those fellows whom you saw bent over the rail were not looking for fish. And you remember how training was conducted for those hardy souls who were still able to sit up. In one corner you'd see a group dutifully listening to the voice that was telling them how much beer they could buy for a shilling, and if you stumbled further down the deck through the mass of humanity, it was common to see a bunch of puzzled faces and unwilling mouths trying to "parlez Francais" in a few not-so-easy lessons.

Then they had Ship's Inspection each day. There were so many people in the inspecting party that it was hard to tell where today's inspection ended and tomorrow's began! You couldn't stay on deck—

they were cleaning it; you couldn't go below—they were inspecting it; and the crew's quarters were off limits. That left one alternative, namely jumping overboard. It's a good thing we were following the southern route; it was easier to swim alongside the ship during an inspection.

This was our first opportunity to buy cigarettes for a nickel a pack, and maybe you think the men didn't stock up. How many of us shed a sympathetic tear for the civilians at home who couldn't buy them at any price. Special Service did a fine job on board ship, showing movies, putting on shows, arranging religious services, providing recreational facilities, and in general, making things as pleasant as possible for the men. The food was good, and on Thanksgiving Day, we were pleasantly surprised to find turkey and all the trimmings awaiting the lusty appetites that the salt air had given us. It was a memorable meal. . . .

The 10th day out, gulls were sighted, and we knew that land could not be too far off. Our destination had already been announced, so that everyone was eager for his first glimpse of England. On the morning of 26 November, land was sighted, and we were soon passing the beautiful Isle of Wight, in southern England. From here on, it was impossible to keep the men from the rails, as no one wanted to miss a moment of it. Remember all those landing barges we saw as we approached Southampton? Could anyone help thinking of all the men who had recently used them to storm the citadel of Hitler's Europe?

On 16 December, we sewed our patches back on our sleeves and were permitted to tell people the identity of our unit. Christmas found us becoming quite British in our manner and having a party for those pink-cheeked English kids, most of them evacuees from bombed areas. Made you a bit homesick, didn't it?

4. V-mail, letters that were microfiched to help the army with mail delivery.

5. Higgins, *Trespass against Them*, 22.

6. Peter Schrijvers, *The Crash of Ruin: American Combat Soldiers in Europe during World War II* (New York: NYU Press, 2001), 112.

7. *Summer Storm* was a 1944 film adapted from Anton Chekhov's *The Shooting Party*.

8. "Eighteen Injured in Georgia Wreck—Fifteen Cars of the New York-to-Tampa West Coast Champion Leave Rails," *New York Times*, November 19, 1944, 37.

9. Carl makes sure to specify "non-tackle." He is almost Pavlovian in his need to preempt this argument.

10. As noted earlier, Carl's grandfather, Harry, came to America and started his dream by becoming a green-grocer and selling food out of a wagon. From there, Harry specialized in meats and eventually opened Sugardale, a meat processing business.

11. Higgins, *Trespass against Them*, 22.

12. Mansoor, *GI Offensive in Europe*, 233

13. George Shank, *I Wrote My Way Out of a Foxhole* (Meridian, MS: Budget Printing, 1991), 76.

14. Robert Nadeau, also a private who joined the 84th Division from the 69th Division, recollects his first day with Company L: "there's . . . 17 men and one second lieutenant. I says this is L Company? They say, yeah. We lost a few men, 105 men yesterday or the day before." Robert P. Nadeau Collection (AFC/2001/001/64383), Veterans History Project, American Folklife Center, Library of Congress.

Chapter 6: The Battle of the Bulge

1. Fussell, *Boys' Crusade*, 96.

2. The climate and terrain of the Ardennes offered numerous challenges:

> The Ardennes is not a distinctively defined region but a continuum of rolling hills and patches of heavy fir trees lying within a swath that starts between Liege and Dinant on the Meuse River and sweeps westward toward the German border. In general, the highest hills stand just inside the German border, and the ground becomes more even as it approaches the Meuse. Roughly a third of the Ardennes is covered by thick forests that stand in scattered patches. A number of rivers and streams flow generally from south to north, often through narrow, steep gorges that are considerable obstacles. Paved roads usually followed high ridges, twisted and turned into river gorges, crossed waterways over stone bridges and eventually led to a number of key road junctions like those at St. Vith and Bastogne. The typically village had a number of stone houses and narrow streets, all centered about a large road intersection, with the largest villages numbering between 2,500 and 4,000 dwellers. The weather in the Ardennes is raw and cold with heavy rainfall, deep snows, and biting winds. In the winter, the days are short with early morning fog and mists that linger well into the morning. . . .

> The nature of the terrain in the Ardennes had a significant influ-
> ence on the conduct of the campaign. Ridge lines tended to block
> and compartmentalize major troop movements from east to west.
> Scattered forests and streams fragmented the lay of the land, making
> command and control and weeping maneuvers very difficult.

Doubler, *Closing with the Enemy*, 201.

3. John S. D. Eisenhower, *The Bitter Woods: The Battle of the Bulge* (New York: Putnam, 1969), 5.

4. Doubler, *Closing with the Enemy*, 246n29. "In late December 1944 the ETO ordered the use of the term 'replacement' discontinued, since it denoted a sense of expendability on the part of those to whom it referred. Instead, the term 're-inforcement' was substituted on grounds that these soldiers should be considered a combat reserve." Mansoor, *GI Offensive in Europe*, 235n74; and Doubler, *Closing with the Enemy*, 247.

5. "The undeniable proof of the dilapidated state of French transportation, however, was what became known among the Americans as the 'forty and eight.' The memory of this standard French railway boxcar—marked 'Hommes 40, Chevaux 8' on the sides, indicating its capacity to hold forty soldiers or eight horses—had been engraved on the mind of the American generation that had fought in the Great War." Schrijvers, *Crash of Ruin*, 44.

6. Mansoor, *GI Offensive in Europe*, 254.

7. Ibid., 7.

8. Frank J. Freese, *Private Memories of World War II: A Small Piece of a Big War* (Madison, WI: printed by author, 1990), 16.

9. Carl's father Leo also had an association with the 84th Division. Leo served during World War I as a Supply Sergeant stationed at Camp Sherman in Ohio, one of the larger facilities for training and staging US forces being sent to Europe. One of the units thus prepared and shipped was the 84th Division. The 84th's World War I service had briefly reentered national consciousness in 1940 because Wendell Willkie, the 1940 GOP presidential nominee, had served in the 84th as a young artillery officer.

10. Theodore Draper, *The 84th Infantry Division in the Battle of Germany, November 1944–May 1945* (New York: The Viking Press, 1946), 1.

11. A. R. Bolling, *Railsplitters: The Story of the 84th Infantry Division* (Paris: Curial-Archereau, 1945), 22, http://www.lonesentry.com/gi_stories_booklets /84thinfantry.

12. Draper, *84th Infantry Division*, 79; Hugh Cole, *The Battle of the Bulge* (Old Saybrook, CT: Konecky & Konecky, 2001), 428.

13. Cole, *Battle of the Bulge*, 577.

14. Citing Supreme Headquarters, Allied Expeditionary Force (SHAEF) documents, military historian Charles B. MacDonald noted that "Casualties through [Jan. 3rd] totaled 516,244, though many of these men had returned to duty." MacDonald, *Victory in Europe, 1945: The Last Offensive from United States Army in World War II* (Mineola, NY: Dover Publications, 2007), 5.

15. Mansoor, *GI Offensive in Europe*, 226.

16. Cole, *Battle of the Bulge*, 269.

17. Among the other shortcomings with Operation Greif was the spelling error in the laminated ID card used for officers. The error was in the official US version, which spelled the word "INDENTIFICATION." The Germans cleaned up the error, giving themselves away. Fussell, *Boys' Crusade*, 137.

18. Mansoor, *GI Offensive in Europe*, 226n52.

19. Perry S. Wolff, *Fortune Favored the Brave: A History of the 334th Infantry, 84th Division* (Mannheim: Manheimer GroBdruckerei, 1945), 43–44.

20. Eisenhower, *Bitter Woods*, 405; "While American forces in the west (the 2d, 3d, and 7th Armored Divisions and the 75th and 84th Infantry Divisions) blunted the spearhead of the German attack, Lieutenant General George S. Patton's Third Army wheeled ninety degrees to counterattack the enemy salient from the south and relieve the encircled 101st Airborne Division at Bastogne." Mansoor, *GI Offensive in Europe*, 228–29.

21. Mansoor, *GI Offensive in Europe*, 229n59.

22. Wolff, *Fortune Favored the Brave*, 73.

23. Shank, *Out of a Foxhole*, 77.

24. Draper, *84th Infantry Division*, 107.

25. "In northeastern France, the soldiers more than once thought they had stepped back in time. In the many tiny villages and hamlets, homes often had none of the comforts that most of the Americans took for granted: no radio, no telephone, no central heating; not even electricity, indoor toilets, bathtubs, or running water. The GIs were shocked to find that families were willing to live under the same roof as their animals." Schrijvers, *Crash of Ruin*, 129.

26. "Replacements traveled for days in unheated French 'forty-and-eight' boxcars, considered suitable for forty men or eight horses, although as Eisenhower wrote Marshall, 'We have reduced the figure to thirty-five enlisted men per car in order that by tight squeezing men can at least lie down.'" Atkinson, *Guns at Last Light*, 410–11.

27. "Across Europe, American soldiers time and time again disapproved of open-ditch sewers, while staring incredulously at toilets with footrests but without either bowls or seats. . . . Moreover, whereas Europe's pissoirs—public urinals

offering little privacy—embarrassed many an American soldier, Europeans proved to be incredibly nonchalant about such matters." Schrijvers, *Crash of Ruin*, 237–38.

28. At this particular location, people didn't use toilet tissue, Carl explained later. They wiped with one of their hands and then wiped the waste on an inner wall of the outhouse. The wall would then be whitewashed every few months.

29. "No chicken found" is likely a reference to "chickenshit," the widely used term for needless petty Army regulations. Fussell provides detail:

> What does that rude term signify? It does not imply complaint against the inevitable inconveniences of military life: overcrowding lack of privacy, tedious institutional cookery, deprivation of personality, general boredom. Nothing much can be done about those things. Chickenshit refers rather to behavior that makes military life worse than in need be: petty harassment of the weak by the strong; open scrimmage for power and authority and prestige; sadism thinly disguised as necessary discipline; a constant "paying off of old scores"; and insistence on the letter rather than the spirit of ordinances; Chickenshit is so called—instead of horse- or bull- or elephant shit—because it is small-minded and ignoble and takes the trivial seriously. Chickenshit can be recognized instantly because it never has anything to do with winning the war.

Fussell, *Wartime*, 80.

30. Draper, *84th Infantry Division*, 111.

31. Ibid., 113. Four basic challenges had to be overcome in the cold:

> Bitter winter weather posed a threat to American troops just as real as German shells and bullets. Field manuals on operations in snow and extreme cold taught soldiers how to function during winter warfare. Four major challenges existed: keeping soldiers warm, moving across snow and ice, transporting and preserving supplies and equipment, and preventing the malfunctioning of weapons and equipment. The army identified four broad categories of solutions to these problems. First, adequate quantities of winter clothing, equipment, and cold weather supplies had to be available. Soldiers also needed training in how to care for themselves and their supplies and equipment. Marching and fighting in snow and ice required special skills and troops needed training on how to keep weapons functioning in bitter cold.

Doubler, *Closing with the Enemy*, 200.

32. Schrijvers, *Crash of Ruin*, 1980. The cold impacted roads, equipment, clothing, and more: "During the Battle of the Bulge, soldiers had to warm up motors at least twice a night if they wanted their vehicles to start in the morning, and even then only urinating on the carburetor and battery could do the trick. Moreover, heavy snow made mine detection nearly impossible and slowed down nervous troops." Ibid., 20n82.

33. Mansoor, *GI Offensive in Europe*, 230.

34. Ibid., 156.

35. "Soldiers had to overcome the tendency to freeze upon initial enemy contact, and units learned to minimize casualties by moving quickly through preplanned mortar and artillery fire and by maneuvering aggressively against enemy defenses." Doubler, *Closing with the Enemy*, 256–57.

36. "The GIs experienced the typical physical symptoms of fear when they eventually faced battle with the Axis foe. Upon nearing the front, hearts pounded and pulses beat rapidly. Some soldiers shook, perspired excessively, experienced a sinking feeling in the stomach, or felt weak or faint. Others suffered from muscular tension, vomiting or involuntary urination or defecation. Tense soldiers chewed gum or stuffed snow into their mouths to detach their tongues from the roofs of mouths that had turned dry from fear." Schrijvers, *Crash of Ruin*, 50n1.

37. Ibid., 67, using multiple footnotes.

38. Ibid.

39. Ibid.

40. *Battle of the Bulge: The American Experience*, directed by Thomas Lennon (Los Angeles, CA: Lennon Documentary Group, WGBH, November 9, 1994).

41. Wolff, *Fortune Favored the Brave*, 71.

42. Schrijvers, *Crash of Ruin*, 4.

43. "Every man has his breaking point. You can hear just so many shells, see just so many torn bodies, fear just so much fear, soak just so much rain, spend just so many sleepless nights." Ralph Martin quoted in Kindsvatter, *American Soldiers*, 159.

44. Eisenhower, *Bitter Woods*, 460; see also chapter 10, letter of July 8.

45. Carl's division was the northernmost American division in the Bulge and his regiment was the northernmost regiment in his division. Right next to him were the British. Indeed, the German planned their offensive to hit the Allies where the American and British sectors joined, in the hope that requirements for US-UK coordination would slow the speed of response.

The confusion of war was made greater by boots. The Americans wore rubber-soled boots. Both the British and the Germans wore hob-nailed boots. On two different occasions, Carl's unit heard hob-nailed boots walking behind the lines. Muscles tensed. Adrenaline spiked. Until British accents were heard. Carl's letter from Britain that he found the British accent fascinating became more than an abstract comment.

Schrijvers discussed the boot confusion: "Belgians who were liberated by the 9th Infantry Division told the Americans how surprised they were by the silence of their footsteps as they had grown used to the intimidating cadence of the German hobnailed boots. The GIs themselves soon also learned to be alarmed by hobnails crashing on stone, and they failed to understand why the Germans had not yet switched to the soft, quiet rubber soles of some of the American footgear." During the parachute assault on Arnhem, British "paratroopers wrapped their hobnail boots in curtain strips to deaden their footfalls." Atkinson, *Guns at Last Light*, 269; and Draper, *84th Infantry Division*, 113.

46. "German losses would be difficult to count with precision.... One postwar analysis put the figure at 82,000, another at 98,000. The official German history would cite 11,000 dead and 34,000 wounded, with an indeterminate number captured, missing, sick, and injured." Atkinson, *Guns at Last Light*, 489.

47. Mansoor, *GI Offensive in Europe*, 216.

48. Draper, *84th Infantry Division*, 107, 121, 122.

49. Ibid., 85, 122–26.

50. Ibid., 122–23.

51. Depending on the situation, if there was a lot of combat going on, Carl would use up three or four magazines in one moment. While combat was not constant and there were periods with no action, the GIs were always on alert, never knowing when fighting would start.

> Ammunition and food would be replenished by a jeep that would stop a half-mile to a mile behind the line. If things were quiet, a few guys at a time could leave the line to retrieve the items from the jeep. That would happen about every three days, so soldiers would take a few days of ammunition and food.
>
> The US Army spent a considerable amount of time and energy on the development of its own packaged rations to ensure that they would be both healthy and tasty. The ten-in-one ration was intended for group feeding in combat situations that allowed a minimum of food preparation. The GIs like them better than any other rations because they contained such frontline delicacies as canned milk, sweet corn, bacon, and sausages. But their weight—45 pounds per cardboard box— often prevented the infantrymen from carrying these rations,

while the tank crews gratefully hoarded them. The C ration was issued as an individual ration in the combat zone. One of its two units contained a 12-ounce can with meat and vegetables. It could be any of four varieties: beef stew, pork and beans, meat hash, or spaghetti. The other unit offered biscuits, coffee, and sweets. The C ration was not to be issued for more than 72 hours in a row. In reality, however, the GIs at the front often lived on them for drawn-out periods, sometimes as long as three months. As a result, many combat soldiers complained about the lack of variety (they especially disliked the hash, stew, and biscuits). In some cases, the prolonged diets of C rations led to vitamin deficiency and nausea. During actual fighting, the Americans subsisted on K rations. They were composed of flat cans with meat, eggs, and cheese as well as biscuits, fruit and chocolate bars, bouillon, coffee, and sugar. All troops disliked the K rations and many GIs upset the nutritional balance of the packages by consuming only what they liked, which was mostly the coffee, the chocolate, and the crackers. Finally, for stopgap use in emergency situations, the soldiers could fall back on D rations. They were nothing more than chocolate bars enriched with vitamin B1 and most soldiers preferred to eat them in between regular rations. They tended to make the men thirsty, however, and in some cases also caused nausea.

Schrijvers, *Crash of Ruin*, 158.

52. Fussell, *Wartime*, 282.

53. Soldiers' letters "are composed largely to sustain the morale of the folks at home, to hint as little as possible at the real, worrisome circumstances of the writer. No one wrote: 'Dear Mother, I am scared to death.'" Fussell, *Wartime*, 145.

54. The Malmedy massacre occurred in Malmedy, Belgium, during the Battle of the Bulge; "As the war dragged on, more and more stories began to circulate among the GIs about German atrocities against POWs. . . . The fear of capture reached an all-time high, however, during the battle of the Ardennes, when news of the Malmedy massacre spread like brushfire." Schrijvers, *Crash of Ruin*, 75–6.

55. Author's interview with Audrey Lavin. She added, "In fact, he had told me that story many times. That combination of powerlessness and guilt really got to him. I don't think he'd ever been in a position before where he couldn't eventually do something."

56. Schrijvers, *Crash of Ruin*, 80; "Not all captured Germans made it into PW handling channels, and some rifle companies developed reputations for taking few prisoners." Doubler, *Closing with the Enemy*, 259.

57. Schrijvers, *Crash of Ruin*, 78–81.

58. Rest areas provided rare and important breaks from combat:

> Unfortunately, America's combat soldiers had few opportunities to get away from the front lines in Europe. The critical situation with respect to manpower left the US Army not much room for allowing the GIs rest periods, passes, leaves, or furloughs. If at all possible, units that had run out of steam were relieved and withdrawn to rest areas for short periods. Those areas that were operated by divisions or higher units were located in large communities. They offered billets in hotels and in buildings with canvas cots and blankets. They also provided hot bathing facilities, mess halls, American Red Cross clubs, movie theatres, and postal and financial facilities. The other rest areas were organized in smaller towns. They were limited to warm billets and facilities for clothing exchange, both baths and warm meals. But combat soldiers usually spent no more than 72 hours in a rest area. Moreover, rest areas were never situated far from the front lines and soldiers were always sent to them on duty status.

Schrijvers, *Crash of Ruin*, 107n17.

59. Ibid., 163–64n77.

60. Draper, *84th Infantry Division*, 131, 133, 140, 146.

61. John D. Campbell and Harold P. Leinbaugh, *The Men of Company K: The Autobiography of a World War II Rifle Company* (New York: William Morrow and Company, 1985), 209.

62. Draper, *84th Infantry Division*, 131, 132. Commanders looked for ways to boost the confidence of their troops in combat:

> Combat was far different from what many soldiers had expected. In peacetime exercises groups of soldiers moved together rapidly in mock attacks, but the opposite was true in battle. The tempo of combat was much slower, with single attacks often taking hours rather than minutes. A myriad of tasks slowed units in battle: gathering intelligence, coordinating direct and indirect fires, evacuating casualties, and handling PWs. Even in small unit actions, detailed planning achieved success more effectively than elan or adrenaline. The battlefield was a lonely place that tended to isolate rather than unify soldiers. Fear and confusion were more prevalent than anyone had expected and tended to hold units back. Much more combat

took place at close quarters than open terrain, and the combat arms had to work much closer than in peacetime. Commanders discovered that combined arms attacks not only increased their combat power but improved soldiers' morale and confidence. Infantrymen felt better with tanks and TDs nearby, while artillery barrages and air strikes gave footsoldiers confidence.

Doubler, *Closing with the Enemy*, 293.

63. Draper, *84th Infantry Division*, 127, 131.

64. Peter Schrijvers, *The Unknown Dead: Civilians in the Battle of the Bulge* (Lawrence: University Press of Kansas, 2005), 325.

Chapter 7: The Battle of the Roer

1. Even more rarely did smaller units or individual soldiers obtain passes, leaves, or furloughs to leave centers or recreation areas. Before the invasion of Normandy, passes in Great Britain could not exceed forty-eight hours and hard-to-get leaves or furloughs were never valid for more than ten days. Not until September 1944 could troops on the continent receive passes of forty-eight hours to various towns and cities. Only in January 1945 were they increased to seventy-two hours. Schrijvers, *Crash of Ruin*, 107.

2. Wolff, *Fortune Favored the Brave*, 79.

3. Draper, *84th Infantry Division*, 131.

4. Atkinson, *Guns at Last Light*, 223.

5. Draper, *84th Infantry Division*, 132, 134; Atkinson, *Guns at Last Light*, 536; MacDonald, *Victory in Europe*, 142–43.

6. Atkinson, *Guns at Last Light*, 537.

7. Draper, *84th Infantry Division*, 133–34.

8. Mansoor, *GI Offensive in Europe*, 240nn6, 7.

9. Is this an oblique reference to the murder of the German POWs? "Nothing revolts the sensitive spirit so much as the bloody and unjust deeds of warfare that leave no trace of guilt in the doers and are from every human perspective unavenged." J. Glenn Gray, *The Warriors: Reflections on Men in Battle* (New York: Bison Books, 1998), 204.

10. Lavin, interviewed by Edmonds, June 18, 1999, 18.

11. Kindsvatter, *American Soldiers*, 68.

12. Carl has switched from being fatalistic about death to the other extreme. "There is a type of soldier who considers death very real for others but without power over him. These soldiers cherish the conviction that they are mysteriously impervious to spattering bullets and exploding shells. The little spot of ground on

which they stand is rendered secure by their standing on it. . . . Since such soldiers are freed from anxiety, they are frequently able to see the ridiculous and amusing aspects of combat life and provide much priceless cheer and humor for their comrades." Gray, *Warriors*, 126.

13. Schrijvers, *Crash of Ruin*, 210. "The result of all this was that most combat soldiers were practically broke. . . . Most obtained what they needed from each other and civilians through barter, an arrangement in which tobacco became the 'gold' of the land." Ibid., 211n97.

14. *Mrs. Miniver* was an Oscar-winning drama about British family stoicism during the war.

15. "In our myopic view, we respected and admired only those who got shot at, and to hell with everyone else. This was unfair to noncombatants who performed essential tasks, but we were so brutalized by war that we were incapable of making fair evaluations." Kindsvatter, *American Soldiers*, 246.

16. MacDonald, *Victory in Europe*, 145.

17. Draper, *84th Infantry Division*, 138, 150–51.

18. Mansoor, *GI Offensive in Europe*, 240. Enemy artillery and bullets fell from the skies, army assault boats drifted downstream, and army engineers gutted it out to build bridges along a "seventeen-mile front." Draper, *84th Infantry Division*, 143–48; Atkinson, *Guns at Last Light*, 538; and MacDonald, *Victory in Europe*, 145, 147.

19. Atkinson, *Guns at Last Light*, 540; MacDonald, *Victory in Europe*, 162.

20. Atkinson, *Guns at Last Light*, 538, 540.

21. Draper, *84th Infantry Division*, 146–73; MacDonald, *Victory in Europe*, 163–67.

22. Draper, *84th Infantry Division*, 160–62.

23. Ibid.

24. Ibid., 166. Six days after crossing the Roer, the 84th gained 20 miles and saw the prisoner count rise to 2,876. Ibid., 173.

25. Ibid., 166. According to Mansoor, the 84th "had executed a major river crossing and advanced forty-five miles in ten days, took 5,445 prisoners, and destroyed eighty-two enemy large-caliber guns, eighteen tanks and assault guns, 159 vehicles, and thirteen supply dumps." Mansoor, *GI Offensive in Europe*, 240–41n10.

26. Schrijvers, *The Crash of Ruin*, 91.

27. Ibid., 91–92.

28. Fraternization with German civilians was not encouraged:

The Twelfth Army Group's pamphlet on nonfraternization lectured: 'Except for such losses of life and property suffered by them, the Ger-

348   mans have no regret for the havoc they have wrought in the world.'
The American soldiers could not have agreed with that observation
more. They were well aware that pleas had not prevented the German forces from invading most of Europe. It therefore upset them that
whenever American troops were about to enter a German community, its inhabitants supposed that showing the white flag or sending
out a delegation of local notabilities was all that was needed to make
the war leave them alone. The GIs had seen the scale of the destruction the Germans had caused elsewhere. They were therefore stunned
by the unperturbed manner in which the Germans dared to ask for
consideration for their own property. In March 1945, the concerned
mayor of a town at the Niers Canal visited a company command post
of the 84th Infantry Division. He wanted help to keep the town's
only factory operational to ensure employment. The German's audac-
ity struck the Americans as even more insulting when they learned
that the factory had been producing nose-cone assemblies for 88 mm
shells.

Ibid., 145.

29. "Whenever American soldiers took over a German town, they conducted
house-to-house searches to collect explosives, ammunition, guns, even knives.
They also confiscated all means of communication, from radio transmitters to
pigeons." Ibid., 191.

30. Atkinson, *Guns at Last Light*, 637. "In the last two years of the war, operations by (Soviet) groups of fronts involved as many as 200 divisions, 2.5 million
soldiers, 6,000 tanks, 40,000 guns, and 7,500 aircraft. Deep operations spanned
frontages of 300–850 miles, thrust to a depth of 300–360 miles, and could destroy
as many as one hundred German divisions." Doubler, *Closing with the Enemy*, 277.

31. Draper, *84th Infantry Division*, 184, 191.

32. Ibid., 184, 195; MacDonald, *Victory in Europe*, 174–76, 179.

33. Draper, *84th Infantry Division*, 191.

34. Pulitzer Prize–winning cartoonist Bill Mauldin (1921–2003) depicted
World War II from the GI's viewpoint.

35. Draper, *84th Infantry Division*, 161, 166, 190.

36. Ibid., 181.

37. Ibid., 190.

38. Ibid.

39. Ibid.

40. "When the GIs moved out of town, they took as much of the foraged food with them as they could carry. They packed boiled eggs, for instance, or rabbit meat they had smoked. Soldiers of the 84th Infantry Division, readying themselves at Grandmenil for the Allied counteroffensive early in January 1945 took time out to butcher and clean a Belgian pig and roped the hindquarters to their packs before jumping off. But these reserves of fresh food never lasted long, and time and again the GIs had to turn to the civilians to replenish them." Schrijvers, *Crash of Ruin*, 161n64.

41. Ibid., 105n11.

42. Draper, *84th Infantry Division*, 195.

43. Ibid.

44. *Watch on the Rhine* is a 1943 film starring Bette Davis, adapted from a play by Lillian Hellman. It was also the German code name for the Ardennes offensive (Wacht am Rhein).

45. "Both civilians and soldiers were right to perceive in the war 'the maximum of physical devastation accompanied by the minimum of human meaning.'" Dwight Macdonald quoted in Fussell, *Wartime*, 143.

46. Schrijvers, *Crash of Ruin*, 211.

47. The interest in collecting souvenirs from German soldiers was common:

> The German soldiers in more than one respect proved themselves opponents worthy to be remembered. That probably helps to explain why the GIs were so eager to frisk or "desouvenir" German POWs in search of mementos. Perhaps they shipped home items as varied as helmets and caps, boots and belts, swastika flags and SS sabres to show material evidence to family and friends of their encounter with the famed enemy. Maybe they collected the fetishes merely for themselves, as reminders for years to come of how lucky they had been to survive the endless series of ferocious battles against a soldier unsurpassed by any other. Whatever the exact reason, the compulsive search for German momentos was testimony of the GIs' fascination with this valiant foe. . . . The most prized trophies, however, were German pistols. Not many GIs were issued sidearms, but they were practical and soldiers preferred them over their rifles for guard duty, for instance. German pistols were excellent souvenirs too. They were rather rare and GIs claimed they were all superior to the American .45 automatic. Both standard German pistols, the Luger (Pistole 8) and the Walther (Pistole 38), were the fashion, but the Luger was unquestionably, as one infantryman called it, the "HOLY GRAIL" of souvenirs.

Ibid., 70.

48. See the letter dated August 12, 1945, page 273.

49. Bill Mauldin's famous cartoon can be found in his obituary, written on January 23, 2003, by Patrick J. Dickson in *Stars and Stripes*. For an online version, see http://flgrube1.tripod.com/id306.html.

50. See letter of April 15, 1945.

51. The third package was sent in response to Carl's December 22 letter from Britain asking for underwear. Months later, his mail is forwarded to him from England.

52. Col. Estes was an officer with whom Dorothy connected while Carl was in Mississippi in some sort of effort to get him transferred. This is also during the time Carl's mother was also talking with Rep. Henderson Carson (see letter dated circa April 18, 1944, page 79).

53. Armed Services Editions were pocket-sized books produced for American soldiers. Over 1,300 titles were produced, ranging from *Candide* by Voltaire to *Blazed Trail Stories* by Stewart Edward White. According to one study, at least, Carl's skepticism made him an outlier: "Combat troops were asked how much prayer helped when things were rough in combat . . . only 6% said it did not help at all." McManus, *Deadly Brotherhood*, 232.

54. The "big one" refers to their silver wedding anniversary. Leo returned to Canton from army service circa 1920 and married Dorothy in 1921, making 1946 their silver wedding anniversary.

55. Frequently, the German soldiers were "men to be remembered" and bore the brunt for it as GIs quickly relieved them of watches, binoculars, pistols, and other mementos. Schrijvers, *Crash of Ruin*, 69–70; "The German soldiers themselves had most often been cleaned out completely by the time they reached the rear as POWs. 'It was an unwritten law with us on the line,' admitted a soldier of the 1st Infantry Division, 'that any prisoners we took ourselves, he was ours to take any thing of his you wanted.'" Ibid., 70.

56. The frequency of Sugardale deliveries and work at the plant was reduced to three days a week during the Great Depression.

Chapter 8: The Battle of the Rhine

1. Mansoor, *GI Offensive in Europe*, 243.

2. Draper, *84th Infantry Division*, 201.

3. Atkinson, *Guns at Last Light*, 567.

4. Draper, *84th Infantry Division*, 201, 203–4.

5. Ibid., 205.

6. Ibid., 204, 209–210.

7. MacDonald, *Victory in Europe*, 386.

8. Draper, *84th Infantry Division*, 209–216.

9. Lavin, interviewed by Edmonds, June 18, 1999, 12.

10. "More recent studies analyzing battles and campaigns in World War II and the Vietnam War find that conservatively 10 to 15 percent of the casualties were caused by friendly fire. . . . About 60 per cent of combat soldiers reported that they had been fired on in some way by our own troops several times, and 20 percent said it happened once." Kindsvatter, *American Soldiers*, 61–62.

11. Fussell, *Boys' Crusade*, 117.

12. Nadeau relates the incident from his perspective, remembering the sergeant as a lieutenant: "There was one that we got wounded in the Pacific . . . and they assigned him to Germany with us and we get there. We're moving to this town here and he gets up. He was on the second floor and, and the Germans were running all over the place and there's someone out in the field hiding behind cows and this lieutenant goes up on the second floor and he starts firing and. We just got into town. And . . . he turn around he shot them right through the wire. He didn't kill them, though, but he's. You know he lived." Robert P. Nadeau Collection (AFC/2001/001/64383).

13. Paul Fussel, *Doing Battle: The Making of a Skeptic* (Boston: Little, Brown & Co., 1996), 82.

14. Fussell, *Wartime*, 281.

15. Doubler, *Closing with the Enemy*, 243.

16. Wolff, *Fortune Favored the Brave*, 113.

17. MacDonald, *Victory in Europe*, 386.

18. The real war was tragic and ironic, beyond the power of any literary or philosophic analysis to suggest, but in unbombed America especially, the meaning of the war seemed inaccessible. Fussell, *Wartime*, 268.

19. Draper, *84th Infantry Division*, 227, 229.

20. "Nix Vershstah" is a mangled attempt at the German phrase *Ich nicht verstehen*, meaning "I do not understand."

21. The SS established the Hannover-Ahlem camp on November 30, 1944, after transferring the camp and its inmates from the Continental Gummiwerke factory at Hannover-Stöcken. In Ahlem the inmates were forced to work in the nearby asphalt tunnels. These were to be cleared for the production of aircraft and Panzer parts for Continental Gummiwerke and Maschinenfabrik Hannover. Salzwedel was a concentration camp for female prisoners. Originally designed for one thousand inmates, it eventually held over three thousand. Michael Hirsch, *The Liberators: America's Witnesses to the Holocaust* (New York: Bantam Books, 2010), 227.

22. Draper, *84th Infantry Division*, 234, 244.

23. Eisenhower on the concentration camps in a letter to Mamie: "I never dreamed that such cruelty, bestiality, and savagery could really exist in this world." Ian Buruma, *Year Zero: A History of 1945* (New York: Penguin, 2013), 227.

24. Lavin, interviewed by Edmonds, June 18, 1999, 22–23.

25. MacDonald, *Victory in Europe*, 443.

26. See Carl's letter dated March 13, 1945, page 184 and subsequent explanation.

27. Carl finally got his motorcycle in his fifties, after the children were grown. He would go to work on his Kawasaki when the weather was good, saving the car for rainy days and the winter months. Like his mother, he was also concerned about his children wanting to ride a motorcycle so he typically stored it at work where it would not become a conversation topic. When Dorothy was ailing and he knew the end was near, he put away the bike because he was concerned that being called to the hospital and arriving on a motorcycle for the death of one's mother would be disrespectful.

28. Draper, *84th Infantry Division*, 238–39, 242.

29. Ibid., 242.

30. Ibid., 243.

31. In 1930s Ohio, "sorry son of a gun" is pretty much as profane as it gets. From my eulogy: "Dad didn't drink, he didn't swear, and he didn't smoke, but let's not dwell on his short-comings."

32. Lavin, interviewed by Edmonds, June 18, 1999, 18. Shooting without hesitation was a trait that commanders tried to encourage:

> Commanders believed that their soldiers did not fire enough and that units needed better fire discipline and training in distributing fire throughout objective areas. Soldiers trained on known-distance rifle ranges found many reasons for not shooting in combat. Instead of placing fire in the general area of the objective, many wanted to identify specific targets before firing, while others preferred to remain under cover rather than exposing themselves while trying to get off a few shots. Some soldiers believed that fire at anything other than a good target was a waste of ammunition. . . . The army adopted a technique known as "marching fire" to increase infantry firepower and aggressiveness. In attacks across open ground, infantry platoons deployed into skirmish lines with their BARs and light machine guns scattered along the line. The idea was for soldiers to keep pressing forward while throwing a wall of lead before them.

Doubler, *Closing with the Enemy*, 250–51; for more info on ratio of fire, see Kindsvatter, *American Soldiers*, 221–23.

33. Nadeau on Gartow, describing both the original assault and the subsequent assault by Company L:

> towards the end of the war there, near the old river that this was on April, on April 22. They had tried to take this town. They went tanks and infantry. They. And they got the tank knocked out and so the third day they just, they just went 22, 20 guys, 20 infantrymen. The, you know, drainage ditch. They got it behind the Germans, went in the house and they, then they would shoot at the Germans at the fox-hole from the houses. So, anyway, what happened is a lot of them took off. Went through, through the old river and went across and there was 35 dead Germans laying around.

Robert P. Nadeau Collection (AFC/2001/001/64383).

34. MacDonald, *Victory in Europe*, 449.

35. Ibid., 447–48; MacDonald uses Draper's language, but puts the chronology before Draper's date of "after May 1" (Draper, *84th Infantry Division*, 246); Atkinson does the same as MacDonald (*Guns at Last Light*, 606–7); chronology differs between MacDonald and Draper.

36. José Ferrer was an Academy Award–winning actor (1912–1992).

37. William L. White, *Report on the Russians* (New York: Harcourt Brace, 1945). White was the son of famed *Emporia Kansas* newspaper editor William Allen White. During the war he served as Roving Editor for *Reader's Digest*. The book was controversial at the time as it offered a critical view of Russia. *Kirkus Reviews* notes: "Those who feel the importance of friendship and understanding with Soviet Russia will find it distasteful and badly timed."

38. He was likely soon disabused of his optimism: "Stalin was vicious, even by his own standards, in his treatment of repatriated prisoners of the Germans. Order No. 270 had designated Soviet POWs as traitors to the Motherland. Every liberated soldier was to be interrogated by the intelligence agencies and, in half of the cases, deposited in a forced-labour camp." Robert Service, *Comrades!: A History of World Communism* (Cambridge: Harvard University Press, 2007), 226.

39. Compare this with Eisenhower's assessment: "In his generous instincts, in his devotion to a comrade, and in his healthy, direct outlook on the affairs of workaday life, the ordinary Russian seems to me to bear a marked similarity to what we call an 'average American.'" Dwight David Eisenhower, *Crusade in Europe* (Baltimore: Johns Hopkins University Press, 1997), 473. One statistic can sum

up the horror that the war brought to the Soviet Union: "Some twenty seven million Soviet citizens died in the war, while combined U.S., British and French combat fatalities amounted to less than one million." Hastings, *Armageddon*, xiv.

40. Draper, *84th Infantry Division*, 247–49.

41. Atkinson, *Guns at Last Light*, 615.

42. Though the project was aborted, Hitler had his own Kamikaze program under which the V-1 flying bomb would be modified to accommodate a suicide pilot. See "The German Kamikazes," *Intelligence Bulletin*, June 1946, http://www .lonesentry.com/articles/kamikaze/index.html.

43. Lavin, interviewed by Edmonds, June 18, 1999, 15–16;

> Probably the most striking event on V-E Day was General Bolling's idea. The towns and villages in our [the division's] sector were visited by Lt. Fritz Kraemer [see below], of the G-2 section [Intelligence], who delivered a brief talk from a sound truck to the townspeople on the significance of the German surrender and the consequences which any further resistance might entail for the German people. On such a day, gathered in the town square to hear such a message, how did the German people react? Most listened quietly, almost rigidly. On the whole their self-control was remarkable. Yet, it was possible to feel that in most towns the capitulation was a relief from the frightful tension and increasing misery of six long years. In some villages, it was also possible to feel that too many people had not learned enough or forgotten enough.

Draper, *84th Infantry Division*, 248.

Lt. Fritz Kraemer was a German refugee who joined the US Army and became Henry Kissinger's mentor, beginning with their meeting and joint work in the 84th. Kraemer was responsible, through the 84th Division, for promoting the careers of two US Secretaries of State: Henry Kissinger and Al Haig, as related in Hubertus Hoffmann's book *On Excellence*: "That I was able to make Alexander Haig the military assistant of Henry Kissinger was pure coincidence. I happened to pass the office of Colonel Hamblin. We had been in the 84th Infantry Division ("The Railsplitters") together where Henry Kissinger was serving too in WW II. He told me that he had been given the job to find a military advisor for Henry Kissinger and had asked the G 1 officer to send him names of seven officers with outstanding military records and a PhD." Kraemer recollected that the Secretary of Defense had, in years past, had an unusually capable staff aide and Hamblin agreed that this individual would be the recommended candidate: Al

Haig. Hoffman, *Fritz Kraemer on Excellence: Missionary, Mentor and Pentagon Strategist* (New York: World Security Network Foundation, 2004, 144),

44. Casualty figures would be significantly higher in the infantry units, and lower in headquarters units, artillery, and the like. Mansoor, *GI Offensive in Europe*, 252.

45. "[After V-E Day] many felt subdued—'curiously flat' in Moorehead's phrase. Elation seemed misplaced. . . . An eerie, profound silence fell across much of the battlefield, and even those astonished to have survived felt too weary, or numb, or haunted for hosannas." Atkinson, *Guns at Last Light*, 627.

46. Ibid., 630.

Chapter 9: Heidelberg and Hamelin Occupation

1. Buruma, *Year Zero*, 70.

2. Earl Ziemke, *The U.S. Army in the Occupation of Germany* (Washington, DC: Center of Military History, 1975), 115.

3. Ibid., 320; by the time the German's capitulated, the size of the US ground forces was considerable:

> Any analysis of army operations in World War II must be made within the context of the tremendous growth and expansion of the ground forces. On 1 January 1941, the authorized strength of what eventually became the AGF (Army Ground Forces) stood at 356,000 troops; by 31 January 1945, the AGF had grown 760 percent and achieved a troop strength of 2.7 million men. The effort to get troops overseas was staggering. AGF training centers handled 2.1 million new soldiers, while service schools conducted specialized training for 108 officers and 229,000 enlisted men. During the mobilization for war the army activated 3,800 ground units with an authorized enlisted strength of 1.7 million men. Between 9 March 1942 and 28 February 1945, the AGF sent 5,900 units with and aggregate strength of 2.1 million men to ports of embarkation and during the same period shipped out 36,900 officer and 726,000 enlisted replacements. . . . The army shipped 89 divisions overseas, and all but one saw combat. Between 6 June 1944 and 8 May 1945, an average of 5,000 Americans per day entered the Continent. When the Germans capitulated, American ground forces in Europe included 61 divisions and all the supporting units, giving the ETO standing strength of 1,703,613 soldiers.

Doubler, *Closing with the Enemy*, 266.

4. Campbell and Leinbaugh, *Men of Company K*, 269.

5. Freese, *Private Memories of World War II*, 23.

6. Ziemke, *Occupation of Germany*, 97.

7. Ibid., 246.

8. The 69th made news across the United States as the first division to link up with the Russian forces on the Elbe on April 25, 1945.

9. Carl was under the assumption that as the war was over, he could freely discuss wartime incidents. Carl was about ten days early. Censorship hadn't formally ended, and army censors were still removing sensitive information.

10. Carl is referring to the Battle of Gartow (see chapter 8, page 210).

11. "SHEAEF anticipated having to release a million and half troops for the Pacific and having to send another 600,000 men home for discharge." Ziemke, *Occupation of Germany*, 328.

12. This might be the sharpest ennui we see from Carl: "'All wars are boyish, and are fought by boys.' Thus Melville in his poem 'The March into Virginia.' War must rely on the young, for only they have the two things fighting requires: physical stamina and innocence about their own mortality. The young are proud of their athleticism, and because their sense of honor has not yet suffered compromise, they make the most useful material for manning the sharp end of war. Knowledge will come after a few months, and then they'll be used up and as soldiers virtually useless—scared, cynical, debilitated, unwilling." Fussell, *Wartime*, 52.

13. Atkinson, *Guns at Last Light*, 544.

14. John Hersey asked the Marines on Guadalcanal, "What are you fighting for?" "A piece of blueberry pie," they answered. "Scotch whisky." "Dames." "Books." "Music." "Movies." Hersey translated these answers into the real one: "To get the goddam thing over and get home." Hersey, *Into the Valley* (New York: A. A. Knopf, 1943), 74–75.

15. Ambrose had a similar view, that the open society of the United States made for a more capable military: "The citizen-soldiers mobilized from the democratic society of the United States were better than those indoctrinated with the fanaticism and racism of Nazi ideology. American soldiers fought because they had to, were held together by small-unit cohesion, and accomplished a difficult job under often brutal conditions." Mansoor, *GI Offensive in Europe*, 10. On a personal level, Audrey related how Dorothy advised her early in her marriage that Carl would never wear clothes that were brown or olive, anything evocative of his uniform.

16. "It is necessary to distinguish the person who is an occasional coward in the face of death from the constitutional coward. In almost everyone at times, there is a coward lurking." Gray, *Warriors*, 133.

17. No matter how well trained, most soldiers found adjusting to life on the front difficult:

> The soldiers of the Western armies were products of modern industrial societies. It is hard to overstate the transition inflicted upon them by warfare. Young men possess remarkable powers of adjustment to new circumstances. British and American soldiers had been expensively trained to endure hardship. But few became wholly inured to battlefield life. They were required to become creatures of the wilderness, perpetual campers and boy scouts, living in fox-holes which allowed their occupants to sleep sitting, but seldom to lie prone. Every soldier spent far more time digging than shooting. It required the labour of many weary hours to contrive a hole deep enough to shelter a man effectively from shellfire. Within days of creating such a refuge, he was required to move on and repeat the process. Soldiers performed every natural function in the open; ate clumsy alfresco picnics of nourishing but monotonous food; lived in filthy and often damp clothing that went unwashed for weeks, even months; and were subject to the arbitrary authority of those appointed to lead them. This allowed individuals negligible discretion over their own lives in small things or large, through the seven days of the week and the eleven months of the campaign. Intelligent men found that among the hardest parts of war was the need to accept orders from stupid ones.

Hastings, *Armageddon*, 140.

18. A reference to Catherine Drinker Bowen's *Yankee from Olympus*, a 1944 biography of Justice Oliver Wendell Holmes Jr.

19. A popular documentary newsreel series.

20. It is unclear if Carl is referring to Carl Engel (1883–1944), Lehman Engel (1910–1982), or another composer with the same, or similar sounding, last name.

21. The command posts of the 84th Division:

23 Dec 44	Baillonville	Luxembourg	Belgium
2 Jan 45	Barvaux	Luxembourg	Belgium
11 Jan 45	Blier	Luxembourg	Belgium
21 Jan 45	Ottre	Luxembourg	Belgium
27 Jan 45	Harze	Luxembourg	Belgium
3 Feb 45	Waubach	Limburg	Netherlands

9 Feb 45	Lindern	Rhineland	Germany
1 Mar 45	Wegburg	Rhineland	Germany
4 Mar 45	Dulken	Rhineland	Germany
5 Mar 45	Krefeld	Rhineland	Germany
2 Apr 45	Lembeck	Westphalia	Germany
4 Apr 45	Appelhulsen	Westphalia	Germany
5 Apr 45	Warendorf	Westphalia	Germany
6 Apr 45	Herford	Westphalia	Germany
8 Apr 45	Lerbeck	Westphalia	Germany
9 Apr 45	Bad Nenndorf	Westphalia	Germany
11 Apr 45	Hannover	Hannover	Germany
12 Apr 45	Burgdorf	Hannover	Germany
14 Apr 45	Beetzendorf	Hannover	Germany
15 Apr 45	Arendsee	Magdeburg	Germany
17 Apr 45	Priemern	Magdeburg	Germany
5 May 45	Salzwedel	Magdeburg	Germany

Draper, *84th Infantry Division*, 212.

22. Carl is referring to the Battle for Gartow (see chapter 8, page 210).

23. A point system determined when a soldier would be sent home:

> Everybody's concern was to get back to the States as soon as pos-
> sible and make up for the time we felt we had wasted in the Army.
> Eighty-five points were needed to get on a boat for home. The point
> system, based on time in the service, overseas time, time in com-
> bat, and number of children, was as fair as the Army could make it.
> Each child counted twelve points, campaigns and medals counted
> five points, and longevity and overseas service were worth a point a
> month. The system proved reasonably fair, but contained inequalities;
> a Purple Heart was worth the same five points whether for a shrapnel
> cut on the arm or a bullet wound through the chest.

Campbell and Leinbaugh, *Men of Company K*, 272.

24. As mentioned in the chapter introduction, as part of army regulation, Carl was not allowed to talk with German civilians. He could only make observations

about them from afar. There were strict nonfraternization rules in place. "Non-fraternization only allowed the GIs to have contact with Germans in matters of official business. They were not permitted to converse with the civilians, to shake hands with them, to accompany them in the streets, to visit their homes, to drink with them, to give or accept gifts, to engage in games or sports with them, or to take part in their social events." Schrijvers, *Crash of Ruin*, 139.

25. "Officers detected a distinct lack of animosity for the enemy among their troops, and postwar surveys revealed that Americans had fairly moderate attitudes toward enemy troops and the German people. A substantial minority of soldiers admitted that some hatred for the Germans motivated them in combat, but most soldiers were not vindictive." Doubler, *Closing with the Enemy*, 258.

26. "As soldiers, the Americans saw a European society that had reached the point of disintegration. As Americans, the soldiers believed that this was the result not only of World War II, but also of the more deep-seated deficiencies that had been eroding the Old World for ages." Schrijvers, *Crash of Ruin*, 108.

> The result was that the war, whether at the front or in the rear, never allowed the American combat soldier to get a well-informed idea of how Europe had looked under the normal conditions of peace. Instead, the GIs saw a society that appeared to be disintegrating and unlikely ever to recover fully again. What is more, the collapse alone could have been responsible for it. They sensed that World War II was merely the terminal symptom of a more complicated European disease, and suspected that the crash was in large measure the result of a much longer and more fundamental process of ruin that had been undermining the Old World.

Ibid., 217.

27. Lavin, interviewed by Edmonds, June 18, 1999, 22.

28. The "relations" were fourth or fifth cousins with the last name of Spitz, of the same family as Olympic swimmer Mark Spitz. When the Spitzes visited the Lavins, Carl had to hide their dog Spitzy. Although the dog was not named after the Spitz family, Dorothy was concerned the family would be offended hearing the call of "Hey, Spitzy, Spitzy, Spitzy," so Spitzy was forced to spend the day with the neighbors.

Chapter 10: Mannheim, Gmund, and Lauda Occupation

1. Ziemke, *Occupation of Germany*, 323.

2. Lavin, interviewed by Edmonds, June 18, 1999, 20.

3. Hamilton, Ohio, is a few miles from Miami of Ohio. The family was attending Fred's graduation.

4. I can relate from a nephew's perspective that Uncle Fred had a pretty sedate personality, so we can guess that there had been a particular incident that troubled Dorothy.

5. Carl is making a joke, as it requires three successful jumps for a paratrooper to win his insignia.

6. "The most available and most heavily attended form of entertainment was the motion picture. Out of a total attendance of 32 million people at all types of entertainment in May 1945, 26 million were at motion pictures. An estimated eight out of ten soldiers saw at least three movies a week." Ziemke, *Occupation of Germany*, 332.

7. *The Keys of the Kingdom*, the 1944 film adapted from a novel by A. J. Cronin, was nominated for four Academy Awards.

8. Carl's affinity for Spinoza in this era of malevolent governments should not be a surprise, given the philosopher's advocacy of rationalism and humanism. Durant explains Spinoza's political philosophy: "Law is necessary because men are subject to passions; if all men were reasonable, law would be superfluous. The perfect law would bear to individuals the same relations which perfect reason bears to passions: it would be the coordination of conflicting forces to avoid the ruin and increase the power of the whole. . . . The perfect state would limit the powers of its citizen only as far as these powers were mutually destructive; it would withdraw no liberty except to add a greater one." The quotation continues with words that must have had a special poignancy for one reading them in the wreckage of Nazi Germany:

> The last end of the state is not to dominate men, nor to restrain them
> by fear; rather it is to free each man from fear that he may live and
> act with full security and without injury to himself or his neighbor.
> . . . The end of the state, I repeat, is not to make rational beings into
> brute beasts and machines. It is to enable their bodies and their minds
> to function safely. It is to lead men to live by, and to exercise, a free
> reason; that they may not waste their strength in hatred, anger and
> guile, nor act unfairly toward one another. Thus the need of the state
> is really liberty.

Walter Durant, *The Story of Philosophy: The Lives and Opinions of the World's Greatest Philosophers* (New York: Pocket Books, 1991), 146.

9. Dorothy actually visited with the Rabbi Lieberman, talked with him about Spinoza and jotted notes on the envelope of this letter (see the letter dated August 6, 1945, page 272).

10. Unfortunately, there is no additional information as to the nature of Dorothy's illness or hospitalization. In her letter to Carl she has downplayed its significance, but Carl is not completely convinced. One hint is offered in Carl's letter dated July 18, 1945 (see page 266), in which he refers to Dorothy's hemorrhage.

11. Since GIs added jelly to their peanut butter sandwiches, they've been credited with helping to popularize the snack.

12. In 1945, Truman changed the Cabinet Secretaries in the Departments of War, State, Treasury, Justice, Post Office, Agriculture, and Labor.

13. "To be sure, there were clues, omens, auguries. Just as surely, they were missed, ignored, explained away. For decades after the death struggle called the Battle of the Bulge, generals, scholars, and foot soldiers alike would ponder the worst U.S. intelligence failure since Pearl Harbor and the deadliest of the war." Atkinson, *Guns at Last Light*, 412.

14. Ziemke, *Occupation of Germany*, 325.

15. Campbell and Leinbaugh, *Men of Company K*, 271.

16. Lavin, interviewed by Edmonds, June 18, 1999, 20.

17. "Special Services stocked 21,000 basketballs, 100,000 dozen table tennis balls, and nearly 350,000 decks of cards, and issued by November 1945, 1443 libraries (each containing 1,000 cloth-bound books), close to 15 million paperback books, and over 44 million magazine. . . . 305 basketball teams had drawn 21,250 spectators, 1,200 touch football teams a mere 1,200, and 90 football teams 379,000." Ziemke, *Occupation of Germany*, 332. We should be skeptical about statistics that show an average of precisely one spectator at each touch football game. But the trend shows what Carl knew in 1940 and what Dorothy feared: Real men don't play touch football.

18. Ziemke, *Occupation of Germany*, 318–19.

19. General Truman described President Truman's visit to the 84th Infantry Division:

In 1945 he [President Truman] was at Potsdam, and Churchill went back to England to get reelected, and didn't get reelected. But while he was gone, Truman came to my area, the 84th Infantry Division area. Evidently, he had told someone that he had a cousin who was chief of staff of one of the divisions, and so he came down. They first stopped at the boundary of the 3rd Armored Division and 84th Infantry Division. Our division commander, [Major General] Alexander

362   R. Bolling, and I had an honor guard there for President Truman, after
       he left the 3rd Armored Division and came into the 84th Infantry
       Division's zone. After the honor guard, I rode in the car with Gen-
       eral Bolling and [General] Harry Vaughan [Truman's military aide] to
       Weinheim. Weinheim is where the 84th Division's headquarters were
       located. We took him to where our staff quarters were, which was a
       beautiful home, a gorgeous home, and that was where we had lunch.
       General Eisenhower, Supreme Commander, was there at the luncheon
       as well as the Secretary of State [James Byrnes], who had wanted to
       become Vice President. . . . Also the Chief Justice [Fred Vinson] was
       there at that time. . . . Also, one of Truman's primary speech writers, or
       one of his advisors, was there. He was a tall thin person [speechwriter
       and Pulitzer Prize–winning playwright Robert Sherwood was six
       foot eight]. . . . President Truman was not there too long. We had all of
       the 84th Division lined up all the way, about ten miles. . .right off the
       Autobahn.

    President Truman reviewed the tanks, self-propelled guns, and other weaponry
as well as the personnel. He had flown in from Potsdam, first reviewed the Third
Armored Division, and then the 84th. Louis S. Truman, "Oral History Interview
with General Louis W. Truman, Independence, Missouri," by Niel M. Johnson,
December 7, 1991, Harry S. Truman Library, Independence, MO, http://www
.trumanlibrary.org/oralhist/trumanl.htm.
    20. Campbell and Leinbaugh, *Men of Company K*, 271.
    21. Between May and September, over ninety-three thousand soldiers were
enrolled: "Plans provided command schools to be operated by units down to
battalion level. The instructors were qualified military personnel and civilians,
including after the non-fraternization rules were relaxed, English-speaking Germans. The command schools were a massive undertaking. Seventh Army issued
packs of 10,000 textbooks to each of its divisions." Ziemke, *Occupation of Germany*,
330.
    22. Ibid., 396.
    23. "Entertainment and recreation programs . . .were continued after the Ger-
man surrender. The sixty-six USO shows in the [European] theatre on V-E Day
played to three-quarters of a million men a month." Ibid., 331.
    24. The weather, the amphitheater, the acoustics, and a first-class troupe all
worked together. Plus Benny, with a genius for comedy, made the main theme of
his routine the GIs. Just months after the end of the war, it was ok to make fun
of the army and to parody the recently sacred war movies. In fact, it was a relief

to do so. And the collective roar meant a collective validation. We made it. We've had enough of the army. And we can show it. At least three other memoirs from the 84th Division describe the event (*Never Tell an Infantryman*, *Foot Soldier*, and *Witness to History*).

25. Larry Adler (1914–2001) was a musician known for harmonica skills and Martha Tilton (1915–2006) was a popular vocalist with a number of chart hits.

26. Billy Conn was a boxer (1917–1993) who won the Light-Heavyweight championship in 1939 and lost the Heavyweight championship to Joe Louis in 1941 and in 1946.

27. A 1944 movie about President Woodrow Wilson.

28. After the war, "looting was so widespread as to be regarded as a soldierly sport." Ziemke, *Occupation of Germany*, 220.

29. *The Story of G.I. Joe* told the story of Ernie Pyle's wartime service. It was nominated for four Oscars in 1946.

30. "The Monkey's Paw," the 1902 short story by W. W. Jacobs.

31. "A Class B allowance is granted when a serviceman makes a voluntary allotment for the support of his dependent parent or parents, brothers or sisters or grandchildren. In addition to the serviceman's contribution, the Government will contribute the following amounts to Class B dependents: $15 to one parent, and an additional $5 for each brother, sister or grandchild, the whole not to total more than $50; $25 to two parents, and an additional $5 for each brother, sister or grandchild up to $50; $5 to each brother, sister or grandchild, if there are no parents." Office of War Information, "Rights and Privileges of American Servicemen," advanced press release, May 1943, http://www.usmm.org/wsa/rights.html.

32. Shep Fields, an American band leader (1910–1981).

33. "Civilian guides conducted tours for three hundred [army] men a day at Heidelberg." Ziemke, *Occupation of Germany*, 332.

34. Despite the hint of this letter, Carl never saw Edith again.

35. Hyman Kaplan was a fictional character of author Leo Rosten in the 1930s. Hyman was a well-meaning but socially awkward Jewish immigrant. His general popularity resulted in *The Education of H*Y*M*AN*K*A*P*L*A*N* being selected as the first Armed Services Edition, the wartime paperbacks published for the GIs. Produced in September 1943, ceremonial copies were presented to President Roosevelt, General Marshall, and Admiral King. Fussell, *Wartime*, 240.

36. *People on Our Side* is a 1944 nonfiction book by journalist Edgar Snow.

Chapter 11: Reims Occupation and Home

1. Lavin, interviewed by Edmonds, June 18, 1999, 24.
2. Ibid.

3. See Frank J. Freese's comments about reinforcements in chapter 6, page 135, from *Private Memories of World War II*, 16.

4. Schrijvers, *Crash of Ruin*, 124.

5. One GI from the 84th remembered fellow soldiers looting a dead German. "First thing somebody done . . . was to kick him over with their foot and look and see if he had any rings on. And somebody . . . cut his finger off and got the ring. It surprised me. I wouldn't have thought about doing things like that.'" McManus, *Deadly Brotherhood*, 75.

6. *Junior Miss*, a 1945 comedy.

7. There is one more German immigrant discussed in the epilogue, see page 313.

8. In 1944, "Frenchmen were willing to pay 50 francs for a pack of cigarettes that Americans could buy from the Army for three francs." Schrijvers, *Crash of Ruin*, 164.

9. France had been the largest economy under German occupation: "Since the economy had been systematically bled dry by the Germans, the black market had already been operating in France for some years." Buruma, *Year Zero*, 58.

10. The official story of destruction of records is from Draper. On the morning of April 16, as the "division's rear echelon was moving from Hannover to Salzwedel . . . mortar shells hit one truck with the personnel and equipment and records of the 335th Infantry and another with ammunition." Draper, *84th Infantry Division*, 239. However, Reid related that the administrative unit of the division believed itself to be surrounded and decided to destroy the records themselves to avoid them falling into enemy hands. It soon became clear that the administrative unit was not in any danger, but they had already destroyed the records. Reid wrote that GIs from across the division were pressed into reconstructing the missing records as it would be unacceptable for a battalion to lose its entire stock of records. Robert Reid, *Never Tell an Infantryman to Have a Nice Day* (Bloomington, IN: Xlibris Corporation, 2010), 161.

11. Premeditated renege is a term relating to the game of bridge; Dorothy was a serious bridge player and was referenced by Charles Goren, regarded as the leading bridge expert in the United States.

12. "The Army's first leave center opened in Paris in late October [1944]. That was followed by the first of fifty-one GI clubs on the Continent. Located in the Grand Hotel on Boulevard des Capucines, the initial club in Paris charged 30 cents a night for a bed; Major Glenn Miller's orchestra played each evening, even after the band leader disappeared in mid-December during a foul-weather flight." Atkinson, *Guns at Last Light*, 400.

13. *Private Lives*, a popular Noël Coward comedy.

14. *Duet for Two Hands*, a play by Mary Hayley Bell.

15. Lavin, interviewed by Edmonds, June 18, 1999, 25. Carl loved to travel and worked in and visited dozens of countries around the world. But he never again traveled by ship.

16. Atkinson, *Guns at Last Light*, 335.

Epilogue

1. Pyle, *Here is Your War*, 325.

2. See chapter 11, footnote 7 for background.

3. Arendt, Introduction, *Warriors*, xi.

4. Samuel Menashe, "The Offering," in *Donald Davie, Samuel Menashe, Allen Curnow*, ed. Carol Ann Duffy, Ursula A Fanthorpe, and James Fenton (Schriftsteller), vol. 6 of *Penguin Modern Poets* (London: Penguin, 1996), 61.

5. McManus, *Deadly Brotherhood*, 294.

6. Lavin, interviewed by Edmonds, June 18, 1999, 26.

Bibliography

Books

Ambrose, Stephen E. *Band of Brothers: E Company, 506th Regiment, 101st Airborne from Normandy to Hitler's Eagle's Nest.* New York: Simon & Schuster, 2002.

——. *Citizen Soldiers: The U. S. Army from the Normandy Beaches to the Bulge to the Surrender of Germany.* New York: Simon & Schuster, 1998.

Arendt, Hannah. Introduction in Gray, *Warriors*, ix–xviii.

Astor, Gerald. *A Blood-Dimmed Tide: The Battle of the Bulge by the Men Who Fought It.* New York: Dell Publishing, 1992.

Atkinson, Rick. *The Guns at Last Light: The War in Western Europe, 1944–1945.* New York: Henry Holt and Co., 2013.

Blunt, Roscoe C., Jr. *Foot Soldier: A Combat Infantryman's War in Europe.* New York: Da Capo Press, 2001.

Buruma, Ian. *Year Zero: A History of 1945.* New York: Penguin, 2013.

Coff, Morris, and John Teare. *Co. K: Our Story, The Men of Trespass Blue King.* Wolfhagen, Ger.; printed by author, July 1945. http://www.69th-infantry-division.com/histories/271/History-of-the-271st-Inf-Rgt-K-Company-July-1945.pdf.

Cole, Hugh. *The Battle of the Bulge.* Old Saybrook, CT: Konecky & Konecky, 2001.

Doubler, Michael D. *Closing with the Enemy: How GIs Fought the War in Europe, 1944–1945.* Lawrence: University Press of Kansas, 1994.

Diehl, Lorraine B. *Over Here!: New York City during World War II.* New York: Harper Collins, 2010.

Draper, Theodore. *The 84th Infantry Division in the Battle of Germany, November 1944–May 1945.* New York: The Viking Press, 1946.

Durant, Will. *The Story of Philosophy: The Lives and Opinions of the World's Greatest Philosophers.* New York: Pocket Books, 1991.

Eisenhower, John S. D. *The Bitter Woods: The Battle of the Bulge*. New York: Putnam, 1969.

Foster, Frank C. *Complete Guide to United States Army Medals, Badges and Insignia— World War II to Present*. Fountain Inn, SC: Medals of America Press, 2004.

Freese, Frank J. *Private Memories of World War II: A Small Piece of a Big War*. Madison, WI: printed by author, 1990.

Fussell, Paul. *The Boys' Crusade: The American Infantry in Northwestern Europe, 1944– 1945*. Modern Library Chronicles, vol. 14. New York: Modern Library, 2005.

———. *Doing Battle: The Making of a Skeptic*. Boston: Back Bay Books, 1998.

———. *Wartime: Understanding and Behavior in the Second World War*. New York: Oxford University Press, 1990.

Ginzberg, Eli. *The Lost Divisions*. New York: Columbia University Press, 1959.

Goldstein, Richard. *Helluva Town: The Story of New York City during World War II*. New York: Free Press, 2010.

Gram, Margaret. "Over There Comes Over Here." In Stepanchev, *People's College on the Hill*, 43–47.

Gray, J. Glenn. *The Warriors: Reflections on Men in Battle*. New York: Bison Books, 1998.

Gup, Ted. *A Secret Gift: How One Man's Kindness—and a Trove of Letters—Revealed the Hidden History of the Great Depression*. New York: Penguin, 2010.

Hastings, Max. *Armageddon: The Battle for Germany, 1944–1945*. New York: Vintage, 2005.

Havighurst, Walter. *The Miami Years, 1809–1969*. New York: Putnam, 1969.

Heald, Edward Thornton. *The Stark County Story*. Vol. 3. Canton, OH: The Stark County Historical Society, 1952.

Henderson, Andrew. *Forgotten Columbus*. Charleston, SC: Arcadia Publishing, 2002.

Higgins, John F. *Trespass against Them: History of the 271st Infantry Regiment 1943– 1945*. Naumburg, Ger.: privately published, 1945. http://www.69th-infantry-division.com/histories/271.html.

Hirsch, Michael. *The Liberators: America's Witnesses to the Holocaust*. New York: Bantam Books, 2010.

Hischak, Thomas. *The Oxford Companion to the American Musical: Theatre, Film and Television*. New York: Oxford University Press, 2008.

Hoffmann, Hubertus. *Fritz Kraemer on Excellence: Missionary, Mentor and Pentagon Strategist*. New York: World Security Network Foundation, 2004.

Howerton, Allan. *Dear Captain*. Bloomington, IN: Xlibris Corporation, 2000.

Keefer, Louis E. *Scholars in Foxholes: The Story of the Army Specialized Training Program in World War II*. Jefferson, NC: McFarland & Co., 1993.

Kenney, Kimberly A. *Canton: A Journey through Time*. Charleston, SC: Arcadia, 2003.

Kindsvatter, Peter S. *American Soldiers: Ground Combat in the World Wars, Korea, and Vietnam.* Lawrence: University Press of Kansas, 2003.

Leinbaugh, Harold P., and John D. Campbell. *The Men of Company K: The Autobiography of a World War II Rifle Company.* New York: William Morrow and Company, 1985.

MacDonald, Charles B. *Victory in Europe, 1945: The Last Offensive from United States Army in World War II.* Mineola, NY: Dover Publications, 2007.

Mansoor, Peter R. *The GI Offensive in Europe: The Triumph of American Infantry Divisions, 1941–1945.* Lawrence: University Press of Kansas, 1999.

McManus, John. *The Deadly Brotherhood: The American Combat Soldier in World War II.* Novato, CA: Presidio Press, 1998.

Menashe, Samuel. "The Offering." In *Donald Davie, Samuel Menashe, Allen Curnow,* edited by Carol Ann Duffy, Ursula A Fanthorpe, and James Fenton (Schriftsteller), 61. Vol. 7 of *Penguin Modern Poets.* London: Penguin Books, 1996.

Miller, Marc, ed. *Witness to History: The World War II Photographs Taken by Maurice Miller.* Revised edition. N.p.: self-published, 2015.

Olson, Lynn. *Those Angry Days: Roosevelt, Lindbergh, and America's Fight over World War II, 1939–1941.* New York: Random House, 2013.

Phillips, Cabell. *The 1940s: Decade of Triumph and Trouble.* New York: Macmillan Publishing Company, 1975.

Pyle, Ernie. *Here Is Your War.* New York: Tess Press, 2004.

Reid, Robert. *Never Tell an Infantryman to Have a Nice Day.* Bloomington, IN: Xlibris Corporation, 2010.

Service, Robert. *Comrades!: A History of World Communism.* Cambridge, MA: Harvard University Press, 2007.

Schrijvers, Peter. *The Crash of Ruin: American Combat Soldiers in Europe during World War II.* New York: NYU Press, 2001.

———. *The Unknown Dead: Civilians in the Battle of the Bulge.* Lawrence: University Press of Kansas, 2005.

Shank, George K. *I Wrote My Way Out of a Foxhole.* Meridian, MS: Budget Printing, 1991.

Stepanchev, Stephen, ed. *The People's College on the Hill: Fifty Years at Queens College, 1937–1987.* New York: Queens College of the City University of New York, 1989.

White, William L. *Report on the Russians.* New York: Harcourt Brace, 1945.

Wolff, Perry S. *Fortune Favored the Brave: A History of the 334th Infantry, 84th Division.* Mannheim: Manheimer GoBdruckerei, 1945.

Ziemke, Earl. *The U.S. Army in the Occupation of Germany.* Washington, DC: Center of Military History, 1975.

Papers, Letters, Collections, and Diaries

Department of Special Collections and Archives. CUNY, Benjamin Rosenthal Library.

Edward, Donald A. *A Private's Diary.* N.p.: printed by author, 1994.

Elder, Tim, ed. "A History of Lehman High School." Last updated January 2014. http://www.cantonlehman.org/docs/history.doc.

Nadeau, Robert P. Collection. AFC/2001/001/64383. Veterans History Project, American Folklife Center, Library of Congress.

Wunderlin, Clarence E., ed. *The Papers of Robert A. Taft.* Vol. 2, *1939–1944.* Kent, OH: Kent State University Press, 2001.

Interviews, Questionnaires, and Oral Transcripts

Lavin, Carl. Interviewed by Franklin L. Lavin, 2005–2008.

Lavin, Carl. Interviewed by Bill Edmonds. Florida State University, Reichelt Oral History Program. June 18, 1999.

Lavin, Carl. Interviewed by Bryant Campbell. 2006. https://www.youtube.com/watch?v=Z9K0owh0Pgk.

Truman, Louis W. "Oral History Interview with General Louis W. Truman." By Niel M. Johnson. December 7, 1991. Harry S. Truman Library, Independence, MO. http://www.trumanlibrary.org/oralhist/trumanl.htm.

Online Sources

"The Fighting 69th Infantry Division." 69th Infantry Division, http://www.69th-infantry-division.com.

"History of the Great Place." US Army. Last updated October 31, 2013. http://pao.hood.army.mil/history.aspx.

Krammer, Arnold P. "German Prisoners of War." *Handbook of Texas Online,* June 15, 2010. Accessed November 10, 2014. http://www.tshaonline.org/handbook/online/articles/qug01.

Office of War Information. "Rights and Privileges of American Servicemen." Advanced press release, May 1943. Reprinted by American Merchant Marine at War. http://www.usmm.org/wsa/rights.html.

"Official Website of Fort Hood Texas." US Army. Last updated June 16, 2016. http://www.hood.army.mil.

Over, William. "Emory Holloway: Biographical Sketch." Adelphi University, Gale Literature Resource Center, Dictionary of Literary Biography database.

Accessed November 10, 2014. http://libraries.adelphi.edu/bar/Whitman/
WhitmanIntroductionEH.htm.

US Army Center of Military History, homepage. Last updated March 21, 2014.
http://www.army.mil/cmh-pg/default.htm.

US Army War College, homepage. Last updated August 20, 2016. http://www.
carlisle.army.mil/.

"World War II Military Situation Maps." Library of Congress, Digital Collections.
http://memory.loc.gov/ammem/collections/maps/wwii/index.html.

"World War II Records." National Archives, Military Records. http://www.
archives.gov/research/military/ww2/.

Miscellany

Special thanks to the *Canton Repository*, 1890s–1960s.

Army Specialized Training Division, Army Service Forces. *Essential Facts about the
Army Specialized Training Program*. Washington, DC: US Government Printing
Office, 1943.

Battle of the Bulge: The American Experience. Directed by Thomas Lennon. Los
Angeles, CA: Lennon Documentary Group, WGBH, 1994.

Bolling, A. R. *Railsplitters: The Story of the 84th Infantry Division*. Paris: Curial-
Archereau, 1945. http://www.lonesentry.com/gi_stories_booklets/84thinfantry.

Canton Official City Directory. Vol. 45. Akron, OH: Burch Directory Company,
1940.

Hoover War History. North Canton, OH: n.p., 1946.

Office for Emergency Management. *Guns Not Gadgets*. Arsenal of Democracy
Series. Washington, DC: Department of the Interior, 1941.

Polaris 1942. Lehman High School Yearbook.

The Stark County Bicentennial Story, 1776–1976. Vol. 2. Canton, OH: Stark Co.
Bicentennial Committee, 1976.

Schubert, Frank N. *Mobilization: The U.S. Army in World War II, the 50th Anniversary*.
Washington, DC: US Army Center of Military History, 1994. http://www.
history.army.mil/documents/mobpam.htm.

Index

CPSIA information can be obtained
at www.ICGtesting.com
Printed in the USA
FFHW02n0251070918
48117648-51846FF